# The Independent Mind
# in British Psychoanalysis

# The Independent Mind in British Psychoanalysis

ERIC RAYNER

Jason Aronson Inc.
*Northvale, New Jersey*
*London*

Library of Congress Cataloging-in-Publication Data

Rayner, Eric.
  The independent mind in British psychoanalysis / Eric Rayner,
    p.  cm.
  Includes bibliographical references and index.
  ISBN 0-87668-560-2
  1. Psychoanalysis.  2. Psychoanalysis—Great Britain.  3. British
Psycho-Analytical Society.  I. Title
RC506.R38  1991
150.19′5′0941—dc20                          91-6403

Manufactured in the United States of America. Jason Aronson Inc. offers books and cassettes. For information and catalog write to Jason Aronson Inc., 230 Livingston Street, Northvale, New Jersey 07647.

# Contents

# Acknowledgements

Many people have contributed to the making of this book so that, though there may be only one writer, the authorship has several, even many, minds behind it.

The original perception of a need for a book on the work of British Independent psychoanalysts came from Robert Young. It was he who persuaded me to plunge into the task and who then kept me going by continuing, generous, open-minded encouragement and penetrating criticism whenever it was needed. I am very grateful to him.

Right at the start I realized that I could not write a book on such a wide subject without help, and I turned to Margret Tonnesmann. She and I have shared the teaching of the theory side of a course on the British Independents at the Institute of Psycho-Analysis in London for a good many years, and I knew that her scholarship was much more careful and consistent than mine. She has spent many weeks giving of her knowledge and searching thoughtfulness. Without her, the book, even if it had been completed, would have been theoretically sloppy and ill-developed. More essential even than this, whole dimensions of thought would have been lacking without the effect of her mind upon the book. I have learnt a very great deal from her.

That the work of the Independents could better be thought of in terms of thematic ideas rather than by considering a sequence of authors was first suggested quite a few years ago by Elizabeth Spillius, and it is this that has given the book its basic shape. I am also particularly indebted to Harold Stewart and David Tuckett, who have taught the sections on technique in the Institute of Psycho-Analysis course on the Independents. What I learnt from their seminars is reflected in the book.

I persuaded a good many of my friends and colleagues to spend many hours reading drafts and advising me: it has been through their efforts that a reasonable enough book took shape. There can be no order of precedence here so I will give their names alphabetically: Christopher

Bollas, William Gillespie, Ralph Layland, Marion Milner (who also brought Chapter 4 alive for me), John Padel (who also instilled some elementary grammar into me), Ray Shepherd, Harold Stewart, Neville Symington and Nick Temple. I also want to thank Enid Balint, Pearl King and Ruth Brook for valuable comments and advice about specific parts of the manuscript. Juliet Hopkins not only read and helped me with large tracts of the draft but also generously allowed a case study of hers (Hopkins, 1987) to appear in the book.

I am acutely aware that, even with all this help, I have done poor justice both to history and to the many fine and sometimes great minds that have made the Independent stream flow in psychoanalysis. I am proud and grateful that I am the richer for knowing many of them in person.

Work on the book could not have started without bringing together a huge bibliography of the works of Independents. This was largely done by my son, William Rayner, with much advice and help from Jill Duncan, librarian at the Institute of Psycho-Analysis. The final abridged bibliography was put together with the very efficient help of Diana Bissett. I would like to thank them all.

My family have all humorously tolerated years of life with a bad-tempered author. Above all, my wife, Dilys Daws, sacrificed many holidays and other necessities. She must have suffered from the writing as much as I have, but with few of the rewards. Nevertheless, she found the heart to read each manuscript, advising and encouraging me at every stage. To round off, Miranda Chaytor was a superb editor.

Finally, I would like to express my thanks to all those anonymous psychoanalysts, Independents and others, who have made me think and stirred the evolution of this book.

# Introduction

PSYCHOANALYSIS IS ABOUT a hundred years old. Its ideas are still in ferment but there is no doubt that it has entered deeply into human culture. Now that the twenty-first century is nearly upon us, it seems appropriate to take stock of where psychoanalytic ideas have been and where they might fruitfully be going. This book aims to be descriptive, to portray the work of some British psychoanalysts during the past seventy years. It does not itself enter upon any evaluation, but there is naturally a hope that the book will be used in future discussion. Debates about ideas are, after all, the essence of any vital body of knowledge.

The book is not a collection of papers, nor is it an exhaustive work of scholarship. The aim has been to portray certain lines of thought which seem to be of sufficiently lasting value to put on record. We have tried to be searching and fair, but the selection is still limited and even idiosyncratic. Injustice will have been done in some way to every author mentioned, and we cannot but feel that they deserve better. Other works with different emphases are likely to be equally, or more, valid. It is to be hoped that these will follow from other pens.

Though the book has one writer, there have really been more than one author. As described in the Acknowledgements, Margret Tonnesmann deserves special credit for her contributions. Much thought from others has also gone into the making. Thus, it seems right to refer to the authorship in the coming pages in the plural, as 'we' rather than 'I'.

Psychoanalysis has never yet been very popular in Britain, even among the intelligentsia and in the universities. However, coming from a small group of people – there have been only a few hundred British psychoanalysts – a wealth of ideas has affected psychoanalytic thinking throughout the world. This is partly due to the fact that Freud himself and his daughter Anna settled in London, and much has germinated from being close to their authority. The freshness of ideas in Britain is also due to others who, like Melanie Klein, came from mainland Europe in the years before the Second World War. Nevertheless, many of the best-known originators have been born in Britain.

The British Psycho-Analytical Society was founded in 1919 and it flourished in the years before the war with an almost exclusively native British membership. However, a considerable number of them learnt their trade in Vienna or Berlin. Melanie Klein came to London in 1926, and, during the 1930s, many refugees from the Nazis arrived. During the war years a profound conflict arose between Melanie Klein and her followers on the one hand and Anna Freud and hers on the other. Two factions grew up and in certain ways these have continued ever since.

The majority of the British Society, particularly those who had been its original members, wished to take sides with neither group. They came to be known first as the 'Middle' group and later as the 'Independents'. All its members are committed psychoanalysts, but it is not a group or school that propounds any one particular theoretical, ideological or technical cause within analysis. It is a rather loose association of people with similar backgrounds and philosophy. Even so, there is a recognizable Independent style. This is hard to define, but we hope that it will emerge as the book describes the work of these psychoanalysts.

It seems that the Independents and their forebears combine specifically British values with the classical tradition of psychoanalysis as developed by Sigmund Freud. The spirit that brings these psychoanalysts together is thus not just British-born; it comes from Europe and other continents as well.

The Independents have developed psychoanalytic ideas in specific ways side by side with acceptance of basic Freudian teaching. They use concepts developed by Klein and her school as well as those of Anna Freud. However, one of their most important contributions has been the exploration of earliest child development and the fateful effects of environmental facilitation and trauma. From this viewpoint arises the proposition that environmental effects upon the individual contribute to traumata that can only be stored in memories which are 'frozen' or dissociated from a person's central ego or functional self. This conception adds to the classical psychoanalytic theory of repression as the prime element in the origin of psychopathology; it does not supplant it. The classical model still applies to conflicts that have reached an oedipal complexity of structure, whereas this aspect of theory developed by the Independents is seen as applying predominantly to disorders of self which first arise before that stage.

The book attempts to show the contributions of the main Independent figures. Jones, Sharpe, Glover, Flugel, Payne, Rickman, Strachey, Brierley, Fairbairn, Winnicott, Balint, Klauber, Khan and Bowlby are now dead, but we will consider also many analysts who are alive today and actively working and contributing. Our aim is not to portray the work of each author in rounded form. Rather, we have selected lines of thought and then shown a writer's contribution to each of these. After an historical introduction there are six chapters on theory. Then, based on these, there are three clinical chapters and one upon the applications of analysis. Lastly, we draw our conclusions. It has been outside the limitations of the book to give critical appraisals of each author, the aim is only to describe and summarize. Critical evaluation and debate must be left to the reader.

There have already been several excellent books published on the work of individual Independent authors: Davis and Wallbridge (1981), Clancier and Kalmanovitch (1987) and Phillips (1988) on Donald Winnicott and Sutherland (1989) on Ronald Fairbairn. Other books, on object relations theory, have described the work of some Independent theorists. These include Grolnik and Barkin (1978), Greenberg and Mitchell (1983), J. Klein (1987) and Hughes (1989). There is also a valuable collection of papers by Independents (Kohon, 1986a). However, there has not yet been a 'history of ideas' of this stream in psychoanalytic culture. It is this which we have attempted by gathering together its main lines of thought in historical sequence.

With the explosion of its concepts all over the world, psychoanalysis might be in danger of losing its own history. This could particularly happen to the Independent stream of thought, for its best-known authors have explicitly refrained from creating any school of disciples solely devoted to the propagation of their own ideas. As with the work of Freud himself, who changed his classical models as new findings made necessary, the contributions described in this book are open to further change and development.

We feel that their exposition is particularly important at this point because the very attitude of open-mindedness of the Independents makes them less striking, and thus less well known, both inside and beyond the British Isles, than the other two groups of psychoanalysts who separately adhere to a more unified approach to some aspects of theory and technique.

The key to an understanding of the Independents is their avowed openness to learning from any psychoanalytic theories. In recent decades the Independents, as well as using indigenous thinking, have drawn ideas largely from America but also from Europe and particularly from France. In order to give space to the main contributors to our theme we have by and large had to refrain from citing authors other than the Independents. Such analysts are likely to have been developing concepts very similar to, and maybe more important than, the ones we are going to describe.

# 1 From Beginnings to Controversy

## THE ROMANTIC AND EMPIRICAL TRADITIONS IN EUROPEAN THOUGHT

IN 1906 WILFRED TROTTER, an English surgeon, when talking to Ernest Jones, mentioned a man in Vienna 'who actually listened with attention to every word his patients said to him' (Jones, 1959, p. 159). This was perhaps the moment when psychoanalysis in Britain began. It was getting on for twenty years before more than a dozen people were practising it here. A 'British School' of psychoanalysis, with certain features of its own, was being identified by some soon after this. Ideas have been coming from this 'school' ever since. Some with originality in them have irrevocably shifted conceptual horizons. The work has come from people of many races and places of birth: English, Scots, Welsh, Irish, Jewish, European, South American, North American, Asian, South African, Australasian. All have had a few things in common: they have been members of the British Psycho-Analytical Society; they have worked together within a European cultural tradition but with a particular, maybe insular, British slant.

The Independent tradition stems from this British school of thought but it is not the only one. It is important to recognize that there has been a dialogue or dialectic process (perhaps better called 'trilectic') over the past fifty years in the British Psycho-Analytical Society among three movements. These have been: the Viennese tradition, led by Anna Freud; the followers of Melanie Klein; and those who wanted to side exclusively with neither. The last group, who became the Independents, are perhaps unlike the other two in particularly reflecting features of a certain British intellectual tradition. They have maybe been both enriched and trapped by it. For this reason Independent ideas cannot be understood in isolation; they originate in Britain, but are born of Freud, Melanie Klein and Anna Freud, as well as many others.

Psychoanalysts in London have firstly seen themselves as Europeans. From the time of Ernest Jones's youth until the 1930s at least, they sought their inspiration from across the water. Most early analysts went to Freud or one of his immediate colleagues in Vienna, Berlin or Budapest for a period of personal analysis.

On the European mainland, it seemed, a particular philosophical tradition had been flourishing for more than a century. Though largely academic in origin, it permeated and inspired much of European intellectual culture. Though perhaps originating in France, it has been said that it also owes its origins to English romantic poets like Keats, Shelley and Byron. The point of departure for philosophical romanticism, as it has come to be known, could be said to be recognizable in the work of Immanuel Kant and to have been predominantly neither French nor English but German.

In philosophical romanticism there is perhaps an underlying metaphysical doctrine that reality is derived from a living Spirit or the Absolute. This is essentially creative so that the ultimate foundation for all things is the urge to self-expression. Nature is one manifestation of Spirit, man another. Essential knowledge must be emotional and intuitive, there must be depth of feeling if reality is to be understood. Reason, being artificial and analytic, is inadequate to the task of comprehending the Absolute. The idealist tradition, stemming from romanticism and led by Fichte, Schopenhauer and Nietzsche, emphasized mind, soul, spirit and life. It stressed the non-sensuous, the valuational and the teleological. Empiricism, in contrast, emphasized the spatial, corporeal, sensuous, non-valuational, factual and mechanistic. The most powerful intellectual tradition of all at the time, the scientific attitude, is naturally more in sympathy with the empiricist than with the romantic point of view.

Freud was born into the heart of these traditions. He received a classical education but became a scientist by conviction. It is none the less easy to see his affinity with self-expression, knowing by intuition and depth of feeling. His dynamic point of view must have roots in teleology. Though he often denied their importance to him, certain central concepts came from philosophical writers. For instance, from Kant came the conception of motive, from Herbart the idea of unconscious processes and from Börne free association (Freud, 1920, pp. 263–5).

British intellectual traditions have differed somewhat from this. They probably rest on the history which was taught over many years in schools – a history which naturally involved an idealization of certain national characteristics and the omission of the nastier, murkier aspects of British culture. According to this historical tradition Britain is insular, and it was imperial and Protestant for over four hundred years. The ideology of British Protestantism drew its inspiration from the idea of the individual's personal, direct, moral contract with God. This inspiration cut across submission to the authority of priests and Pope. It was probably one of the foundations of the modern conception of the individual having personal responsibility for his own rules of conscience. In the late sixteenth century, when Protestantism was at its freshest, England particularly was mercantile and seafaring. Thrusting outwards, many people were identifying with its own separate national character which was expressed in the great literature of the time, the age of Shakespeare.

The following century, the seventeenth, was perhaps the greatest in British history for its flowering of ideas and cultural movements. It was also one of the stormiest. One of the kings of this time, Charles I, of Catholic inclinations and believing in the divine right of the monarch, clashed with the gentry and the merchants led by the House of Commons. In the Civil War which followed, a revolution of a very bloody nature, the king was defeated and publicly beheaded.

The Commonwealth that ensued was a time of the flowering of a multitude of original political ideologies. One influential movement was known as The Independents! But the government was oppressive and became loathed by lords, gentry and commoners alike. The son of the late king was asked to return, and there followed two and a half decades of easygoing stability. Towards the end of the century, however, a king came to the throne who threatened to turn the clock back to authoritarianism. Their ideals of freedom threatened, the lords, gentry, merchants and common people joined together and ousted James II in the 'glorious' bloodless revolution of 1688. Never again did they want the authoritarianism of Catholicism, the instability, as they saw it, of a republic or the tyrannies of enthusiastic ideologies. A constitutional monarch was found and the age of stable parliamentary government came into being. Political liberalism with its principles of social justice was born.

The aristocracy and middle classes at least were tired of the divine right of church or state. In principle they loathed ideological authoritarianism of any sort – they were not so bothered about this so long as they remained the masters on their own estates or slave-maintained colonies, of course. They disliked complex, closed systems of theory perhaps because they savoured of authoritarianism. They were sick of extremism – 'please to God, no enthusiasm' was often quoted. Romanticism with its enthusiastic ideology, which came later, was alien to this spirit, as also were charismatic movements.

There was, however, a dream of a quiet debate, dialogue and discourse that would lead to discussion. Here is the ideal or myth of British compromise, social justice, democracy, give and take, and fair play. This political liberalism has affinities with the empiricism of English philosophers of those centuries, such as Locke, Berkeley, Hume and J. S. Mill (whom incidentally Freud, as a young man, translated). Here knowledge tended to be seen as arising from perceptions and experience, not from innate ideas. Conflicting perceptions could, in a way, be sorted out by debate and compromise between the senses within the mind like social discussion between people. Empiricism has an affinity with the scientific attitude, with its evaluation of hypotheses in the light of factual evidence.

Here is empiricism, and pragmatism, in practice. Love of it brings a natural leaning towards experiment and trial and error. When using this mode of learning, the experience of error is often as valuable as correctness. We will find this philosophy in the Independents' approach to psychoanalysis as a therapy as well as a theory. These attitudes were – and are – of course ideologies, often based on myths, but they are none the less really powerful in British intellectual life.

Freud's ideas, with scientific methodology modulating the perception of emotionality and the psychodynamics of the unconscious born of romanticism and idealism, must have intrigued and disturbed the empirical, pragmatic-minded British intelligentsia. His underlying vision of an encompassing general psychology of the mind based upon psychoanalysis was alien to their nature. Even so, those who committed themselves to psychoanalysis in Britain at the start were almost pure English, Welsh or Scots. Their backgrounds were middle class, mercantile and professional, with some from the gentry. Many had deeply Protestant religious backgrounds, some were scientific, others literary and artistic. These early analysts were not themselves insular: they looked outwards with open minds. They were also deeply attuned to English empiricism and they disliked romantic ideologies that could be tainted with fanaticism. They sought discussion rather than combative and competitive debate, for this could deteriorate into ideological battle.

Ernest Jones, who could be called the father of the British Independent tradition, was by nature an autocrat, but in intellectual philosophy he was scientifically open-minded. In this at least British empiricism was deeply ingrained in him.

Thus, it is the empirical tradition of open-mindedness which provides a core inspiration and ethic for the British Independents. Incidentally, it was, we think, William Gillespie who first formulated this idea – though no written source has been traced. Independents come together because they are all committed psychoanalysts in the first place, and then, not because they espouse any particular theory within it, but simply because they have an *attitude* in common. This is to *evaluate and respect ideas for their use and truth value, no matter whence they come.* Here the positive use and enjoyment of doubt is essential. Ideological certainty and factionalism are alien to their spirit. Where differences occur the Independents prefer to settle them by discussion and compromise. This attitude is sometimes seen by other analysts as a sloppy eclecticism. It can certainly deteriorate into this, but essentially it requires careful scholarship and intense intellectual discipline. The demands upon an Independent mind are very high.

The Independent tradition stems explicitly from the 1940s when the majority of the British Psycho-Analytical Society wished to side exclusively with neither Melanie Klein nor Anna Freud. But the tradition really stretches back further to the time around the founding of the Society in 1919. We shall be introducing many of the early pioneers, for British psychoanalysis cannot be understood without them.

The original psychoanalysts in Britain were steeped in classical theory and technique and passed this on to their students (see Fenichel, 1946, and Greenson, 1967, for expositions of classical theory and technique). It cannot be overemphasized that the British Independents have always had the classical fundamentals of psychoanalysis in common: the existence of the unconscious, the theory of instincts, childhood sexuality and development, defence, displacement, symbolization, symptom formation, repetition, transference, resistance, transference neurosis and working through (King and Steiner, 1990). In other respects they may differ widely: some are hardly distinguishable from colleagues of Klein, others are closer to Anna Freud, while many use the ideas of both equally, as well as others from anywhere in the world. The Independents are thus not a close-knit group but a collection or at most an association of individual psychoanalysts.

Their ideology is a humanistic, decent-minded, democratic, kindly philosophy, and it is strong enough to inspire a way of life. But, by itself, it also has weaknesses. As in any democratic-minded philosophy which values individual freedom and responsibility, people can very readily fly in widely different directions. They can then become unsupportive strangers to one another. Original ideas may be born, but readily wither. Dislike of system-building, often characteristic of empiricism, can bring about neglect of coherent theory, which at best can give strength to the practice of a difficult technique in the face of adversity. Many Independents are seriously ignorant of their theoretical roots.

It is thus to a loose collection of individualists that we must look when setting out to search for and abstract the most important, vital and long-lasting themes or lines of thought which characterize the Independent tradition. We think we have found not only some of these, but also a particular attitude to, or idiom of, work, and this should emerge in the pages of this book.

## THE BEGINNINGS OF THE BRITISH PSYCHO-ANALYTICAL SOCIETY

It was Ernest Jones who founded the British Psycho-Analytical Society. His forebears were Welsh artisans. Brilliant scholastically, he gained scholarships and prizes as he went through school. At sixteen he started medical studies and qualified in London, with a gold medal, in 1900 at the age of twenty-one. Passionately devoted to science, he saw in it the hope for mankind's future. He read voraciously in all forms of literature and explored the arts. Determined to become a neurologist, he came first upon the work of Kraepelin, then upon the hysterical symptoms and problems of some of his patients, and then the work of Freud.

He went to Switzerland and met Jung in 1907, and in 1908 he travelled to Germany to study with Kraepelin for some months. In the summer of that year he attended the International Congress of psychoanalysis and met Freud for the first time. He read a paper there in which he introduced the new term 'rationalization'. For two or three years he seems to have hesitated between Kraepelinian psychiatry and psychoanalysis, and it was on the strength of the former that he was offered a post running the new psychiatric clinic of the Toronto medical school in Canada. There followed a most fruitful period of his literary output – dozens of papers explained analytic principles, with others on applied analysis as well as character analysis (Jones, 1948, 1974a, 1974b). Being without analytic colleagues in Canada, he must have worked out his new-found ideas by writing to a wider audience. Each summer he returned to Europe and increased his acquaintance with Freud and his circle. In 1910 he was the main founding force of the American Psychoanalytical Association.

Jones found Toronto 'provincial' and by 1913 moved back to London. During that year he founded the London Psycho-Analytic Society of about a dozen interested people. Among these was David Eder, a general practitioner in Soho, and Douglas Bryan, another GP from Leicester, who moved up to London to practise as an analyst. In 1914 the First World War isolated London from Freud. Dissatisfied with many of the members of the London Society who had followed Jung, who remained in contact with London, Jones saw no point in continuing dialogue with them. Thus, in 1919, he called together those still in agreement with him about psychoanalytic principles and together they voted to disband this Society and to found the British Psycho-Analytical Society. By this means the new Society had a membership of those of whose consistent understanding and furtherance of psychoanalysis Jones was sure. Full membership was effectively now open only to those who professionally practised psychoanalysis.

The group which assembled under Jones's leadership had brilliance. Between 1919 and 1924 most of those who were to become prominent in the next twenty years joined the British Society. By 1925 the Society had fifty-four members. Among them were David Eder and Douglas Bryan from the old London Society; J. C. Flugel, a distinguished academic psychologist; Joan Riviere, a gifted woman from a distinguished family; James Glover, a remarkable Scottish doctor who died young, and his brother, Edward, also a doctor; the writers James and Alix Strachey, members of the 'Bloomsbury Group'; Ella Sharpe, a teacher of literature and head of a teachers' training college. There was also Susan Isaacs (Brierley as she then was), an educational pioneer; Sylvia Payne, a doctor fresh from running wartime hospitals; William Stoddart, a well-known psychiatrist; John Rickman, a Quaker who had been organizing medical services in Russia; and Adrian Stephen, brother of Virginia Woolf, and his wife Karin. Melanie Klein and then Donald Winnicott came to the Society later, in the 1920s, as did Marjorie Brierley. Ronald Fairbairn, William Gillespie and John Bowlby came in the 1930s.

Jones was a strict professional, proud of his medical background, and he drove people to study medicine if at all possible. However, he saw, like Freud himself, that psychoanalysis would benefit from a wider base of skill and knowledge, so non-medicals, both men and women, were allowed to join the Society from the start.

The *International Journal of Psycho-Analysis* was founded in 1920, and at about the same time the publication of books in English was started. In 1924 the Institute of Psycho-Analysis, legally empowered to handle business transactions, was formed. This cleared the way for the start of the International Library of Psycho-Analysis. It was John Rickman, once a law student, who masterminded much of this administrative creativity with Jones. Perhaps following from this early example, the Independents have a strong tradition of administrative service and competence. In 1926 the London Clinic of Psycho-Analysis for low-fee patients was founded, and Rickman was its first director. At the same time a formal training in psychoanalysis was instituted with a training committee consisting of Jones, Rickman, Glover, Flugel and Bryan. Thus, by the mid-1920s, the Society had established itself. Its form and functions remain very much the same, sixty years later.

In 1925 news had come from Berlin, where many British aspirants went for analysis with Abraham or Sachs, of Melanie Klein's work with children. She had felt spurned in Vienna and isolated in Berlin even though appreciated by Ferenczi and Abraham. Her first visit to London was orchestrated by Alix Strachey who was in Berlin at the time. Jones himself was hesitant to start with, but Klein came over in 1925 to lecture and was much appreciated. Jones now was enthusiastic, and in the following year Klein came over to settle, was well received and clearly well liked. There are references to her in the British literature from 1927 onwards.

Her analyses of small children, of two years old and upwards, opened up a new realm, the small child's phantasy world. The enthusiastic response of the British analysts of the time came from the informed; Isaacs and Sharpe, for instance, were distinguished professionals in the field of child development and education.

Klein's first point of departure from classical analysis at the time was to treat children's play as equivalent to the free associations of adult patients. She revealed the presence in very young children of complex systems of phantasy which had not been conceived of before. These were sometimes consciously reported but were more often inferred by Klein from the child's play. Naturally no data were received directly from children under two years old, but Klein saw good reason to interpolate backwards and infer *systems of unconscious phantasy* in the early weeks and months of life. (Here we must pause for a moment to explain the British usage of 'phantasy' as distinct from 'fantasy'. 'Fantasy', for the British but not the Americans, tends to have the connotation of a caprice or fanciful whim. 'Phantasy', on the other hand, is thought of as deeper, as imagination or a visionary notion. Since the psychoanalytic concept is concerned with imagination, the British tend to use the term 'phantasy' (Rycroft, 1968b).)

Klein soon began to conceive that it was the child's own destructive impulses deflected from sources in the death instincts that created most anxiety and were thus a primary pathogen. With this in mind she became convinced of the necessity for early interpretation of destructive and hate-laden phantasy, particularly in relation to the analyst, even in the first session. This was a technique which was contrary to Freud's classic teaching that mild positive transference feelings should not be interfered with and that feelings about the analyst, the transference, should be interpreted only when they were emerging as resistance to progress.

By the mid-1920s, after Freud's *Mourning and Melancholia* (1917) with its concern with loss, and at the time of *Inhibitions, Symptoms and Anxiety* (1926) with its new concept of signal anxiety, the atmosphere in Vienna and Berlin was tending towards interest in environmental instigators of neurosis. This was not the direction of Klein's interest. However, Jones and many of the British were also particularly interested in hate and aggression as manifestations of innate instincts and as determinants of behaviour rather than as environmental stress-activated aggressive responses.

In 1926 Anna Freud published her book on child analysis. Her views, for instance on the nature of early fantasy and on the transference of children, were very different from those of Melanie Klein. At a meeting of the British Society on the subject, Klein trenchantly attacked Anna Freud's contentions, agreeing with very few of them. She was supported in these criticisms by Riviere and Sharpe and finally by Jones himself (King and

Steiner, 1990). The proceedings were published in the *International Journal of Psycho-Analysis* (1927, p. 330). Freud himself took pains to remain neutral. It seems likely that the Freuds' antipathy to Klein and their suspicion of the British Society were beginning to crystallize at that time. It can be reasoned that Klein was simply making honest scientific criticisms, but their sharp form was probably received in Vienna as going beyond this. The fact that many of the London analysts spoke in agreement with her is also likely to have fuelled Viennese suspicion of the British Society as a whole.

Up to 1934 Mrs Klein had read eleven papers and other communications to the Society in London. She was appreciated as an outstanding contributor, though not always uncritically, and she was regarded as an equal and valued colleague. But as yet she had no particular body of followers.

By the 1930s the atmosphere between London and Vienna was so tense that a series of exchange lectures was arranged to inform both sides. There were differences not only about Klein's views, but also about female sexuality and the manifestation of the death instinct. Debate on these last two issues was led by Jones in person and had little to do with Klein. Jones's ambitiousness was also well known and the Viennese were likely to have been suspicious of this. The exchanges began, but world events prevented their completion. The subject Jones took up for his part in the exchange was female sexual development (1935). Arguing quite openly with Freud, he disagreed with his phallocentric theory and asserted that little girls had an early awareness of the vagina. Their body feelings, said Jones, are not the same as those of boys in the pre-oedipal years – as Freud had proposed. Jones quoted the evidence gathered by his formidable group of female analysts, Payne, Brierley, Klein, Sharpe, Riviere, Isaacs *et al.* (see Chapter 5). Although Freud did not agree with Jones, he seems to have been undisturbed by the debate. This was to be expected in view of the fact that Jones was completely loyal to Freud personally.

In his running of the British Society Jones was a most efficient organizer, but he was an autocrat and was often resented for his arrogance and high-handedness in public dealings. He was respected but hardly loved, for he and Edward Glover, who became his right-hand man after Rickman had resigned from many of his administrative posts, made no secret of their belief that they held a monopoly in the referral of patients.

Jones was thus feared especially by the non-medical analysts. He was punctilious, did not suffer fools, encouraged those seen as clever but was impatient with those he thought little of. However, as well as being a brilliant administrator, he was generous with time and money, extraordinarily brave and loyal, single-minded, and gifted with intelligence and inexhaustible vitality. He was a man of rare stature.

In 1933, the Nazis came to power in Germany. As President of the International Association, Jones set about finding ways to help refugees leave Germany and settle in England and other countries. In this he and Anna Freud co-operated closely, even though they were on opposite sides in the Klein debate. The correspondence between them at this time shows two profound and brave people.

In 1938 the Nazis entered Austria and marched into Vienna. Jones immediately went straight there and Rickman followed soon after. It was largely Marie Bonaparte with her Greek royal connections and the American diplomat William Bullitt who persuaded the Nazis to let Freud go, but it was Jones who persuaded Freud himself and obtained visas for him and his family. Two months later the Freuds came to London. Nearly all the analysts from Vienna came at about the same time. Most then moved on across the Atlantic – among other reasons, there is little doubt that Jones felt there was not much room for more competition in London. But some, including Anna Freud, stayed. What had been a disagreement over a thousand miles was now one over a distance of a thousand yards.

## THE CONTROVERSIAL DISCUSSIONS OF THE 1940s

In the later 1920s and early 1930s Klein had begun to be more definite about the dating of the origin of neurotic conflicts. She took them back in time far earlier than Freud, for instance placing the origins of the Oedipus complex in the earliest months of life (Klein, 1928). If this triadic set of relationships comes so early, it could not have been developed over time in a family environment, as in Freud's view of the complex. For Klein it was much more endogenous to the infant. By the mid-1930s, she was turning her investigations (Klein, 1935) to the part played in depression by destructiveness, derived from the death instincts, and to the importance of remorse and concern about this in both normal and pathological development. At that time she introduced the concept of the *depressive position* (Klein, 1935, 1940), and this has played a large part in much British thinking. According to Klein, this position is reached when the infant realizes that his or her love and hate are directed to the same object, mother. He is thus beginning to experience ambivalence and also his own effects upon another object. Klein was the first to point to the importance of the unconscious impulse to repair objects felt to have been damaged by the destructive attacks of hate. This is intrinsic to depressive responsiveness.

It will be noted that Klein was invariably concerned with the individual's relation to objects: hence she was epitomized as an 'object-relations theorist'. But she was primarily interested in primitive instinctual impulses and their phantasied effects upon *internal* objects. She was not so interested in the details of how real external objects might contribute to phantasies and to pathology in general. She envisaged real objects as having an ameliorating effect upon pathological anxieties. But the origins of anxiety lay in aggression – which was fundamentally innate and founded upon the projection of the death instincts from the self. In other words, many analysts felt that, for Klein, real external parents tended to be viewed as 'good' objects, but their traumatizing or 'bad' aspects were often ignored. This question later came to be one of the focuses of contention with the Independents, particularly Winnicott and Fairbairn. It has been said, for instance, that many of Winnicott's original theoretical papers are, in effect, addressed to Klein in an attempt to convince her to modify her point of view.

It was not till the later 1940s and 1950s that Klein turned her interest fully towards schizoid phenomena (1946). In the 1930s she had led Ronald Fairbairn towards consideration of depressive states; in the 1940s it was his turn to point out the importance of the schizoid position and the central role of splitting of ego and object in it. She, however, took a vital further step which Fairbairn had not envisaged. This was to point out the importance of denial and projection of parts of the self in schizoid mechanisms. This is now usually referred to using the term projective identification.

We have noted how Freud, though careful not to take sides, became suspicious of Klein, especially after the public attack by her upon Anna in 1927. He seems later to have gone as far as to suspect that she was deviating to create an alternative theory that destroyed essentials of psychoanalysis. Klein always denied this and no doubt felt hurt, but in the

London of the 1930s she was well protected by Jones and others. From 1938, however, the hostile Viennese had become part of the British Society. It was very soon clear that all was not going to settle down happily. It might have been expected that the coming of the Second World War would have served to settle differences, at least for the time being, but it was not to be. With the war, psychoanalytic practice was most seriously disrupted. Many members, like Rickman, Foulkes, Stephen, Scott, Rosenberg (later Zetzel) and Bion (who was still a student), went into the medical corps. Here, imbued with the urgency of war, they started a vigorous analytic interest in group, community and institutional phenomena. Analysts worked in close co-operation with social scientists for the first time. In the Tavistock Institute of Human Relations, formed after the war, this co-operation has continued (see Chapter 11).

Anna Freud stayed in London to found the Hampstead Nurseries. Melanie Klein and some of her main colleagues left London. The two sides began to draw into themselves – into battle order. It is remarkable how the Viennese, refugees and in London for only a year, had managed to go on to the conceptual offensive. But by now they had a few strong, anti-Klein supporters in the British Society.

As early as 1935, Klein's daughter, Melitta Schmideberg, who, though young, had already published many papers, had begun to dispute with her mother in scientific meetings. These disagreements reached levels of unpleasant invective, on Melitta's part at least. Edward Glover, earlier a supporter of Klein, joined in Schmideberg's attacks. They were supported by Friedlander and Low and then by the Viennese.

Jones left London in 1939 to practise in Sussex. Though still President of the Society, he left the running of many meetings to Glover. By early 1940 tension had reached sufficient proportions for James Strachey to write the following letter. It reflects the sentiments of those, the majority of the British Society at the time, who later became Independents. It crystallizes the emotions felt by many for much of the next forty years (it is here quoted in full by kind permission of the Archives of the British Psycho-Analytical Society).

Dear Glover,                    April 23rd 1940.
  I'm celebrating the arrival of spring in bed with some sort of feverish cold - so I'm afraid there's no chance of my getting to London for the Training Committee tomorrow.

I should rather like you to know (for your personal information) that – if it comes to a showdown – I'm very strongly in favour of compromise at all costs. The trouble seems to me to be with extremism, on *both* sides. My own view is that Mrs K. has made some highly important contributions to $\psi\alpha$, but that it's absurd to make out (a) that they cover the whole subject or (b) that their validity is axiomatic. On the other hand I think it's equally ludicrous for Miss F. to maintain that $\psi\alpha$ is a game reserve belonging to the F. family and that Mrs K's views are fatally subversive.

These attitudes on both sides are of course purely religious and the very antithesis of science. They are also (on both sides) infused by, I believe, a desire to dominate the situation and in particular the future – which is why both sides lay so much stress on the training of candidates. Actually, of course, it's a megalomanic mirage to suppose that you can control the opinion of the people you analyse beyond a very limited point. But in any case it ought naturally to be the aim of a training analysis to put the trainee into a position to arrive at his own decisions upon moot points – not to stuff him with your own private dogmas.

In fact I feel like Mercutio about it. Why should these wretched fascists and (bloody foreigners) communists invade our peaceful compromising island? But I see I'm more feverish than I'd thought.

Anyhow, I feel that any suggestion of a 'split' in the society ought to be condemned and resisted to the utmost.

Yours Sincerely,
James Strachey

By 1941 the atmosphere in scientific meetings was becoming electric. Eva Rosenfeld, who, like Rickman, had had analysis with both Freud and Klein, recalled them as 'the nightmare years' (personal communication). It is puzzling that there should be such passion on matters of theory in the midst of a world war. The situation was that London was being bombed nearly every night, and many did not know whether they would survive, let alone what would happen to analysis – to which they had given their lives. They felt they were the protectors of precious ideas which were threatened not only by bombs but from within their colleagues and themselves. Also, it was hardly possible to go on practising analysis, which is vital to keep coherent analytic ideas alive. Ideological

venom and character assassination were released under these circumstances. Where many people found a new communality under the threats
of war, the opposite happened to psychoanalysts in London.

The records of the Society show that there were other issues active as
well as the Freud–Klein dispute (King and Steiner, 1990). Glover, one of
the main protagonists in the quarrel, was disliked for his high-handed,
anti-democratic running of the Society. A constitution for the Society
had been drawn up in 1920 but in it there had been no provision for
limitations to the tenure of office-holders. Jones had in effect created the
Society and then run it autocratically from then on. Why this was
tolerated by the membership for so long is an interesting question. He
was President continuously for twenty-seven years in all! What is more,
both Jones and Glover were thought to be aloof and high-handed in their
handling of relations with the public and other professions, and many –
being sensitive to the communal spirit of wartime – were incensed by this.
A new constitution was in the air, and questions about power were being
asked. A priority was the question about who should be empowered to
train students. It was with them, after all, that the future of analysis lay.
This was one of the deep-seated reasons for the ugliness of the Freud–
Klein dispute.

In 1942 there was a series of business meetings, very acrimonious
indeed, but chaired by Ernest Jones with courtesy and fairness. In these it
was decided to hold a series of theoretical discussions to air the controversial views. It was agreed that two of Mrs Klein's closest collaborators
should pre-circulate papers formulating the main tenets of Kleinian
thought. These were Susan Isaacs and Paula Heimann, who had come as
a young analyst from Berlin ten years before. She had a second analysis
with Klein and became her closest assistant. Later, in the 1950s, she
broke away and was a leading influence with the British Independents for
many years. The papers – on primitive development, on the nature of
phantasy and on introjection and projection – have become milestones in
the history of psychoanalysis. A committee was elected to organize the
discussion of these papers, and replies to them were carefully prepared
beforehand by participants. A main point at issue was whether the
phantasies described by Klein as occurring in the first year of life were
valid inferences – for inferences they must be. Anna Freud was certain
they were not valid. It was also contended that Klein's stress upon
destructiveness as the primary pathogen drew attention away from infan-

tile sexuality. Closely allied to this was disquiet at Klein's dating of various developmental events. The Oedipus complex, for instance, was seen by her as occurring in the early months rather than early years. Likewise, the organization of the super-ego was, according to Klein, reached much earlier and very differently from in Freud's model.

Anna Freud, Glover, the Schmidebergs and their collaborators (the Hoffers, Friedlander, Low, Burlingham and Lantos) objected vehemently to the Kleinian papers. Isaacs is remembered for the debating brilliance of her defence of Klein. Other analysts, the ones later to call themselves Independent, representing the majority of the Society, took a measured approach: they disagreed with Klein on some issues and supported her on many others. The contributions of such as Payne, Brierley, Sharpe and also Balint, Bowlby and Gillespie are models of careful thought. These discussions, documented verbatim, are now published (King and Steiner, 1990); Hayman's paper (1989) is also useful.

The Controversial Discussions, set up as an intellectual and not as a psychotherapeutic venture, were probably doomed from the start if resolution of conflict was the aim. However, they still served to clarify conceptual issues. Jones left the chairing of the crucial discussions to Glover who was thoroughly partisan.

## THE GENTLEMEN'S AGREEMENT

The Society was still riven by dissent. A general meeting appointed three open-minded and respected members to work out a new constitution. These were John Rickman, Sylvia Payne and William Gillespie. Incidentally, these three names are not renowned for their literary output, but, as well as for the constitution, they are all, especially Rickman, quite separately remembered by many for their outstanding generosity, sense of fairness and wisdom. Such qualities do not often get the publicity that well-known writers receive, but the character of the British Society has rested on such as these. The constitution was drawn up in 1944, a democratic one with regular elections. Glover, probably responding to his unpopularity and seeing that he had no hope of being elected president, resigned from the Society. It thus lost a remarkable, independently thinking mind. In 1946, after the war and with members returning to

London, Jones, president for so long, stood down. Sylvia Payne, respected for her administrative fairness, was elected president.

Meanwhile a new training structure was being worked out to find a compromise between the interests of Klein and Anna Freud as well as the neutral British. A scheme was devised whereby there were two streams of training for students. There was the 'A' stream for students with British and Kleinian training analysts and the 'B' stream for Anna Freud's and her colleagues' students. As the main body of the British were determined not to lapse into 'extremism' they insisted that, while a student's first supervisor might be Kleinian or Anna Freudian, the second supervisor must come from neither camp. It was laid down that they must come from the 'middle'. Thus, upon a matter of training principle, was born the 'Middle' Group. The stipulation about a middle-group second supervisor lapsed in the mid-1950s, but most analysts, whether involved in training or not, had by then definitely begun to identify themselves as 'Kleinian', 'B' or 'Middle' Group. Although it has never been written into any formal constitution, a 'gentlemen's agreement' then grew up which in effect divided the Society into the three groups, each having a carefully maintained equal status in the selection for administrative posts. The Middle Group later came to call themselves Independents. This term was chosen to emphasize the philosophy that, given a basic commitment to psychoanalysis, each analyst should be free to develop and decide upon his further identifications and loyalties.

The group structure brought a new stability – it was 'good old British compromise'. Other institutions from other nations might have split and gone their separate ways and this might have been better. The British saw, and still see, the grouping as no more than a necessary expedient. The tripartite division has been maintained to the present day. Members of the different groups are often long-standing intimate friends and colleagues who have, through the shared worries of work, developed a trust for each other that transcends group allegiances. Even so, there is frequent acrimony about group-ideological matters. Many voices now say that the division has outlived its usefulness and that the time has come for change.

The end of the war brought a flood of new recruits to analysis. In the country at large, social, medical, welfare and psychological concerns were at the forefront of everyone's minds. It was a socially optimistic

time, and analysts became innovators in the application of psychoanalytic concepts in various fields. The late 1940s and 1950s were the time of
a great flowering of the British Independents, and it is to the main lines of
their thought that we will direct our attention now.


## ANNA FREUD, KLEIN AND THE INDEPENDENTS

It must be made plain that, whatever the achievements of Independents in
their own right, these have come in part from a creative interplay with
ideas stemming from Anna Freud (1926, 1936, 1965, 1971) and her colleagues on the one hand and the Kleinians on the other. Independents
have used ideas from both schools in varying proportions as well as ideas
of their own and from other countries. This mix, in the setting of the
Independents' own particular philosophy, is evident in many publications.

The theoretical contributions of Anna Freud in the field of analysis of
defence are regarded by many Independents without controversy and as
forming a basic core in their everyday work. Her work on developmental
lines is well recognized, accepted and used also without controversy. The
later work on development by her colleagues is also used. American ego-
psychology and self-psychology are perhaps less well mastered by many
but none the less used. It must be emphasized again that Independent
thinking takes basic classical psychoanalytic theory and technique as
axiomatic: the characteristics of the unconscious; defence and resistance;
interpretation and the transference; metapsychology. All these may be
reinvestigated but never dismissed.

There is no doubt that the contributions of Klein and those who have
come after her – Bion, Rosenfeld, Segal, Money-Kyrle, Bick, Thorner,
Joseph, Meltzer (Spillius, 1988a, 1988b; Hinshelwood, 1989) – have been
major sources of inspiration, in varying proportions, to many Independents. They adopted Klein's ideas of systems of phantasy and particularly
of the importance of the mechanisms of denial, projection and introjection creating splits for defensive purposes in the personality. The conception of projective identification is used with facility by many Independents. Klein gave the Independents her unique vision of the internal
world with its vital complexity.

Many Independents think that Fairbairn's (1940, 1944, [1952]) specific
contribution on splitting was as important as Klein's. We have noted that

he introduced the idea of the *schizoid position* to Klein, and he also dealt with psychic structures emanating from it more systematically than she did. He used the term schizoid to describe the early events where the infant interprets rejection and frustration as being because his love is destructive of his mother's love. There is then a reaction to this by the splitting of both the ego or self, and also its corresponding object, into discrepant good and bad parts. From these fateful events, Fairbairn thinks, arise many aspects of the multiplicity of character structure. He thus saw these early events as arising out of *environmental* provision and traumata and developed a model of the mind out of this in a systematic way. However, Fairbairn did not emphasize the importance of projections in schizoid mechanisms; this was one of Klein's great contributions.

The early origins of guilt, out of a two-person relationship, and defences against it, together with the emergence of Klein's depressive position, are widely agreed – though Winnicott and some Independents preferred to use the term 'stage of concern'.

However, Independents do not widely subscribe to Klein's particular theory of neonatal development, either in her dating or in the means by which one position is said to succeed the other. Thus, many do not subscribe to her description of the early infantile central predominance of the *paranoid-schizoid position*. This was formulated by Klein (1946) as being the result of the mode by which the infant deals with his innate destructive impulses by splitting of ego and object into good and bad parts. The destructive impulses are then projected on to the bad objects by whom he then feels persecuted. It constitutes the infant's first attempt to master his death instinct. Independents would agree that the paranoid-schizoid position itself is of great importance, but largely, as we have just noted with regard to Fairbairn's view, as a *reactive* development consequent upon infant–environment interactions and *trauma*. Fairbairn, for instance, would agree that the schizoid precedes the depressive position as part of development, but Balint and Winnicott consider it to be largely a pathological byway, very common but not essentially prior to depressive experience.

Summarizing, there is a strong line of thinking among the Independents that affirms the central importance of both the paranoid-schizoid and depressive positions in pathology and sees both as reaction patterns to traumatic impingements. There is doubt whether the one must succeed the other in normal primitive emotional development. This may be the case, but our knowledge of infancy is felt to be still insufficient to be definitive about the issue.

Though most Independents may subscribe to the idea of innate propensities, they tend not to agree with Klein's assumption of a quite highly articulated inborn ego with well-developed complex patterns of motive and affect – such as innate envy. To them envy is an emotion, more complex than a drive, which is what Klein would see it as. Nor do they agree with the correlative idea of a well-developed innate body image.

Perhaps most important is the disagreement concerning the origin of psychopathology. It seems that ultimately Klein sees pathology as rooted in a conflict between impulses, originally between life and death instincts. These then transform into conflicts between love and hate in relation to objects. The mental representatives of these impulses take the form of phantasies, often very frightening. There are specific defensive structures against these experiences which in themselves have phantastic content. Experiences with real external parents can ameliorate pathology, but they themselves are not viewed primarily as pathogens.

Independents, on the other hand, vary in their thinking but tend to conceive of the crucial origins of pathology as lying, as we have already noted, in the first place in real external object-relations. Phantasy then arises out of these. They would probably argue that all imagination, and hence phantasy, is an 'inference' or 'interpretation', however instantaneous or mistaken it might be, which includes an idea of things outside the self. Imagination or phantasy thus probably arises out of the interplay between infant and environment and has no meaning as an innate faculty.

Kleinians today often emphasize that they too do not ignore the environment. This is clearly true in their clinical presentations and also in such theory as Bion's (1963) conception of mother as a 'container'. Independents reply that there must surely be a connection between this newer emphasis and the well-known arguments on the subject in the 1940s and 1950s by such as Bowlby and Winnicott. These are rarely acknowledged by the Kleinians as having been important to them.

Fairbairn, Winnicott, Bowlby and Balint all unequivocally see the origins of much pathology in infantile traumata. These are often seen as arising from various forms of loss of real intimacy with parents – particularly with mother. Such early intimacy, when working well, seems likely to have its own special form or emotional patterning of delight – even perhaps its own experience of primitive beauty or something close to it. Loss of the assurance of such experience constitutes a trauma.

Alternatively, traumata may arise from distortions of reality and from overstimulation. Fairbairn, for instance, goes on to propound that the individual thenceforward searches in one way or another for his lost intimacy or its substitutes. The human being is, in this sense, 'object-seeking' rather than simply pleasure-seeking. The so-called 'British School', in which Kleinians and Independents are often muddled together, is inevitably associated with the 'object-relations' point of view. Like most psychoanalysts, Independents are likely to hold to the classical view of the importance of body functioning and of drives arising from it. But they often assign equal motivational strength to desires for and about objects, both in the form of external things and people, and as internal structures and their associated phantasies.

The differences in view about sources of pathology have led to some important and deeply felt differences in views about the technique of analysis. For instance, it has already been noted that Kleinians tend to concentrate upon what the patient's destructive impulses, with their innate basis, have done to his internal objects. Many Independents tend to think that this concentration upon innate destructiveness and hate can lead to a patient's false conformity during psychoanalytic treatment.

The Independents, tending to see pathology as arising from real, faulty object-relations, are more concerned with the repetition of these bad object-relations, first in psychopathology and then in the developing drama of the therapeutic relation. Thus, they are likely to believe in forming a working alliance and waiting for the individual structure of this drama to evolve before starting formal interpretations. In this way they are closer to classical analytic technique, which waits for the transference neurosis to develop, than they are to the Kleinians' approach. Both Independents and Kleinians, however, nowadays equally stress the fundamental importance of the countertransference. Nevertheless they use it rather differently: the Kleinians tend to view the analyst's countertransference feelings as having been created predominantly by the patient's projective activity. The Independents are more likely to view the analyst's feelings as having been created both by the patient and by the analyst himself within the setting of the particular pattern of their relationship at the time. They often perceive this as a repetition of early mother–infant emotional encounters.

We have tried to summarize the main hallmarks that identify the theoretical and also technical positions of the three groups which constitute the British Psycho-Analytical Society. In the following chapters we will discuss in some detail the contributions from those early analysts whom we have regarded as independent in spirit. Then comes the portrayal of the work, over the last forty-five years, of Independents who have carried forward the spirit of open-mindedness that prevailed before the tripartite structure had to be evolved.

# 2 Emotion, Object and Person

## EARLY THINKING ABOUT AFFECTS

THIS CHAPTER CONFINES itself to introducing the ideas of affect, self, object-relations, their numerosity or condition with respect to number, and the alternatives of internal–external. These concepts are much used, even if often only implicitly, by Independents.

Taking the lead from Kant, philosophers in the last century tended to conceive of the mind as divided into thinking, willing and feeling. The early psychologists Latinized the terminology into cognition, conation and affect but kept the same order of classification. Cognition tended to become the preserve of the academics while conation or willing was a field naturally worked over by Freud and psychodynamic theory. Affect and feeling remained somewhat poor relations.

The definitions of affect, feeling and emotion are vague. Affect has sometimes been used specifically of the experience associated with desire, but more usually it is a generic term covering any emotional state or mood, whereas feeling has been more widely used to refer to any experience of the self and its body sensations. However, they are frequently used synonymously with the idea of emotion, and we will continue this usage here. It is interesting to note that the term 'emotion' is sometimes usefully reserved, by T. S. Eliot for instance, for the act of communication of feeling.

The concept of affects has played an important part in psychoanalytic theory from the beginning. Freud first conceived of psychic conflict as being between ideas with incompatible feeling charges. Ideas became dynamic from their feeling charges.

With the development of instinct theory, affect was understood as the qualitative expression of the quantity of instinctual energy and its fluctuations (Laplanche and Pontalis, 1973). Here affects are conceived of as psychic tension states which compel towards motor, secretory and circulatory discharges and which result in an internal alteration of a person's body (Brierley, 1937).

In 1915 Freud stated that instinctual impulses in conflict give rise to a call for defensive action. Ideas representing the impulses are retained in the unconscious while the quantitative factor, the affect, is consciously experienced but mainly transformed into anxiety. Thus affects presuppose a quantitative theory of cathexis, and Laplanche and Pontalis (1973), for instance, consider that this is the only theory which can account for an affect's apparent independence of its various specific manifestations.

When he introduced his second theory of anxiety in 1926, Freud maintained the quantitative aspect of affect and its close link with physiological phenomena. He then suggested that affects are reproductions of very early pre-individual experiences of vital importance which orientate the ego towards adaptation. He differentiated between traumatic and signal anxiety. Traumatic anxiety is a biological event where psychic functioning cannot cope adaptively with a massive flooding of anxiety; signal anxiety on the other hand consists of the release of a smaller quantity of affect which activates appropriate adaptive ego functions.

At this time Freud also introduced a developmental theory about that aspect of affect which is directly experienced. Here separation anxiety is the earliest anxiety. This undergoes a developmental sequence: first there is dread of loss of the object – mother; then of loss of the love of the object; and later comes anxiety about loss of the love of the internalized object, the super-ego. From this point of view Freud saw castration anxiety as a form of separation anxiety. It can be seen that, while Freud continued to maintain the quantitative theory of affect as a tension state and disturbance of functioning, he also saw the actual experience of affects as a means of orientation towards living (Green, 1977).

Turning now to developments in Britain, in the 1920s there was, under Jones's leadership, a particular interest in the work not only of Freud but also of Abraham and Ferenczi. Ferenczi particularly turned a detailed eye on the clinical complexities of emotional states. His influence was reinforced when Balint came to Britain from Hungary in the late 1930s. Jones himself wrote 'Fear, guilt and hate' in 1929. Here he shows how diverse affects can influence, or cover up, one another. It is of interest to note that specific affects are here beginning to be used as basic *units* in the conceptual building of a piece of theory in psychoanalysis.

From the point of view of the development of Independents' thinking in this region it was Brierley (1937) who was seminal, but to understand this it is valuable to describe the work of two of the people who influenced her. The academic psychologist William McDougall (1908) was, unusually in England, a theoretical system builder. He constructed a model of the mind by defining in detail an array of specific biologically based instinctual patterns. These were: reproductive, parental, pugnacious, gregarious, acquisitive, playful, imitative instincts and the like. They were based on innate tendencies but modifiable through experience. What is more, these primary instincts could combine and modify each other to a well nigh infinite extent. The main point of interest for us is that McDougall envisaged each instinct pattern as giving rise to its own specific experience of emotion. There were thus simple emotions based upon the primary instincts and also complex emotions and sentiments which were the experiential aspects of combinations of instincts. McDougall's work seems now to have disappeared from sight and is of historical interest only, but he was used by Jones. Moreover, he was a deeply formative influence upon Flugel, who studied under him, and upon Brierley who was Flugel's student. He also influenced both Glover and Rycroft.

Flugel, both an academic and a practising psychoanalyst, illuminated the common ground between academic psychology and psychoanalysis in the region of drives, affects and emotion. In his *Studies in Feeling and Desire* (1955) we see McDougall's and Freud's conceptions being repeatedly compared and contrasted together with efforts to integrate them. Flugel's role as a mediator between two cultures was acknowledged as important between the 1920s and 1940s, but his work is little referred to by later authors.


## BRIERLEY

### AFFECT AND OBJECT RELATION

Flugel's student, Marjorie Brierley (1937), is a very important figure in British Independents' clinical thinking (Hayman, 1986). She showed how affects, in surrendering pride of place to the instincts, had been neglected by psychoanalysis. They are not simply energy-discharge phenomena but, as Freud had begun to investigate in 1926, highly complex functional *ego* activities in everyday adaptation. What is more, she explicitly ties primary affect development to *object relations*. In making this step she was a co-founder of object-relations theory. She speaks of the object cathexis of affects rather than their energy charge.

Brierley formulates an important hypothesis about experience in infancy: that in the beginning the *object is indistinguishable from the affect*. The infant is aware of feelings, which are body feelings of course. They are the main objects of his subjective experience to begin with: the infant's object *is* the affect. Thenceforward, as objects come to be discriminated as outside the self, they are known mainly from the particular patterns of affects evoked in and around them. By stressing the object relation in affect Brierley epitomizes the main thrust of the British School of the time, Melanie Klein being then one of them. The French analyst André Green (1977, p. 144) says 'for writers of the English school, it is not a question of pushing back affect towards biology, but rather of setting it in a framework of primitive sensibility, the vestiges of which must be sought by the analyst in the analytic situation through the transference and counter-transference'.


## GLOVER

### AFFECT AND INSTINCT

Perhaps because of his rather ignominious role in the Controversial Discussions and his subsequent departure from the British Society, Edward Glover is not much quoted by later Independent writers, but his scholarly influence was great throughout the 1920s and 1930s. In some of his most important papers (1932a, 1932b, 1939, 1943) he spells out the central function of affects within his rigorously classical model of the mind. It bears striking similarities to that of McDougall, and Glover was indeed working closely at the time with two of McDougall's pupils, Flugel and Brierley.

With the precise and closely packed reasoning typical of him, Glover investigates the many ways in which affects can be studied (1939). Introspections must be the starting point, but then affects can be described individually and labelled. From this they can be classified as fixed or labile, as positive or reactive, by reference to instinct or as simple or compound, and so on.

He points out (1932b) that even in earliest infancy every instinctual *impulse involves a specific ego function.* More specifically impulse frustration and gratification *create* particular ego functions. This is close both to Piaget's description of earliest learning and to an operant conditioning model. He uses already a kind of modern control-systems thinking which makes it plain that there can be no goal-directed behaviour, as in any drive, without a feedback control system. Here he is close to Fairbairn who also saw that every drive must involve an ego function – a control system, however limited its scope (see Chapter 7). In the neonate, Glover, probably mistakenly on recent evidence (Stern, 1985), sees little sign of an overall organizing ego. But he does specify, much less controversially, an array of simple, largely reflex-bound drive or instinct patterns which are controlled by *ego nuclei.* These would include, say, a hungry infant rooting: head orientating towards the breast, finding it, then sucking. Another example would be the sequential constriction and dilation of the sphincters with evacuation of a full bowel or bladder and so on. The individual's *experience* of the bodily urge to carry out, and then of the act itself, has its own specific quality and is termed a *primary affect.*

With development these disparate functions combine into higher or more integrated organizations. The ego nuclei always remain active. In health they are never destroyed. However, with growth a central ego becomes a superordinate organizing structure. And, just as the ego nuclei combine, so too naturally must their representatives in experience also join together so that *compound affects* develop. The memories of affects then become data for later use by the ego. An affect points to possible *future* qualities of pleasure, pain, anxiety and so on.

Glover goes on to show how compound affects can be analysed into their simple components, whereas simple affects are unanalysable. For instance, he led the way in showing how envy is complex, with its comparison of qualities possessed by self and object: it is readily analysed into simpler components. It is thus a compound not a simple affect, hence unlikely to be a basic mental element as proposed by Klcin. The main thrust of what Glover pointed out was that a feeling is of a more complex nature than its component desire.

Jones's, Flugel's, Brierley's, and also Glover's work, all had implications for clinical practice. They provided the impetus for the closer study of the central importance of emotions in the psychoanalytic situation. For instance, Freud (1910a) had understood countertransference as a predominantly neurotic phenomenon within the analyst which he must overcome or else it would limit his work with patients. Following Ferenczi's detailed studies, it was Michael and Alice Balint (1939) and also Winnicott (1949a) who first pointed out that the analyst's emotional responsiveness to his patient, his countertransference, is essential for the psychoanalytic process to unfold. Countertransference is thus not just a pathological aspect of the analyst hindering his understanding. Paula Heimann's paper (1950) on countertransference, written when she was still a collaborator with Klein, has become a classic. Other papers by Little (1951), Limentani (1977) and King (1978) study the subtle interpersonal affects between patient and analyst, and particularly the possibility of the analyst's contribution to the affects of the moment. There is no doubt that, alongside Racker (1968) in South America, it was Independent analysts who brought about the widespread discussion, and later acceptance, of countertransference affects as essential tools for the analytic task. (Kohon (1986b) summarizes this; see also Chapter 9 of this volume.)


## BOWLBY

### AFFECT AS AN EGO-FUNCTIONING STATE OF EVALUATION

John Bowlby has studied feelings and emotions from a wider perspective. In the first volume of his trilogy, *Attachment* (1969), *Separation* (1973) and *Loss* (1980), he examines the biological survival value of feelings and their communication. It is a core aspect of his theoretical position. He draws upon the work of the American philosopher, Susanne Langer. It is not widely recognized even by Independent analysts how much her work has influenced their analytic thinking. Bowlby uses her work on feeling (Langer 1942, 1953, 1967, 1972, 1982); Milner and, particularly, Rycroft have both used her studies on affect and symbolization (1942); Matte-Blanco (1975) drew upon her exposition of symbolic logic (1967) to develop his concept of logical symmetry.

Following Langer, Bowlby observes that feelings, in both man and animals, are states of *appraisal*. Here the individual is aware of himself and the world in several directions at once in the same instant. In an inward direction there is awareness of his self, his body, its urges, movements and biochemical changes. At the same instant, in an outward direction he is aware of the objects, surfaces, spaces and movements of the environment.

Bowlby makes clear that affects or feelings are *intuitive evaluations* of the overall state of the individual in his or her environment. This is of his body functioning, his self, his memory with internal objects, and the environment with its objects, their emotions if any and the spaces between them. Feelings contain object relations and, being usually evaluative, they include a sense of the *future*. For instance, anxiety, dread, determination, eagerness and despair all definitely have 'futurity' in them; with some other emotions this is less immediately apparent. In a feeling the experiences of body, self and environment come together as a unit or whole. Feelings must have some 'unit' status because they can, if sufficiently differentiated, be represented by symbols. The proper study of such symbolization of affects is the domain not only of psychoanalysis but also of aesthetics (see Chapter 4).

Introspection will easily draw attention to what is being felt at any present moment – in both an outward and an inward direction. If one 'subtracts' and concentrates on one direction only, body feeling only, say, it will be found that the overall emotion is flattened. Continued narrowing of the field of awareness seems to make feeling disappear and only sensations or perceptions are left. Relaxation of this focusing lets the various aspects come together again so that the whole feeling returns. Affect seems to be the result of an integrated activity. It is not abstractive as is a cognitive activity such as thinking, which deals with and operates upon specific concepts. But it is a preliminary evaluative stage, in which there is potential imagination or fantasy, from which thought may emerge. Being a state of appraisal, affect occurs, both at the beginning and culmination, in each phase of any well-rounded, 'whole' thought process which could be called 'wise'.

We can abstract a feeling and conceptualize about it. 'Love', for instance, can be thus thought, talked and generalized about. But a particular child's real actual affection for his parents, their loving their child or a person's love for a partner, say, is an experience of a pattern of appraisal that is different from feelings of love for any other person. It contains a unique network of object relations and is thus concrete, not abstract. However, that which is *in common* between all the different feelings of love for particular people and things can be *abstracted* and used in symbolized abstract thought.

In summary: it seems that feelings are ego states *par excellence*. From them emerge 'predictive' ideas: trepidations, anxiety, excited anticipation or delight. Such appraisals may be mistaken: they can obviously be grossly distorted by fantasy or they can be unrealistic – as in neurosis or psychosis. They can be grossly one-sided – as in prejudices, and by splitting and denial vast tracts of reality can be ignored. But within the feeling itself there can be instantaneous integrated appraisal. In its way it has certain efficiencies lacking in abstractive thought.

Desires, wishes, instincts and drives are core aspects of any feeling, but we have noted other aspects: body sensations, fantasy and perceptions of the environment, for instance. The motive aspect is only part of a feeling. We have also shown that feeling is an essential, albeit intuitive, preliminary stage in any rounded thinking. This view is a long way from the post-Kantian division of the mind into will, feeling and thinking. The subsequent emphasis upon different 'regions' of the mind, the academics working predominantly with cognition while analysts stressed willing or conation, might have been a necessary developmental step at the time. But it meant that it took some time before the understanding of real personal experience and dynamics could be considered.

By 1926 Freud had overcome the bias of the times when he stated, in his modification of his theory of anxiety, that feeling is an essential ego activity. Thirty years after this, Langer, having studied Freud closely, concluded her comprehensive proposals about feeling, symbolization and thinking. Ten years later Bowlby brought them back to psychoanalysis.

It is of interest that Langer's own trilogy *Mind: an Essay in Human Feeling* (1967, 1972, 1982) goes so far as to propose that feeling, in its breadth and depth, is the first characteristic to examine when distinguishing the mind of man from that of other animals.

## AFFECTS, OBJECT RELATIONS AND THE LOGIC OF RELATIONS

It is a distinct feature of early British analysts that they have conceived of all affects as containing object relations. It will be noted that the conception of an object relation bears a clear resemblance to the structure of a logical relation. Formal logic is based upon primary propositions in the form: subject–object and the relation between them. Object-relations theory makes propositions like this, but confines itself to the realm of emotions. It also centres its concepts around one sort of subject only – the self. Object-relations theory always uses 'units' of self and object and the relation between them. Hence, just as in logic where there can be no subject without an object and its relationship to it, so in psychoanalysis there can be no conception of an object relation without a self. Winnicott was in effect saying this when he made the famous point that '"there is no such thing as a baby" – meaning that if you set out to describe a baby, you will find you are describing *a baby and someone*' (Winnicott, 1964, p. 88).

It may also be worth noting that in object-relations theory the objects of the self may be *external* people or things and also conditions between concrete objects: thus the sea and the air we breathe are objects. However, body parts are also objects of the self, and so may feelings be. These objects may be experienced as *internal* to the self or as external. They may also be felt as somewhere in between, in which case they are transitional (Winnicott, 1951, 1971a). Memories contain object relations, and much unconscious phantasy is also structured in object relations (these would all be predominantly internal in nature). What use the study of formal logical relations may have for psychoanalysis, and vice versa, will be discussed in the next chapter. If one were asked wherein lay Winnicott's particular greatness it would be hard to be specific. It was perhaps in the way he showed how special ordinary, real human relationships were. He dwelt most upon mothers and children, of course, but he highlighted many others in any place or time. Freud, and then Klein, had illuminated the individual unconscious and inner world. Winnicott showed how these determine and are determined by our myriad interpersonal relationships.

## BALINT AND RICKMAN

### THE NUMERICAL ASPECT OF OBJECT RELATIONS: ONE-PERSON, TWO-PERSON, THREE-PERSON AND MULTI-PERSON THEORY

Much of psychoanalysis is naturally concerned with unconscious, phan-tasied self–object relations that are conceived of as internal to the psyche.

Though it does not ignore the environment, Kleinian thought is particularly centred upon these internal object relations. It thus tends towards being a one-person theory, for the reality of other people is secondary in it. However, the question of the environment interacting with the individual has been a keystone of one line of Independent thinking in the past forty years. It is not the defining characteristic of an Independent – some are not particularly interested in research in this area – but it is where Independents have made core contributions both to analysis and to culture generally. Clarification of certain presuppositions underlying these ideas may be useful.

A well-known observation was made by Balint (1950) at about the same time as it was expounded rather more fully by Rickman (1950c, 1951b). It is one that is often referred to in the literature.

Balint pointed out that it is always important to be aware of the *number of people related to within the patient's imagination* and also of the number able to be used and comprehended in the *external world* at any one time.

He says that the young infant, in not distinguishing between self and object, mother say, is working in a one-person frame. Later, the infant will begin to distinguish himself from his mother but this is all that can be comprehended at any one moment. It is only later still that three-person relations can be conceived consistently. There is usually great resistance to it when intense emotions are involved. It is of course the hallmark of the *oedipal* level, where the conception of the two parents doing things together independently of the child must be experienced and assimilated.

Balint used this measure a great deal clinically. In diagnosis, students were consistently taught to estimate the level of emotional complexity of a patient's communication. Was it more or less totally solipsistic or one-person? Was it ignoring all else in the world except the self and one other involved person? Or were social situations between self and two or more other people felt about articulatedly from various points of view? When deciding upon whether a prospective patient could use 'focal therapy' for instance, this question was rigorously asked and discussed. For focal therapy to be usable, it was reckoned that evidence of capacity to use three-person relations was essential.

Rickman had rather wider vistas in mind in his thinking on the subject of numerosity. In considering the nature of the human sciences, Rickman (1950b, 1951a) directed his attention naturally towards psychology. He pointed out that the *breadth* of the *field of observation* by researchers varied markedly and that their theories varied in consequence. Although under the one title of psychology, each form of theory called for slightly different disciplines. Some considered the events *within one* body, others in the *interaction of two* together, others in *three*, and yet others in a multiplicity of people.

Of these approaches Rickman asserted that none was intrinsically better than another: they furnished different data and, in matters of theory, also informed us differently.

A one-body psychology concerns itself with what goes on inside one person, viewed in isolation. Its purview is neurophysiology, sensation, perception, memory, certain aspects of thinking and introspection. The ideal observer for this, Rickman says, is a robot, unaffected by the object of observation except to record.

A two-body psychology observes the *reciprocating*, or interacting, relations between two people – one of whom may be the observer himself, who would then be called a participant observer. It thus sees *two systems*, two organizing *egos* interacting. Theory about a patient in an analytic transference with his analyst in a consulting-room is an epitome of a two-body psychology.

However, Rickman points out, the two-body analytic relation is not really quite closed upon that. What the patient says and does in the consulting-room depends upon what is happening at the time with other people – his wife, for instance. Hence, even though there are only two people in the room, a third is influencing them. It then becomes a triangular, or three-person, situation. This is epitomized by the oedipal situation.

As an example of an analyst observing in a three-person situation, Rickman cites Winnicott in his baby clinics, seeing the baby with the mother and thus naturally conceiving of them as a unit. In other words, the level of much of Winnicott's data was different from that of a paediatrician who examined the baby and gathered data from that source alone. The nature of the paediatrician's theory arising from this would consequently be slightly different.

From a three-body scope, the data in the analyst's mind can expand to four or more bodies, when naturally the study becomes that of groups. Findings in one discipline may be of great use in another, but they can never provide an adequate framework for theory in the other. Thus,

Rickman says, psychoanalysis can be very helpful, with its insights, to anthropology, say, but its theory will never be both necessary and sufficient for it.

Rickman has made plain that the immediate scope of an analyst's *observation*, as he sits in his chair, is intentionally limited to a *two*-person one. In so far as he aims to be opaque like a mirror (Freud 1912a, p. 118), dwelling focally only upon the patient's unconscious, then his *theoretical imagination* about the patient is striving towards a *one*-person psychology.

Freud's original seduction theory of neuroses, incidentally, was a two- or three-body one – the nature of the parents or nursemaids as causative agents was paramount. When he turned away from this with the realization that many patients' tales of seduction were phantasies, his theorizing became predominantly a one-term psychology – with a focus upon internal psychic mechanisms. This was one of the most important steps that Freud took, for psychoanalysis is, above all else, a mode of insight into individual internal processes. However, he seems to have begun to return, in part, to a two-person theory with signal anxiety (1926) where interest in the maternal environment comes to the fore. Even here, some say it is the rising tension within the infant when the mother is absent that is causative, not so much the absence itself, in which case we are back to a one-body theory again.

Melanie Klein steadfastly followed in Freud's footsteps in being essentially a one-person psychologist. It was not that she did not believe in the importance of the child's environment for normal development, but it was theoretically more or less ignored. Many Independents, led by Winnicott and Bowlby, were dissatisfied with this. They felt that, if the effect of interacting with others was ignored, then an aspect of the truth was also being ignored. It was wrong both theoretically and therapeutically. Such tunnel vision can make the analyst prone to ignore the truth of influences, traumatic or seductive, with which a patient's ego has to cope. This can leave a patient with the feeling that his analyst wants to know only some of the truth about him.

With this in mind, many Independents tend towards two-, three- and multi-body psychologies in some aspects of their theories. Here, more than one mind, ego or control-system is involved. This gives dimensions of thinking that may escape those who adhere more or less exclusively to one-body psychology.

In this context a recent paper by an American philosopher (Cavell, 1988) is of interest. She points out that much of the tradition of psycho-analytic theory is of a one-person sort, and this is essentially solipsistic. It is based, she thinks, upon a Cartesian theory of mind. Its *'cogito ergo sum'* expresses the notion that the only thing we can know for certain is our own thoughts, and these come only from within the self. It is a one-person or solipsistic theory of knowledge. Cavell points out, however, that Wittgenstein, followed by Donald Davidson, disputed this by contending that both thinking and language fundamentally take the same logical forms. They argue that it is possible to conduct a process of thinking only after having communicated in language first at some time in life, and this involves a process of the *interpretation* of symbols between at least two people. Thus, thinking is not basically a one-person activity, it is rooted in *dialogue*. Solitary thought is internalized dialogue. It is developed socially, but when mature it proceeds between parts of the self.

Cavell then moves back to psychoanalysis and suggests that object-relations theorists have intuitively grasped this two-person basis to thought. Without knowing it they have moved in the Wittgenstein–Davidson direction and away from a Cartesian theory of mind. This would be particularly true of Winnicott with his 'There is no such thing as a baby without a mother', which is close to 'There is no such thing as thinking without another person in dialogue'. We were making a similar point earlier when it was said that 'there is no such thing as a self only one in relation to an object, and vice versa'. The philosophers would add to this by saying further 'There is no such thing as a word – to be meaningful it must be a word in a sentence'. It is a relativistic form of thinking. Klein, unlike Winnicott, was, with her unique concern with phantasy, much more traditionally Cartesian in her thought. However, it could be said that Bion broke away from this mode.

## MOVEMENT OF THOUGHT AND EXTERNAL REALITY

If we consider the *span of comprehension* of an individual's imagination – one-, two-, three- or multi-body, not about the number of persons, but about the number of *physical objects* and their relations to each other, we can see that people vary enormously in their facility to deal with the logical structures that are involved in such matters. Mathematicians and workers in the physical sciences must be particularly talented in conceiving of numbers of objects, at least within a specialized field. The psychoanalytic thinker, however, is concerned with the person's scope of comprehension of real people and their internal representations, psycho-analytic objects in other words, who have *experiences* of their own separate from one another. This requires *movement in imagination* on the analyst's part – identifying with one person, moving to observing him, then looking at self, identifying with another as to how the first might affect him, and so on, then gathering these impressions together and forming new conceptions of things. Not only must this be an intellectual movement, of the kind the physical scientist is adept at, but it must also be movement in and out of different *affects* – the weaving and combining of rich and complex multidimensional emotional maps. Padel (1985a) has written on this; see also Abelin (1981) for an American view on this question and Britton (1989) for a Kleinian perspective.

Without this potentiality, an individual's sense of *external reality* is impaired – at least that aspect of external reality which is other people with feelings, experiences and characters of their own. It is interesting to note that the ultimate test of sanity, a reality sense, depends paradoxi-cally on something very close to madness – the ability to 'become' some-one else. In psychological health it is transient and reversible; in illness it is involuntary and even irreversible.

The question of the sense of external reality is an important one for analysts who deal with madness and its borderlands, yet it is little thought about theoretically. Two books by Independents include it in their titles, Rycroft's *Imagination and Reality* (1968a) and Winnicott's *Playing and Reality* (1971a).

The functioning of a reality sense, or reality testing as it is often called in psychoanalysis, depends upon some crucial factors. Thinking that is realistic must be open to *sensory* impact, to feedback data mediated by the relevant *exteroceptors*. This is at least partially absent in delusion and hallucination. The realistic individual must have imaginative 'hypotheses' and *test* them in two directions, namely the effect of the environment on the self and also the effect of the self upon the environment. Exclusive sensitivity to the first of these two directions of effect, that upon the self, is a mark of a predominantly paranoid-schizoid position. Under patho-logical conditions, it can intensify to 'ideas of reference'. Attention to the latter, the effect of self on others, signals more depressive-position thought. Intrinsic to this position is, of course, the surrender of omnipotence. Things that are real may be affectable by desire, but they must be recognized as not inevitably controlled by it. This line of thinking has been a major Kleinian contribution.

The loss of omnipotence is achieved only painfully, often with the arousal of violent grief, rage and mourning. Thus the steady recognition of reality is contingent upon the tolerance and use of one's own hostility and the ability to bear loss. Winnicott (1950b) has stressed that the sense of reality develops from the infant's repeated experience of the survival of the primary object ('mother' or 'breast') after his cavalier treatment and attacks upon it. For him, it is not so much awareness of the loss of the object that constitutes the sense of reality but rather the object's survival. This fosters basic trust (Erikson, 1950) and the object can then be released from the infant's omnipotent control and placed into external or *shared* reality.

It is this imaginative movement, by both analyst and patient, between reality and phantasy, between external and internal, as well as between one-person and multi-person thinking, that has been of particular interest to Independents and has become one of their hallmarks.

# 3    Abstraction and Symbolization

## INTRODUCTION: SIGNS, SYMBOLS AND MEANING

THE DECODING OF symbolization lies at the heart of psychoanalytic theory and even more so at the heart of technique, so it is necessary to approach this question now, for all later chapters rest upon it.

By the beginning of the twentieth century the importance of symbolization was beginning to be generally evident. Charles Peirce and Edmund Husserl were laying the foundations of semantics. The study of symbolism is intrinsic to many disciplines like epistemology, linguistics, mathematics, anthropology and aesthetics, but we will naturally confine ourselves to psychological definitions (we draw particularly upon Langer, 1942, 1953, also Cassirer, 1953).

When anything has *meaning* it is a sign, signal or symbol *of* something *to* someone – this could be to the person himself. A *sign* indicates the existence of a thing or event. The *interpretation* of signs is the basis of animal intelligence. Their misinterpretation is the simplest form of *mistake*. Truth and falsehood are thus born of the interpretation of signs. Not only can animals be adept at interpreting signs of things in their environment, they can also actively make *signals*.

*Symbolization* is a different order of activity. It is probably the almost unique preserve of humankind. It is the basis of reflective thinking. A symbol can be made in the *absence* of the event it stands for. It does *not evoke action*. It is a vehicle for a *conception* of an object. Signs announce their object, symbols lead people to conceive their objects. It is conceptions, not the things, that symbols directly mean.

Such conceptions must originally be derived by a process of *selection*, which involves a process of sensory *abstraction*. Here certain qualities, characteristics or features are drawn out or abstracted from a field of data to form into the conception. Conceptions can be evoked by the presentation of an appropriate symbol, which can happen at amazing speed. When conceptions are used together in pure thought, without the actual presence of the objects, we speak of *concept* use. These concepts will have been derived by primitive processes of selection or sensory abstractions that are present in infancy. Later, pre-conceptual abstraction must certainly take place by the time of the coming of the use of words, for this rests upon such abstraction (Piaget, 1950, 1953). This leads ultimately to fully abstract thought – or abstract operations as Piaget calls them. Here, purely abstract concepts, ones that have no tangible examples, may be used as elements in thinking.

There is one order of symbols which *resemble* the things they stand for. They are usually visual images, but they can be verbal, like 'bang' and 'splash'. It was these symbols, as they occur in dreams, that first drew Freud's attention. They are *isomorphic* with what is symbolized; there is an element of identity of form between the two. Most verbal symbols, however, bear no resemblance to the things symbolized. They must thus have arisen by *convention* through social discourse among people.

The realm of psychoanalysis bestrides, or is transitional between, both forms of symbolization but it has one particular area of interest: this is referred to as psychoanalytic symbolism, which is usually of an isomorphic form. From the early days psychoanalytic symbolism was defined as the representation of some object or activity which remained *hidden* to the user of the symbol. The symbol itself may or may not be consciously perceived. It is a special kind of indirect presentation which can be distinguished from various other forms of pictorial presentation of thought.

## FREUD AND JONES

When Freud (1900–1) investigated his and his patients' dreams as a means of exploring the manifestations of unconscious processes, he found that dreams make use of a symbolism that is already present in unconscious representations. He saw that there was a remarkable constancy in the relationship between the manifest dream symbol and that which was symbolized. He then suggested that this was due to the psychic mechanism of displacement.

In analysing his patients' dreams he became aware that there were elements to which they could not associate and yet this could not be accounted for by resistance. He came to understand that these elements were symbols which were the same for all individuals and were to be found in neurotic symptoms but also in myth, religion and folklore. He envisaged that a primary process made use of such symbols for the discharge of psychic tension states without the dream censor being involved, but the dream censor may also make use of them. Freud saw that the symbols were manifold, but that which was symbolized was restricted to body sensations and parts, and primary objects. By this means, erotic experiences may be signified in a non-sexual way. The dreamer was never aware of the meaning of the symbol and interpretations often met with a patient's resistance against acknowledging them. Freud suggested that such universal symbols evolved in the course of development of language. In time, by inheritance of acquired characteristics, these symbols became genetically rooted. In this context he pointed out that the differences between the original objects and their symbols are of no interest: only their identical features, or isomorphisms, are responded to. Freud also conceived that there are typical dreams which are common to mankind, which can be understood without recourse to a patient's associations.

In an encyclopaedia article he categorizes this symbolism and says:

In the course of investigating the form of expression brought about by the dream-work, the surprising fact emerged that certain objects, arrangements and relations are represented, in a sense indirectly, by 'symbols', which are used by the dreamer without his understanding them and to which as a rule he offers no associations. Their translation has to be provided by the analyst, who can himself only discover it empirically by experimentally fitting it into a context. It was later found that linguistic usage, mythology and folklore afford the most ample analogies to dream-symbols. Symbols, which raise the most interesting and hitherto unsolved problems, seem to be a fragment of extremely ancient inherited mental equipment. The use of a common symbolism extends far beyond the use of a common language.

(Freud, 1923a, p. 242)

Freud also pointed out that neurotic symptoms can be the symbolic manifestation of an unconscious conflict. In his paper on 'The unconscious' (1915d), he gives the example of the neurotic inhibition of an obsessional patient who put on his socks and then, to undo the act, took them off again. This he repeated several times. The action symbolically represented sexual intercourse and aroused intense anxiety. He contrasted this with the schizophrenic patient who cannot put on the socks because, when he pulls them up, he fears that thousands of holes will become visible. There is here a representation of the vagina. However, Freud points out that the symbolic representation is not the thousands of holes in the fabric of the sock but the word 'hole' which is symbolically equated with the vagina in this case.

Freud's first main aim was centred on this symbolic representation of unconscious objects, processes and conflicts. But then, in *Beyond the Pleasure Principle* (1920a), he relates the example of an eighteen-month-old baby who, when his mother was absent, played with a cotton reel to which a string was attached. The boy threw the reel away, saying 'gone', but then recovered it, using the string, and said 'there'. This game was repeated time and again. Freud used this example to explain repetition compulsion: the aim was to master a painful traumatic event – mother's absence. The important function of the game was that the boy symbolized the trauma by using the acts and words. It must be emphasized that Freud was not, on this occasion, particularly concerned with the symbolism of the function for he was using the example to explain how a mastery of a trauma was achieved by repeating a form of the unpleasant event. It is likely that he did not enter into the detail of this particular symbolization because, as will be remembered, it was not until 1926 that he introduced his new theory of anxiety. It was then that anxiety was seen as a signal to deal with either intrapsychic or external danger, in the first instance separation anxiety when the infant was in the helpless state of dependency upon mother.

Ten years prior to this revision of the theory of anxiety and before the coming of Freud's structural theory (1923b) it was Ernest Jones who brought symbolism into focus with his paper 'The theory of symbolism' (1916). Here he expanded and considerably added to Freud's conceptualization at that time. The paper is widely known as a classic, even though some of the findings have been seen as limited since the development of object-relations theory. It was a combative paper, given to the London Psycho-Analytical Society after the disagreements between Freud and Jung, and when the membership of the Society was divided by the discord. Jones's aim was to differentiate the Freudian conceptualization of symbolization from the Jungian. We will describe this paper at some length, for upon it rests much later work.

Jones points out that civilization rests upon symbolism and that humanity is ceaselessly occupied by the task of replacing one idea by another. It is the fabric of all language, art, religion and science. Jones then sets about differentiating symbolization in the broadest sense from the particular form which is psychoanalytical symbolism. Maybe provocatively, he also called this 'true symbolism'.

He states that a psychoanalytic or 'true' symbol has the following characteristics: 1. it is a replacement for something hidden; 2. it thus represents something unconscious that has been repressed; 3. when the original meaning is revealed to the symbolizer by interpretation of the symbol there is incredulity and resistance; 4. the displacement is unidirectional – from the unconscious idea to the symbol and never the other way round, thus a church spire may symbolize a penis, but a penis never symbolizes a church spire; 5. the things symbolized are few; these are the sensations and acts by the body or its parts in relation to primary objects, or near relatives in other words; the acts are of feeding, excretion, erotic love, procreation and death; 6. their symbols are many but not infinite.

These symbols emerge through the mind's capacity to use similarities, to identify one object with another. Jones, following Freud, postulates that symbolism is the remains of an identity that once existed in the history of the race and of the individual. Thus psychoanalytic or 'true' symbolism is regressive to a primitive mode of functioning. In this view, the primitive mind tends to note resemblances and ignore differences. Here the pleasure principle is dominant. Jones thought that there were probably survival values in the unidirectional thrust of symbolization in primordial times. For instance, by the repression of sexual urges, and then their displacement on to ordinary objects, the gruelling toil of everyday life was made tolerable by its being infused, albeit unconsciously, with some sexual pleasure.

True or psychoanalytic symbolism arises, Jones maintained, from the unconscious intrapsychic conflict between repression (this term was used then to cover any form of defence) and that which is repressed. Jones goes on to distinguish true symbolism from sublimation. In the 'true' form, the affect which invests the symbol is unaltered, while in sublimation the original affect has undergone a modification.

With regard to the process of the formation of a symbol Jones says:

In so far as a secondary idea B receives its meaning from a primary idea A, with which it has been identified, it functions as what may be called a symbolic equivalent of A. At this stage, however, it does not yet constitute a symbol of A, not until it replaces A as a substitute in the context where A would logically appear.

(Jones, 1916, 1948, p. 139)

Jones thinks, further, that there is an overflow of *feeling* and interest from A to B and this makes it possible for B to represent A, but the essential element is the *inhibition of affect* in relation to A. He goes on: 'When the inhibition is at its maximum there arises symbolism in its most typical form' (1948, p. 139). What is more, Jones wishes to reserve the term true symbolism for this phenomenon. The two cardinal characteristics of this are, first, that the process is completely unconscious and, second, that there has not yet been that modification of affect from the original to the symbol that is indicative of sublimation. According to this view, 'true' or psychoanalytic symbols occur when sublimation cannot be achieved.

With this in mind, Jones questions the validity of Silberer's concept of *functional symbolism*. Let us investigate this issue with some care. First, summarizing Jones again, psychoanalytic symbols are related to three sorts of psychic phenomena: unconscious conflicts, inhibiting influences and sublimations. Sublimations as well as symbols are derived from intrapsychic conflicts. The actual material 'chosen' for the symbol is taken from the sublimated tendencies; the inhibiting influences are to some extent represented in this formation, but the dynamic force which creates the symbol comes from unconscious complexes.

Silberer conceived that certain higher mental functions, as well as unconscious instinctual complexes, could be represented, symbolized he said, by *visual* images which were akin to psychoanalytic symbols. Thus his functional symbolism was a regression from higher forms of thought to a more primitive one. He described how, when he had engaged in a difficult problem and was fatigued and drowsy, a visual image appeared which, on self-analysis, was a representation of the problem and thought in question.

An example of this might be that of the famous chemist Kekulé who is said to have had considerable difficulties when trying to work out the structure of the benzene molecule. Depressed, he dozed off in his laboratory and dreamt of a snake circling round upon itself to bite its own tail. He woke up refreshed, went back to work and shortly after discovered the circular form of the benzene ring.

Jones agrees with Silberer that a symbolic image may be used to represent an inhibiting force as well as being sublimatory material, but he maintains that it is then a *metaphor*, not a psychoanalytic symbol. With a metaphor, all that psychic processes can do is select a symbol that has already been created by unconscious complexes; they can never create a true symbol anew. Jones says:

> The essential function of all symbolism, using the word in the broadest and most popular sense, is to overcome the inhibition that is *hindering the free expression of a given feeling-idea* [our italics], the force derived from this, in its forward urge, being the effective cause of symbolism. It always constitutes a regression to a simpler mode of apprehension. If the regression proceeds only a certain distance, remaining conscious or at most preconscious, the result is metaphorical, or what Silberer calls 'functional', symbolism. If, owing to the strength of the unconscious complex, it proceeds further – to the level of the unconscious – the result is symbolism in the strict sense. The circumstance that the same image can be employed for both of these functions should not blind us to the important differences between them. Of these the principal one is that with the metaphor the feeling to be expressed is over-sublimated, whereas with symbolism it is under-sublimated; the one relates to an effort that has attempted something beyond its strength, the other to an effort that is prevented from accomplishing what it would.
> (Jones, 1948, p. 144)

From this point of view Kekulé's dream must remain inconclusive. Was the snake in the dream a visual image of the sought-after benzene ring? If so, then Jones would say it was a metaphor and Silberer would call it a functional symbol. Or was it also a psychoanalytic or 'true' symbol? In this case it would have represented an unconscious conflict of Kekulé's. We will never know the answer to this, for the dream was, of course, never analysed.

Jones's paper has remained the authoritative one on the classical psychoanalytic theory of symbolism. Let us emphasize again that Jones was at pains to show that metaphor and psychoanalytic symbolism were both in the service of expressing impeded feeling-ideas. This historic contribution has not been seriously contested but, with the coming, some years later, of the structural theory of the mind, and then the 'absence' or separation theory of anxiety, object relations began to come to the centre of attention. Jones's theory of psychoanalytic symbolism as the 'true' symbolism was then regarded as too narrow to work with. In Britain it was Ella Sharpe (1929) and, shortly afterwards, Klein (1930) who were the first to broaden the concept from an object-relations point of view.

## KLEIN AND SHARPE

In 1930 Klein was in no doubt about the importance of symbolism in early development and in psychic functioning generally, for she affirms that it is the source of all the talents and all sublimations. She, like Jones, is interested in the instigation of the transformation from primary to secondary objects, and goes on to extend his theory that unconscious conflicts, impeded from expression, provide the impetus for the creation of symbols. She suggests that it is out of anxiety about oral sadism that the infant turns away from the original object. He denies the existence of his impulses towards this original object. Then, by the use of symbolic equations, he moves these impulses to a new object and so on. Note that Freud and Jones had used the term symbolic equivalence to indicate the same process. But the word 'equation' seems more used now, and Klein's paper was the start of much fruitful work, particularly by followers like Segal (1957), on this subject of symbolic equations.

At the same time Sharpe (1930) was directing attention to the function of symbolization in sublimation. Observing the Altamira cave paintings of 17,000 years ago, she points out the images of men in ritual dance playing at imitating, at *being* the animals they would hunt. There is the delusion – she calls it this, we would say illusion now–that the man *is* the animal. By this means man has overcome the limits of his own body in space and time and, in a sense, triumphed over his own mortality.

In such serious play, Sharpe sees the root of dance, drama, poetry, song and the visual arts. In this paper and others (1925, 1929, 1935, 1940), she makes it plain that this sublimating symbolism involves movement in and out of mimicry and imitation. Here there is *synchrony of rhythm*, or attunement (Stern, 1985), with the object. It is pantomime, she says, which everyone intuitively understands. Her stress upon the aesthetic importance of rhythmic form is of great interest and will be discussed in the next chapter. She is one of the first analysts in a tradition of seeing *imitation* as an aspect of symbolization in the roots of play and sublimation. This of course is not only British nor only psychoanalytic: it is basic to Piaget in Europe and many others in America. It emphasizes how play uses the sense of *identity between people*, between self and another, and not just between things. Sharpe is here presenting the view that symbolization can be conceived of as representing an absent object and not only a repressed one.

Though both Freud and Jones saw that symbolization was based on identification, it remained for the early object-relations theorists to develop conceptualizations to include interpersonal identifications. With this, imitation and play were fully recognized as symbolic activities. This was Sharpe's prime contribution.

Sharpe also directed attention towards further analytic understanding of metaphor. After Jones, she was a pioneer in this. She pointed out (1937) how dreams have many elements in common with poetic diction and also with visual artistic creativity. From her work on dreams also come suggestions about how manifest content may represent present life situations and not just instincts and primitive objects. The form of a patient's predicaments can be portrayed by the form of the dream images. This is what Jones would have called a use of metaphor rather than 'true' symbolism and is close to Silberer's observations.

With regard to the development of metaphor, Sharpe sees the child's ability to use this mode emerging during the second anal stage: she postulates (1940) that the creation of metaphor cannot arise until sphincter control, that is until the child has learnt to control himself and carry something, as a metaphor does, from one place to another.


## MILNER AND RYCROFT

The first written critique of Jones (1916) came from Milner in her paper on 'The role of illusion in symbol formation' (1952). She agrees with him that transference of interest from a primary object to a secondary one is essential. But she then departs from him and suggests that psychoanalytic symbolism should not be restricted to the products of repressed unconscious conflict. Symbolism, even as it arises in dreams and analytic practice, is not confined to this source. Symbolism may be regressive but that does not make it less valuable to the mature mind. What is more, restricting the usage of psychoanalytic symbolism to Jones's 'strict' definition creates an unnecessary cleavage between psychoanalysis and other disciplines. By this means psychoanalysis can become isolated.

Milner then reasons along much the same lines as Sharpe had done twenty years before. The finding of identities, equations or samenesses is not simply pathological. It can be adaptive and creatively valuable. She stresses the importance of the experience of *fusion* with, and then separating from, another person. The emotion of this fusion is often an ecstasy, and, like genital orgasm, it may be regressive but is biologically adaptive and hardly pathological. The fusion or illusion of identity can occur not only with people but also in experience of things. The merging across boundaries transcends the common-sense ego but is needed in order to find the familiar in the unfamiliar. For acts of creativity, therapeutically or in art, Milner thinks there needs at times to be an acceptance of return to oneness. The important issue for normality lies, perhaps, in the *reversibility* of the fusion–separation dyad. Milner's idiom about these issues is close to that of Winnicott. They were friends but it seems they were coming to their ideas almost independently, only later seeing how close they were.

At about the same time, Rycroft (1956a) was also addressing the question of symbolism in a comprehensive paper. It was an attempt to reconcile analytic with non-analytic usage on the basis of primary and secondary process symbolism. Rycroft's view is that symbols do not necessarily represent 'hidden' or repressed objects. There are, in fact, many ordinary people who can be aware of the underlying meanings of psychoanalytic symbols. For them the unconscious may be available without their being psychotic. Most symbols, he says, have both primary and secondary process elements within them – at least potentially. However, their admixture can vary: for instance, bizarre symbols contain little secondary process manifestation, whereas logical symbols would naturally be dominated by secondary processes. Rycroft comes to the same conclusion as Milner (1952) and also Segal (1957), namely that symbolizing is a general, normal process of value and that Jones's (1916) definition of 'true' symbolism is too narrow.

Rycroft reasons that defence is naturally of vital importance for all pathology, but what it casts a shadow over is the *affective* meaning of the symbol, not the cognitive nature of the symbol itself. Thus, it is affective depth and breadth which are truncated and distorted by repression or defensive processes. Jones did himself point in this direction in 1916, but it was not an aspect that was particularly taken up then. Rycroft goes on to say that, only in states of extensive malfunctioning of the ego, such as in psychosis, is the cognitive content affected as well.

The prime contribution of these papers is the clarification that psychoanalytic symbols are essentially representations of affects. As pointed out in the last chapter, these affects are structures which contain experiences of self in relation to body functioning and also to internal and external objects.

Rycroft (1962b) refers further to Langer's (1942) theories. He shows that she makes a crucial distinction between *discursive symbols* and *non-discursive* or *presentational* ones. Discursive symbolism is that of conscious or preconscious rational thinking in which words or other definable symbols are presented successively in accordance with *conventional* rules such as grammar or syntax. It is the equivalent of the highly refined secondary process. It provides the medium of dialogue and hence of thought process.

Presentational symbolism, on the other hand, is the same as psychoanalytic or isomorphic symbolism and involves more primary process than does the discursive form. It uses visual or auditory images rather than words, though poetic and dramatic diction contain strong presentational elements. The presentational symbol pattern appears at a single instant rather than in sequence. The symbols have no grammar or syntax, and they cannot be used alone in rational discourse or argument. Such symbols constitute the imaginative material of dreams and art. These images symbolize affective states. They are, Rycroft is at pains to point out, very *efficient communicators* of feeling. They can contain great densities of affective data. A picture, a tone of voice or rhythm of a tune can convey more of an emotion than strings of logically ordered words. They are of prime use in emotional dialogues.

In conclusion, presentational, isomorphic or non-discursive symbolism complements discursive symbolism with its dialogue and logical thought. The two probably share common roots but they function with different qualities and serve different purposes. As a means of communication of feelings, even those of the most profound nature, presentational symbolism has no equal. Psychoanalytic object-relations theory lays stress upon both forms of communication, and in analytic therapy there must be continuous movement between and combination of the two. This point of view is central, if often implicitly, in much Independent theory of technique (see Chapters 8, 9 and 10), and it also makes an important contribution to creativity and aesthetics (see Chapter 4).

## MATTE-BLANCO

We now come to the contribution of a colleague who has not worked in Britain for many years. Though he is a long-standing member of the British Society who rightly calls himself an Independent, neither his idiom nor his subject matter has been in the British Independent mainstream. However, we are going to place him here because the present writer (Rayner, 1981; Rayner and Tuckett, 1988) and other Independents (Arden, 1984; Casement, 1985) have used his work. Matte-Blanco's explorations of unconscious functioning are extensive and, to give the reader a useful exposition, it seems necessary to present his theories in some detail. Moreover, the present writer's mode of thought, reflected in this book, has been informed by his approach, so it seems fitting to discuss him rather fully here.

In the 1950s Matte-Blanco (1975) was considering the main characteristics of the unconscious as described by Freud (1900, 1915d): particularly displacement, condensation, timelessness, absence of negation and replacement of external by internal reality. Freud had made it plain that these did not obey the ordinary rules of logic. But, Matte-Blanco argued, they must obey some rules, for unconscious processes were at least sometimes understandable – and this would be impossible without rules.

He then moved temporarily from a psychodynamic mode to one of formal logic. He noticed, as Freud had done, that schizophrenic patients made *category errors* in their thought disorder. For instance, one patient saw a very tall man and concluded 'He must be very wealthy'. The patient here was making a category error about an abstract attribute, 'largeness' or 'high quantity of', and thus making a very inappropriate inference.

Matte-Blanco then reasoned that, if psychosis is a breakthrough of unconscious process, then perhaps the unconscious generally is prone to making category errors. He thus turned to the mental activity of categorization or classification and investigated it with the use of mathematical set theory. It is the choice of this mode that makes him difficult. (Summaries are available in Rayner, 1981; Rayner and Tuckett, 1988.)

Matte-Blanco does not set out particularly to examine symbolization but a process upon which he thinks it must rest. It will be recalled that both

Freud and Jones recognized that a psychoanalytic symbol appeared to be 'chosen' by the unconscious on the basis of its *similarity* with the thing symbolized. We also noted that the selection, or sensory abstraction, of certain characteristics or qualities to form a conception must precede any symbolic representation. It is this that Matte-Blanco has explored.

It will be evident in a general way that the mind, be it animal or human, is continuously classifying. Management of the objects of the environment requires constant *recognition*. Without this everything would have to be repeatedly learnt anew. This 'same again' experience involves classificatory activity. Any classification involves the registration of a sameness of identity. However, relating to the world also entails the discrimination of differences, that is, of the relations between subject and objects, and between the objects themselves – without this the environment would be untraversable. Matte-Blanco thinks that unconscious processes are variants of these universal and everyday activities but operate with their own logical rules.

The fundamental axis of Matte-Blanco's (1975) proposal is as follows:

> Most relationships that can be discriminated about the physical world are what can be termed logically asymmetrical.

A logically asymmetrical relationship is one whose *converse is not identical* to it. Some examples will make this clear.

A is to the left of B has the converse B is to the right of A.

A is after B has the converse B is before A.

A is eating B has the converse B is being eaten by A.

Here the converses are not identical to the originally proposed relationship: they are thus logically asymmetrical relations.

This sort of discrimination is, of course, essential to recognition of, and thought about, the external world.

Some perceived relations are, however, logically *symmetrical*. A symmetrical relation is one whose *converse is identical* to it. Here are some examples.

A is near B has the converse B is near A.

A is touching B has the converse B is touching A.

A is in synchrony with B has the converse B is in synchrony with A.

Matte-Blanco now makes two hypotheses which are as follows:

1.   Ordinary logical thought, which is primarily scientific logic about the physical world, must usually entertain propositions about asymmetri-

cal relations. Here the mind must be able to conceive of relations whose converses are not identical. The functioning of this logic is virtually synonymous with secondary process.

2.   The unconscious, however, often treats the converse of a relation as identical to it when ordinary conscious logic would discriminate asymmetry. It selectively treats asymmetrical relations as symmetrical. This very simple proposal is the keystone of Matte-Blanco's work.

For general purposes it is usually sufficient to understand that, in the realm of experience, symmetry = sameness and asymmetry = difference. Note that similarity, which includes differences in its meaning, is not identical with symmetry or sameness.

The apparently inappropriate mixing or 'insertion' of symmetrical into the mind's experience of asymmetrical relations is called *symmetrization*; the alternative term, homogenization, is also used. When such insertions into ordered thinking take place very odd things happen. For instance, when a symmetrization intrudes into an awareness of time, sequential order disappears. When this happens the registration 'a is after b' is not distinguishable from 'b is after a'. It could be said that only 'afterness' is known. In the region of the symmetrization the time sense has now disappeared. In like manner it can be shown that the sense of space can be 'un-ordered' or disappear with symmetrization.

It can also readily be shown that, by the same process of symmetrization or homogenization, whole objects may come to be experienced as identical to their parts. This is observable often enough in *emotional* experiences. It is usual in sexual thoughts, for instance, to recognize that the penis is a part of the body in a certain location. But in dreams and in psychosis it is quite common to experience penis, whole body and self as undifferentiated, identical or interchangeable. In muted form it is common enough in neurosis, as when an excited patient complains that his whole body or mind feels like an ejaculating penis. Matte-Blanco investigates this disappearance of order over many modalities of thought and affect in great detail.

The equation of part and whole can also occur with regard to awareness of, or expressions about, *classes* of objects. De Gaulle, for instance, did this with the idea of himself and the class 'France' in his well-known phrase '*Je suis la France*'. More commonplace is the thought, 'Oh, it's a woman, must be a bad driver'. Here an individual driver is equated with two classes, women and drivers, and the two classes are also equated.

Probably Matte-Blanco's (1975) most fundamental contribution has been to demonstrate that Freud's, apparently disparate, main characteristics of the unconscious (condensation, displacement, absence of mutual contradiction, timelessness, etc.) can be understood in terms of symmetrizations or homogenizations of ordinary logical thought. It is the 'business' of the unconscious for these symmetrizations to occur there. The unconscious *is* logical but with its own particular rules which involve insertions of symmetrical thought.

Different patterns of the *interweaving* of symmetrization with asymmetrical logic can be shown to create different forms of unconscious process. For instance, various defence mechanisms can be understood in terms of differing patterns of this kind (Matte-Blanco, 1988). Thus, projective identification can be seen this way. Briefly, when this takes place there is *first* the (unconscious) registration of a symmetry or sameness of an attribute in common between the self and another person. The quality is then disavowed or *denied* with regard to the self, but *not* with regard to the object. For instance, the self and a friend may both be felt to be 'mean', say: this is a symmetrical relation. Meanness is then denied with regard to the self but not about the friend. The result of such denial has the effect of projection: the friend is mean but not the self. There must then be continued efforts to reinforce this denial, of course. Other defences have been investigated in the same way.

Turning to a consideration of emotions generally, it is necessary first to recall that, when a symmetrization occurs within an act of classification, there is then *no discrimination between the members of the class.* A member of a class is known only as identical to the whole class. The subtlety of a sense of similarity then disappears and only a crude sameness is known.

This often seems to happen at emotional levels of thought (Matte-Blanco, 1975). It was noted in the last chapter how a real and particular affect about a person is a complex pattern of appraisal: it has a uniqueness about it and is not a generality. But, especially in excited states and in hysteria, affects can be abstracted and generalized very easily into ideas of love, hate, envy, melancholy and so on. When this happens, differences readily disappear. Crude, extreme feelings, which know no subtleties born of discrimination but which are ruled by symmetrizations or homogenizations, then come to the fore. This was noted in such an experience as equating penis, whole body and whole self, or de Gaulle saying he was France, or all women being conceived of as bad drivers.

Thinking about this *part = whole* vein, whose logic seems to rule in crude emotion, Matte-Blanco noted that, in mathematical set theory (for our purposes a set is a collection of any sort, and a class is thus a set), a subset is equivalent to (i.e. has as many elements as) the whole set *only when* the set is *infinite*. Here then, in mathematical logic a part can equal a whole. Very oddly, this is the same as what we have seen happening psychologically as the result of symmetrization. By this means Matte-Blanco has introduced the concept of infinity into psychoanalytic thinking.

Let us look at some of the consequences of this. For instance, omniscience clearly has an infinite basis. An omniscient notion contains the idea 'I can know everything that is possible to know' or 'there is no limit to my knowing'. Omnipotence likewise involves an infinity, 'I can do all conceivable things'. Impotence also can at root be seen as 'I cannot do everything conceivable'. In idealization too, the self or an object is endowed with infinite wonderfulness.

Omnipotence, omniscience, etc., can be recognized as *feeling states*, albeit often of a pathological kind. Consider a few other extremes: for instance, being in love. It would carry no impact for a lover to express his feelings by saying 'I am in love with you for only a finite time in a specific location'. Rather, the true, passionate, perhaps hysterical lover experiences his love as being as good as timeless and no matter where the lover might be. At its height the loved one's beauty is all beauty and the lover's love is boundless, infinites hold sway, parts tend to be identical to wholes, time and space stand still. Idealization with its sense of infinity dominates being in love. In extreme or hysterical fear, too, the individual is not afraid of a specific limited robber or murderer but of the essence of an unknowable threat. Grief, on the other hand, is a result of an experience in time, of loss: it thus does not start with an infinity, but, at its height, it irradiates so that everything good can be felt as lost for all eternity.

These extreme emotional states display qualities of irradiation and maximization. Also, time and space tend to disappear. If general or extreme emotions are contained as nuclei within any feeling, then we may conclude that, in their cognitive aspects, all affects contain elements of symmetrization.

Thus, Matte-Blanco concludes that both affects and unconscious processes involve infinities.

What has Matte-Blanco done for the study of symbolization? His way of thinking has shown that any symbol, even one that refers to the most specific thing, stands for an *abstracted* characteristic or attribute and that abstraction is intrinsic to all classificatory activity. What is more, the unconscious is marked by the occurrence of symmetrization, of the registration only of sameness where the conscious mind might detect differences. So, unconscious processes involve variations upon classificatory activities which can be specified in logical terms.

It is now possible to see that psychoanalytic or isomorphic symbols are the product of symmetrization or homogenization. Such an isomorphic symbol has at least one attribute that is the same as the thing symbolized. They belong, in a wide sense, in the same class together. Thus a spire has erectness in common with the penis. Symbols that have arisen by convention on the other hand need have no such identity with the thing symbolized.

The symbolic activity in *imitation* and hence in all *play*, first pointed out by Sharpe (1930), can be seen from the logical point of view as a symmetrization of self-with-other. At a moment of make-believe the actor *is* his character. If he is sane, he will also know he is not, of course. Here we have *symmetrization between persons*. Another way of thinking about this is to say there is *attunement* between the persons (Stern, 1985). From the logical point of view this is also what happens in any mutual empathy. Here we are at the borderline, or transition, between a one-person and a two-person psychology.

Matte-Blanco's new 'calculus' for the study of unconscious and emotional processes is a conceptual horizon-shift. It adds the logical point of view to metapsychology, but it still probably appeals to very few therapeutic minds. It casts existing psychoanalytic theory into a new light, but it replaces none of it, so most analysts can still work without it. Some practising clinicians find his logical mode an invaluable advance, particularly when at work with borderline processes. But it is still seen by many as having little immediate relevance to their clinical work.

## WINNICOTT

Winnicott (1951, 1971a; see also Davis and Wallbridge, 1981; Phillips, 1988), like Matte-Blanco, speaks hardly at all about symbolization as a subject on its own, but he is centrally concerned with its development and experiential conditions. Matte-Blanco, with data from adult patients on the couch and a conceptual armoury from mathematics, investigates the logical form of the structures that give rise to symbolization. Winnicott, with data from the couch and paediatric clinics, and an armoury from general medicine, investigates the *developmental lines* which lead to symbolic activity.

In this section we will discuss his conceptualization of what he called the *third, or intermediate, area* of experience to which inner reality and external life contribute. This is the area of what he named *transitional phenomena*. Winnicott was first and foremost a paediatrician who saw thousands of mothers with their babies and young children in his clinics. He became interested in the effect of the environment from observing ordinary health hazards. Then, later, focusing on psychological growth, he naturally saw the importance of the environment for emotional development. His mode of conceptualization therefore centres upon a developmental frame and, because he investigated the earliest roots of the development of differentiation of self in relation to objects, his theoretical discourse is most often couched in terms of infant and mother.

Being a physician, he thought psychosomatically as a matter of course, but his poetic style of writing resembles that of the Bloomsbury circle. Seeing newborn infants daily, he noted their individuality of movement, and he then conceived of this as evidence of *innate potentials* to create a particular self style or *true self* unique to that individual only. This potentiality was met by an environment, mediated by the nursing mother, which could be facilitating or impinging.

Winnicott conceptualizes the very beginning of the infant's life as a mother–baby unit, hence his saying (as already quoted): 'I once risked the remark "There is no such thing as a baby" – meaning that if you set out to describe a baby, you will find you are describing a baby and someone. A baby cannot exist alone, but is essentially part of a relationship' (1964, p. 88).

To begin with, the infant can integrate only a little with his environment, and mother gives ego-cover to allow a growing of cohesion to sensori-motor elements. In time the infant becomes a unit, and with this comes the beginning of inner psychic reality and its complement, shared external reality. However, it is Winnicott's thesis that there is another area of experience which is neither inside nor outside, but in between. He felt that Freud neglected this when he conceptualized development from the pleasure principle to the reality principle. It is this area, the potential space, which develops between infant and mother from the beginning and which mediates development towards acceptance of shared reality. Important emotional development and earliest object relating take place by this means.

At first, there is the baby who experiences a spontaneous sensation – a want of satisfaction, say, as he feels hungry; with this there is mother who adapts and presents the breast. Winnicott thinks that the infant's experience is then that he has 'created' the breast. There is here a paradox and illusion and the developmental stage of *omnipotence*. The breast has become a *subjective object* for the infant.

At the beginning the infant needs mother's total adaptation so that he does not have to cope with 'not-me' aspects too early in life. In time the infant may experience a sensation, say hunger again, and mother might not be quite ready yet to present the breast to him. It is at such moments as this that the infant begins to become aware of 'not-me' aspects. For a time the infant can *create* breast-feeding satisfaction in imagination or, as Freud said, he can hallucinate the breast. But, when it is not forthcoming within a certain time, distress and then rage break out. Winnicott's term 'creation' is not quite the same as Freud's 'hallucination' (Davis and Wallbridge, 1981): 'creation' starts earlier, at a time when reality and omnipotent illusion are still the same.

When the infant creates the breast which is absent, he weaves 'me' and 'not-me' elements into the fantasized creation in a 'potential space'. At such a time his hands, face and mouth will grasp something, and he will 'find an object' which is, and is not, himself: these are the 'me' aspects. But it is also mother and yet not her: these are the 'not-me' aspects. Such a paradoxical object Winnicott called *transitional*, as it facilitates transition from the omnipotence that must occur in relating to a subjectively created object to relating to mother as an object who is 'objectively perceived', seen as in external reality (1951, 1971a).

Transitional objects must have certain attributes which stand for, or remind him of, mother, like smell or the texture of a blanket or the bit of wool picked from one. Winnicott emphasized that ordinary 'good-enough' parents intuitively know the vital importance of such things to a child. Once a baby has indicated that he has taken possession of it, they know that it has to survive and be available at all times as long as he needs it. However, Winnicott explains, it is not only such concrete objects that serve transitionally. Many infants do not seem to be particularly attached to such concrete things but, for them, special sounds, sights, lightings and postures serve the same aim. All these may contain something of mother and stand for possession of and union with her, yet they are also 'not-me' in the child's area of illusion.

To the observer such use of an object is an illusion but to the infant it is real. Hence Winnicott calls attention to the paradox 'It is neither me nor not-me' and we would not ask the child the question 'Have you conceived of this or was it presented to you from without?'. It may be a symbol, Winnicott says, but it is its actuality that is the point. He sees this third, transitional, area as the root of symbolism.

We have already mentioned that a mother's adaptation to her baby needs to be nearly complete at the early times of absolute dependence. In time, however, the mother will inevitably begin to disillusion her baby, by letting him wait, say. This will elicit rage, that is, an attack towards the mother who is experienced at that moment as a not-me object. With care by the mother, the baby will, however, understand that she, the 'environment-mother', can survive these attacks. This will enhance acceptance of shared reality as trustworthy. Winnicott stated that this was the time of the development of the depressive position (Klein, 1935; Winnicott, 1949b, 1954).

The transitional object stands for all the stages on the infant's way from absolute dependency to relative dependency upon mother, and also for the change from relating to the subjectively conceived object to relating to what is objectively perceived as in external reality. Winnicott lists its attributes as follows:

1   The infant assumes rights over the object, and we agree to this assumption. Nevertheless some abrogation of omnipotence is a feature from the start.

2   The object is affectionately cuddled as well as excitedly loved and mutilated.

3   It must never change, unless changed by the infant.

4   It must survive instinctual loving, and also hating and, if it be a feature, pure aggression.

5   Yet it must seem to the infant to give warmth, or to move, or to have texture, or to do something that seems to show it has vitality or reality of its own.

6 It comes from without from our point of view, but not so from the point of view of the baby. Neither does it come from within; it is not a hallucination.

7 Its fate is to be gradually decathected, so that in the course of years it becomes not so much forgotten as relegated to limbo. By this I mean that in health the transitional object does not 'go inside' nor does the feeling about it necessarily undergo repression. It is not forgotten and it is not mourned. It loses meaning, and this is because the transitional phenomena have become diffused, have become spread out over the whole intermediate territory between 'inner psychic reality' and 'the external world as perceived by two persons in common', that is to say, over the whole cultural field.

(Winnicott, 1971a, p. 5)

Thus, as the child's experience widens and transitional phenomena are spread out into play, transitional objects themselves sink into limbo. However, if a concrete transitional object is maintained into later life, negative use can be made of it, perhaps as a fetish. Hence, addictions and perversions are related to it.

Critics have said that transitional phenomena arise when the introjection of a good object has failed. Winnicott saw things differently: the transitional object, the first possession, is not a projected good object. It serves spontaneous experiences of actuality and creativity. Without it there would not be any experience of self. Its origin lies at the *birth* of self and not-self, and this differentiation is presupposed in the very concepts of introjection and projection. Thus it could be said that projection and introjection occur when transitionality has failed, rather than vice versa.

The experience of the third area, potential space, remains, in a child's further development, between that which is definitely 'me' or psychic reality and 'not-me' shared external reality. When the early transitional phenomena widen, play takes place in this potential space. It is the child's play which in time unfolds into contributing to society and culture. This is also the area of ego relatedness where meaningful, affectionate, sharing-yet-separate friendship, companionship and loves take place. It is the area of experience in which play and illusion are maintained in the spontaneous, creative activity of the healthy. Milner's concept of fusion and de-fusion is near to Winnicott's concept of the potential space.

Winnicott summarizes the essential features of play when he says:

To get to the idea of playing it is helpful to think of the *preoccupation* that characterizes the play of a young child. . .What matters is the near-withdrawal state, akin to the *concentration* of older children and adults. The playing child inhabits an area that cannot be easily left, nor can it easily admit intrusions. . .This area of playing is not inner psychic reality. It is outside the individual, but it is not the external world. . .the child gathers. . .phenomena from external reality and uses these in the service of some sample derived from inner or personal reality. Without hallucinating the child puts out a sample of dream potential and lives with this sample in a chosen setting of fragments from external reality. . .the child manipulates external phenomena in the service of the dream and invests [them] with dream meaning and feeling. . .There is a direct development from transitional phenomena to playing, and from playing to shared playing, and from this to cultural experiences    Playing implies trust, and belongs to the potential space between (what was at first) baby and mother-figure. . .Playing involves the body [but] bodily excitement in erotogenic zones constantly threatens playing and therefore threatens the child's sense of existing as a person. . .in seduction some external agency exploits the child's instincts and helps to annihilate the child's sense of existing as an autonomous unit. . .instinctual arousal beyond a certain point must lead to. . .climax [or] failed climax and a sense of mental confusion [or] alternative climax (as in provocation. . .). . .Playing can be said to reach its own saturation point, which refers to the capacity to contain experience. Playing is inherently exciting and precarious.

(Winnicott, 1971a,, pp. S1–2)

## RECENT WRITERS

Chrisopher Bollas (1989), following Winnicott, has suggested that it is useful to distinguish transitional phenomena, which largely concern that which lies between the self and the outside generally, from what he calls *intermediate* phenomena. These are events that lie specifically between two or more people – in the potential space between them. It is in this space that true communication takes place, says Bollas. Most important to analysts is the idea that it is here where the minds of patient and analyst meet. It is a transitional or intermediate, multidimensional 'screen', as it were, between them, upon which the one projects for the other to 'read'. This will be considered further in the chapters on technique.

Recently Independents have been examining this intimate interpersonalness and the need for it in symbol development. For instance, Enid Balint has been writing in this vein for some years, about the need for a mother and child to echo or mirror each other (E. Balint, 1963, 1972, 1973). Kenneth Wright (1976, 1990) has very recently been writing about symbol formation and the development of the self. He uses Winnicott and transitional phenomena extensively. He also draws on existential and phenomenological ideas, particularly those of Sartre, a social-psychology perspective from Mead and Cooley and writing about language from such as Cassirer and Langer.

Peter Hobson (1985, 1989a and 1989b), investigating symbol formation, and its lack, with autistic children, is convincing about the necessity of what he calls *social referencing*, which is real interpersonalness. As Frances Tustin (1981), a Kleinian child therapist who also uses Winnicott, has also pointed out, autistic children do symbolize, but in very limited and repetitive ways. This seems to be related to their grave incapacity to empathize or identify with other points of view. Taking a lead from the psychologists Heinz Werner and Lev Vigotsky, Hobson argues that, in order to symbolize, functional conceptions must be formed and these are based on the process of abstraction, as discussed earlier in this chapter. What Hobson's research shows is that this capacity to abstract usefully in a functional way depends upon the individual being able to take up and integrate data received from *different points of view*. Thus, we can develop a conception of space only by viewing objects around us from different points. Hobson's central point is that, although much development of this can, and needs to be, done in solitude, the experience of the *concurrent* points of view of other persons is also vital. Without this social referencing bizarre autistic symbols may be formed but not functional ones. (See also Abelin, 1981; Padel, 1985a; Britton *et al.*, 1989.)

We think this chapter shows how, in the course of historical development, object-relations theory has helped to widen the psychoanalytic conception of symbolism and reassessed its assumptions and clinical relevance.

# 4  Creativity and Dreams

IN ITS BROADEST sense a created product must have something of a new form about it. Its newness makes it distinguishable from repetition or reproduction, but it is the production of a unique form that is of the very essence of creativity. Much technological work that can genuinely be called creative is concerned with producing forms that are usable in everyday life. The arts, on the other hand, aim to produce forms that have beauty in them. There is a mystery about what constitutes a beautiful form: it is sensory and can be quite simple, but it is never unidimensional; it always has a dense combination of elements in it – and a unique wholeness or 'gestalt' quality. It is valuable to distinguish the sense or *appreciation of beauty*, whose study is the business of aesthetics, from the desire and ability, or otherwise, to carry out the *production of beauty*, which is artistic creativity. It is with the latter, with production, that sublimation is concerned.

The underlying sense of, and desire for, the experience of beauty of form is profoundly felt by many people. It is probably universal and of very early origin in both the history of mankind and of each individual. Its importance stretches beyond the tastes of a cultured élite. This has recently been succinctly stated by Bollas (1987, 1989), Milner (1987) and Likierman (1989) among others.

Along with its aesthetic qualities a created production must possess a validity or authenticity which achieves a 'fit' with reality. It has been said that, to be truly artistic, a product must be congruent with an emotional or inner reality, while in technology and science it must accord with external physical reality. Creativity is not just fantasizing. A true creation has something convincing, compelling, wonderful, even awesome about it: these qualities are summed together under the idea of beauty. Perhaps this naturally arises with many things that are new and will have some surprise in them. More mundanely, from the psychological point of view, the very newness of a created thing implies that it must be a product of imagination.

It has been said that creativity is the ability to form symbols. Without the free use of symbolic thought there can be no creativity. But ordinary creativity does not necessarily involve the forming of new symbols. A mechanical invention, for instance, must have employed symbolic thought, such as applied mathematics, say, but need not be concerned with new symbolic forms. Intellectual and artistic creativity, on the other hand, does involve the production of new symbols.

Classical analysis has been careful from the start never to give the impression that psychoanalysis could evaluate the aesthetic qualities of a work of art, but Freud made valuable contributions to thought about the dynamics acting within the individual when creating. In 1908, and later in his *Autobiographical Study* (1925b), he suggested that, in the painful transition from the pleasure to the reality principle, instinctual satisfaction has to be renounced. It is here that fantasy and imagination provide substitutes. The neurotic finds these only in the asocial products of daydreaming, but the artist is able to turn them back into the realm of reality. He does this by arousing a sympathetic response, one of similarity or resonance, in others who experience the artistic creation.

The neurotic and the artist are both trying to find compromise formations which represent the satisfaction of unconscious forces together with those of repression. However, the artist, unlike the neurotic, is able to sublimate the erotic impulses by transforming both their aims and their objects. For Freud, these are mainly suppressed, pre-genital, perverse sexual excitations which are transformed by the sublimation so that they can be used for cultural pursuits of all sorts. Laplanche and Pontalis (1973) have drawn attention to some other assumptions on sublimation that Freud came to later in his life. With the introduction of the idea of narcissism and then the structural theory, he postulated that libidinal investment in objects is withdrawn into the ego and so becomes de-sexualized. It is thus narcissistic libido which is the source of sublimated activity.

As we have just said, Freud stressed that psychoanalysis had nothing to contribute to literary criticism or to aesthetics as such. Mannoni (1971) has pointed out that Freud's study of works of art aims only at gaining further knowledge of the unconscious. In *Leonardo da Vinci and a Memory of His Childhood* (1910b) he investigated the origin and vicissitudes of the epistomophilic drive. Freud suggests that Leonardo had succeeded in sublimating this extensively, but that he had also inhibited part of it in his life. For instance, Leonardo stayed abstinent, made narcissistic object choices, preferring friendships with younger men, which showed some signs of repressed homosexual strivings, and he also suffered from considerable work inhibitions. Freud suggests that these may have been due to a trauma of his childhood. Leonardo was illegitimate and much loved by his mother. He was taken away from her by his father when he was about five years old.

It is in this paper that Freud stresses the limits of psychoanalytic investigation in creative activity. He says that sublimation lies 'in the organic foundations of character on which the mental structure is only afterwards created. Since artistic talent and capacity are intimately connected with sublimation we must admit that the nature of the artistic function is also inaccessible to us along psycho-analytic lines' (1910b, p. 136). On the other hand, Freud was stressing the fateful influences of early childhood experiences upon the person's whole life: 'The apportioning of the determining factors of our life between the "necessities" of our constitution and the "chances" of our childhood may still be uncertain in detail, but in general it is no longer possible to doubt the importance precisely of the first years of our childhood' (1910b, p. 137).

In his monograph, Freud deals with many of Leonardo's character features, as well as patterns of work, which are then related to his childhood experiences. However, it is now well known that Freud's investigations into the relevance of a particular childhood memory were based on false premises because of a translator's mistake. Mannoni points out, and we agree with him, that this does not diminish the importance of Freud's contribution to the study of creativity.

Some decades later, Melanie Klein (1935) added new dimensions to the understanding of the desire to create and of impediments in its path. Whereas the earlier Freud was naturally concerned with the vicissitudes of libido in creativity, Klein focused upon destructiveness. She showed how the urge to create could arise in attempts to make reparation for destructive phantasies. Creativity thus emerges only with the depressive position. It could be viewed as a sublimation of the destructive impulses.

In contrast to the tentativeness of both Freud and Klein, there has been a strong Independent tradition centring much attention upon the creative aspects of mental life and upon the use of aesthetics to understand psychoanalysis as much as the other way round. The psychoanalytic process itself is, for instance, often viewed with aesthetic considerations in mind. It is interesting that an original background in literature or the humanities is very common among many of the most original Independent writers. Sharpe, Strachey, K. Stephen, Fairbairn, Rycroft, King, Klauber, Khan, Padel, Coltart, Symington, Bollas, Mitchell-Rossdale, Casement and Parsons all studied such subjects at university before turning to the caring professions and then to analysis. The link between the poetic, literary and psychoanalytic mind is obvious – it has after all been said that Shakespeare was Britain's greatest psychoanalyst. The Independents trained in the humanities seem to have a natural ease and a generative idiom in their thinking which suggests that a core natural language for analytic theory is poetic, dramatic and historical.

## CREATIVITY AND DREAMS

### SHARPE

It seems apt here to interweave dreaming on the one hand and creativity on the other, as the mutuality of the two comes up repeatedly in Independent writings. We will largely dwell first upon creativity and then on dreaming. This separation is an artefact for ease of presentation, but also dreams are put second because some interesting aspects have emerged only very recently.

Though she obviously owes much to Jones, her early mentor, and to Sachs, her analyst, Ella Sharpe must be accorded pride of place in this particular stream of interest. In the late 1920s she wrote a series of general theoretical papers on creativity and sublimation. Her later psychobiographical papers in the genre of Freud's 'Leonardo' will be mentioned in our last chapter on applications of analysis. Sharpe's general theoretical papers however must be addressed here. As already mentioned, they start with an imaginative exploration of the nature of the 17,000-year-old cave paintings at Altamira in Northern Spain. She takes these as more or less the first works of art known to us. These are naturalistically beautiful renderings of the animals that lived around the cave artists and which they must have killed for food. But they also include more formalized pictures of men ritually dancing – where some play the part of hunters and others, wearing animals masks, are the hunted (1930).

Here, thinks Sharpe, is the first evidence of dance, imitation, play and make-believe, albeit in a ritual form. The drama is about the animals that are vital in life and death to the dancers. No doubt in dread for their lives and recognizing their dependence upon the animals whom they killed for food, or who might kill them, the dancers 'become' the animals of the hunt. Sharpe concludes that this is a *magical* act, 'delusion' of being the animals, an omnipotent means of overcoming primitive men's powerlessness. This early evidence of culture, of sublimation, rests upon acts of killing and being killed.

Sharpe now turns to the personal analyses of actors and artists of various kinds to show how they too, in their sublime activities, are *being* the characters they portray. It is this 'being the other' that Sharpe calls a delusion of unity with the animate object of their play. Later work by other writers refers to such play activity many times but calls it an *illusion* of unity. The use of the two words is in line with the paradox that the actor both *is* the character he is playing and yet is not so. As we have seen, a simultaneous symmetrization and asymmetry (Matte-Blanco 1975, 1988) takes place between the actor and his part, and this puts it in the third area of the mind – the realm of transitional phenomena (Winnicott, 1951, 1971a).

Sharpe points out her debt to Klein by showing how many sublimations spring from the same roots as delusions of persecution, that is, from fears of death and of retributions for killing. In a later paper (1935) she begins to examine the very particular qualities that distinguish the creative artist from other people. She suggests that the artist is often portrayed as a person of loose morals. This might be so by ordinary standards, but in its own particular area the ethic of an artist must be more stringent than that of other people. It is an ethic devoted to good *form*. The criteria are: line, colour, harmony, melody, texture and so on, depending upon the medium of the artist. In this sensory world, the harnessing of and living in *rhythm* is paramount. As far as we know, this was seen by no analyst before Sharpe, but it has been memorably emphasized also by Milner (1950a).

The chosen world of the artist is a sensory one, whether musical, verbal or visual, so that his rigorous ethic must be a demand of and for the senses. Sharpe points out that, this being so, the artist is dwelling in a *pre-verbal* realm to a much greater degree than other people. The artist's ethic generates a *compulsion* to create to the edge of life and death itself: he 'can do no other'. It is close to obsessional neurosis but is free of its sterile repetitiveness.

In the mid-1930s Sharpe gave lectures to students which formed the book *Dream Analysis* (1937). This is a small work of art in grace of style as well as content. Though many of her points had been made by Jones (1916), and no doubt by Rank and Sachs, probably nowhere before had the importance of the interdependence of dreams and creativity been expressed in the English language with such clarity.

Stressing that the latent content of a dream is derived from *experience* of some kind, Sharpe points out that this is both of memories of actual past occurrences and also of the emotional states and bodily sensations accompanying such occurrences. She goes on to point out: 'In this respect one may make a comparison between dreams and works of art' (Sharpe, 1937, p. 13). She surmises that a creative artist's past knowledge is like the reminiscent process of the dream, and notes that this must be occurring in Rembrandt's use of lighting and Turner's introduction of a bridge in many of his landscapes. To support this suggestion, which is the same as that made by Freud about Leonardo's capturing of the *Mona Lisa*'s enigmatic smile, she gives examples worked out with artists in analysis with her. She goes on to emphasize how this use of creative processes in dreams helps us not only to get in touch with memories of past experiences but also to correlate these with immediate affects towards the analyst – in other words with the impact of the transference.

Taking this lead into dreaming as a creative process she explores dream mechanisms from the point of view of certain well-known laws of aesthetics – those of poetic diction, which had been codified by academic critics. Their use is not sufficient, of course, to produce good poetry but they are necessary for it. Sharpe maintains 'The laws of poetic diction, evolved by the critics from great poetry and the laws of dream formation as discovered by Freud, spring from the same unconscious sources and have the same mechanisms in common' (1937, p. 19).

The simplest of all poetic devices, she says, is the simile. This is the equation of two otherwise dissimilar things by means of a common attribute.

> Blue were her eyes as the fairy flax,
> Her cheeks like the dawn of day,
> And her bosom white as the hawthorn buds
> That ope in the month of May.

(Sharpe, 1937, p. 20)

Where the words 'as' or 'like' are omitted we have the most universal poetic device – metaphor: 'The ship ploughs the sea', 'a stone she was cast on the shore of life'. The symbolization of emotional states by means of images of concrete things, omnipresent in dreams, is silent, implied metaphor. For instance, 'his hawk mind tore their composure to pieces' uses full verbal metaphor in description, while a dream of a hawk tearing at flesh might well represent latent dream thoughts about someone likewise being destructively critical. There are other poetic devices: metonymy is a figure of speech in which a specific object stands for a general function, as in the use of 'the throne' or 'the chair'. There are also synecdoche, onomatopoeia and punning, all of which can be shown to occur regularly in dreams. Matte-Blanco has suggested that the equation, or identity element, in otherwise dissimilar things, in simile and metaphor, again shows the operation of symmetrization. Other poetic devices can be shown to use it also.

Sharpe argues a case for the recognition of the dream as a creative and *dramatic* process with convincing clinical material. She does not seem to have thought she was saying anything new, but it was to be many years before her reasoning about creativity, drama and dreaming was taken up again. Fairbairn (1944) was the first to do this, then, much later, came Joyce McDougall's *Theatres of the Mind* (1985) from France. Segal (1981) and Meltzer (1983) have approached the subject from the Kleinian point of view. Similar observations were being made by Milner (1950a, 1969, 1987) about visual art.

## ARTISTIC CREATIVITY

### MILNER

After starting to train in infant teaching Marion Milner turned to psychology and was one of Flugel's many students in the 1920s, then an industrial and educational psychologist, before training as an analyst in the 1940s. She was inspired first by Grace Pailthorpe, a psychoanalyst, and painted a great deal with Sylvia Payne and Margaret Little. Her work has been professionally exhibited in the West End of London. Her drawings are evocative, vital and humorous. We will draw upon only three of her books here (1950a, 1969, 1987) – these dwell upon the creativity of both the visual artist and the psychoanalyst.

Her famous and popular book, *On Not Being Able to Paint* (1950a) is a study of her own drawings. She was training as an analyst at the time and developed a method of near doodling – of allowing her hand to wander spontaneously over the paper, making what it willed, as it were. The result was a series of funny drawings which illustrate the argument of the book. This derives from introspection and analysis of both the content of the drawings and what her mind was doing at the time of creating them. The drawing forms an equivalent to free association. She is particularly interested in what stops her from drawing and also in what emerges when something interesting appears on the paper. She concludes that the drawings portray not only external objects but, more importantly, the *structure* of her own – often unconscious – *feelings and thoughts*. This is close to Silberer's ideas. In her many books Milner is concerned with several main ideas,

one of them being the question of how a wide focus of attention, comparable to that made use of by Freud in his listening with free-floating attention, and alternating with the narrow focus of logical verbal thought, can be used – even must be used for the full appreciation of the world. This includes that bit of the 'outer' world that is the sensations of one's own body from the inside including, of course, breathing. These sensations are, naturally, only 'outer' from the point of view of the observing self.

(Milner, 1989, personal communication)

*The Hands of the Living God* (1969) is a detailed study of the analysis over many years of a young woman who had been diagnosed as schizophrenic by a psychiatrist but might better be described as suffering from a borderline illness. The book is illustrated by dozens of doodle drawings by the patient. Though prolific – Milner received about four thousand in the course of a few years of analysis – the drawings are sometimes of a striking unusualness and humour. Milner's detached account of her clinical work with this patient gives a moving record of a patient communicating feelings through the medium of drawing when she had lost the verbal language to do so. When she became more able to talk meaningfully she lost interest in the use of the drawings and even, for some years, in drawing itself. This book can be read as a study in aesthetics or as a detailed case report of the successful treatment of a very ill woman.

*The Suppressed Madness of Sane Men* (1987) collects together Milner's main observations on the subject of creativity and psychoanalysis developed over a long lifetime. We shall attempt to summarize just a few of them here.

Milner dwells almost exclusively on visual art and psychoanalysis. Nevertheless, many of her observations could apply to other media. In contradistinction to the early analysts, she uses analysis to investigate the creation of beauty itself and also vice versa – she thus appeals to aesthetics to illuminate analysis. For her, aesthetic worth is of vital importance. Our criterion of newness, mentioned earlier, is affirmed; but there are others for her, and she would probably assent to Schopenhauer's well-known aphorism: 'Thus, the task is, not so much to see what no one has seen yet; but to think what nobody has thought yet, about that which everybody sees.' But, as well as this, *truthfulness of expression* in the *elaboration of reality* is essential for Milner. Though the artist may be portraying an object out there in space, the essential truthfulness must concern the artist's own affective experience. The work of art is a symbolization of feeling by means of *rhythmic* form. This naturally concurs with Langer (1967). It is also an expression of the self feeling something and, if it portrays this truthfully, it could be said to be an expression of the 'true self' (Winnicott, 1945b, 1950b, 1971a), a concept which we will mention later. Such true expression is to be contrasted with a drawing of a failed artist that copies another in a slavish way, is derivative or compliant, to a fashion for instance, and which would then be false to one's true feelings.

Milner says, 'Psychic creativeness is the capacity for making a symbol. Thus, creativeness in the arts is making a symbol for feeling and creativeness in science in making a symbol for knowing' (1950a, p. 148). But Milner the artist is most concerned with the personal experiences in creating things. Intimacy with one's own body sensations and movements is essential. It is upon the bedrock of his own body, its sensations and affects, that the artist bases his work. She emphasizes that 'The most assured stability comes, not only in the establishing of reciprocating body rhythms with a devoted carer, but this can also lead to a reciprocating interplay with the particular qualities of a chosen medium – whether by sounds or visual shapes which would be in some form of adaptable medium, especially toys in childhood' (1989, personal communication).

Repeatedly in her work (see especially 1950a), Milner points out how the *spontaneous* aspect of drawing is 'like dreaming when awake but with a responsive bit of the outer world, the medium, to receive the dream images in some external form and thus modify them through its inherent qualities, just as the analyst does with the patient's words or gestures' (1989, personal communication). Sharpe made the same observation.

Another essential in creativity is *idealization*, not of one's own body, particularly, but of the object of one's study – one falls in love with the object and with one's own portrayal. There is an illusion of loving and being loved in this. But alternating with it must be a disillusionment, even denigration of – a falling out of love with, the object and the work of art. Thus *reciprocation of passion* must go on.

In the necessary state of in-loveness there is, Milner thinks:

> A feeling representation of a kind of orgasm, and ecstasy (what Winnicott called an ego-orgasm). The work of art then contains a symbolization of this kind of ecstasy (even an ecstasy of hate) which is achieved by a harmony of form or wholeness, this being an essential part of what beauty is in a work of art.
>
> (1989, personal communication; see also Milner 1950a, 1958, 1987)

She points out that the emotion of idealization, so necessary in creativity, is often understood by analysts simply as a defence against ambivalence. It is obviously frequently used in this way, but the blissful experience of orgasm *really* is a marvellous feeling, worthy of ecstasy and idealization. It is then not a manic defensive delusion (1950a).

There are necessary anal elements in creative production. The obsessive devotion, being unable to rest until the creation has been completed, is one aspect. The idealization of one's product is another. Here Milner points out how, not only is the anal orgasm of defecating a blissful feeling, but the establishment of body control is a wonderful achievement in itself for both mother and child. It is worthy of idealization. However, it readily over-reaches itself, as when a child idealizes merely the products of his achievement, the faeces themselves. When the idealization has become defensive, Milner thinks of it as a grandiose obliteration of the child's experience of separateness. There is then a denial of vulnerable loneliness, when isolated from the parents with their life and intercourse together.

In the act of creation, as perhaps in any ecstatic-orgasmic experience, there is a loosening of the differentiation of self and object – there is a transient sense of fusion or unity. We noted in the last chapter Milner's stress upon this in another context, that of analytic therapy and symbol formation (Milner, 1950a, 1952, 1969, 1987). Both in therapeutic change and in artistic creation there is not only a de-differentiation of subject, or self, and object, but also between different objects where they are recognized as alike in ways not seen before. This de-differentiation must also occur between unconscious and conscious levels of the mind.

Sharpe referred to an experience like this as a 'delusion' of unity of self with object, and we suggested the use of Milner's term – an illusion of unity. The term 'illusion' is used widely by Independents – by Winnicott, Rycroft and Klauber as well as Milner. It does not have quite the same meaning as the Kleinians' 'phantasy' which refers to the unconscious psychic representation of a drive and is predominantly internal. Illusion, rather differently, is pointing at a phenomenon that is close to, even partly is, both internal and external reality. The term illusion thus refers to 'the third area', that which is felt as within the self and also of the external world. We are in the region of paradox – Winnicott's transitional space.

With the presence of illusion in art, Milner makes it plain that the provision of a *frame* for the created work is often necessary to protect the sanity of the experiencer of the work. With a painting an actual frame informs the viewer that the area within it portrays an illusion: the work of art is not actual external reality but a portrayal of it. Even if there is no actual frame there is a recognizable edge somewhere. The frame for a theatrical performance is the stage with the actors on it; that of a book is given on the cover, saying whether it is fiction or not. A similar frame is created for the drama of analysis. This is provided by the setting established by the analyst from the start – the layout of his room, his self-contained, reflective manner of speaking and so on. Milner describes this, as does Rycroft (1958). Heimann (1957) talks similarly but of 'figure and ground' rather than of frame.

There may be an illusion of unity, or an experience of the real actual aspects in unison – between self and object, or between objects, or between parts of the self. But for true, sane creativity this must be *transient*. We have mentioned already how Milner spells out how a *rhythm* of oscillation or *reciprocity* between differentiation and fusion must take place. With the mind settling into one position, either of differentiation or its opposite, then a delusion is in the ascendant. It will be evident here why creativity is so difficult and frightening. With the boundaries of self being in flux we are at the borderline of psychosis – hence Milner's book title, taken from Santayana, *The Suppressed Madness of Sane Men* (1987).

Milner recognizes the significance of self–object de-differentiation, homogenization or symmetrization as Matte-Blanco calls it, between selves. She sees clearly how this is a phenomenon stressed by mystics throughout the world over many centuries. She explores and agrees with many of the ideas of Christian, Hindu and Taoist writers about the finding of creative enlightenment with the 'destruction' of the self–object divide (Milner 1987). Zen writers like Suzuki (1953) speak similarly.

Not only must one risk forms of madness in true creativity, it is also necessary to endure *emptiness*. The mind must find its state of 'pregnant emptiness' divested of prior conceptions for it to be able to be filled by fresh created imagination. This may be 'a dreadful emptiness' – the fear of irreversible depression that must be mastered. Milner refers here to 'the abysmal depth of dread'. She thinks that this comes about by the artist needing to exercise his omnipotence and then, within a rhythmic cycle, to loosen its grip to allow the dreaded feeling of total impotence. This sequence is also close to much mystical experience. Moreover, it is consonant with Bion's injunction to the analyst to divest himself of 'memory and desire' when approaching a session.

In summary, it is only by rhythmic reciprocity, in analysis or art, between fusion and differentiation, that new insight can come about. This involves perceiving something common in mental structures which had hitherto been seen as different. Likewise, something different may be discovered in that which had only been known as the same. However, meaningful creativity involves much beyond such simple newness. Thus, a memorable work of art brings together many insights, in highly condensed form, into one symbolic pattern. Because of its density of expression a great work cannot be fully described by the discursive logic of ordinary verbal descriptions, it can only be indicated and alluded to by them.

Milner sees that, since the artist needs to master profound psychotic and depressive anxieties, and harness these with great density in expression, he needs a strong ethic, self-discipline and courage within his chosen medium. Perhaps in reaction to this particular severity he may be lax in other fields (1950a, 1987). Ella Sharpe (1935) and Enid Balint (1989, personal communication) emphasize the same point.

HEIMANN

An example of development in an author's thinking can be seen with Paula Heimann. Her first paper on sublimation and creativity (1942) was written when she was one of Klein's collaborators. Here, like Klein, she saw the importance of *reparation* of internal objects. The assimilation of damaged and damaging objects leads to creative freedom of the ego. Fifteen years later she had returned to basic Freud and attempted to integrate it with later findings (1957). She conceived of two sources of sublimation: one which stems from object love and object conflict and which serves their mastery; a second she terms ego sublimation where the ego has a relation with itself and asserts itself to create something of importance.

In this, the creative person must be capable of being 'object-hostile'. The artist, for instance, must be able to treat his human objects with a certain indifference or opposition. This is not quite ruthlessness, which implies cruelty, but an absence of compliance or concern so that he can get on with his *solitary* creative activity. Heimann points out that this opposition to others is first healthily manifest in the anal stage (1962b). At this stage the infant needs to produce in his own time without compliance with others. Such activities strengthen identity formation. She also draws attention to the mastery of locomotor activity during the anal stage which allows the child to assert his independence against his mother's wishes. These are 'I against you' activities which strengthen identity formation.

Heimann throws light on the necessary obsessive elements in creative activity. For her, narcissism is not just a stage of development towards object relating, as in classical theory, but has its own developmental lines leading to mature narcissism. Narcissism and object-relating thus grow hand-in-hand, and one cannot develop without the other. The necessity for a solitude in creativity emphasizes its autonomous functioning. This can be accompanied by regression to auto-erotism, which is similar to Milner's findings about pre-genital orgasm.

We have shown Heimann turning to find roots of creativity in things other than just classical sublimation as a form of instinctual defence or Klein's concept of reparation. Heimann sees creativity as also having innate origins that are not defensive. This is in line with a marked direction of thought in the Independents. It was emphasized in Milner, we see it in Balint and, most markedly of all, early origins are stressed by Winnicott.

## BALINT

Michael Balint's (1968) frame of reference is developmental like Heimann's, and speculates that even before birth the infant must be strongly pre-object-relating to its uterine environment. However, in this phase and after birth also, there is no awareness of separateness. He calls this the area of creation. It is out of this non-separateness or fusion, which he conceives of as the infant's original state of harmonious mix-up with the environment, that creative acts, in their widest sense, must emerge. He is of the opinion that a transient return to this pre-object state occurs in any creativity. It is interesting to note that Balint does not idealize this state: an act of creation need not be beautiful, or truthful, but it does produce something new. Associated with this is the stage of primary love. Here love is *not* felt as directed *towards* another object or person: what is desired is to *be* loved. Balint rejects the idea of the phase of primary narcissism since he sees the infant as being emotionally related to a pre-object environment (1951, 1968).

The basic idea of early non-differentiation or fusion is, of course, held by many authors in addition to the Independent writers whom we have mentioned: Mahler *et al.* (1975) is close to it, and so is Piaget (1951, 1953). Stern (1985) has, more recently, questioned its being developmentally prior to differentiation.

## WINNICOTT

Artistic creativity is not Donald Winnicott's primary focus of interest. He wishes us to look at something much more general – at ordinary creativity which he thinks is potentially present in everyone and is the defining hallmark of health itself. This is one of Winnicott's crucial visions (1971a).

Freud's psychodynamic point of view sees life as wrestling with incompatible desires – man is ambivalent from the cradle to the grave. Winnicott, at heart a British Darwinian, sees things in terms of survival in the environment. But it is survival of the *authenticity of the self* that he is concerned about. The experience that comes from authenticity is 'feeling real' and its loss is associated with feelings of unreality. Winnicott does not disagree with Freud; he is simply pointing towards something else without negating Freud (Phillips, 1988).

The self is central to Winnicott's theorizing. He uses this word to connote both the I as agent, where the term ego (the English translation of Freud's *Ich* – I) has classically been used, and the self as object. No doubt 'ego' was too formal a word for Winnicott's informal and spontaneous idiom of writing. As described already, the vital self is rooted in its own pattern of innate potentials. This localization in 'dwelling-in-the-body' is the beginning of the true self (Winnicott, 1945b, 1947a, 1947b, 1950b). It cannot be known directly, only inferred. The very particular patterning of movements, different from all others, that each individual infant has is a close manifestation of it. Survival of the true self is associated with authenticity.

At birth, and probably before, the individual self meets its environment. This is usually mediated by mother whose *adaptiveness* to her baby's true potentials is enhanced by that pronounced single-mindedness of late pregnancy and the early months which Winnicott termed *primary maternal preoccupation* (1956b). Optimally with his mother's adaptiveness, as described in the last chapter, the momentarily frustrated baby 'hallucinates' satisfaction from mother and then, if at that instant he is actually satisfied by her, his hallucination comes true, imagination and reality coincide. This process is called *realization* by Winnicott. The discovery of reality and the sense of reality are *created* out of imagination. At this early stage the adaptiveness of the mother must be well nigh total. If it is, then the infant can discover which of his imaginings are realized, that is, are confirmed by events, and which are not. Normal health is intrinsic to this creativity. If in this alternation of satisfaction and frustration a sense of *continuity* of self with objects is maintained, then the mother has been good enough (Winnicott 1964, 1965a, 1965b). Note that Winnicott differs markedly from Freud here. For Freud, creativity is a later development, the fruit of sublimation; for Winnicott, it is of very early origin and primary to ordinary health.

Where maternal adaptiveness is not good enough, the hallucinations following frustration are not followed by a realization with satisfaction but by continued frustration and thus more hallucination. An infant can stand quite a lot of this, Winnicott thinks, but his tolerance is not unlimited – when the limit has been passed the infant has been *trau-*

*matized*. The environment has *impinged* (1953). The experience is seen by others as extreme distress and may be felt by the infant as what Winnicott calls *unthinkable dread*, which is psychotic anxiety. Under this circumstance, *continuity* of process which is necessary for the growth of realistic imagination and thinking has been fractured. The outcome of gross traumatization is damage to innate or true-self body–mind potentiality and then the development of 'false' self structures (see Chapters 6 and 7).

In the early months of life the infant is clearly in a state of *total dependence* upon his mother. It is to manage this that the mother is optimally in a state of maternal preoccupation. Through the months of infancy and then childhood the individual slowly learns ways to be able to be gradually less dependent upon mother. What Winnicott maintains here is that every individual has a *drive to develop* independence, to 'become isolated without being insulated'. This drive is biologically rooted, and it must be inferred as one of the innate potentials of the true self. But it is not specifically a libidinal drive in the Freudian sense. It is prior to infantile sexuality. This vision of a drive to grow up is intrinsic to Winnicott's object-relations point of view and lies outside classical instinct theory.

Where continuity has been maintained, then the true self is enabled to interact with the reality of the environment within the transitional area. As we showed in the last chapter, this is where the means of symbolizing is found, and it is this that is within the essence of culture and creativity, be it purely artistic or more ordinary. It is with the artist that Winnicott and Milner meet. She does not write with the dramatic phraseology of Winnicott but their thinking has much in common.

**BOLLAS**

Christopher Bollas (1989) has taken Winnicott's formulation of true and false self several stages further. More systematically than Winnicott did, he spells out the theory of innate potentiality of the true self acting in a dialectic with the environment. He sees the dangers here of impingement and the psychosis-rooted false self. Bollas says that every person potentially has his own *idiom*, his own potential ego patterning of imagining and responsiveness. He then goes on to consider two concepts new to psychoanalytic thinking – destiny and fate. We have already mentioned how Winnicott conceived of a drive to develop; Bollas takes a logical step on from this. In so far as development is rooted in spontaneity of expression of bodily based true-self potentials, in interaction with the environment, then the individual can be conceived as fulfilling his destiny. It is thus meaningful to speak in this case of a *destiny drive*. However, where the individual's true self has been lost and he is at the mercy of his compliance with environmental demands then, Bollas suggests, he is *fated*. A person who finds his destiny is *actively* discovering aspects of the environment to *use* creatively in the fulfilment of his potentials that is his destiny. In contrast, when a person is fated he is passively driven by forces that are outside his foresight and span of decision.

In an area related to creativity but not quite synonymous with it, Bollas (1987) has a new theoretical view about *aesthetic* experience which is likely to be important. To begin with in Bollas's model, following Winnicott, innate true-self potentialities encounter environmental factors. Some of these may be deleterious impingements, while others will be more benign. Next, an environmental factor or object that evokes a *change* to a *new form* in an individual's *ego* is called a *transformational object* by Bollas. Thus any object that transforms an individual's ego functioning is a transformational object. In the case an infant many of the effects his mother has will naturally be transformational. Note that this change is to a new form and will thus not be due to traumatic impingement, which by its nature is shattering rather than transformational.

The next proposition by Bollas is a crucial one: that the experience of *ego transformation* is essentially felt as an *aesthetic* one. Thus, in so far as it is transformational, interplay with mother is the infant's *first aesthetic*. This is not to say that the young child experiences fully articulated conscious feelings of beauty: far from it. However, the roots of ideas of beauty must stem from such times. Bollas suggests that anything of true beauty is evoking, however minimally, some ego change in the experiencer. Such considerations as this naturally must have a direct bearing upon the understanding of creativity, for much creative effort is expended in pursuit of producing something that will 'move' other people – that is, transform them in some way, however small. If what Bollas says is correct, then aesthetics is assuredly a matter of everyday concern for everyone and not just a luxury indulged in by a few favoured with leisure and sensibility.

**ENID BALINT**

Though her individual writing is still perhaps less well known than that of the others mentioned here, Enid Balint has continued a particular line of thinking about creativity that is primarily clinical in nature (1963, 1972, 1973). She has noted from the analysis of artistic people that many had severe inhibitions of their creativity. However, often against paralysing fears, they felt their honesty, as it were, insisted that they should go on trying to portray an aspect of the world as they really saw it. She also noted that many of these patients grew up in their early years with a primary care-giver mother who loved and looked after them, but who seemed lacking in some feature of the capacity to perceive their child as they really were. Balint feels that the paralysis of creativity must be deemed neurotic, but not its apparently obsessed quality. This seems to stem predominantly from a profound need to express a truthfulness of perception which is essentially healthy.

## DREAMS

The contribution by Independents to investigations of dreams does not, at first sight, seem vast when compared to the volume produced upon some other subjects. What is more, it perhaps reflects something of a British insularity in its slowness to pick up findings from other countries. For example, dream laboratory work has been available for a quarter of a century, but it is not centrally used to reassess our dream theories. Thus, the recent findings about REM (rapid eye-movement periods) dreaming and memory systems have hardly been used even though there have been, since Fisher's (1965) pioneering studies, works from America by analytically minded writers to point the way (e.g., Hartmann, 1984; Palombo, 1978). However, even though it may ignore some results from abroad, work in Britain does contain a vital line of thought.

**SHARPE**

It will be remembered that Sharpe's unambitious aim was to inform students about dream analysis and that she succeeded in giving probably the best exposition of classical theory on dreams after Freud himself.

However, while probably hardly aware of it, she was beginning to extend the boundaries of analytic theory.

Freud demonstrated that dreams have understandable meanings which can be interpreted. He then followed this by formulation of the topographical structure of dreams. Thus, dreams have a manifest and latent content which can be understood only by interpretation. The activity of the dream work converts latent content into manifest dream and the main thrust of classical interpretation was towards understanding the latent content. From the therapeutic point of view, interest centred on the dream work only in so far as it created a resistance to the uncovering of the latent thoughts. When these had emerged, the analyst's task was completed and the patient was left free to get on with his own life, hopefully through the better sublimation of impulses contained in the hitherto latent thoughts.

The Independents have, on the other hand, been particularly interested in the dream work itself as a creative activity, and the seeds of this can be seen in Sharpe. Thus, not only did she unravel the functioning of processes in common between dreams and poetic diction, like metaphor, but she also began to investigate other functions, particularly those concerned with the analytic transference. She pointed out how in analysis the dream could be used as a 'thing', as a love gift, say, or to placate, or in the service of other dramatic or manipulative gestures to the analyst. Furthermore, she began to see that examining the manifest *structure* of the dream had value – it could indicate the nature of the *psychic situation* of the dreamer in such a way as to illustrate progress in the analysis.

To summarize this, at the end of her book Sharpe recounts the following dream. It was told her by an eighty-one-year-old woman three days before her death – she did not regain full consciousness again after telling it.

> I saw all my sicknesses gathered together and as I looked they were no longer sicknesses but roses and I knew the roses would be planted and that they would grow.

> (Sharpe, 1937, p. 200)

Clearly we could say that the transformation of the illnesses into roses was a wish-fulfilment, but the point Sharpe makes is that the dream perhaps *also* portrays a reality in her situation – that she has in fact planted things in her life, in other people's minds for instance, which will grow after she is gone.

## FAIRBAIRN

We shall be discussing Fairbairn's (1952) central contribution to the understanding of schizoid processes and the theory of psychic structure in Chapter 7. We confine ourselves here to his use of dreams in approaching psychic structure. His contribution is brief but important. We can best recount a dream he used to illustrate his points.

> The dreamer saw the figure of herself being viciously attacked by a well-known actress in a venerable building which had belonged to her family for generations. Her husband was looking on; but he seemed quite helpless and quite incapable of protecting her. After delivering the attack the actress turned away and resumed playing a stage part, which, as seemed to be implied, she had momentarily set aside in order to deliver the attack by way of interlude. The dreamer then found herself gazing at the figure of herself lying bleeding on the floor; but, as she gazed, she noticed that this figure turned for an instant into that of a man. Thereafter the figure alternated between herself and this man until eventually she awoke in a state of acute anxiety.
>
> (Fairbairn, 1952, p. 95)

Fairbairn shows how the characters in this dream drama classically represent the patient's husband, mother, father and the analyst. But as well as this, each character represents an *aspect of the ego functioning* of the dreamer herself. What is more, the dramatic structure of the dream, a product of the dream work, is a representation of the actual internal interactions of different aspects of the dreamer's ego. The structure of *the dream drama represents psychic structure*. What was mentioned almost in passing by Sharpe is now explicitly central and remains so in Independent thinking. It demonstrates the quintessence of the working of the internal interactions of self–object relations.

## KLAUBER

For nearly two decades, years which were perhaps the most creative in the history of the British Society, interest in dreams was at a low ebb for some reason. However, John Klauber (1967) then takes up a theme briefly pointed out by Sharpe thirty years earlier. He asks the question – why is a dream reported by a patient on one day and not another? He goes on to point out that Freud was interested in uncovering the symbolic meaning of the fragments in a dream rather than the function, not only of the dream as a whole pattern, but also the psychology of its being reported. Paula Heimann (1956) was making the same point some years earlier when she stressed that a dream in analysis is shaped in order to be a communication from patient to analyst.

Klauber says: 'A dream is a private work of art. Like all art it is, in Picasso's phrase, a fiction that brings us nearer reality' (1981, p. 31). He goes on to explore why a dream story or drama might be recounted at a certain time, and comes to the conclusion that it happens when the patient cannot report some state of affairs by the ordinary logical use of words. The patient then resorts to that mixture of primary and secondary processes that is afforded by the dreaming mode. Hence the report of a dream implies the following.

1   There is a conflict impinging upon the conscious/preconscious systems.
2   But there is an increased confidence in the ego being able to withstand the conflict.
3   However, there is still a barrier against integration: non-adaptive defences are at work.
4   The titillation of a dream report indicates that crude energies are interwoven with neutralized ones.
5   Synthetic functions of the ego may be paralysed at the moment, but there are attempts by the ego to integrate functions of the id, super-ego and external reality.

## KHAN

At about the same time, or even a bit before, Masud Khan (1962a) was thinking about the overall functions of recounted dreams. In asking about the nature of 'the good dream', he is working along very similar lines to Klauber. He examines the 'whole pattern', the gestalt, of this sort of dream and concludes that the dreamer's ego is alerted but not too disturbed by threatened breakthroughs of the id. This sort of dream is an indication that the ego is working on the material.

Khan continues his investigation into the overall pattern of dreams in a later paper (1976). He points out how Winnicott (1971b) distinguishes between 'fantasying' and dreaming. In that paper Winnicott quotes a patient who had spent long hours throughout her life day-dreaming, but it had a sterile, repetitive quality to it. It was isolated and compulsive – in no way creative. In the course of analysis this began to give way to remembered dreaming and, in conscious life, to a parallel freeing and use of her imagination.

Winnicott goes on to suggest that, in the sterile fantasying process, a patient is manically, omnipotently controlling his internal objects, doing what he calls 'object relating'. When dreaming comes with imagination, this omnipotence is loosened and objects attain a freedom. With this, people can be used as real separate objects with qualities of their own. Winnicott calls this 'object usage'. This notation is sometimes felt to be rather confusing, for 'a person being used' means in common parlance something very close to what Winnicott calls object relating, and vice versa. The usage is derived from his differentiation of the mother who is the object of instinctual satisfaction, to whom the infant relates, and the environment-mother who is used in imaginative elaborations.

Khan takes this idea up where Winnicott left off. He recognizes that the creative imagination which Winnicott was highlighting involved freedom by the patient to use transitional phenomena – to use the third area. It also seems that this creativity is involved in dreaming. Thus, just as a child in therapy uses the space of a blank sheet of paper to make it his own as a transitional potential space, so perhaps a 'dream space' can be used transitionally. Khan goes on to make an interesting distinction between the 'dream process' and his newly coined 'dream space'. The dream process is biological, and its characteristics are well investigated in dream laboratories. The dream space is a much more problematic acquisition: Khan thinks it is an individual achievement of ego development. Those who have not developed its use are, like people who have been unable to be free in usage of real objects, prone to *act out* the latent content of their dreams. Those who do use the 'space' for dreams move into creative imagination.

We can now draw several strands together: as distinct from object relating, which involves manic-magical control of internal objects, creative object usage requires the functioning of a transitional mental potential space. It seems to us that this must have a *neutral* quality, in which the protagonists, parts of the self, can meet and mingle. It is close to Lewin's (1948) 'dream screen'. Bollas (1987) has extended this concept of a potential space to one between patient and analyst. This interpersonal area he has called 'intermediate space'.

It seems to the present writer that an exclusive use of spacial metaphors about these transitional phenomena can be restricting. Maybe the neutrality of the ground in these spaces for discourse is provided by the activity of paradox. A commonality or sameness, and at the same time a separateness, is registered between the 'protagonists' who are in communication. This is provided by their being subject simultaneously to both symmetrization and asymmetrization. The 'protagonists' may be different parts of the self-with-internal-object or, in other words, affect structures. However, they may also have interpersonal aspects, as in social, or analytic, situations.

## STEWART

In the decade after Khan was thinking along these lines, Harold Stewart contributed to the ongoing discussion in two papers (1973, 1981). He reviews the use made of dreams in analysis since Freud's day and points out how different from Freud are the techniques of many analysts today. Freud took a dream as a special communication, different from other associations, treated it as an honoured guest, and formally asked for associations to each part of the dream. By this means, elements of the latent content would slowly emerge. In contrast to this, Stewart observed, some analysts treated a dream on a par with any other association: they dwelt upon the motive for bringing up the dream at the time and so on, but sometimes seemed to ignore the content of the dream itself. Some had even become so cavalier with dreams that they seemed to concern themselves only with the manifest content and its form, interpreting this while ignoring the slow, quiet search for latent meanings. Stewart is also convinced of the value of investigating the form of the drama of the dream, and what he calls the 'experience' of the dream.

His conclusion is that Freud's classical method must not be abandoned but that we should equip ourselves to use the whole array of approaches that are now available to us, both new and more classical.

Furthermore, Stewart, following in Sharpe's footsteps, is concerned with the meaning that can be attached to the overall mood and pattern of a dream – it is this that he calls the dream 'experience'. He is at pains to point out how uniquely valuable the analysis of a dream can be, with its access to memories from different stages, in regaining the meaning of the *continuity* of life. The dreamer's experience of a dream can also provide an estimate of the *state of his ego* and its capacity to find this sense of continuity. Stewart investigates the dreams of various patients and suggests that dreams where 'distancing' is paramount, where the dreamer is looking at rather than participating in the manifest content, are indications of withdrawal. They are facets, he thinks, of the operation of schizoid mechanisms. When this withdrawal begins to break there is a likelihood of psychotic processes and tranference psychosis coming to the fore. This is often heralded by the experience of being 'overwhelmed' in dreams. When the ego has achieved a greater coalescence and continuity, the presence of a transference neurosis is signalled by the experience of the dreamer becoming an active participant in the dream drama.

The dream is just one aspect, albeit an important one clinically, Stewart thinks, of the *experience* of psychic structure. His interest in this is seen in his consideration of the characteristics of different levels of thought (1968), and also in his work upon the ways in which different qualities of psychic space can be experienced (1985). These, as well as structure, can be portrayed in some dreams. He is close to Khan here.

## DREAMING, CREATIVITY AND AESTHETICS

### RYCROFT

One of the foremost Independent thinkers and contributors in the 1950s and 1960s, Charles Rycroft, was even then particularly interested in the nature of dreaming. But it was the late 1970s before he brought out the only book (1979) exclusively devoted to the dream by a British Independent analyst since Sharpe.

By the time of writing his book, *The Innocence of Dreams* (1979), Rycroft had withdrawn himself from the British Society and appeared much more critical of Freud's work than most of us would feel is justified. However, this should not blind us to the importance of the contribution that Rycroft's book makes to our understanding.

Rycroft is critical of Freud for concentrating too exclusively upon causal factors in the constitution of a dream. If a dream can be interpreted, Rycroft says, if it has meaning, then it must be the *creation* of an agent or *person* who *endows it with a meaning.* If dreams are phenomena simply with causes then they must be explicable in terms of prior events without reference to a person or creative agent. He seems to think that causal and meaning explanations are mutually exclusive, rather than complementary as others would argue. Rycroft wholeheartedly espouses a creative explanation and asks – for what purpose is the dream created?

He then sets out the evidence for arriving at the following proposition:

the meaning conveyed by them [dreams] tends to be of a kind that the sleeping and later waking recipient is reluctant to understand, and that therefore the division of the self into two parts that occurs during dreaming tends to be such that the agent who constructs dreams tends to possess insights into the person's true nature which the recipient, i.e. the person's waking self, is reluctant to acquire.

(Rycroft, 1979, pp. 47–8)

We can see from this that Rycroft is quite clear that a dream is a *communication from one aspect of the self to another.* It is interesting to note how this follows naturally from Fairbairn's proposal that the dream represents different aspects of the self. However, he did not go so far as to say that a major function of the dream is to communicate between them as Rycroft does. It is also clear that Rycroft follows on from Winnicott's conception of the true and false self. The agent who constructs the dream in Rycroft's quotation could easily serve the true self. Rycroft is clear about this link with Winnicott, just as he is clear that he is borrowing from Jung as well. He agrees with Calvin Hall who says 'A dream is a letter to oneself. It is not a newspaper story or a magazine article' (1966, p. 12).

In the communication from one aspect of the self to another, the unconscious dreaming self utters from a *timeless, total position,* while the conscious recipient is in time and can thus manage only one thing at a time *in sequence.* This is an observation that is also made from quite different premises by Matte-Blanco (1988), who studies it in detail using the mathematical logic of multidimensionality.

Rycroft does not attempt such mathematical matters but confines himself to the use of ordinary verbal syntax. He suggests that the grammar of dreams consists of a mixture of discursive, verbal-level logic and non-discursive, isomorphic symbolism (these concepts of Langer (1942) were introduced in Chapter 3). Rycroft thinks that the unconscious agent can represent certain aspects of its data by means of non-discursive symbolism alone, but of course the conscious recipient is on the whole in poor shape to comprehend its code.

Rycroft examines the use of metaphor in dreams and waking life. In waking life, a speaker will search for a metaphor to enhance his communication about some affect of which he is fully conscious. In dreams, it is the unconscious agent that seems to use the metaphor and the waking self often cannot understand it. Poets, Rycroft thinks, are nearer to the dream process, for their imagery is usually so dense that they cannot be fully conscious of its whole meaning. He, like Sharpe, Klauber and others, affirms that the dream is akin to involuntary poetry.

Rycroft goes on to say that it would be an over-simplification to think solely in terms of communication between only two aspects of the self – the unconscious or true self and the conscious recipient. It must be an open question as to how many agents and recipients there may be. However, he does stress that the 'two-way traffic', from body-to-self-to-outside-world and from outside-to-self-to-body, is of fundamental importance. The communication *to* the body is just as important in dreams as that *from* the body to the self, and so on. Rycroft astringently points out how Jones's paper (1916), which insisted on a one-way traffic only in the symbolizing process, for years held the clock back on the further understanding of dreams.

For all its valuable qualities, Rycroft's book is often ignored among analysts. Perhaps this is because it is sometimes unduly dismissive of Freud, but also, at times, it may seem too popularist and elementary for professionals. This is a pity, for embedded in it are serious and important observations and arguments.

**BOLLAS**

The most recent contribution to the discussion of theories of dreams is by Christopher Bollas. He was originally a historian, but has researched and lectured on the psychology of literary criticism and has worked with schizophrenia and autistic children while he was taking up psychoanalysis, so he is of the arts and humanities background of many Independents. His important book, *The Shadow of the Object* (1987), is only in small part about dreaming, but it crystallizes much of what has been discussed here, and his conclusions bear many affinities to those of Rycroft.

We will first consider Bollas's ideas about Winnicott's true self; this is a key concept for him. Our description now repeats Bollas's, given earlier in this chapter. According to Winnicott, the true self originates in the patterning of an infant's inherited potential. At and after birth, the baby with his potentiality 'meets the mother'. Bollas conceives her to be, in the first instance, not so much a solid, specific thing out there as an 'environment-mother' – experienced by the infant as an array of potentials to *transform* things for the baby. A transformation may be that of changing the blood glycogen levels by feeding, or it may be giving the baby new glimmers that there are other people in the world like him by smiling – and so on. As it is in the nature of a mother to bring about changes for good and ill in her baby, Bollas refers, as mentioned earlier, to this early mother as a *transformational object*. Since she arouses changes, some pleasant, some not, she is met with delight, desire and dread.

The innate potential of the infant will thus be met by his environment-transformational-mother and she, depending upon her character and handling, will facilitate the growth of his true-self potential in some ways – and not others. In other ways the mother, with her assumptions about living, may impinge so that compliant false-self modes emerge. This is what Winnicott has described in his work on early development. Bollas now takes over: the mother and child function together with reverie, rapport and lack of them. This whole experience is, he thinks, the first human *aesthetic*. It is, as it were, the human being's first drama, and this primary aesthetic experience is then re-established and reworked time and again through life. The profundity and beauty of madonna and child painting throughout much of Christian history perhaps attests to this proposal about the original aesthetic.

An aesthetic is that setting and patterning of stimulations which evoke an *aesthetic moment* in an individual. Bollas's thinking is here close to that of Milner with her ideas of ego-orgasm, ecstasy and beauty. They agree that this aesthetic experience is profound and unique. It need not be happy but beauty is in it, albeit often a terrible beauty. An experience of truthfulness and newness seems to be in it also and, Bollas suggests, a true-self experience with the environment must be present. Winnicott referred to authenticity here. In so far as compliant, false-self experiences are paramount, the aesthetic moment is absent.

What can we know of the nature of an experience of beauty? The aesthetic of a poem lies in its rhythmic structure and choice of evocative words. We have seen from Sharpe that it is the task of the critic to investigate the rules of poetic diction that contibute to it. The aesthetic of a play is achieved by the form of drama given by the writer, together with the structuring by its director of the performance and so on. Bollas contends that a dream also has an aesthetic. He says:

> I regard the dream as a fiction constructed by a unique aesthetic: the transformation of the subject into his thought, specifically, the placing of the self into an allegory of desire and dread that is fashioned by the ego. From this point of view, the dream experience becomes an ironic form of object relation, as the part of the self in the dream is the object of the unconscious ego's articulation of memory and desire.
>
> (Bollas, 1987, p. 64)

Here, unequivocally laid out, is the bringing of aesthetics to the dream, just as the dream is brought to aesthetics. It is what has been stated, albeit hesitantly and in different language, since Sharpe – by Milner, Heimann, Klauber, Winnicott, Stewart and Rycroft. Among many other things, Bollas stresses how the dreamer is *transformed into his thought*: a symbol for this then becomes an object of the dream. The subject becomes an object, a character who plays the self. This was first clearly spelt out by Fairbairn. Bollas, like Rycroft, stresses the two-way 'conversation' between aspects of the ego. He adds that this is essentially *ironic*, indicating the elements of confrontation between aspects of himself in the dreamer's dream.

Here is a trenchant exposition of the aesthetic and creativity of dreams. Bollas's introduction of the idea of the aesthetic seems a conceptual leap forward – it has a precision that the more general idea of creativity lacks, but, as we have seen, it rests on quite a long history rooted in Sharpe, Milner and Winnicott. Bollas, like Rycroft, also offers a critique of Freud, but perhaps with more care, pointing out how Freud stuck to the particular meanings he could find in the content of dreams but left the form of their aesthetic aside. Bollas says that a dream aesthetic is a mode of transforming thought into dramatic representation: it is how 'the thematic is transformed by the poetic'. A dream is highly sophisticated theatre, albeit a private one.


## CONCLUSION

The very strength, longevity and fruitfulness of this line of investigation of dreams from the point of view of creativity and aesthetics attests to its value. Interestingly, it stems at present almost exclusively from analysts who originally had backgrounds in the arts. Perhaps it is because of this that the biology of dreaming, with its scientific discipline, has been neglected by British analysts. A bridge between the two form of disciplines is perhaps now called for.

The following line of thought might be interesting: in sleep, non-REM mentation takes place but it seems to lack symbolization and certainly lacks dramatization which occurs exclusively in REM periods. Thus the dream work, its dramatization and aesthetic must be a function related to REM. The question then arises – can there be a connection between REM and symbolization, with its aesthetic and dramatization, during waking hours when REM is apparently in abeyance? Another somewhat speculative question is the following: dramatization is often associated with the 'normal' functioning of hysteria, and hysteria is associated with genital-phallic activity that has 'gone wrong'. Now, REM, with its attendant dreaming and dramatization, is known by dream researchers to be associated with genital engorgement and arousal. Is this just coincidental? Perhaps a meeting between biology and the arts will be useful to answer this.

Reconsidering the subject matter of this whole chapter, it becomes evident that there is a strong undercurrent of thought concerning itself with aesthetics, creativity, dreaming and the psychoanalytic process. Milner (1952), Bollas (1987) and, most recently, Likierman (1989) have all reasoned at length about how important underlying questions of beauty and creativity are in any psychoanalysis. If this is so, then it is not an esoteric subject, of interest only to a refined élite, but an everyday concern.

# 5 Development – Environment, Libido and Aggression

## DARWINIAN ROOTS

THE DARWINIAN INHERITANCE of the British Independents must not be underestimated: survival in a habitat or environment is an abiding concern. However, it is the instinct for survival and development of the individual, of the self, not particularly of the species, that interests them.

Classical psychoanalysis saw human development as governed by instinctual strivings and their vicissitudes. Freud's developmental theory was biologically informed and envisaged development as a succession of typical instinctual patterns which facilitate human growth. Here, objects are sought to give pleasure by the satisfaction of an instinct; adaptation to reality is painfully learnt by renouncing pleasure. The ego is built by identification with objects that have been given up. If satisfaction is given too abundantly, or is too much frustrated, then the instinctual strivings will remain fixated in their primitive state. Integration will then be only partial, and this may give rise to pathology later in life. The infant's world of external objects is seen, in this view, as supporting or hindering normal developmental lines.

Melanie Klein's main interest was rather more specific than this: it was with the representations of instinctual strivings and their objects in intrapsychic systems of phantasy. As we have already indicated, Independents reacted to her and her followers' relative lack of interest in the self's interaction with the environment, so that a debate or dialectic process has been going on in Britain for the past forty years. The four main Independent authors in this debate have been M. Balint, Fairbairn, Bowlby and Winnicott. Heimann, Khan, M. James, Stewart, E. Balint and many others entered the debate with them.

It has been said (Phillips, 1988, p. 10) that 'it was to be part of the contribution of what became known as the British School of object-relations theorists, to translate psychoanalysis from a theory of sexual desire into a theory of emotional nurture'. Though Klein was one of the originators of the object-relations movement, it has largely been in debate with her and her followers that the theories of emotional nurture within the habitat of the family and beyond have been forged, largely by the British Independents.

The interest in environmental effects upon the individual may also have its roots in the British empirical tradition. Here philosophers, like Locke, Berkeley and Hume, often wary of theories about innate faculties, envisaged the mind, even as a *tabula rasa* at birth, waiting for the environment to imprint upon the memory.

It was with the desire to understand environmental influences in mind that British analysts stretched beyond the consulting-room. If they could pick out causative foci of developmental disability or agents of destructive potentiality, perhaps they could then have some hand in initiating prevention at source. The aim here has been to inform social policies. To Independents this has always seemed an honourable use of psychoanalytic understanding. This was what John Bowlby quite intentionally set out to do forty years ago, and, certainly more than any other analyst, he has met with a large degree of success in directly effecting changes in social policy about the care of children. But he has tended to be ignored by many psychoanalysts who have criticized his theories for lacking evaluation of intra-psychic processes. This is largely because analysts had not understood that his work was not primarily aimed at contributing to the one-to-one analytic treatment situation. They then failed to realize how important findings like Bowlby's in the field of the applications of analysis can be to psychoanalytic theory itself.


## HUNGARIAN ROOTS

There is another basis to the Independents' biological interest which is recent in origin and specifically psychoanalytic in nature. Bowlby, for one, acknowledges his debt to a line of thinking in Budapest during the 1920s and 1930s. Sandor Ferenczi (1926) coined the phrase 'the confusion of tongues' between parents and children, and it was his interest in family influences that inspired the work of a small group of Hungarian analysts.

Their spokesman was Michael Balint (1952) and he tells how their interest in the environment started from a clinical base. They were looking at the *formal* elements in the analytic situation, that is, at phenomena of the transference. They argued that, if members of the group compared notes and observed which of individual patients' defence patterns fell away during the analysis, then maybe the form of what remained could be regarded as a general human quality. From this starting point, the group turned outwards to evidence about general human qualities from other disciplines.

One member of the Budapest group was Imre Hermann. He was the first analyst to study primates as well as humans (Hermann, 1936). He observed that the infant monkey instinctively clings to its mother for at least the first two months of its life. There is, he says, an innate pattern of *attachment* between mother and infant. The human infant is forcibly separated from this attachment. However, the *wish* to belong again to this unit continues in finding substitutes and symptoms, such as sucking and clinging. John Bowlby has used some of Hermann's findings in his own research.

Alice Balint (1939, in M. Balint, 1952), Michael's first wife, took comparative pedagogics as her field of study. She showed how a child loved his mother from a very early age as a definite object, but without a consistent reality sense. What is more, the mother's love for the infant was an almost perfect counterpart to the infant's love for the mother. Furthermore, she found that disturbances in the mother's patterning were matched by disturbances in the infant. She was also here clearly a forerunner of Bowlby and Winnicott.


## LIBIDINAL DEVELOPMENT

The Independents have always been concerned with libido theory. It is, after all, about the pattern of life itself. But, working in a later era than Freud himself, they have not necessarily accepted concepts of the classical instinct theories of energy discharge. These seem tied to the laws of the science of that earlier time. The Independents' object-relations view of instinct, for instance, is close to a control-systems model of mismatch reduction, even though the psychoanalytic ideas often pre-date this form of theory. This is not to say that the Independents denied the importance of tension reduction through the release of libidinal impulses, but they did not see them as the only sources of object-seeking.

What is more, with their biologically oriented minds, concerned also with the individual in his environment, they were inevitably interested in the interplay between libido, as manifest in biological drives, and the effects of environmental influences upon it. It is because of their interest in this correlation that Independents, at times, have been accused of down-grading the importance of internal psychic structures and phantasy. This seems a mistaken criticism since, for instance, Fairbairn is one of the most original systematic thinkers about internal psychic structure after Freud. And Winnicott's concepts arising from early development have changed many views about the internal world.

In the 1920s, in Berlin, Abraham was unfolding his theories of psychopathology based on psychosexual phases and developmental lines. In Budapest, Ferenczi was thinking about psychosexual development over a much longer evolutionary time base. In *Thalassa* (1952), inspired by Haeckel's idea that ontogeny recapitulates philogeny, he was thinking about reproduction from the most primitive organisms to man. He saw the coming of life from the sea to dry land as a fateful moment in sexual history. This somewhat amateur biological thinking has fallen into disrepute, but it was taken up by the young Balint. His early papers on biological parallels with psychosexual development clearly contain the germ of much of his later theories of technique, of the 'new beginning' for instance, and these have been of central importance in some Independents' thinking about analytic practice in more recent years.


## FEMALE SEXUALITY:
## THE VIENNA-LONDON CONTROVERSY

Jones, at heart a Darwin-orientated evolutionist, was nevertheless not particularly interested in environmental influences: his interest lay in libidinal development. In this he was a true classical analyst. In London, he was not only closely following what was happening on the continent but was also ambitious to make the British Society foremost in the world.

He particularly admired the contributions of the outstanding women who had gathered with him: Sylvia Payne, Ella Sharpe, Barbara Low, Mary Chadwick, Nina Searl, Susan Isaacs, Joan Riviere, Karin Stephen, Alix Strachey, Marjorie Brierley and of course Melanie Klein. Under the influence of their thinking Jones began to take issue with Freud about female libidinal development.

It was a historic first debate in which the British played a key role. In it both Freud and Jones maintained their respect for each other's viewpoint while being clear about their differences.

In his earlier work Freud felt that mystery enveloped the sexual life of women. In *Three Essays* he wrote that the sexual life of men had 'alone become accessible to research. That of women . . . is still veiled in an impenetrable obscurity' (1905, p. 151). It was only in 1925 that Freud wrote his first comprehensive account of female sexual development. In his editor's note (Freud, 1925a, pp. 244–6), Strachey points out that Freud had from early on discussed some characteristics of female sexuality, but that this paper linked them up for the first time. From 1905 onwards, Freud had maintained that the little girl's leading sexual organ was the clitoris, and, as a consequence, her sexuality had an overall masculine character. According to this view, a wave of repression at puberty is necessary before the vagina takes on the leading genital role in femininity.

In 1925 Freud repeated his other, earlier thesis that, for both a boy and a girl, a child's first love object is mother's breast. From this, both sexes show the same libidinal development to begin with. However, Freud now makes plain that there are two prerequisites for the girl before entering into the phase of the positive Oedipus complex. There must be a change in body cathexis by renouncing her clitoris and also a change of her sexual object. It is during this pre-oedipal phallic phase that both boys and girls discover the real nature of the genitals of the opposite sex. This, Freud thinks, is the *primary cause* of the girl's developmental change to femininity. At this time the girl experiences her clitoris as inferior to a penis and feels castrated. It is this sense of castration with its consequent penis envy which activates a transformation, of her hitherto masculine-active wish for a penis into a passive-feminine desire to have a baby.

At this time, an aspect of the girl's penis envy is changed into jealousy so that resentment of mother is enhanced. With this the girl turns her libidinal love away from mother towards her father, and so her positive Oedipus complex becomes established. Whereas the boy's Oedipus complex is dissolved under the impact of this castration anxiety, the girl's complex often lingers on and dissolves only gradually. Further development depends on the course of indentification. In so far as the girl identifies with father, this will lead to masculine character traits; if she identifies with her mother, the transformation of her wish for a penis into a desire for a baby and a husband will be strengthened. If she experiences disappointment in her father she may return, even in adulthood, to dependency upon her mother, and this can have fateful consequences for marriage.

Freud reasoned further that, since the boy dissolves his oedipal strivings under castration threat and by incorporation of a powerful father, then the super-ego of men, and hence their ethical attitudes, will be rather different from those of women, whose oedipal fate has been different.

Freud maintained this 1925 position on female development. In fact, he elaborated it in two later papers (1931, 1933). In the first of these particularly, he criticized those analysts who differed from his view of female sexual development. He reiterated the importance of the castration complex and penis envy as *primary* for female development, and rejected the conception of them as secondary regressive defences against anxieties very early in female development.

In one of his last papers (1937) he was still actively considering these questions. Freud thought that clinical work had proved most difficult with male patients manifesting a 'masculine protest' as a defence against repressed passive-feminine wishes, and also with female patients who showed a strong desire for a penis as defence against repressed castration feelings. With both of these, only partial results are likely to be achieved.

In 1927 Jones wrote 'The early development of female sexuality' which arose out of his having had five female active homosexuals in analysis at one time. From this clinical starting point he investigates his view of the vicissitudes of female sexual development. His argument is complex, and we cannot attempt to summarize it but only to pick out one or two essential points.

Jones sees female homosexuality as a 'solution' to ineffable predicaments and anxieties. He suggests two different directions the homosexual solution can take for a woman. One is to become interested in being a man with men. The other, more common 'solution' is to disavow any sexual interest in men and to invest all her sexual love in women. The latter particularly devolves upon the *denial* of any desire for contact between vagina and penis and also the denial of a wish to have a penis herself. This also involves the projection of sexual parts of the self, both male and female, upon the partner. The partner then becomes a narcissistic object and sexually exciting for this very reason.

The interest of this lies in two directions: first, Jones introduces the concept of *aphanesis* for the first time. In doing so he is beginning to contradict Freud. He suggests that a girl cannot be driven by castration anxiety when she already knows she is castrated. It thus cannot be fear of castration that is basic in the female half of humankind: it must be more general, and Jones suggests that it is fear of the total extinction of any sexual, or erotic, satisfaction. Only the male version of aphanesis takes the form of castration anxiety. There is a similarity here between aphanesis and several theories of psychic cataclysm, like Balint's catastrophe of the loss of primary love, Winnicott's unthinkable anxiety and Fairbairn's loss of intimacy. However, these are object-related concepts, while Jones's, in true classical tradition, is simply instinct-related. Though clearly a meaningful idea, aphanesis has never really caught on conceptually.

This paper begins Jones's major argument with Freud. Some women had begun to challenge Freud's theory. Karen Horney in Berlin had been arguing that Freud's phallocentric theory of female development was mistaken in certain basic ways. The little girl, she insisted, is aware of her vagina from the start. There are thus definitely different lines of psychosexual development for boys and girls from the beginning. They do not start the same and then diverge on the discovery of penis-lack, as Freud proposed. Jones took this up and most specifically agreed with Horney. But he also goes further by using Klein's insights into the girl's primitive feelings, not just about her own body, but about her mother's. Thus the homosexual woman's anxieties, for instance, do not concern simply anger with mother for her failure to give her a penis, but much darker fears about her own insides. Her vagina in particular is felt to be dreadfully vulnerable to attack by her mysterious mother. These attacks would come in talion for the attacks she has, in feeling and phantasy, been wreaking in the first instance upon her mother's insides. Not only is Jones's avowal of a girl's own separate sexual development of note, but he is also beginning to put the importance of the mother–child relation into the centre of his considerations.

A few years later came one of Jones's finest papers, 'The phallic phase' (1933). In this, Jones spells out Freud's theory of psychosexual development again (perhaps making it more phallocentric than it actually was). He argues that the phallic phase is at the very axis of normal development for Freud. Jones disagrees on two counts. First, as in his previous paper, he asserts the separate development of boy and girl so that female sexuality has a course in its own right. Next, he does not see the phallic phase as central to *normal* development. Rather, it is a neurotic byway, present in all of us but more pronounced in some than in others. Phallicism, Jones says, is a character pathology with certain essential manifestations: exaggerated omnipotence, exhibitionism, self-centredness and being less related to other people.

Thus, he again takes sides with Horney about separate male and female development and furthermore spells out Klein's findings. He agrees with the Kleinian view about the importance of sadistic attacks upon the mysterious body of the mother and feared retaliation for these. He thinks that they are more likely to provide the first impetus into phallic narcissism than does the simple phallocentric theory. Jones is in full agreement with Freud about the final path of the Oedipus complex and the crucial role of ideas about father in both sexes, but it is over the precursors that he takes the side of the evidence presented by the women analysts.

His third and last paper on the subject, 'Early female sexuality' (1935), was read to the Vienna Psychoanalytic Society. It was part of the exchange between London and Vienna, attempting to iron out the growing differences and tensions between the two societies. These centred only partly upon Melanie Klein. There were other components of theoretical and technical difference and moreover some rivalry between them. Jones and Riviere read papers in Vienna, and Robert Waelder came to London, but to no avail: in some ways the controversies continue today.

Jones's Vienna paper is a distillation of his previous two. He spells out Freud's theory of female development and carefully takes issue with it. After the 1930s hardly any British analyst was likely to be an uncritical supporter of Freud's theory of female psychosexual development in its phallocentric aspects, and by the 1980s it is regarded by many analysts as more dated than most of Freud's theories. Of the women analysts participating in this debate it was Sylvia Payne (1935, 1950) perhaps who continued to contribute most along these lines. A fitting sequel to this debate on a world-wide stage has been Juliet Mitchell's writing on feminism (1972; 1974; Mitchell and Oakley, 1978; Mitchell and Rose, 1982). There is a valuable description of the Jones–Freud controversy by her (1974, p. 121). It was at about this time that she was moving from her original, rather Lacanian position to a later British Independent one.

## GILLESPIE'S LATER SOLUTION OF THE CONTROVERSY

It remained for William Gillespie to write the last chapter of this piece of history – many years later (1969, 1975). He summarizes the arguments of the 1920s and 1930s and points out the consequences of Freud's sexual theory for the mature woman in a way that was not raised by Jones. Gillespie says:

> I refer to Freud's view that the female must not only change the sex of her love object, but must also overcome an initial phallic stage of development in which the leading erotogenic zone is the clitoris and the aim an active one directed towards the mother in the first instance: she must, said Freud, substitute the vagina for the clitoris as the leading zone, and accept a passive aim in place of her original active one. This can be accomplished successfully in such a way as to produce a truly mature woman only if she can succeed in overcoming the very strong earlier attachment to the clitoral zone with its active aim, which many women fail to accomplish satisfactorily.
>
> (Gillespie, 1969, p. 32)

Gillespie then goes on to consider the detailed physiological evidence of Masters and Johnson (1965). As is well known, they make plain that stimulation of the clitoris is central to any female genital orgasm, whether so-called vaginal or not. Thus Freud's theory of arousal being only at first centred upon the clitoris, which state of affairs must then be overcome to end the phallic phase, is physiologically incorrect. Vaginal arousal may be, and obviously is, avoided by many women, but the clitoris still remains a centre of arousal, whether via vaginal stimulation or not.

It is in Gillespie's second paper on this subject (1975) that one finds the best extant summary of the controversy of the 1930s and a direct comparison of this with the findings of Masters and Johnson. He then adds some afterthoughts. One is that Michael (1968), another British Independent, has shown that the sexual activity of the male rhesus monkey varies not with his own hormonal state but with that of his female partner. Here is *interpersonal* sexuality *par excellence*. Gillespie suggests that this should make us wary of formulations which simplistically ascribe sexual activeness to males and passivity to females.

Gillespie ends with an intriguing speculation, which harks back to the days of Ferenczi's *Thalassa* (1925) and its ideas about life coming to the dry land from the sea. He notes the recent work of biologists showing that female fish have, and need to have, as strong an ejaculatory orgasm as the male – for sperm and ova both need to be ejected into the water at the same time. Going up the evolutionary scale, we find that most female mammals do not show sexual orgasm, as it is not necessary for the purposes of internal impregnation. The human female is an exception. Perhaps, Gillespie thinks, the human female has recently relearned how to have an orgasm – with the aid of just those muscle groups that go into action during the male orgasm. The suggestion from these ideas is that 'Woman's dissatisfaction with her role is rooted a great deal more deeply than mere envy of the male's possession of the imposing external genitalia. . .they are demanding to be liberated from that unfair share in the reproductive process which evolution has imposed on the female of the viviparous species' (1975, p. 7).


## VIEWS ON LIBIDINAL DEVELOPMENT

For Balint (1937) the aim of all human striving is to find harmony with the environment – to live in peace. This biological situation serves as a model for the distribution of the libido, so cathexis of the environment is intense. It forms the basis of object-relations development. Balint's distinctive view on this will be described in the next chapter. He also wrote informatively upon genitality (Balint 1947), though this work is biased towards masculinity and is now mainly of historical interest. His thesis is that genital behaviour in lower animals, particularly in the male, involves quick arousal and culmination: it is all-consuming and concerned only with completion of the act. The so-called human 'genital' character on the other hand is a 'gentleman' who is thoughtful and considerate of his mate as well as his offspring. Genitality in the human thus involves unselfishness, and this must be a product of civilization, of learning – even of masochism. It is thus not the simple unfolding of a biological instinct but is the fruit of engagement in complex object relating. Enid Balint, who spent many years developing and working upon the therapy of sexual problems, wrote 'Technical problems found in the analysis of women by a woman analyst' (1973), which might at first sight seem like a sequel, but it differs markedly from Michael Balint's approach in being also a careful and unusual clinical study of some women's problems of genitality, with interest in depressive concerns about very early faulty maternal identifications.

Winnicott took libidinal development for granted and, whereas its biological base was recognizable in the background of all his work, his main concern was early self–object development.

All of Fairbairn's (1952) theory, though about the development of object relations, evolves from a libidinal base. In the first instance everything is subordinated to the infant's libidinal satisfaction with his mother. It is disturbances of this that create the first psychic structures. Fairbairn took issue with Abraham about the nature of the phasing of developments in the second oral and anal phases and from this worked out his own model. Like Balint's and Winnicott's, his theories rest upon libidinal conceptions, but Fairbairn does not add to them specifically except through object-relations theory.

Heimann (1989), after leaving the Kleinians, went back to basic Freudian theory of libidinal development and added to it to bring it into line with object-relations theories. Following Freud's statement in 'Analysis terminable and interminable' (1937), she saw the ego and the id, with the latter's close representation of somatic developments, as having their own separate, innate characteristics and as being subject to their own developmental lines. They are, however, continuously interlinked. She postulates that narcissism, in another dimension as it were, has its own developmental line that is linked to, but distinct from, object-love developments.

In her paper on the anal phase (1962b), Heimann investigates with great sensitivity the toddler's predicament during the anal phase and draws important theoretical conclusions from it. She shows that a profound paradox is inherent in the anal phase: the child's desire to copy and please mother is in contradiction to the desire of the child to be free to do things, to create in his own way and in his own time. She shows too that anality is a time and a body zone of crucial *narcissistic* sensitivity. The links she makes between the self state of narcissism and the body state of anality are rarely made. Heimann goes on to look at anality in creativity, particularly in its necessary obsessive features. With clinical detail she describes several writers in the travail of their productions fearing the conceptual mess they are making, their ideational constipation, their need to retain and withhold their intellects, their fear of being robbed and the under- and over-valuation of what they have to produce. She shows the value of aggressiveness – the non-ruth, or *benign aggressiveness* as she calls it, to protect the solitude necessary for all creative productiveness.


## AGGRESSIVENESS

The death instincts

is the name given to a basic category: the death instincts, which are opposed to the life instincts, strive towards the reduction of tension to zero-point. In other words, their goal is to bring the living being back to the inorganic state.

The death instincts are to begin with directed inwards and tend towards self-destruction, but they are subsequently turned towards the outside world in the form of the aggressive or destructive instinct.

(Laplanche and Pontalis, 1973, p. 97)

In its original form, and with the Eros–Thanatos duality, this notion has never appealed to many British Independents. Ernest Jones was always quite explicit that he did not agree with it. For him it was not biologically based and was more of a metaphysical speculation which had little to commend it. A Darwinian background emerges in other writers. The first to address the question with biological care was John Pratt (1958). He showed both logical and biological flaws in the Eros-Thanatos theory, demonstrating that it had the appearance of an empirical theory but that it wanted substantive evidence. It was a misfortune that he died before he could complete his line of thought.

William Gillespie (1971), in much the same idiom as Pratt, has perhaps best summarized the thread of many Independents' views of the death instinct. After describing Freud's view, he says that probably 'most analysts have compromised with the death instinct by accepting the theory of a primary instinct of aggression, but rejecting or at least ignoring the self-directed death instinct theory'. But he says that this is not the case with Melanie Klein: she took the death instinct as a vitally important fact in the psychology of the individual, rather than seeing it as a cosmological concept. Within this framework, a 'bad' object is one into which the aggressiveness of the death instinct has been projected. Seen from this point of view, the ultimate 'badness' is the death instinct which is an integral part of the infant himself – a sort of original sin. The explanatory use she makes of the death instinct theory inevitably gives the impression that ultimately it is this inherent 'bad' element in the infant that gives rise to the trouble, rather than, for example, any failure in mothering.

Gillespie concludes with a crucial examination of theory. He suggests that all drives or instincts in the psychoanalytic sense are *homeostatic*. Freud had not heard the term of course, except perhaps as an old man, but it is implied in the idea of '*Triebe*'. Cybernetic or information-control theory would say that psychoanalytic instincts involve feedback or mismatch-reduction processes. In these there is a 'criterion' built into the organism's central nervous system. When this criterion is not being registered, the organism is active until it is found again, and then becomes quiescent. New factors may occur by which the organism departs from the criterion state, it is then prone to be active again until that state is re-found, and so on. Now death, *per se*, cannot be such a criterion within a feedback or homeostatic system. For, once found, death cannot be departed from and then re-found. But this re-finding is intrinsic to homeostasis and hence to instinct, so death *per se* cannot be an instinctual aim.

Some Independents do subscribe to the death instinct theory very much in the form that Klein took it from Freud. But Gillespie's view, both about the idea of the instinct itself and with regard to its consequence that aggressiveness could then be seen as an original sin of a sort, would probably be subscribed to by the majority.

A basic, almost philosophical difference of outlook between Kleinians and Independents is epitomized by this difference of attitude to the death instinct theory. For Kleinian theory, destructiveness is an innate propensity which each individual ego is fated to wrestle with within himself from the start. It is thus fundamentally intra-psychic. The environment may help or hinder pathogenic aggressiveness, but in the last analysis it is peripheral.

In contrast to this, the main thrust of Independent thinking has been more biological. Anxiety arising from fear of environmental provision is itself the pathogen. Aggression in all its varieties may stem from this and thus is rooted in *survival* mechanisms. It is essential in healthy activity and secondary to, an *adjunct* of, libidinal and developmental drives. When these, or the integrity of the self, are impinged upon and threatened, then aggression may be aroused. This would be part of fight–flight reactions. In states of trauma the violence of these reactions will go beyond any survival value in the response mechanisms used. It is here that many of the roots of pathology are seen. This difference in outlook between Kleinians and Independents may have consequences for the theory of technique of analysis which will be considered later.

It has been suggested (Grotstein, 1981) that the phenomenon seen as the death instinct is not a searching for the inanimate state. Rather it is a biological instinct, on the lines Bowlby expounds, rooted in predatory patterns, or protection of self from predators, which has innate components. This is then a death-dealing or death-avoiding instinct. Some Independents would probably find such an approach compatible with their point of view.

## BALINT

For Balint it is primary love of object and the environment generally that is basic to the individual, and this does not in the first place involve aggressivity, for only omnipotence functions within it. At this level the individual needs objects desperately, but this is denied by the omnipotence which is a fundamental characteristic of primary love. However, these demands inevitably lead to frustrations, and the response to these is noisy, vehement aggressiveness. Frustrations of demand lead to hate. This is a *defence* against, an omnipotent denial of, the pain of the realization of dependency. Persistent hate is always the sign of an immature ego.

Aggressiveness, which is clearly linked to survival mechanisms, is for Balint (1965, 1968) to be distinguished from innate sadistic tendencies. In this he is clearly close to Klein, whereas his treatment of aggressiveness is more biological. If frustration reaches traumatic proportions at a very early age, a *basic fault* forms in the character structure. Here aggressiveness and distress are not *active*; there is only passive resignation or despair. The emotion of hate only develops later than at the time of the formation of basic fault structures. The reasoning here is that hate is an object-related emotion – one always hates something. Hate thus requires a self–object differentiation of some stability before it can be experienced, and this is not manifest in the early days after birth.

For Balint, hate is a fundamentally healthy protective device which can, however, get grossly distorted. It is an essential element in the experience of psychic conflict and thus occurs at the three-person oedipal level of neurotic problems. A problem of such a level involving hate, is approachable by the classical, verbal only, technique of analysis. But problems at the level of the basic fault, being pre-hate and conflict, can be approached only by the experience of a change in the environment provided by the analyst, which allows a regression to a state of primary love and what Balint calls a 'new beginning'.


## WINNICOTT

For Donald Winnicott (1945b, 1949a, 1950b, 1951, 1971a) aggression has two meanings. The first is somatic expression in vigorous muscular movements, already detectable in the womb. This muscular movement meeting opposition is enjoyable and makes for the feeling of 'real'. It is visible also in ordinary, eager, greedy, libidinous sucking and chewing.

Many other object-relations analysts see aggressiveness simply as a reaction to frustration. Winnicott insists on its dual background, for he does not disagree with the frustration theory but sees the aggressiveness produced as not the only kind. For instance, he sees rage as a *true-self-protective* activity. It is a response to environmental *impingement*. If the child is so immature as to be in a state of absolute dependence then the result of environmental impingement is false-self formation, which is a defence organization. If the child is more mature – self–object differentiation being more stable – then hate is the natural response. Hate can, however, itself be cataclysmically overwhelming, especially when the child feels that his mother's love is not surviving his hate. In so far as she is felt to survive the hate, the child *loves* her the more.

More basic than survival of hate, for Winnicott, is the survival by the mother of the infant's vigorous muscular aggression. This is aggression of the first sort just described. Here the infant attacks his mother, not necessarily in rage, and discovers that she has survived it. He has then begun to realize that his mother is not inside his omnipotent control and so begins to love her as an external object. Hence, Winnicott maintains, it is the aggressive attacks on the mother, and her survival of them, which facilitate the infant's recognition of external, shared reality (1969, 1971a). This is a different conception from that of classical analysis, where reality is perceived in the context of frustration of impulses and the painful renunciation of pleasure.

With this reality development, an important step is achieved towards the infant's recognition of the permanence, or constancy, of the object as separate. At this time, not only does the sense of trust in the object, as a 'not-me' person, develop, but also the discovery of 'me' and a feeling of 'being real'. The infant can now feel safer to hate, and thence to rebel against a mother whom he or she also loves. Under these circumstances, attacks are no longer magical, so that it becomes possible also to tolerate actual aggressiveness towards shared reality.

With the discovery of the shared reality world of objects comes a growing capacity to relate by, what Winnicott (1971a) called, 'cross-identification'. This is the capacity to 'stand in the other person's shoes'. The previous state to this was one where magically destructive attacks took place on incompletely differentiated 'subjective objects'. Here the attacks had a 'pre-ruth' quality to them. Now, with cross-identification, *concern* develops for the well-being of the objects of shared reality. It is only with the development of this as a potentiality, Winnicott thinks, that we can, at times, talk of a person's ruthlessness.

Returning to the pre-ruth stage, if the 'subjective-object-mother' of that time is unable to survive the infant's attacks, in particular if she retaliates, then *actual* destructiveness becomes a feature. This can be defended against, of course, and aggressiveness will either be grossly inhibited or it will be actualized by the individual becoming the object of an aggressive attack. It is with this in mind that Winnicott maintained that, in the clinical situation, the more aggressive child is often the healthier one (1969, 1971b).

One of the most crucial failures of the early 'not-good-enough' mother is an inability to disillusion her infant as she fails to facilitate that growth process in the infant which makes shared reality real for him (1960c, 1965b).

It is of interest to note how similar are the origins of Balint's basic fault and Winnicott's false self (they will be discussed further in Chapters 6 and 7).

## BOWLBY

John Bowlby (1969, 1973, 1980) likewise sees aggression as essentially reactive. It is manifest in the sequence observed after separation: rage-protest, despair, apathy. He also indicates its initial healthy survival value in eliciting the parent's, or attachment object's, attention.

## FAIRBAIRN

Aggressiveness is also seen as essentially reactive by Fairbairn (1952). It is a primary dynamic factor in so far as it cannot be resolved into libido. But it is subordinate to libido – its servant, as it were. No infant directs aggressiveness to an object without frustration. In this, Fairbairn seems to be in disagreement with Winnicott, but clearly Fairbairn is discussing only rage-aggression and not the vigorous muscularity that Winnicott is pointing out.

Aggression is not for Fairbairn the prime cause of psychopathology: this, as we have pointed out, is the feeling that infant's love has destroyed mother's love. Hate comes later, in the second oral stage, presumably after the ego, or self, is sufficiently differentiated to feel it. Its feared effects can then become the source of profound anxiety. Fairbairn thinks that the feeling that hate has destroyed the prime mother object's love is the fundamental root of melancholia and, derivatively, other depressions.

## HEIMANN

In her 1964 paper, Paula Heimann revised her previous assumptions about life and death instincts, which she had upheld when a Kleinian, because clinical work did not confirm that particular distinction. She thinks (1964) that maybe the human being is endowed with two forms of aggression: one serving survival, active assertiveness and healthy narcissism. The second form is seen in cruelty, which is specifically human as no other species practises it. This is seen by her as the result of problems of adaptation during early development. When there are early traumata, the infant experiences death-like somatic sensations and these leave somatic memories. They then manifest themselves in phantasies of death, anxiety about death and the wishes to die which underlie depressive states and which we all have at times in dreams. Cruelty probably involves a projection of such experiences in order to get others to suffer in a reversal of roles. Cruelty and sadism, Heimann says, point to environmental failure in care.


## STEWART

Harold Stewart does not speculate theoretically about the innate basis of aggression or otherwise. His concern is always close to clinical experience and here he sees aggression working pathologically, but also in healthy ways. One of his interests, over several decades, has been control and collusion, both interpersonally and between parts of the self. For instance, one of his earliest papers speculated that both Jocasta and Oedipus are portrayed as knowingly colluding in their sexual crime (1961). Likewise interested in control and collusion were papers upon hypnosis (1963, 1966). Here he noted that, when a patient was freed to contradict and hence be consciously aggressive to the hypnotist, then the hypnoid state was broken. Further hypnosis was impossible so long as the aggressiveness remained free. In a later paper (1977) the same questions of control and collusion are addressed, this time with regard to hysteria. Again the need for freedom of aggressiveness, within the limits necessary to counter the influence of the controllingness, is seen as healthy.


## CONCLUSION

Reviewing the themes of the whole chapter, it seems that all the authors referred to assume and use a basic, underlying conception of the libido in its widest sense. They also give centrality to aggressiveness. It is universally seen in pathological form in depression, but most authors also stress its normal functioning. The importance of death-dealing impulses (Grotstein, 1981) is affirmed, but there is variance in opinion about the form of the innate basis of these. Very little assent is given to Freud's, and hence Klein's, original speculation about the death instincts as instincts to return to the inanimate state, which may then be projected, nor to the Eros–Thanatos dichotomy.

Independent analysts have written a numer of books and papers about various aspects of development: James (1960, 1964) on pre-adolescence; Evans (1982b), Hayman (1969) and Tonnesmann (1980) on adolescence; E. Balint (1973) and Main (1989) on marriage; Douglas (1956, 1963), Birksted-Breen (1975) and Raphael-Leff (1984) on motherhood; Layland (1981) on fatherhood; King (1978, 1986) and Hildebrand (1988) on mid-life and Gillespie (1963) on the end of life. Rayner (1971, 1986) has produced an elementary textbook on development from birth to death.

# 6 Development – Self and Environment

WITH THE COMING of psychoanalytic investigation into early development, interest shifted somewhat away from the instinct theory of classical orientation with its emphasis on libidinal development. The Independents came naturally to conceive of a 'self–object' relation form of theory. Here the dynamics of desires and wishes are still paramount, but different ego aspects, or parts of the self, come to be seen in dynamic interaction with one another and with complementary internal or external objects. The most cogent and systematic thinker about the object-relations theory of dynamic psychic structures was Ronald Fairbairn.

The self is now envisaged as a crucial agent in motivation. It still, as in Freud's model of the ego, has to compromise between outside and inside. But now the sense of self is seen as being referred to in any wish or desire. It might then be said that there is no emotion without self and no self without emotion. The most dramatic propagandist of the self was of course Donald Winnicott with his concern for the development of the true self. Winnicott, in effect, pointed out how profound could be the desire and drive towards the development of the self, as well as how powerfully it might be hidden or falsified. His work has been followed up by Bollas's formulations of destiny and fate (1989). This is the British equivalent, in some of its aspects, of American self-psychology (Kohut, 1971), but in a different idiom. It is concerned, of course, with narcissism, with the self as object, and encompasses normal as well as pathological functions.

The self is seen as a relatively autonomous agent which in health has continuity throughout life. But it is always interacting with the environment and the people in it – modifying and being modified by them. The Independents on the whole do not support a solipsistic theory of psychology, which they conceive of as too exclusively preoccupied with internal phantasy only.


## BALINT

We shall discuss here only that aspect of Balint's theory which is concerned with the self and environment. This is very largely confined to reconstructive consideration of the earliest days and months of life, for Balint thinks residues of these live on in us timelessly.

It will be recalled that Michael Balint's theoretical conclusions were derived from his work with the Budapest group. He reasoned (1937) that an interacting object relation with his maternal environment was important for an infant from before birth. He thus took issue with Freud's concept of primary narcissism (1914a): that the infant's love of self, associated with auto-erotism, precedes object love. Instead, he proposed that a desire to *be loved* was a primary form of love.

However, Freud himself clearly agrees with what Balint is arguing when he says:

> It will be rightly objected that an organization which was a slave to the pleasure principle and neglected the reality of the external world could not maintain itself alive for the shortest time, so that it could not have come into existence at all. The employment of a fiction like this is, however, justified when one considers that the infant – *provided one includes with it the care it receives from its mother* – does almost realize a psychical system of this kind.
>
> (Freud, 1911, p. 220 fn.)

It is the 'care it receives from the mother' with which Balint is concerned. Balint (1952, 1968) reasons that the early biological situation serves as a model for the location of libidinal investment in the first instance. Even in utero there must be intense cathexis of the environment, but so far there is no self–object differentiation. Environment and self are experienced as interpenetrating in a *harmonious mix-up*: amniotic fluid, placenta and infant's body are undifferentiated in experience. The harmonious mix-up alters dramatically at birth. Birth is a trauma that upsets this equilibrium by changing the environment radically and enforces, under the real threat of death, a new form of adaptation, exchanges with the environment through the lungs. This starts off, or at least accelerates, the separation of self and environment (1968).

Even after birth, so long as exchange of substances is not severely impeded, there is no great discrimination, and self and environment are still in harmonious mix-up. However, frustration is inevitable, and homogeneous flux is no longer the rule. Self and objects then come to be contrasted and differentiated. The ego or self tends to develop a conception of itself and withdraws into itself to regain, albeit transiently, the previous oneness of being.

At first, objects are experienced as indifferent or frustrating, but some are satisfying. Towards these objects something of the previous undifferentiatedness is felt and with it *primary love* is transiently regained. Such primary objects, mostly aspects of the maternal environment, are assumed to be present for the purposes of the self. No consideration is given to them; they are not conceived as having separate interests. The ego's attitude to them is thus one of *omnipotence*.

Serious trauma at this developmental level creates a *basic fault* in the structure of the infant's psyche. This is envisaged by Balint (1968) as a *mood* deficiency or fault. It is not thought of as a split or fracture, but a faultiness of the sort that permeates a whole material, rather like the misordering of the structure of the molecules in a faulty crystal or the mismatched genetic coding that can occur in chromosomes. A person manifesting a basic fault has an underlying feeling that something is wrong about him. He is neither bitter nor angry nor determined, but simply feels there is nothing he can do about it. The only cure lies with the environment. It is because of this helplessness that Balint sees it as basic: it is primitive, originating before the stable differentiation of self and objects. It will be noted that the very sense of the person's helplessness is close to its opposite, the omnipotence that rules in the state of primary love. This is naturally a theory of pathological character structure (see Chapter 7).

With the coming of object differentiation, Balint (1959) sees two characteristic modes of relating to the environment that act as *defences* against psychotic or cataclysmic anxieties. The one is to love, even to cling to, be intensely involved with an dependent upon, the newly emerging objects: this he calls an *ochnophilic* attitude. It bears a resemblance to Bowlby's concept of attachment. The other, termed *philobatic*, is to dislike attachment to objects but to love the *spaces* between them. It involves a partial return to harmonious mix-up. Objects may be related to and satisfied, but with the aim of freeing again the open space which is explored and mastered. Instead of investing in objects, the philobat cathects his own ego skills.

Balint has little to say about the object differentiations of later child-hood except to stress the fateful shift from two-person relating in infancy and toddlerdom to the beginning of three-person experience with the coming of the Oedipus complex. Here, as already mentioned, Balint emphasized the child's need to tolerate at least two other parallel objects. This brings with it all the well-known affects of jealousy, envy and hate. These arise in particular when the two objects, the parents, are satisfying each other together, with the child left out and alone. Later still, adult love is aimed, with an active striving, towards re-establishing aspects of the *unio mystica* – towards the harmonious mix-up of earliest times but now in the setting of, and interpenetrating with, other complex object relations.

It is of note here that, while both Fairbairn and Winnicott explicitly use and take account of Klein's depressive position, Balint sees what he calls 'normal depression'. This is linked to reality testing and the accep-tance of a frustrating and hurtful reality. In its developmental aspects he conceives of both Kleinian positions, the paranoid-schizoid and the depressive, as parallel phenomena arising out of the infant's dawning reality testing (1952, 1965).

## FAIRBAIRN

For Balint, the libido was his starting point. Fairbairn also started there but his thought developed differently, for he was interested in forms. It is in his understanding of form, and thence of mental structure, that his contribution lies. His work is contained mainly in one book (1952), which is closely reasoned and not easy reading. He achieved a remarkable intensity of systematic thought about analytic matters. He did this largely alone, for, living in Edinburgh, he had little contact with colleagues in London.

Fairbairn's main contributions were written close together between 1940 and 1944. The first is his introduction to the features of the schizoid

personality. The second is a systematic psychopathology. He sees schizoid splitting as most basic to the fate of a person. It is only after this, and
built upon it, that depressive reactions mediating destructiveness emerge.
These may be followed by the neuroses which can all be seen as different,
specifiable patterns of elements reactive to schizoid or depressive experiences. Fairbairn's third contribution is a re-examination of defence
mechanisms, and last comes his finest and most difficult contribution –
on psychic structure itself. As all four concern character structure and its
disorder, they will be discussed in Chapter 7. Here we will consider only
his ideas about the self and environment.

Fairbairn is the most forthright of the object-relations theorists. The
continued interaction of the ego (he uses the term 'ego' throughout) with
the environment is stressed. He sets his sights against the classical model
of pleasure coming from drive-energy discharge. He uses such phrases as
'The libido is primarily object-seeking (rather than pleasure-seeking as in
classical theory)' (1952, p. 82). By this he means that pleasure is gained by
the quality of the state of an ego–object relation – internal or external –
rather than in discharge of energy. Likewise anxiety is reduced by a
change in object relation rather than by any discharge of energy. Thus, a
baby stops crying, not after feeding but on sight and smell of the breast,
at a moment when it is doubtful whether there is any particular discharge
of energy. In turning away from an instinct-energy-discharge theory,
Fairbairn is implicitly using a control-systems form of theory, though this
was before information-systems theories had been formally conceived.
The change of focus from energy discharge (boiling tea-kettle theory, as
Bowlby calls it) marks a leap for psychoanalysis.

Fairbairn gives an example of the object-relations view when he tells of
a patient who often complained of nausea. It was clear that this arose
from fellatio phantasies about her father's penis which was identified with
a bad breast. But it was also related to the 'emotional badness' of the
person of her father, a whole real object.

Fairbairn is sometimes remembered for theoretically pointed remarks
like those indicating that there is no such thing as the id (1944). By this he
meant that he did not believe in a mental representation of an underlying
seething, or structureless, cauldron of energy or impulses. He did not
mean that the mind was unconnected with the body, for his theory always
relates ego activity to physical functions. He was meaning that motiva-

tion is spurred, not only by neuro-physiological conditions, but also by the state of mismatch between ego and external and internal objects – or with other aspects of the ego. The demands between these sub-systems create the dynamic structure that is the personality. 'Whole person' motives could be just as powerful as body needs.

For Fairbairn, the original blissful object relation is *intimacy* with mother. It is a state between objects who know each other, not just of feeding pleasure, etc., though these are essential aspects of it. Intimacy with mother or other objects is always being searched for – even if it gives more pain than pleasure. Fairbairn stresses that sexualization is often not so much a breakthrough of libido, but rather a frantic substitute for personal intimacy.

The fundamental schizoid reaction, upon which all pathology rests, is a reaction of withdrawal from, which is a primitive defence against, the trauma of not feeling intimately loved. 'The type of mother who is specially prone to provoke such a regression is the mother who fails to convince her child by spontaneous and genuine expressions of affection that she herself loves him as a person' (1952, p. 13). The child comes to feel 'that his own love for his mother is not really valued and accepted by her' (1952, p. 17).

In so far as a child feels that his *love has destroyed* his mother's feeling for him then Fairbairn thinks we have the origin of a schizoid state. In so far as a child feels his *hate has destroyed* his mother's feeling for him then we have the origin of a depressive state. We can compare this formulation with Klein's on the paranoid-schizoid and depressive positions. Fairbairn is clear that he is using Klein's idea concerning the psychic 'positions', the depressive position particularly. Until the time of his paper on the schizoid personality, she referred only to the paranoid position. It was from him, she acknowledges, that she borrowed the term 'schizoid' with its stress upon splitting. Fairbairn agrees with her that the schizoid position is prior to the depressive. It is present in all of us to a greater or lesser degree. But, rather unlike Klein, who stresses aggression as the crucial pathogen, he sees the schizoid position as a pathological *reaction to environmental failure*. As in Balint's concepts of primary love and the basic fault, intimacy with mother is the natural or normal base for development: damage to this is the instigator or cause of pathological reactions, which are schizoid in the first place. It is of note here that Winnicott did not agree with either Klein or Fairbairn that the schizoid position necessarily preceded the depressive position. For him it was important in pathology but was a byway from normal life, a dead-end not a stage in development.

We can see that 'Fairbairn faced squarely something that few other analysts have tried to deal with theoretically: the basic and structural effects on the personality of bad or defective mothering, the forms taken by the psychological diseases due to environmental deficiency' (Padel, 1972, p. 25).

What is more, Fairbairn repeatedly makes it plain that 'analysis is about the real situations that patients have actually lived through and (partially) assimilated, transformed, or rejected during their early development' (Padel, 1972, p. 20). This is why reconstruction of past events is seen by Fairbairn as particularly vital therapeutically.


BOWLBY


A child psychiatrist before training as an analyst in the mid-1930s John Bowlby signalled the direction of his work for much of the rest of his life in his monograph 'Forty-four juvenile thieves' (1944). In this he spoke of being struck by the statistic that a very high percentage of the young delinquents he studied had spent early childhood without a consistent mother figure. Some years later came his historic WHO monograph, *Maternal Care and Mental Health* (1951). His essential conclusion in this book is: it is believed to be essential for mental health that the infant and young child should experience a warm, intimate and continuous relationship with his mother (or one person who steadily mothers him) in which both find satisfaction and enjoyment.

The child who does not have such a provision is likely to show signs of either *partial deprivation* – excessive need for love or for revenge, gross guilt and depression, or *complete deprivation* whose signs are: listlessness, quiet unresponsiveness and retardation of development. This is the anaclitic depression of Spitz (1965). Later such deprived children show signs of superficiality, want of real feeling, lack of concentration, deceit and compulsive thieving. Bowlby's book is an important review and description of the large researches, mostly from America, upon which his conclusions are based.

He continues by specifying that the lack of any attachment opportunity for at least three months during the phase of life from six months of age to three years is likely to result in the most common form of deprivation characteristic – the affectionless character. Bowlby concludes with suggestions for social policy changes, to help families and to help helpers.

His findings have been criticized (Rutter, 1972) but their main thrust has never been overthrown. More recent criticism has come from some feminists, and also from some policy makers, because he shows how it is usually optimal if possible for mothers to be with their children at home for much of the day when they are young. However, there can be no doubt that Bowlby's observations and advice have become part of society's discourse on child care, at least in the western world.

His work following on from this was much aided by Anna Freud and her co-workers, in particular, of course, by the films on separation and deprivation by James and and Joyce Robertson (Robertson, 1958, 1982).

Bowlby's work is essentially concerned with the necessary conditions of normal child development, especially with the child's needs, in common with the young of other species, for secure relations in his or her environment. Loss of this security is envisaged as the primary pathogen.

**ATTACHMENT**

Bowlby's trilogy, *Attachment* (1969), *Separation, Anxiety and Anger* (1973) and *Loss, Sadness and Depression* (1980), is a carefully researched and comprehensive study in the field of attachment and loss.

In *Attachment*, he draws attention to Freud's increasing recognition of the environmental factors in ontogenesis, especially after he had written *Mourning and Melancholia* (1917). However, he emphasizes how Freud and the early psychoanalysts used data drawn only from the treatment of adult psycho-neurotic patients and those suffering from narcissistic disorders. They were thus arriving at conclusions by working backwards. Bowlby, on the other hand, gives his attention directly to loss of attachment figures in childhood and then works forward. His attachment theory is thus based on direct observation, and is both clinical and statistical. It is derived from biology – the attachment behaviour of mammals and the Darwinian survival value of attachment patterns. Being biological, and specifically ethological, it uses cybernetic and control-systems theory extensively.

Attachment theory is firmly about causation. Clinical psychoanalysis, Bowlby points out, being retrospective, can use only a historical method and thus suffers from the inability to determine the relative importance of different causative factors. His theory, based on direct statistical observations of childhood environmental impingements or trauma, does not suffer from this disadvantage.

His model, as mentioned already, is a control-systems or cybernetic one. Like Fairbairn, he points out that a baby stops crying because he sees his mother, not because psychic energy has been exhausted or discharged. Hence the concept of feedback or mismatch reduction is quite central to Bowlby's way of thinking.

The whole quest of his book is towards explaining the detachment and disturbance of the human infant after separation from mother for lengths of time, as he had ascertained so carefully in his WHO book.

He starts his main argument by examining instinctive behaviour as observed by biologists. There are recognizable, regular patterns of behaviour, more complex than reflexes, common to all members of one sex of a species, and seeming to contribute to the survival of that species. These are called instincts. They are not simple responses to a stimulus, but sequential patterns of responses. They become apparent for what they are when they are seen to arise in the absence of opportunities for learning, though they may be modifiable by learning. They are thus a product of genetic endowment in interaction with the effects of the environment. Human behaviour compared to that of lower animals is very variable, but not infinitely so: commonalities can be discerned, such as mating, feeding, care and attachment by the young. Hence, instincts operate in humankind as well.

Bowlby describes these instinctive patterns in terms of behaviour systems of complex chains and networks of hierarchies of feedback arcs. He suggests that an affect in any species is a high-level state of appraisal which discriminates instantaneously the status of the environment and at the same time that of the internal physiological economy. These states of appraisal can be communicated quickly and efficiently to other members of the species. Alarm calls are perhaps the most obvious affect communications (see also Chapter 2).

To the biologist, instincts, as described here, are not the same as psychoanalytic instincts. The latter are better termed drives but came to be called instincts in the English translations of Freud (see Freud 1915b).

The first specific proposition of the theory of attachment is that the child's tie to the mother is the product of the activity of a number of instinctive systems that have *proximity* to the mother as the predictable outcome.

These proximity-seeking patterns are observed in birds, mammals and in primates. For instance, the rhesus monkey spends three years in close proximity to its mother after several months of actual clinging to her – often by sucking a nipple. Baboons spend the first year with mother and the second with peers. Durations vary from species to species but the attachment is universal in primates. When proximity behaviour wanes, the young wander away from mother but will search for and return to her immediately when alarmed.

Man is a primate, and typical primate clinging and proximity behaviour is manifested in most human societies. It is not fully manifest until a child is walking, that is, until the second year. As with other primates, there is an increase with alarm. This behaviour is clearly exhibited until the third year. The behaviour towards the mother also displays an instinctive patterning: calling, crying, smiling and other facial gestures will bring mother to the child and so on. Subsidiary attachment figures may be established by young children who are secure with their mother. Fear of strangers is also related to the attachment system.

Bowlby reasons that attachment is an instinctive pattern independent of feeding satisfaction and he refers to Harlow's famous experiments with young monkeys. When offered a wire dummy 'parent' with a teat and a plentiful supply of milk, they would spend a few minutes getting enough food and then turn to another dummy parent, this one covered in fur, to cling to for the rest of the day. Many other observations of animals and humans support this contention. It is thus clear that attachment behaviour is not secondary to a feeding drive, nor is it a symbolized derivative of it. In humans, frustration of attachment certainly arouses anxiety, and this may be soothed by thumb-sucking, but this does not mean that the attachment pattern itself is derivative from feeding.

Bowlby thinks that the attachment pattern itself has survival value for group-living animals, as a protection from predators. It seems likely, however, that there are other functions operative as well. Sexual behaviour and attachment are distinct behaviour systems but are readily interwoven.

The fundamental departure from ordinary psychoanalytic theory, as Bowlby knows, is that he has ascribed complex biological instinctive patterns to man in a much more specific and detailed way than Freud envisaged. He is perhaps closer to the line of thinking of William McDougall (see Chapter 2).

## SEPARATION

In Bowlby's second volume, *Separation, Anxiety and Anger* (1973), he starts his investigation with detailed reportage of Anna Freud's and her colleagues' work on brief separation, particularly that of Christophe Heinicke and James and Joyce Robertson. From these and other sources he defines a specific sequence of responses in separated infants and young children who had no alternative attachment figure. This is: separation – protest – despair – detachment.

Freud (1926) introduced the notion that separation and loss may become principal sources of pathology. When he introduced his revised theory of anxiety, he conceived of separation anxiety as the first and basic anxiety – *signal anxiety*. In this, Freud and Bowlby would agree – not so Melanie Klein, thinks Bowlby. She envisaged aggression as the ultimate source of anxiety, not separation itself. This might, however, arouse aggression.

Bowlby goes on to describe and investigate in detail the many researches carried out comparing behaviour of the young with and without their mothers in various species of animals and in humans of various races. The attachment – separation – protest – despair – detachment sequence seems universal, at least in primates.

Bowlby takes issue with both Freud and Klein whom he thinks did not believe in any reality basis to neurotic *fear*. But, he argues, fear in children is very often triggered by anticipated or actual loss of an attachment object, and this, in a sense, is a realistically based fear. He then proceeds with a detailed investigation of infantile and animal fears, their ontogeny and vicissitudes.

Bowlby next discusses the question of the actual structured quality of an individual's attachment to his own parent figures. He, with his well-known original co-worker, Mary Ainsworth, distinguishes the chronic state of *anxious attachment* in many children. This seems to arise from abandonment threatened by acts, gestures, implications or actual threats by attachment figures. In the course of these investigations it became plain that an attachment figure need not necessarily be the mother, even though it usually is. It can sometimes be father, grandmother or other intimate and consistent helper.

A great deal of research has been done, mostly in the United States, by Ainsworth's co-workers, particularly Mary Main, on the attachment patterns of children who have on the whole not physically separated for long periods from their parents. They particularly enquire into the causation, consistency and longevity of these patterns.

Mary Main (Main *et al.*, 1985), for instance, distinguishes four main forms of attachment in young children: anxious-avoidant; secure; ambivalent/anxious; disorganized. The last of these is not a distinguishable pattern but rather an absence of one. Recently a new subcategory of anxious-avoidant attachment has been isolated. This is 'reverse attachment' where the child clings to *acts of parenting* the parent.

The distinct patterns are based on quite remarkably high correlations between ratings by independent observers. They have a high degree of consistency and longevity in individual children. What is more, the children's patterns can be correlated to the behaviour patterns of the attachment figures. For instance, predictions of type of attachment pattern, based on videotapes of attachment figures' behaviour when the child was eighteen months of age, correlated significantly with attachment patterns of the child at five years old.

Bowlby, in a discussion on anger and attachment, suggests that there can be a real survival value in anger: this is to alert the parent who has withdrawn and regain attention. However, when loss has become permanent and the parent irrecoverable, the anger is no longer functional though often still present. Bowlby is thus strongly inclined to agree with the Balint–Fairbairn frustration-aggression hypothesis and not with Klein's concept of aggression and anger being an expression of a deflected death instinct impulse. But he does point out that felt hostility increases anxiety. The book ends with a survey of phobias in childhood and a thorough review of relevant literature.

## LOSS

The last of the trilogy, *Loss* (1980), contains a wide and authoritative review of the literature of psychoanalytic, psychiatric and ethological studies on grief and loss. He introduces again his information-control-systems, or cybernetic, framework of investigation. For instance, his specification of the information that can be handled by conscious processes, in contrast to different levels of unconscious process, is an original contribution. It is unlike most psychoanalytic language, with the notable exceptions of theorists like Peterfreund (1971) and Palombo (1978) in America. Yet it is not far from what Rycroft and Bollas say about the communication patterns between different parts of the self in dreams (see Chapter 4). Bowlby uses his framework to investigate mourning, which is first seen in terms of an information-processing system within the individual that has been built up in relation to an important external 'other' which then becomes suddenly partially redundant because of loss of the other.

In direct clinical studies of loss, grief and mourning, Bowlby draws not only upon such as Lindemann (1944) but also particularly upon work by his colleague Colin Murray Parkes (1972) and follows him in distinguishing the following bereavement sequence in adults who have suffered profound loss: 1) numbing; 2) distress and anger; 3) yearning and searching; 4) disorganization and despair; 5) reorganization.

This is similar to the protest – despair – detachment of the young child who has lost an attachment figure. The disordered variants of mourning are then considered in detail: for instance, physical breakdown of health; suicide; chronic mourning; displacement of the lost one into other people; introjection into the self with attendant euphoria; and so on. Bowlby then goes on to consider therapeutic measures, from those that can be carried out by friends and relatives, to those that require skilled help.

Bowlby systematically shows that *children mourn* in the same way as adults if given adequate information and care. The belief that children cannot mourn is based no doubt upon the fact that children often cannot find words for their intense feelings. Bowlby, together with all the researchers whom he has gathered together in the pages of his book, makes it clear that this belief is a cruel fiction.

There is much in Bowlby's point of view that seems somewhat alien to basic psychoanalytic thinking. It is not essentially derived from the therapeutic situation, free association, dreaming or fantasy. It is thus not primarily a theory about the hidden meanings of manifest ideas or actions. It is a causal theory about the effect of real life events upon the individual in the creation of disturbance and disability. It is also a biological theory, having a form derived from that used to understand the behaviour of lower animals.

Bowlby's work on attachment, separation and loss has been appreciated by only a few psychoanalysts as an important contribution to our theory and to our clinical work with patients. He has postulated that attachment is a human instinct which is also present in lower animals. It seems to us that the understanding of its experiential manifestations can widen and enrich our comprehension of psychic functioning in the analytic situation. Moreover, if deprivation of attachment figures has been shown to have causative effects on individual development, its recognition in our therapeutic approach, and hence in analytic theory, seems to be essential.

Here is an example by Juliet Hopkins, a child psychotherapist, that illustrates the use of Bowlby's work. It shows the treatment of a child with an avoidant attachment who came to be able to express her need for attachment when distressed, first to the therapist and then to her own mother.

Clare was referred for psychotherapy at the age of six on account of night terrors. Her mother reported that she had resented her arrival and found her physically repellent as a baby, though she had gradually come to enjoy talking and playing with her. She had always propped Clare's bottle and kept her in a playpen all day until she started nursery school. She thought that Clare had always resisted being cuddled. As soon as Clare could walk she walked away from her mother and was liable to get lost. She had always been stoically independent, never asking for help except when she had hurt herself . . .

The psychiatrist who assessed Clare described her as having a false personality (Winnicott, 1960d). She was strongly identified with her mother whose phrases and gestures she accurately reproduced. It seemed that she did not need mother because she had become her. Similarly, in therapy, Clare took over my capacity to make interpretations and gave them to herself so that she would not need to depend on me. Once, when I spoke to her about her hidden wish to cry, Clare explained, 'I never cry because if I started I would never stop'. I understood this to mean that she feared there would never be anyone to comfort her.

Clare often spoke of her worry about lepers which gave her bad dreams. She explained that lepers were contagious which meant that 'if they touch someone they die'. She thought they could be cured by the laying on of hands. As therapy proceeded Clare became aware that she felt herself to be a leper whom no one wanted to touch because she would kill them, and she also became aware of her longing to cry and be comforted. In the sessions she was tortured by the longing to touch and be touched by me which conflicted with her terror of it . . .

After nearly a year of therapy Clare allowed an accident to happen which enabled her to translate some of her longings into action. She fell heavily from my desk onto the floor. As she lay there she raised her arms beseechingly towards me and burst into tears. I picked her up and she sobbed for some minutes on my lap, though keeping her head averted from me.

Clare's mother reported that the day after this event Clare came to her to be comforted in distress for the first time. Mother, who had been greatly helped by her own therapist, was ready to respond to Clare and thereafter Clare continued to turn to her mother when upset and began for the first time to confide her worries to her.

(Hopkins, 1987, p. 8)

## WINNICOTT

In his professional life Donald Winnicott worked simultaneously as paediatrician, child psychiatrist and psychoanalyst. He had a small number of borderline patients as part of his analytic practice. He himself said that deeply disturbed regressed adult patients on the couch can

teach the analyst more about early infancy than can be learned from direct observation of infants, and more than can be learned from contact with mothers who are involved with infants. At the same time, clinical contact with the normal and abnormal experiences of the infant–mother relationship influences the analyst's analytic theory since what happens in the transference (in the regressed phase of some of these patients) is a form of infant–mother relationship.

(Winnicott, 1965b, p. 141)

This unique combination of working with infants and mothers, and with disturbed adult patients, is the ground from which Winnicott's conceptualization arose. He saw all disorders of the self as instances of what he called *environmental deficiency diseases* which include a whole range from chronic schizophrenic to false-self living.

At the very beginning, the infant's development evolves from the infant–mother unity, and from this Winnicott assumes three main functions which facilitate healthy development: holding-integration; handling-personalization; and object-relating (1960c, 1962a). Let us examine these in turn.

### HOLDING-INTEGRATION

At the start the infant is unintegrated most of the time. Since there is, in effect, no ego, there is no id yet. The mother holds the infant both physically and figuratively and so gives cohesion to his or her sensori-motor elements. The mother does this, Winnicott says, through the means of her *primary maternal preoccupation* (1956b). This ordinarily starts towards the end of her pregnancy and continues for some weeks post-partum. It is a state of heightened sensitivity to her own self, her body and the baby, and is often manifest as a state of withdrawal from, or loss of interest in, other activities.

Under these sensitized conditions, the infant will naturally give expression to a spontaneous impulse which will be manifest in the form of a gesture which the mother meets with an expression of her own in response. This is likely to give him a feeling of magic and omnipotence. It will be one of the first elements in the 'making sense' of his gesture for the infant. With regard to this 'making sense', it will be remembered from Chapter 4 that Winnicott often conceptualized in terms of the infant and the breast. Thus, at the time of feeding the infant was seen as creating the breast, which was there to be created. Whether the breast had been created or was there already was noted as a paradox about which the baby must not be challenged too soon. Like the breast, the mother's response to her child's gesture also provides a paradox that is not to be challenged too soon. If it is, the infant must cope prematurely with an external factor, a 'not-me' impingement.

Winnicott sees the meeting of the infant's spontaneous gesture with a gesture from mother as a function of the 'environment-mother': this is to be distinguished from the 'id-mother', which is the object of instinctual impulse satisfaction. In brief, it is the id-mother who produces the milk of the breast whereas it is the environment-mother who responds, in her own pattern, to the infant's initiation of the sequence of being fed to give him his primary experiences of magical omnipotence. We have already spelt out how important Winnicott thinks these are. They give rise to ego nuclei which in time will become integrated to the degree that the infant can experience 'I am', and this will feel *real* to him. This feeling real, or feeling alive, is one of the basic properties of what Winnicott called the *true self*. Thus, when the infant's gestures are met by those of the mother in such a way that 'me' and 'not-me' do *not* have to be negotiated, there is, paradoxically, a facilitation of 'me' and 'not-me' development. As a result of sequences like this, in so far as the state of 'I exist' is securely reached in development, the true self becomes more firmly established.

On the way to this stable differentiation, the infant experiences partial integration states which are more or less independent of each other. Thus, being bathed will not at first be linked with being fed, and so on. Winnicott has postulated that *return* to states of un-integration is important for both infant and mother. This is what periods of rest are needed for. Ensuring such repose, free of threats to the infant's personal continuity, is one of a 'good-enough' mother's reliable 'holding' functions (Davis and Wallbridge, 1981, p. 49). This experience, Winnicott thinks, is the precursor of the adult's ability to relax and have a capacity to be alone (1958b).

**HANDLING-PERSONALIZATION**

Whereas the holding just described facilitates integration towards the 'I am' state, the mother's *handling* - her good-enough active adaptation of her body and limbs to the infant's body needs - facilitates *personalization*. This is the 'in-dwelling' of self in the body to achieve *psychosomatic unity*. Winnicott calls this a 'psychosomatic collusion' (Davis and Wallbridge, 1981, p. 40). It was mentioned in Chapter 4 that a potential true self expresses itself at the beginning of life in the infant's own particular pattern of motility. Good co-ordination and muscle tone are the achievement of personalization. Psychosomatic unity is essential for healthy living, and it is a precondition for total involvement with shared reality. Even after psychosomatic in-dwelling has been reached, the psyche may lose touch with the body, and in extreme states it may not be easy for them to return to each other. Winnicott gives the example of an infant screaming very hard, with pallor, sweating and even vomiting, to such a degree that mother or other onlooker worries that the baby is dying.

**OBJECT-RELATING**

We have already described (Chapters 3 and 4) how Winnicott sees object-relating evolving from the experience of magical omnipotence. This holds sway when objects are not yet differentiated from the self, and are thus called *self-objects* under these conditions. It will be remembered that it is muscular attacks on the mother, and her survival of them, which facilitate the infant's developmental step of releasing her from his omnipotent control. With this, integration to the 'I am' state is achieved, and the true self can feel 'real'. Mother can now be perceived as a separate person in shared reality. She, as an object, is now 'out there' and can be *used* properly in reality and not in an illusory or omnipotent way. Winnicott called this *object usage*, whereas he called the mode of treating the self-object in a magical way *object-relating*. We have already noted the unusualness of this notation, and many readers have been confused by it, but it is simple enough once grasped. It will also be recalled from Chapter 3 how development of the articulation of both the external and internal worlds is mediated by experiences *in between* the two, by the *transitional* objects and phenomena of the third area.

The growth of reality sense, of 'internal' and 'external', and of self and object, involves psychic continuity. For this, satisfaction and coherence need to come with predictability. If psychic continuity is achieved then the task of the good-enough *environment-mother* (or substitute) is being achieved. Bollas (1987) has referred to her at this stage as a *transformational* object, for she is not necessarily known as a concrete 'thing out there', but rather as an initiator of changes of state or transformations.

Winnicott states that, when the environment is good enough, the infant is not aware of its separateness at the beginning. A baby's own biological mother is likely to provide the best environment for her baby, but not necessarily so. It is most likely that she will serve best because of her propensity to merge with and respond to the innate potentials, the true self, of her baby which have been within her since conception. This propensity *to be with* the other, Winnicott calls a *pure female element*. This is in contradistinction to *doing with*, which is associated with muscular forcefulness and hence aggressiveness. Winnicott refers to this as a *pure male element* in the personality. He stresses that these two propensities, or elements, function together in healthy life in both males and females (1971a).

It is the mother's holding, not only not her physical prehension, but also in her *comprehension*, her holding in mind, of the true self of her child that is the prerequisite of healthy or true development. De-adaptation by mother (and/or substitutes) constitutes the early reality principle. Here relative failures, especially of impulsive desires, are not only inevitable but also necessary for health. Where such inevitable failures are *repaired* – by the mother allowing *regression* to temporary fusion and merging to the state of absolute dependence – then the failures are benign and enhance reality sense. When failure is not mended in this way there is *deprivation*. Failures later in childhood come to matter less and less, so that overprotective and highly indulgent mothers may stifle a child's authentic creative living in heathy, age-appropriate play activities.

Frustration of desires is inevitable, Winnicott stresses: without 'id frustration' there can be no forsaking of omnipotence and no growth of reality sense. However, id frustration must be distinguished from frustration of *ego need*. This occurs where a child's knowing, as opposed to willing, is impinged upon or confused. It is the frustration of these ego needs that is essentially damaging. When there is *traumatic impingement*, the ego is affected, the infant's sense of *continuity* and predictability is then broken. This gives rise to feelings of annihilation, going to pieces, falling for ever, disorientation, withdrawal, isolation and non-communication. The not-good-enough environment-mother may fail in her 'holding' function and allow these psychotic anxieties or unthinkable dreads to occur as breaks in the child's self-defences.

Winnicott conceived of the coherence of the innate potentials of the original true self being shattered by fateful traumata – the original environmental failures, in very much the same way as described by Balint, Fairbairn and, particularly, Bowlby.

### PRIMITIVE BREAKDOWN

Winnicott (1960c, 1962c) thinks that a catastrophic primitive agony during the stage of early partial integration results in disintegration, which, in the worst event, leads to a fragmentation in the line of continuity of being. In other cases, it sets in motion psychotic self-defences which are organized in such a way as to protect the self from experiences of 'unthinkable' anxieties. His well-known phrase 'Clinical fear of breakdown is fear of the breakdown that has already been experienced' (1962c, 1973) explains this. The defence is organized as an illness and can be conceived of in terms of distortions of ego organization.

Under these circumstances dissociations and splitting may then manifest themselves during childhood as infantile schizophrenia or autism. Later they may appear as latent schizophrenia, and also as schizoid personality disorders, which are less extreme and compatible with sanity apart from a hidden schizoid element.

### FALSE SELF

The main aim in all these illnesses is organization towards *invulnerability*. Winnicott always maintained that psychotic self-defences are extremes of universal normal phenomena. For him there is no sharp dividing line between what he considered to be environmental deficiency diseases and ordinary health.

If a trauma, occurring in the stage of an infant's absolute dependence, lies in environmental deficiencies affecting object relating, a self-defence in the form of a *caretaker* self will develop. This caretaker will be a *false self* in that it is not the true or authentic self, but one that protects the integrity of the true self which can thus remain hidden (1960c, 1960d, 1971a).

Winnicott saw the aetiology of this lying in the not-good-enough mother's repeated failures to meet the infant's *gestures*; this, incidentally, is very close to Stern's (1985) theory of attunement. Winnicott continues his explanation by suggesting that if, instead of *meeting* her child's gestures, she uses only her own, *in vacuo* as it were, these then have to be made sense of by the child. He cannot do this by reference to his own gesture and his bodily state that lies behind it, so he resorts to a compliance which has mimicry in it but which is alien to his own true self. Under these circumstances the mother's gesture has the quality of an *impingement*.

Gross impingements at this earliest stage of development result in a pathological extreme of false-self organization. Winnicott's view of deficit in symbol formation can now be understood. The infant's gesture is a signal of his internal state to the good-enough mother which she responds to with her gesture. Her gesture is thus a signal back to him that adds her comprehension to his understanding. There is in this case a benign circle, as it were, of meaningfulness in the signals. It is of note that this is likely to be the rudiment of the symbolization of a feeling state. With the 'meaningless' gesture of the not-good-enough mother, this benign circle of meaning growth does not get started, symbol usage is thence impaired and with this the likelihood of psychosomatic illness is increased.

Under these circumstances, the compliant infant will live, but lives falsely. Winnicott says:

> The protest against being forced into false existence can be detected from the earliest stages. The clinical picture is one of general irritability, and of feeding and other function disturbances which may, however, disappear only to reappear in serious form at a later stage.
>
> (Winnicott, 1965b, p. 146)

When the mother cannot adapt her responsiveness well enough,

> the infant gets seduced into compliance, and a compliant false self reacts to environmental demands and the infant seems to accept them. Through this false self the child builds up a false set of relationships, and by means of introjections even attains a show of being real, so that the child may grow up to be just like mother, nurse, aunt, brother, or whoever dominates the scene.
>
> (Winnicott, 1965b, p. 146)

The false self has one very important function, Winnicott thinks, namely to *hide* the true self by compliance with environmental demands. The false self is one instance of a split in the infant's personality. He also presented another character disorder, the 'anti-social tendency'. This is caused by deprivation, that is, a failure of appropriate environmental ego cover *after* the child has reached unit status. This, and other environmental deficiency diseases, as Winnicott calls them, are phenomena of privation (1956b). We come to them further in the next chapter.


## MARTIN JAMES

There have been notable contributions to the theory of the environmental facilitation of development by Martin James. One of particular importance has been his well-known paper 'Premature ego development' (1960). In this he reports observing a child who, for the first three months, had been rigidly fed by a nurse. The infant was chronically hungry and also in a chronic tension state. The baby showed strong indications of premature ego development, and James suggests that this may have been due to the premature 'tolerance' of delay which had been enforced upon her by the rigidly timed and inadequate feeding.

At three months old the baby was markedly hypersensitive and also alternated between quiescence and hyperactivity. At eight months she showed a precocious facility in identification and in reactivity to the environment. Over a longer period of study in her childhood, she showed a noticeably narcissistic development, with a low ability to relate realistically to objects. She was unusually clumsy and showed signs of subtle disorders of motility. However, her mental activity was remarkably mobile; magical ideas were often running away with her. The case material, incidentally, could be read as a typical example of Winnicott's false-self defence organized before the child reached unit status.

James then discusses the biological and metapsychological consequences of environmental impingements in the earliest stages of primary narcissism. He points out that, in the stage of primary narcissism, severe chronic environmental failure can set constitutional neurological patterning into abnormality. It is likely, he thinks, that this can be reversible only at the time and is not retrospectively reversible, by psychoanalysis for instance, because the patterns are not in symbolic form. What is important is whether a pattern can become symbolic or not. If not, a psychosomatic process will ensue. In like manner, early ego nuclei can normally become linked to other and later nuclei, or they may stay dissociated, split off and uncathected. During the early, undifferentiated state, James thinks, a transition takes place from biological to psychological experiences.

James places emphasis upon *specificity* of recognition. Thus an infant's growing ability to *recognize mother* as different from other women brings an increased capacity to delay and to *anticipate* when with her. The development of the specificity in delay depends, to some extent at least, on the nature of what handling is presented to the infant by the environment – by mother in particular.

The little girl quoted by James, who missed the 'protective shield' (Khan, 1963) or ego-cover (Winnicott, 1965a), was forced to take on a protective ego-cover of her own very soon. She developed, one could say, a false self. This was why she developed narcissistically – for the normal development of 'body-ego relish' needs satisfaction – and this comes, as we have just described, from the attention of other objects and their meeting of the infant's gestures with appropriate gestures. These were largely missing; the environment was not facilitating to her here.

James also points out, metapsychologically, that the infant's chronic tension state stimulated *regression* from motor discharge to the *sensory end* of the psychic apparatus, which is rather similar to what occurs in dreams. Here there is a hypercathexis of memory and perceptual storing functions, with a lack of facilitation of progressive means of discharge. This lopsided overstimulation then led to premature access to images which began to organize into thoughts with little discharge content to them. As a consequence, the little girl tended to manipulate images instead of engaging in, and manipulating, shared reality objects. She often treated intra-psychic events as reality. Ideas took on a substantial existence and, with this, words became like things. The little girl also employed a sort of 'organ speech' in her movements, which often seemed to have a magical function to them.

James suggested that treatment of such cases can succeed only if the pathological patterns have reached symbolic levels. He suggests that *management* of such cases should include regressive handling at the time of the trauma, by means of narcissistic gratifications, to avoid precocious reactions which are not phase adequate.

## MASUD KHAN

Khan developed two interlinked concepts: *cumulative trauma* (1963) and *maternal complicity and seduction* (1978). Both of these signify failures of maternal facilitation during infancy and childhood.

### CUMULATIVE TRAUMA

Khan says:

The concept of cumulative trauma tentatively offers, in terms of early ego-development and in the context of infant–mother relationship, a complementary hypothesis to the concept of fixation points in libido development. In this sense it tries to map out what were the significant points of stress and strain in the evolving mother–infant (child) relationship that gradually gather into a dynamic substratum in the morphology of a particular character or personality.

(Khan, 1974b, p. 55)

Khan explores the role of mother as a protective shield and states that a cumulative trauma is the result of many breaches in the protective shield from childhood to adolescence: a single one may be insignificant by itself, but this, together with others, may produce a sum that is damaging. Khan stresses that these breaches are both qualitatively and quantitatively different from gross impingements of intrusions. They have the quality of strains which do not so much distort ego development as bias it. However, cumulatively and in retrospect, they have the effect of a trauma.

Cumulative trauma starts when there are frequent impingements upon the infant's psyche-soma which the infant has no means of eliminating. (In effect, the mother is failing, perhaps imperceptibly on each occasion, in her function as a shield.) These set up a nucleus of pathogenic reactions, which in turn sets in train a process of interplay with mother which is distinct from normal, protective-shield adaptation to the child's needs.

These pathogenic reactions can have any or all of the effects that Khan lists as: 1) premature and selective ego-development; 2) a specially sensitive responsiveness to mother's moods which creates an imbalance in the integration of the aggressive drive; 3) dissociation with either an archaic dependency bond or precipitate independence; and finally 4) an attitude of exaggerated concern for mother with craving for concern from her instead of age-adequate disillusionment. In all these an 'ego interest' has substituted for true object cathexis: a precocious cathexis of, and acuity about, external or internal reality supplants subjective, affective awareness as a coherent experience. The most important effect, however, is on body-ego development in the growing child. Over the course of maturation these residues are likely to coalesce into a specific type of body-ego organization.

Once this interplay between mother and child has started, all new developmental experiences and object relations tend to be drawn into its sphere. Here there appear to be attempts to correct earlier distortions, but in fact they only complicate the pathology. It will be noted that this is a form of repetition compulsion. Khan goes on to qualify this picture: he emphasizes that an infant or child usually has great inherent resilience and can, not only recover, but also use breaches and strains as nuclei for growth so as to arrive at fairly healthy functioning. However, under acute stress and crisis in adult life, this achievement can break down.

Turning to the prevalence of patients presenting with schizoid character disorders, Khan suggests that the investigation of the history of disturbances in the mother–child relationship, within a cumulative-trauma framework, may help to evaluate these disorders. It was to this task of investigating and reconstructing the aetiology of these schizoid character problems that Khan devoted much of his work. We will address ourselves to this further in the next chapter.

### MATERNAL COMPLICITY AND SEDUCTION

A counterpart to cumulative trauma is not traumatic *per se* but almost the opposite. This is seductive sexualization and spoiling, enhancing of omnipotence, or other chronic indulgence by parents – mother particularly. Khan covers this under the title of complicity. While not itself traumatic, such parental seduction leaves the child open to traumata from other ordinary, everyday events. He draws attention to the important area of the awesome tasks that many children's immature egos have to face when inundated by the peculiar characteristics of their parents, psychotic, perverse, anti-social and neurotic, as they try to grow through childhood. It is still poorly researched.

## HEIMANN

With regard to the effects of the environment, Paula Heimann (1989) developed a view basically similar to that of Winnicott. She maintains that the infant does not introject a bad object, but may suffer intrusions against which he is helpless. This creates a bad object in the psychic structure which is not assimilated and stays dissociated, but influences id, ego and super-ego structures. Rather like Khan with his cumulative trauma, she sees the importance of chronic pathogenic effects in later, as well as in early, childhood.

## ENID BALINT

Enid Balint is best known for her careful studies of persons in the clinical analytic situation, but these usually include reconstructions of the early interpersonal qualities of object relations between parent and child. She is an unabashed object-relations theorist here. One quality she notes in several papers is the inability of some mothers to know what their child's experiences, feelings and thoughts really are at the time of their happening. She is convinced of the pathogenic nature of such maternal incapacity, and that it shows its effects in later life (1963, 1973). In another paper, 'Fair shares and mutual concern' (1972), she argues that children brought up in a family climate which allows personal freedom of choice, together with mutual concern in the earliest years, seem to be well equipped to withstand the inevitable later personal frustrations in life where 'fair shares for all' is the optimal social norm.

## CONCLUSION

The body of opinion of the authors discussed here is unequivocal that environmental, particularly parental, factors are vital for healthy growth. If they fail they become operative in disease and disorder in later life.

Though other contributing factors are not ruled out, psychopathology is traced by all our authors to traumata of various kinds. A trauma occurs when the continuity of the self, of ongoing development of a person's mental and emotional life, is disrupted.

Traumata are envisaged as often originating very early in life in the times of a child's well-nigh total dependency. They are seen as being caused by various events, such as separation from primary care-givers beyond the span tolerable for the infant's development at the time. Traumata may also arise through deprivation of 'good-enough' (Winnicott, 1941a) parental loving care – like chronic lack of empathy, hostility, denigration, cruelty, sexual abuse, unreliability, deceit, withdrawal and others.

However, traumata may come not from one set of events but from an accumulation over many years. Thus, very early disruptions are not the only causes of pathology. What is more, parental over-indulgence and over-stimulation, beyond the child's capacity to process excitement, are seen as creating vulnerability in a child. Sexual abuse of children would seem both to create vulnerability and also to be traumatic to the child's integrity and identity.

The long-term result of these traumata, the creation of pathological psychic structures, has been mentioned on several occasions. For instance, attention has been drawn to the schizoid character, the basic fault and to the false self. It is pathological character structures such as these that seem to lie at the heart of chronic individual disturbance and will next be considered.

# 7    Character and Its Vicissitudes

THE QUESTION OF character is paradoxical, for it is both at the core of a person's individuality and yet very often that which is categorizable and thus general about him. Freud thought of character as compounded from two sources: first, from early ego identifications, that is, the ego built up of object relationships that have been given up. Second, character is seen as habitual modes of defence, together with other vicissitudes of the libidinal drives.

Individual character has fascinated humankind from the earliest times. Bards and playwrights have portrayed its varieties for thousands of years and novelists for hundreds. But it has perhaps not been until the coming of psychoanalysis that an individual person's character has really been engaged with, with the aim of substantial understanding and change. Much of analysis is character analysis, and the British have played an impressive part in this endeavour.

Ernest Jones's 'The God complex' (1913b) is perhaps the first study of the narcissistic character. He points to the marked self-admiring features that often seem to fall together in one person. He portrays the lofty arrogance, contempt and grandiosity that commonly go with withdrawn self-absorption, the demand to be loved and inability to love others. Jones continued in the same line with his paper on 'Anal-erotic character traits' (1918) and essays upon the Welsh, Irish and English characters.

His study of 'The phallic phase' (1933), however, contains more than descriptive typology. It develops a theory about the *dynamic structures* that seem to be involved in phallic characteristics. It is to such structural questions of various configurations that Independents have mainly contributed. Glover followed Jones's example with papers on the oral (1925) and neurotic (1948) characters. Since then, though there have not been many papers by the British on this subject, some have been important.

## FAIRBAIRN

### THE SCHIZOID CHARACTER

More than almost any other British analyst since Freud, Fairbairn was a systematic thinker about those dynamic structures that make up the personality, and we will now consider his work in some detail (Fairbairn, 1952; Guntrip, 1973; Padel, 1972; Goldberg and Mitchell, 1983; Hughes, 1989; Sutherland, 1989).

During the 1930s Fairbairn had been impressed by Klein's work on early phantasy and particularly that on aggressiveness, depression and the depressive position. However, he came to the opinion that schizoid mechanisms were the more basic, and it was largely he who stimulated her later work upon these mechanisms. Working at the time in a psychology department, he was closely in touch with McDougall's ideas and thus came easily to the view that sexuality may not be the only source of satisfaction (Sutherland, 1989).

Fairbairn first developed his conception of the *schizoid* personality, and it was out of this that his *endo-psychic structure* unfolded. However, for ease of comprehension, we will approach structure first.

The dream of the actress which Fairbairn (1944, 1952) related has already been recounted (Chapter 4, p. 00). In the manifest dream there were several characters: the dreamer herself, her husband, a well-known actress and an unknown man. From this and from the patient's associations, Fairbairn derived three sets of interpretations. One was about her current life and marriage, the second about her childhood oedipal relation with her mother and father, and lastly he showed that the structure of the drama of the dream represented certain essentials of the patient's own psychic structure. The figures of the dream are thus not only internal objects, but also represent different parts of the ego which have structured relations with each other. There are also often drives to change aspects of the parts in relation to others, so the psyche is said to be *dynamically* structured. It is of interest to note that the idea of structure implies continuity and, if this is habitual, then it is called an individual's character.

Fairbairn thus introduces the notion that each individual experiences himself with a *multiplicity* of egos (Fairbairn's usage of the term 'ego' and not 'self' is continued here). The basic psychic elements which, Fairbairn suggests, are used in the structure of the mind are in effect *ego-and-object* relations. These are affect structures (see Chapter 2), and close to Glover's model of affect and ego nuclei.

Fairbairn stressed that any one mind is a complex somato-psychic structure of smaller dynamic systems. He maintained that the notion of the id as discharging energy was obsolete. In effect, he saw that every feeling, with every motive in it, had a feedback system. There was for Fairbairn a nucleus of an ego system to every drive or desire, and each ego nucleus could be conceived of as an information-control system.

With his rejection of the value of the psychic energy-discharge model, motivation arising from discrepancies between ego and others, each seen as a whole character, became important for Fairbairn. Object relations, either internal or external, were thence as compelling as physiological drives. Neither psychological nor physiological drives took precedence. In both cases the primary process reigned supreme at unconscious levels. For Fairbairn the experience of intimacy with mother was paramount; feeding satisfaction from her breast was, at times, secondary to this. His view was the reverse of Klein's. She saw greed for the maternal breast as primary. For him, this greed could often largely be a consequence of loss of intimacy with mother.

### ENDO-PSYCHIC STRUCTURE

Fairbairn's dynamic structure is inspired by and very close to Freud's ego, id and super-ego, but Fairbairn specifically elaborated this into a number of primary ego-object structures. A diagram (Figure 1) conceived by John Padel (1972) portrays the comparison with Freud. For Fairbairn, a *libidinal ego*, mediating libidinal desires, relates to libidinally *exciting objects*. This is matched by, and in continuous conflict with, an *anti-libinal ego* linked with *rejecting objects*. Mediating between these and also relating to ideal objects and objectives, and to the external world, is the *central ego*. This is not originally derived from the other ego structures but is conceived of as being present in primitive, undifferentiated form from the start. This differs rather from Glover's conception of early ego nuclei where a central ego plays little or no part (1939, 1956, 1968). For Fairbairn, a central organizing agency is a characteristic of a living thing, otherwise the organism would disintegrate into its parts.

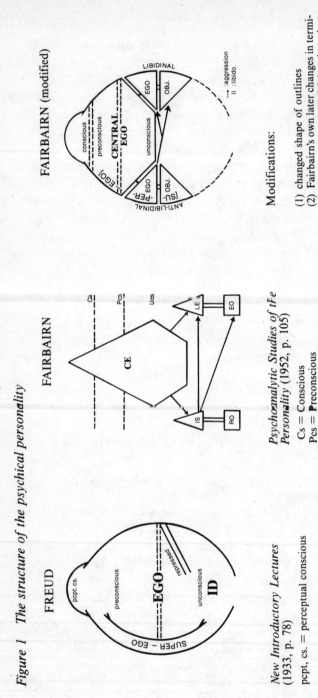

Figure 1   The structure of the psychical personality

FREUD

FAIRBAIRN

FAIRBAIRN (modified)

*New Introductory Lectures*
(1933, p. 78)

pcpt, cs. = perceptual conscious

*Psychoanalytic Studies of the
Personality* (1952, p. 105)

Cs = Conscious
Pcs = Preconscious
Ucs = Unconscious
CE = Central Ego
IS = Internal Saboteur
LE = Libidinal Ego
RO = Rejecting Object
EO = Exciting Object
→ = aggression
|| = libido

Modifications:

(1) changed shape of outlines
(2) Fairbairn's own later changes in termi-
    nology and SUPEREGO written in.
(3) dotted line = ideal object
    = accepted object

*Note*   This comparison and modified diagram is by Dr John Padel and is reproduced here by his kind permission.

The different ego-object structures are envisaged as originally arising out of *splitting*, that is, out of primitive *defensive* activity. This in turn will have originated from forms of loss of optimal intimacy with primary objects like mother. Being based on splits, psychic structure, though often normal, is seen in large measure as a schizoid product. In this context, looking again at Fairbairn's actress dream, it is possible to distinguish his three major ego structures portrayed by the characters of the dream. Thus, the structure of the drama of the dream, its *aesthetic* as Bollas (1987) calls it, portrays those aspects of the psychic structure of the dreamer that are active at that time.

Even though many clinicians may not explicitly use the particular specifications of the details of Fairbairn's tripartite structures, the idea of a dialectic between libidinal and anti-libidinal, for instance, is implicit in much analytic thinking. What is more, the general idea of a psychic structure of multiple conflicting ego-object systems which are portrayed by the dramatic form of dreams is probably used every day.

With such a multiple ego-object system in mind, any manner of defensive manoeuvre can be conceived of as being used by any part-ego upon any other parts. Thus, as worked out later in Kleinian theory, splittings, denials, projections, introjections and displacements of parts of the ego can be noted at any time occurring within the psychic structure and also between it and the outside world.

**THEORY OF PSYCHOPATHOLOGY**

At the same time as developing the structural model, Fairbairn thought about the process of neurosis generally (1943). Taking his cue from Klein, he saw evaluative activity, particularly the simple splitting into good and bad objects, as primary. He conceived of neurotic disturbance as being the result of the *return* of previously warded-off bad object experiences to conscious levels of the ego.

He also attempted a comprehensive view of psychopathology, using this good–bad dichotomy (1941) as a basis for patterns of defensive manoeuvre that are characteristic of each pathological category. In brief, schizoid illness comes from the sense the infant feels that his *love* for mother is *bad* and destructive for her. Depressive illness is derived from later in infancy and comes from the experience that the baby's *aggression* or hate has been *bad* for and destroyed mother. The neuroses are derived from later developments still, when the child is in a 'transitional state' (Fairbairn used this term slightly differently from Winnicott) between total and relative dependence. Paranoia arises by the *anal* expulsion or projection of bad objects to the outside world so that the ego is kept purely good and free of evil. Hysteria, on the other hand, is of more oedipal origin, whereby both good and bad objects are externalized so that the ego is made small and sexually predominantly innocent.

According to Fairbairn, the structuring of the mind involves the division into separate ego-parts and this must take place first by splitting. Freud's view was slightly different: for him a split was the *result* of a defensive process, particularly of denial. This is perhaps the better formulation. At all events, emotional levels of the mind originate for Fairbairn in the *schizoid* process. This is both *the* basic pathological syndrome and also a core origin of the internal world and psychic structure. Schizoid process is both valuable and dangerous.

In Fairbairn's classic paper (1940), schizoid conditions are seen to constitute the most deep-seated of all psychopathology, so they provide unrivalled opportunities for the foundations of the personality. Schizoid people are often more capable of truthful insight, or lack of it, than others more integrated. It is not only in psychosis, but also in hysteria, phobia, obsession and simple anxiety, that underlying schizoid mechanisms can be seen to operate.

The overtly schizoid individual can be described as someone who is often mystified about himself and also mysterious. He is frequently transiently disturbed about his sense of reality, or there is a sense of unfamiliarity with the familiar, or familiarity with the unfamiliar. Characterologically speaking, agitators and fanatics are found among schizoid individuals, and so are intellectuals, where they live with lofty detachment from the common man. Three characteristics are sufficiently prominent to warrant special attention: an attitude of omnipotence, isolation and detachment, and a preoccupation with inner reality. They are close to Jung's introverted type.

The fundamental schizoid phenomenon is splits in the ego. The basic developmental position of the psyche is a schizoid one, and more fundamental than the depressive position. The 'looking on at oneself' from a distance is basically a schizoid mode. Dreams, too, have something of this looking at oneself about them. The dream drama is a universal schizoid phenomenon.

The schizoid position originates in the early oral phase and is essentially an oral incorporative phenomenon: the mouth is thus its chief organ. The oral-libidinal attitude is one where taking predominates over giving. It is directed fundamentally towards mother as a whole person, but as an object she is objectified by an abstraction – 'the breast'. In this position the self and people are related to as part-objects, 'partial' Fairbairn calls them, so people are thought of and manipulated and treated as organs, things or animals.

The type of mother who provokes such schizoid regressions is one who fails to convince her child by spontaneous affection that she herself truly loves him as a person in his own right. Instead of real emotional openness, the schizoid individual then often uses *techniques* of relating to others. One is that of *playing roles*. This seems close to the characteristics of Winnicott's false self. There is no doubt a schizoid ingredient to be found in any dramatic role-taking, and it is certainly evident in hysterical behaviour. Another technique is an *exhibitionistic* one, where high levels of literary or artistic excellence may be striven for in order to fascinate others without being more than marginally involved with them. The reason for this distancing is because the child, and then the adult, has come to believe that loving relationships are bad, or at least suspect.

Withdrawing from intimate relationships, the schizoid person often overvalues intellectualization. Thought becomes libidinized and abstract ideas are then valued above people. Where schizoid individuals become charismatic and involved with social policies, they are prone to be ruthless and ideologically bound to a closed political system. The number of their victims, Fairbairn notes, may then run into millions.

The tragedy of the ordinary schizoid individual is that he believes it is his love that destroys. He must thus neither love nor be loved: 'Like the Troubadours (and perhaps the dictators), he can only permit himself to love and be loved from afar' (1952, p. 26). Since the joy of loving is barred to him, he gives himself over to the joy of hating and gets what satisfaction he can out of that. He thus makes a pact with the devil and says, 'Evil be thou my good' (p. 27). The moral motive in this perhaps is that it is better to destroy by hate and risk being depressed than to destroy by love – which is what he feels his fate has handed him.

# BALINT

### CHARACTER FAULTS

The concept of the basic fault (1968) has already been discussed (Chapter 6). We quote here Balint's description of its emergence in the clinical situation.

> Then at some point, suddenly or insidiously, the atmosphere of the analytic situation changes profoundly. . .[the] interpretations given by the analyst are not experienced any longer by the patient as interpretations. Instead he may feel them as an attack, a demand, a base insinuation, an uncalled-for rudeness or insult, unfair treatment, injustice, or at least as a complete lack of consideration. . .on the other hand [they] may be experienced as something highly pleasing and gratifying, exciting or soothing, or as a seduction; in general as an irrefutable sign of consideration, affection, and love. . .Moreover – and this is not so easy to admit – the patient somehow seems able to get under the analyst's skin. . .apparently from an uncanny talent that enables the patient to 'understand' the analyst's motives. . .[which] may occasionally give the impression of, or perhaps may even amount to, telepathy or clairvoyance. . .If now the analyst fails to 'click in', that is, to respond as the patient expects him to do, no reaction of anger, rage, contempt or criticism will appear. . .The only thing that can be observed is a feeling of emptiness, being lost, deadness, futility, and so on, coupled with an apparently lifeless acceptance of everything that has been offered.
>
> (M. Balint, 1968, p. 18; see also E. Balint, 1963)

The basic fault is seen by Balint as originating when an individual experiences a rupture in his trusting of primary love during early development. The instigating cause has been described as similar to that of Fairbairn's schizoid position and Winnicott's false self. But Balint's syndrome is not conceived of as a structure of splits like Fairbairn's. It is a *mood* that may permeate more or less the whole of the personality. Balint maintains that every individual is likely to suffer some infusion of a basic faultiness, but for some it becomes a major characteristic of their sense of living and the whole self.

We have also noted Balint's (1959) proposal that there can be two particular *character-defensive modes* of reaction to this basic environmental failure. Both are mood responses aiming to restore certain aspects of the primary love state between self and environment while denying others. When pronounced as a character trait, the *philobat* loves open empty spaces and the freedom and apparent safety of the space between objects. He is an optimistic action man, an acrobat, a climber, height-lover or explorer; he cathects his own ego skills and avoids objects. The typical *ochnophil*, on the other hand, loves concrete objects and clings to them to protect himself and them. He tends to be phobic, unadventurous, doubtful and pessimistic, and is prone to be a feeling and thinking person rather than a doer. Here the individual is holding on to his objects to control them in the state of primary love again. Most people are of course mixed in their reactions. These concepts of Balint's are not used by many analysts. Perhaps this is partly because he uses unevocative, neo-classical terminology, but the ideas behind them seem important and contribute to the understanding of some patients who present difficulties in the clinical situation.

## WINNICOTT

**FALSE SELF**

The last chapter has already discussed the aetiology of false-self structures (1960c). Here we will be concerned with their various manifestations. As we have said, false-self structures may organize when the infant has been exposed to traumatic impingements which have threatened true-self activity. These problems belong, Winnicott says, to infant-to-mother living and

> not to the theory of early mechanisms of ego-defence organised against id-impulses, though of course these two subjects overlap. . .It is essential to take into account the mother's behaviour and attitudes because it is in this field that dependence is real and near absolute. It is not possible to state what takes place by reference to the baby alone.
>
> (1965b, pp. 144–5)

Winnicott defined the true self, as we have seen, as coming from the aliveness of the body tissues and their functions. One could say that it is the infant's vitality. He also emphasized that understanding the true self is necessary before attempting to comprehend the false self. He adds that it might be more true to say that the false self hides the infant's inner reality rather than his true self.

In the course of development the feeling of being real is strengthened by the child's increasing ability to tolerate two sets of phenomena. The first is breaks in the continuity of true-self vitality of living. The second is reactive, false-self experiences of compliantly relating to the environment. He gives the example of a child who is taught to say 'ta' before his first birthday. In other words, an infant of this age can be taught to acknowledge the existence of an environment that is just becoming intellectually accepted. True feelings of gratitude may or may not follow (1965b, p. 149).

It may be thought that Winnicott underestimates the usefulness of compliance since he often seems to equate it with the false self. However, he makes it clear that, provided the infant has developed a healthy ego organization which is adaptive to the environment, the true self has a compliant aspect. That is, the infant has an ability to comply and not to be exposed: this ability to compromise is an achievement. However, in the healthy person this compromise ceases to be allowable to the self when issues are felt to be crucial. The true self then, in health, can override the compliant self.

It is interesting to note that Winnicott rarely systematically compared and contrasted his formulations about developmental sequences with those from the classical theory of libidinal development. But it would seem likely that, though their roots lie, for Winnicott, very early in infancy, compliance, falsity, protest against it and authenticity are clearly and crucially visible in toddlerhood, that is, in the anal phase.

Winnicott has given a classification of false-self organizations.

1   At one extreme: the False Self sets up as real and it is this that observers tend to think is the real person. In living relationships, work relationships, and friendship, however, the False Self begins to fail. In situations in which what is expected is a whole person the False Self has some essential lacking. At this extreme the True Self is hidden.

2   Less extreme: the False Self defends the True Self; the True Self, however, is acknowledged as a potential and is allowed a secret life. Here is the clearest example of clinical illness as an organisation

with a positive aim, the preservation of the individual in spite of abnormal environmental conditions. This is an extension of the psycho-analytic concept of value of symptoms to the sick person.

3　More towards health: the False Self has as its main concern a search for conditions which will make possible for the True Self to come into its own. If conditions cannot be found then there must be reorganised a new defence against exploitation of the True Self and if there be doubt then the clinical result is suicide. Suicide in this context is the destruction of the total self in avoidance of annihilation of the True Self. When suicide is the only defence left against betrayal of the True Self, then it becomes the lot of the False Self to organise the suicide. This of course involves its own destruction, but at the same time eliminates the need for its continued existence, since its function is the protection of the True Self from insult.

4　Still further towards health: the False Self is built upon identifications (as for example that of the patient. . .whose childhood environment and whose actual nannie gave much colour to the False Self organisation).

5　In health: the False Self is represented by the whole organisation of the polite and mannered social attitude, a 'not wearing the heart on the sleeve', as it might be said. Much has gone to the individual's ability to forgo omnipotence and the primary process in general, the gain being the place in society which can never be gained or maintained by the True Self alone.

(Winnicott, 1965b, pp. 142–3)

An example, given by Winnicott, of a false-self personality may be useful at this point.

Ellen, aged ten. . .It can be taken that this child was physically, emotionally and intellectually normal at one year. At that time, however, the mother left her husband and took the child away, after which the father only saw her at intervals. When the child was 6¼, the father arrived, unannounced, and picked his daughter up in his car as she was on her way to school. The child came away without a murmur, and was contented to be brought back to London. After this father started divorce proceedings. When she was nine, the father remarried, this time making an excellent choice. The child's home background now became good for the first time since she was one year old.

The complaint was that Ellen was artificial. She was nice, and good, and intelligent. The only thing was that 'you could not get on to a sincere basis with her' as her father said. In addition, she was childish for her age and it was said that one could never predict from her mood on rising what might or might not happen in the course of the day. . . Her parents said that if caught off her guard she would usually be found to be sorrowful. Her real mother's moods were also unreliable.

Superficially the child was very happy with her father and especially with her excellent step-mother, to whom she clung. Yet it was easily found that she mourned the loss of her real mother, who had been anything but a reliable parent to her.

(Winnicott, 1954 [1958a, p. 71])

It is of interest that the crucial trauma for this false-self formation was apparently not any particular one from the very earliest months of complete dependency to which Winnicott often pointed, but more chronic or cumulative ones from the second year onwards. It is a good example of the sort of evidence that convinces many Independents of the importance of the long-term pattern of the interacting characters of both parents in the environment of a growing child.

Winnicott thinks that the 'mind' can be the location of the false self. This would occur when there is a dissociation between the activity of a fine intellect and the person's somato-psychic existence. Clinically, it may be manifest in feelings of being a phoney as the person becomes more successful. There are also people who show promise but sooner or later destroy themselves. In typical cases this failure often produces shock among people in their environment. Winnicott was of the opinion that people suffering from false-self organization could respond to treatment only through allowing regression to dependency in the therapy (see Chapter 9).

### ANTISOCIAL TENDENCY

Winnicott thought that all character disorders are distortions of ego structure. They will have first occurred in connection with the child's attempt to accommodate to developmental deficiencies, and are seen by Winnicott as being due to environmental failure along the lines we have considered earlier in this chapter. However, these character disorders are seen as arising from traumata *after* the age when the child began to experience himself as a whole person. They would none the less have been deprivations enough to stunt and distort further ego development.

Winnicott thinks that all character disorders show some antisocial tendency, but it may be hidden in a reaction-formation, or in a complaining attitude, which then develops a grievance, which will naturally have an antisocial aspect. The tendency may be hidden by symptoms like daydreaming, bed-wetting, compulsive masturbation, lying, etc. – periodically in this case there is likely to be stealing or compulsive aggressive activity and destruction (1956c, 1958a, 1963c, 1965b).

It will be emerging that Winnicott links any character disorder with an antisocial tendency. Such a disorder is a hidden illness in an intact personality. There is always a distortion as a result of the antisocial tendency. He emphasizes that this tendency always expresses *hope*. It is the child's communication that all *was* well before the trauma, and it is an attempt to get back to pre-trauma life. Character disorders really need to be treated at the time when the trauma occurred, otherwise the ego will exploit its distortions by secondary gains. The severity of the illness that lies hidden can vary considerably. The character disorder can cover unconscious psycho-neurotic conflicts, or, at the other end of the spectrum, it can hide psychotic processes. In the latter case the hidden illness lies in the very ego structure itself and shows symptoms like dissociation, depersonalization, regression and omnipotent dependence.

We saw earlier that Winnicott viewed the antisocial tendency as starting in the environment's failure to adjust to the child when dependence has become relative. At the developmental stage after this, the family may fail to recognize the child's predicament and so leave the ego distortion unhealed. At a later stage still, it might be the wider society, taking the family's place as the child grows older, which fails to meet and heal the distortion. Psychoanalysis will inevitably make such patients ill and is thus to be approached only when there is some suffering present at the outset.

As the original trauma has occurred within the family, Winnicott said that the symptoms of stealing or compulsive destructive behaviour can often be cured *within* the family, by giving special attention to the trauma by allowing regression and even 'spoiling' the child. He presented a great deal of case material on this subject and shows how, when he simply helped the parents by giving them advice about how to handle their child, the stealing or misbehaving was often cured and the antisocial tendency disappeared.

If the child is not given attention at the right time, secondary gains from the symptoms and from the ego distortions will then make it necessary to manage the children in institutions. As these often fail in the crucial attempt to deal with the antisocial tendency, the next step is likely to be prison in adulthood. Some individuals succeed in avoiding prison but nevertheless can show severe psychopathy in their living in the community. Winnicott thinks that psychotherapy at this time is bound to fail unless the patient is first placed in an institution, from where the therapy can be arranged. The question of treatment of character disorders arises again in Chapter 10.

## MASUD KHAN

### CHARACTER PATHOLOGY

With the exception of Padel (1972, 1986), Guntrip (1973) and Sutherland (1989), Khan has used Fairbairn more systematically in his writings than anyone in Britain. We are exclusively concerned here with his earlier work that appeared in his books *The Privacy of the Self* (1974b), *Alienation in Perversions* (1979) and *Hidden Selves* (1983). In his later years, Khan suffered from a disabling illness and, shortly before his death, he seems to have dissociated himself from the clinical aspects of psychoanalysis. His earlier theoretical contributions, based on a wide knowledge of the analytic literature and extensive experience of clinical practice, are fine literary works and most valuable to analysts.

He uses Fairbairn's thinking about the schizoid personality as the starting point for a far-reaching theoretical point of view about perversity, of which Fairbairn himself may have had little inkling.

Khan (1960a, 1974b, 1979) starts by describing Fairbairn's basic idea about the schizoid position and then focuses upon two crucial points, namely the schizoid techniques of playing roles and of exhibitionism. He notes a similar point brought out by Helene Deutsch (1942) about the 'staged' quality of the 'as-if' personality, which is close to a schizoid state. He then points out the high *suggestibility* of such people. This suggestibility is, Khan thinks, a form of ego passivity that serves to avoid any strong feelings. You don't have to feel about the other person if you imitate him.

This brings Khan to the vital step of seeing this 'as-if' quality and suggestibility as being similar to Winnicott's false self (Winnicott, 1948b, 1949b, 1951, 1953, 1960d). The schizoid propensity to be suggestible, to imitate, to play roles and be 'as-if' is pointing to the same mechanisms as those of false-self formation.

Khan schematizes the features of the transference behaviour of a particular type of schizoid patient in analysis. These are briefly:

1  They tend to provoke or seduce the analyst.
2  Instead of communicating they exhibit psychic contents.
3  Affects have a discharge urgency about them.
4  Narcissism is patently deficient, and their auto-erotism is compulsive.
5  They lean on others and are prone to act out.
6  They need the analyst desperately but only with limited involvement.
7  They cannot tolerate anxiety and will wildly use a variety of defences, particularly splitting, projective identification, denigration and idealization.

In a later paper, Khan (1969b) goes further into the facets of schizoid functioning. He notices certain patients who have an eerie scatter of a few intense personal involvements interspersed with long times of nothingness. They are earnest and candid in analysis and establish an agile, positive working relationship – yet nothing changes. They get attached to the analyst but remain impervious and disassociated. He says:

> I was a mixture of a nagging nanny and a comforting transitional thing-person-object of whom they had little perception or affective awareness as a person. . .they *compelled* a role upon me quite different clinically from the neurotic's familiar projection of early object relations on to the analyst.
>
> (Khan, 1974b, p. 84)

The patients had been, Khan thinks, gifted and over-sensitive children. They had been 'special', as described by Main (1957). Their mothers had, it seems, been vital and sensitive, and a bond of adaptive, precocious, mutual sensitiveness had continued for much longer than was developmentally necessary. There was thus over-libidinization at every developmental stage; with this there was a *failure to integrate aggression*.

With regard to this failure of aggression, 'The object is here not a firmly established separate not-me person, nor is it as yet a stably internalized object. The real talent of these mothers lay in maintaining this most important *position* of the object throughout the childhood of the child' (1974b, p. 86). By this means the children formed only a diffuse perception of their mother. A consequence was that repression was not so much used as a stable defence as were denial, incorporation, splitting and negation.

It is stressed that the mothers seemed to shirk every form of aggressive confrontation with their 'special' and gifted children. The result seems to have been that in adolescence these children became moody, self-absorbed, intense and phobic.

The function of these phobic mechanisms is pursued in detail (Khan, 1966). The role of the phobias is not so much to distance from objects, but more to *cling* desperately to their primary *internal* object representations. The mechanism is thus established in order to continue a link between a primary, now idealized, state of the object and the narcissistic self. A particular counter-phobic technique is then established – the patient's social experiences take on the active characteristics of a *happening*. A sudden intense climate of specialness is actualized. It is of interest to note here the similarity of the mood to that which Balint described as in the area of the basic fault. Khan, however, sees that by making the object special they become special themselves. By this means self-absorption is changed to elation. But when *emotional surrender* threatens, then the relation quickly dissipates. Khan sees this 'happening' as the very means by which true emotional interdependency is avoided.

Khan observes that at least some of these schizoid 'special' patients, though in intense symbiotic attachment with their mothers, had often been suddenly separated from them. When this happened surrogate mothers were usually quickly found to be special with. 'They had internalized the idealized mother and the child-self attached to her. They had then colluded with the environment and the caretaking person in "nursing" this internalized *special* ego state' (1974b, p. 77).

Khan's studies of the schizoid personality integrate much that has been gathered from other Independents – from Fairbairn and Winnicott, of course, and also from Main (1957) on the need to be special. The work of

Bowlby, on attachment and separation (1951, 1969, 1973), also springs to mind, as does that of Balint on the basic fault.

## BOLLAS

### NORMOTIC, GHOSTLINE AND ANTI-NARCISSISTIC CHARACTERS

The work of Winnicott and Khan has found a valuable sequel in Christopher Bollas's writings. He also draws widely from others like Bion, Heimann and Limentani.

We have already drawn attention to his basic use of Winnicott's theory of innate potentials being the origin of true-self activity. He also assumes the creation of false-self structures which aim to protect yet impede its development. Thus Bollas's mode of thinking is basically a developmental one. He directs attention to various vicissitudes of both true- and false-self developments. He describes (Bollas, 1987, 1989) among other things three variations of character akin to false-self creation but with definite differences.

In the *normotic character* (1987) he notes patients with a general deletion of subjective factors in their awareness. What is being used, he thinks, is a form of manic defense (Winnicott, 1935) wherein the purpose is to be rid of intra-psychic life. Such a character is abnormally normal, stable, secure, comfortable and extravert. He is interested in objects but concerned predominantly with their 'thingness' aspects. There is a transfer of subjective states of mind into the materialness of external objects. There is thence a de-symbolization of the mental aspects of content. With such a person introspection is rare. It does not occur to him seriously to enter into arguments of feeling as might occur in family quarrels. Being without an experienced inner world, he is *moodless*. He lacks internal space as described by Winnicott (1971a), Khan (1974b) and Stewart (1985). There being an absence of a subjective world, the affective aspects of transitional phenomena are not used. However, he is not without identity: he has action as a defining quality of his life. This is real, not false or as-if, neither is he robotic, so it is not true to say that he is a false-self character. A clinical description illustrates this.

It is striking that such a person does achieve something of a state of reverie. A female patient wanders from one store to another in the course of her day. She might find herself in a supermarket for an hour or more, not because she is in particular need of any food or other items but because the material aesthetic of the supermarket, resplendent with its vegetables, cereals and canned goods, is soothing.

From the supermarket to the pet shop: from the sportsware store to the large hardware shop: . . .from a tennis match to the jacuzzi: this person *can* live a life without ever blinking an eye. If his mother or father is dying the normotic does not feel grief, instead engages in a detailed examination of the nature of the disease.

(Bollas, 1987, p.139)

This form of personality is, Bollas says, close to Joyce McDougall's (1986) 'anti-analysand'. He goes on:

What is lacking is that originating subjectivity which informs our use of the symbolic. The normotic does not see himself other than as an object (ideally smart and spruced up, productive and sociable) among all the objects of the material world. Since he does not perceive himself as a subject, he does not ask to be seen by the other, nor does he look into the other. . .the normotic has only partly developed the capacity to symbolize the self. In Bion's language there is an impoverished production of 'alpha elements', a term which he uses to represent that mental transformation whereby emotional experiences become a possibility in the first place.

(Bollas, 1987, p.141)

Another clinical description may illustrate this.

The patient was an adolescent who had attempted suicide by cutting his arm from the wrist to the elbow. This event had followed a disappointment in school when he felt he had failed people. For several days. . .he had become 'dreamy'. . .He then attempted suicide and would certainly have died had he not been discovered. . .After less than a month, he was released from the hospital. Within a few days he was re-admitted following another serious suicide attempt. . .Before seeing the patient I imagined him to be a rather depressed looking and hopeless chap. . .I was quite surprised when he entered the room and strode confidently to his chair. Sitting next to me was a handsome, athletic, wholesome looking lad, neatly dressed in cotton trousers, tennis shoes and stylish short-sleeved shirt. . .Tom behaved as if nothing was at all unusual in his immediate history. . .it was clear that he had felt terribly isolated since moving to his new school, and had entered into athletics in an effort to find friendship. He had never been allowed to mourn the loss of his friends from the previous school, for his father led the family with clichés about how strong people put things behind them. . .we were all moved by the utter failure of Tom's family to *think* about what they had all been through.

(Bollas, 1987, p.148)

Less common in its grosser forms is what Bollas calls the *ghostline personality*. To explain what he means, he returns to Winnicott's famous model of the infant's first creation being the hallucination of the breast which may then be affirmed in reality by the mother. Creativity originating from such experience as this is needed in an imagination which functions in the *use* of any objects from infancy onwards. Objects to be used ordinarily have at some time transitional status, that is, they intermingle with the self so that the objects enter into the self's imagination. Some children, particularly autistic ones, do not develop this imagination in the proper use of objects. Tustin (1981), Bollas tells us, explains how symbolization is then non-existent or stunted so that objects are manipulated only for their sensations and not their use. Thus, a key will be used for sensations only: its meaning as a door-opener does not emerge. Transitional activity has not taken place.

There are, Bollas thinks, similarly stunted alternatives to transitional activity that may operate in people who seem more normal. One such mode seems schizoid in nature. Here the individual creates an *alternative*, make-believe world in which to live. This imagined world can usually be seen to be derived from real people and experiences but is made up of characters who then take on a life of their own and the patient lives with them. Imagination is used alternatively to, not for use in, reality.

Here is one of Bollas's descriptions.

Mary was an exceptionally gifted philosophy student who felt suicidal. I discovered that along with two female friends she lived in a pretend alternative world. They had created their own private language (more complex than black slang), had invented names, and discussed purely imaginary characters who constituted a sort of ongoing soap opera. They had a group name and were almost inseparable.

(Bollas, 1989, p. 122)

He continues his argument:

> Adrienne established an alternative world complete with alter selves
> and other that was profoundly refusing of the actual world. There was
> something ghostly about these internal objects – we could say that
> Adrienne was a ghostline personality. What do we mean by this? . . .If
> these internal objects are derived from real people (including the per-
> son's self), then they are rather like the common notion of a ghost as
> the spirit of that which has lived.
>
> (Bollas, 1989, p. 125)

Bollas speculates about the early environment of people who create these
alternatives. He thinks, following Heimann (1956), that their mothers
may have been prone to disown their children's bodies and hence portrayed them as alien to the maternal environmental world. Other mothers
seem not to have been actively alienating like this but to have been so
depressed as to be lifeless or dead to their children. Without life in
external reality to take up and contain the vitality of the child he finds an
alternative world for his interest and pleasures.

Yet another character is discovered and portrayed by Bollas, the *anti-
narcissist*. Often adored by mother, the sufferer's narcissism becomes a
bloated burden to himself and has to be chronically attacked. This is less
of a borderline character problem than the other two described, but is
equally intransigent to treatment, for negative therapeutic reactions are
often the order of the day. The anti-narcissist, Bollas suggests, must
systematically destroy his destiny and convert himself into a fated person.
By this means his old, apparently stable internal chemistry is conserved,
but only in the way a dead thing is.


## PERVERSIONS AND ADDICTIONS

A special case of character pathology is perversity, and Independent
analysts have contributed to its theoretical and practical understanding.
Glover (1932b, 1939, 1943, 1956, 1968), Gillespie (1940, 1952, 1956a,b),
Limentani (1968, 1977, 1979a, 1979b) and Khan (1974b, 1979, 1983) have
all written extensively about the subject.

## GLOVER

Edward Glover's (1939, 1956, 1968) original accounts of classical theory and ego development apply to all branches of psychopathology, including the perversions and addictions. He meticulously examines the many anxiety situations against which perversions are a defence and a form of prophylaxis. It was he who emphasized, perhaps for the first time, the importance of the *sexualization of anxiety* as the basic act, safety valve and self-saver, of the pervert. Khan utilizes this in his theory, and it is this, perhaps more than anything, that distinguishes perversion from neurosis and psychosis. By sexualization fears of annihilatory intensity are temporarily stilled by orgasms emerging from an intensely exquisite erotic experience.

Glover also introduces us, as early as 1932, to one central function of this sexualizing, or eroticization, process: this is the *preservation of the reality sense*. It has been emphasized since by Khan and, later, by Joyce McDougall (1986). Glover also draws our attention to the central part played by *castration anxiety* in the perversions. What is more, in seeing the dread of annihilation at the core of the castration anxiety, Glover readily spots the psychosis inherent in perversions and how the sexualized act can act as a preservation of sanity. As Glover says, *Perversion covers a flaw in the reality sense*. It may be added that, classical theorist as he was, he paid little attention to environmental factors while Khan, as we shall see, was very concerned about these.

In his use of ego-developmental lines he sees drug addiction as intermediate between perversions and neuroses. Addictions, like perversions, are means of preserving the reality sense in the face of psychotic anxieties, but here there are present also strong repressions – of pronounced homosexual fears, for instance. This time it is pharmacological effects that are used to promote manic ecstasies rather than sexual acts with a compliant partner, as happens in the perversions.

By his meticulous attention to detail, Glover reminds us that perversions always involve sexual acts with real other people or real objects, animate or inanimate. However, in these acts the core genital-to-genital arousal of male and female is avoided. It is recognition of this that keeps a focus upon the fear and horror of the genitals and embedded in this is the crucial element of castration anxiety.

## GILLESPIE

Summarizing analytic thinking on perversions, William Gillespie (1956) brings this up to date with his own conclusions illustrated from his clinical work. He starts by taking us back to Freud. In *Three Essays* (1905), Freud saw the perversions as representing the persistence into adulthood of polymorphous-perverse infantile sexuality at the expense of mature genitality – these impulses having *escaped the defences* that might otherwise have been converted into neurotic symptoms. However, in his paper on Leonardo (1910), Freud had begun to see that perversions might also act as defences in their own right. Sachs (1923) then continued the line of thought. In neurosis, Sachs noted, repressed phantasy breaks through only as a symptom that is *ego-dystonic*, whereas in perversion it is ego-syntonic and even pleasurable. Sachs saw perversion as the preservation in consciousness of a specially suitable piece of infantile material on to which special pleasure is placed.

Gillespie points out that in Freud's later writings the super-ego does not come into his argument on perversions. This is surprising because, given perversion's oedipal roots, one might expect a particularly close connection. However, in other classical writings this connection becomes quite clear – perversion constitutes a defence against guilt as well as against annihilation and castration anxiety.

Gillespie summarizes by enlarging on Sachs's main thesis that a perversion consists in the acceptance and adoption of certain elements of infantile sexuality while other aspects are repressed or warded off in other defensive ways. What will pass into perversion is dictated in part at least by what will please the super-ego – this being particularly clear in masochism, but it is seen in other perversions as well. He stresses that castration anxiety is always a paramount experience. Within this, oral sadistic regressions contribute intensively to enhancing the castration anxiety. Like Glover, Gillespie emphasizes that the quintessence of perversion is the sexualization of this anxiety with consequent acting upon it.

He goes on to show how *splitting*, denial and omnipotent idealization play strong parts in perversion formation. Here he is drawing upon Klein and agrees with her that these are *schizoid* phenomena. In the 1950s Gillespie is opening the way for Khan's formulations twenty years later.

Gillespie, like Glover, emphasizes the closeness to psychosis. He notes that in perversion there is a contrasting combination of repression and psychotic-level defences. Here it is splitting that holds the day, and he points out how Freud (1940), as well as Klein (1946), introduced us to this concept. Gillespie summarized much in the metaphor of the pure 'upstairs' always being safely present to allow the darker deeds to go on 'downstairs' with equanimity. Concluding, he again stresses the castration complex, but then moves across to see that fetishism at least involves a certain use of transitional objects. He does not go further, but Khan and also Phyllis Greenacre (1968) have worked this out more fully.


## LIMENTANI

Adam Limentani's papers on both perversions and addictions are based on extensive clinical experience over many years (1966, 1976, 1979a, 1979b, 1984; see also his collection *Between Freud and Klein*, 1989). About *addictions*, he brings together much clinical material which lends support to recognizing the core importance of *manic* mechanisms. This is a line of thought which was first put forward by Glover.

### TRANSSEXUALISM

He has also written clinically upon transsexualism. Being clinical, these papers tend to eschew theory, though Limentani does feel it important to argue against Stoller's (1974) theory on this subject. He puts forward the view, backed by case documentation, that transsexualism develops on a background of profound early disturbances of *symbol formation*. These disturbances arise out of phantasies involved in a *symbiotic fusion* with the mother. This is enhanced by intrusive or absent *paternal* influence.

Limentani is at pains to tell the reader how difficult it is to convey the distress that goes with the transsexual's belief that he possesses a mind that is alien to his body. Here Limentani, unlike some other authors, sees no particular desire for revenge upon women nor latent hostility to men in the transsexual. What he does see in the male is that the mother has become part of the narcissistic self-organization of the young boy. The transsexual then delegates the *masculine* side of himself to her. In both male and female there is an apparent strength and depth of identification with the parent of the opposite sex, but Limentani, again unlike other authors, does not think that envy plays a large part in this. Rather, in his view, the lack of a firm, consistent or loving *father* is of particular importance in the transsexual outcome. Father's role is vital, he thinks, for the control of cross-gender identifications and projections, and in transsexuality these have become very seriously disordered. He does not think that it is right to regard such sufferers as psychotic, but the annihilatory fears that pervade their lives are of a psychotic intensity.

**BISEXUALITY**

In considering bisexuality, Limentani, as is his custom, investigates common aetiological factors behind the condition. He says there is usually evidence of severe personality disturbance in one or both parents. Patients tend to be highly intelligent, but often precociously so. There has often been evidence of exquisite awareness of early bodily experiences, and also of early unbearable separation anxiety. Splitting of male and female elements in the personality figures prominently, and the patients have a marked capacity to dissociate the male and female parts of themselves. If the heterosexual aspect is viewed separately, it has a definitely 'pseudo' quality about it.

The object choice of bisexuals can be classed as either of the 'attachment' or of the 'narcissistic' type. The two types coexist and usually alternate in any one individual, very often with protracted and recurrent promiscuous sexual behaviour. Bisexuality cannot be regarded simply as the result of unresolved oedipal conflicts. Rather, if transference manifestations are any guide, bisexuality represents a desire to keep control of and gain satisfaction equally from *both mother and father*. There is an inability to give up either. Impressive heterosexual exploits suggest a pseudo-genitality and a predominance of pre-oedipal dependency disturbances. Even here, however, this does not mean that father is unimportant; bisexuals often show intense desire for an ideal father. In fact a history of ineffectual or absent fathers is common. But low frustration tolerance, possibly of a constitutional kind, is also common. Limentani thinks that, as with other borderline conditions, therapeutic prognosis is often doubtful, but he is more optimistic than some authorities – so long as the transference is worked with intensively.

## HOMOSEXUALITY

Limentani affirms that, in normal conditions, a homosexual nucleus originates in the formative years and then, if repression is adequate, it will act as a psychic regulator which may be a source of enrichment to the personality. In more abnormal states the nucleus of homosexuality can reinforce other shaky neurotic defences and its removal needs to be approached with caution. If the homosexuality is holding a latent hetero-sexuality at bay, then the prognosis for therapy may be good. But where there is no such latent heterosexual core, when the individual can be termed 'truly' homosexual, then there is little likelihood of change to a true heterosexuality.

## VAGINA-MAN

Another valuable concept introduced by Limentani is that of the vagina-man (1989). Such a character is the male counterpart of the phallic woman. He is basically narcissistic, intelligent, charming and friendly. He is easily affected by contacts with people, when he can often get engulfed or engulfing. He is usually very attentive to women, so that his sexual performance is better than average, but his partner is often a masculine woman who prefers the more feminine male anyway. An outstanding attribute of the vagina-man is his passivity, which well matches the more masculine woman that he tends to prefer. On the other hand, his passivity is unwelcome when he is relating to men, especially those in authority. The essence of the vagina-man is his desire to participate in using a perfected vaginal activity. He can only do this by displacement, of course: by the use of, not only anus or mouth, but other receptor organs as well – eyes, ears, touch and nose. It is his fascination with receptivity that accounts for his overriding passivity.

# KHAN

## NARCISSISTIC REPAIR AND COLLUSION

Using Fairbairn's original framework, Khan (1979) investigates the per-versions as a special case of a schizoid structure.

There is, Khan thinks, a pronounced reparative drive in perversion formation. But it is an attempted *repair of a narcissistic feeling* about the self, and not only about the object – as Klein had originally said was the main function of reparation. In Khan's experience of patients with perversions, he noted that they had all been much loved by their mothers. There was lavish body-love but in an *impersonal* sort of way. They were 'idolized' by their mothers, rather than idealized, as could sometimes happen with the schizoid 'special' patients. With this body-idolization there is a dissociation between the feelings of body and of self. Mother and child gradually turn each other into accomplices in this. An absence of imaginative, thoughtful playing together and of creative transitional activity is noticeable. Although remarkably intuitive to their mothers' moods, such children tend to become passive and lacking in initiative towards her. In puberty they seem to have very little capacity for masturbation with imaginative sexual reverie. They feel full of themselves – they are special, but with not much to offer. However, when they find a partner, they unerringly find someone who is drawn to, and has a talent for, playing the part of a sort of transitional object – a thing to be manipulated. It is interesting to note that Khan's formulations bear comparison with Laufer's (1984) concept of the central masturbatory phantasy which has a form closer to classical theory.

What seems to be re-enacted here is a recreation of the mother's idolization of the child's body as her own created object – another sort of transitional object. Both partners have a secret, silent, ritualized acceptance of the make-believe quality of the relation. Both have a sense of its special reparativeness and the sadism involved is kept to a minimum. Though both promise eternal fidelity, they both know that separation will come and it will not be too traumatic. It is a relation that is engineered from the head and acted upon, exploited in the service of pre-programmed, orgasmic sexuality. The overt fantasies and imaginings of perversions remain banal, compulsive and limited.

Drawing upon Gillespie (1952) and Glover (1943, 1956), Khan goes on to look further into the intimacy and mutuality of complicity in the perversions. It is of interest to note how there is here a distinctly two-person theory, also an omnipotent manipulation of whole people to be like things, which shows perversion's closeness to psychosis. Further, there is an exploitation of acts of sexuality to still all mental pain and anxiety. In doing this the danger of breaking into psychosis is reduced. Perversion formation preserves the reality sense.

Intimacy can be a special perverse technique. Lacking a true capacity to focus upon and relate emotionally in the ordinary run of life to loved people, the perverted person *plays* at being intimate instead. In this he 'tries to *make known* to himself and *announce and press into another* something pertaining to his inmost nature as well as discharging its instinctual tension in a compulsive and exigent way' (Khan, 1979, p. 22). A make-believe situation is offered in which the two individuals temporarily renounce their separate identities. Joyce McDougall is close to this formulation when she describes the neo-sexualities (1986); Chasseguet-Smirgel does likewise (1984). In this intimacy there is experience of idolized over-valuation of self and object, insatiability, solitary play – and with over-valuation there is envy. It is this envy which often makes perverts behave viciously towards their objects. Khan stresses the charade involved: it is auto-erotism *à deux*.

'The pervert's loved one has essentially the value of a transitional object (Winnicott, 1951). 'Through its (his or her) readiness to comply it lends itself to be invented, manipulated, used and abused, ravaged and discarded, cherished and idealized, symbolically identified with and deanimated all at once' (Khan, 1979, p. 26).

## MANIC DEFENCE AND ACTING WITH ANOTHER

What makes the difference between this perverse play and the transitional phenomena of true creative play? Khan suggests the following are critical: perversion is a sexual variant of the *manic defence*; there is a flight of external from intra-psychic reality; there is also an omnipotent manipulation of the external object to conform with inner reality so that this can be held in suspended animation. This allows for the *denial* of profound affects, particularly of depression. There is thus crucially a holding at bay of the feelings of loss, guilt, responsibility and accepting reality, whose exercise is essential to the full functioning of a *depressive position*.

All this is achieved in the *acting out* of the pervert. Affect and need tensions are displaced and projected into external reality – in this case another external person. Passive experience is then transformed into more tolerable action. It is essentially a counter-phobic activity of avoiding the fear of the self's own nothingness, but also it obliterates its own aggressiveness. At the same time there is a semblance of communication with another real person.

## ACTING OUT AND THE COLLAGE OF THE PERSONALITY

The continuous proclivity to act out means that a perverse person's feeling structure is not integrated; rather, the affective self-object parts form a *collage* (1979). Here, each part has its own form, but it is not coherently related to other parts. If we borrowed Bollas's terms, we could say that the 'aesthetic' of the interpersonal-emotional aspects of the personality is fractured. Khan summarizes matters in a slightly different way.

> The ego of the pervert acts out his dream and involves another person in its actualization. It is possible to argue that if the pervert dramatizes and actually fufils his body-dreams with a real person, he also cannot wake out of them. Here we meet another formidable therapeutic task in the treatment of the pervert: how to wean and wake him from his specific mode of dramatizing his dreams.
>
> (Khan, 1979, p. 30)

Khan goes on to note that perverse elements are often detectable in other schizoid patients who nevertheless differ from the true pervert. There are certain schizoid people who appear at first like normal effective people. But polymorphous and bisexual strivings, arising out of *body-image confusions*, play a part in these people's lives. This sort of schizoid person seems friendly, clever and well turned out. But they have a compliance and apathy that can readily give way to aggressiveness and hostility. In analysis they easily become flat, silent, self-pitying and morose.

However, they readily get passionately involved with people, and this is pursued with manic intensity while it lasts. Every such experience is ecstatic and grossly sexualized. Unlike the true perversions, these states usually occur with an ordinary sexual partner and, though ecstatic at the time, they are felt with bewilderment and shame afterwards. Such acts are thus both acceptable to one part of the self and quite unacceptable to another. One particular feature is often the special desire for anal intercourse with a person of the opposite sex. Likewise, the mouth is often compulsively used for direct genital orgasm. Contact and penetration with and between different body parts thus seems to be compulsively and ecstatically vital, not just in foreplay but in culmination. In this Khan thinks the schizoid person is trying to find again some aspect of his own body experience which has been fractured, lost or never developed. 'I am trying to find out something. I know my body from outside only. I have no sense of being in it. Also I know other people exist, like my wife exists, but I have to *feel* it before I can be sure of her existence' (1979, p. 36).

Khan here thinks that the mothers were adequate in infancy but failed in something in toddlerhood. In the anal stage particularly the mother seems to have maintained a primarily auto-erotic relation with her child. She seems to disregard separateness because of her need for the service of ecstatic auto-erotic intimacies. This seems to give rise to body mis-identifications with mother, but at the same time with his own body also. There can thus be a boy's estrangement from his penis, or an over-idolization of it; it would be likewise with a girl and her vagina. These patients seem over-eager to explore their insides but unable to find coherent representations of their mothers with their bodies in their inner world. In a seductive relation with mother, the experience of conflict with her and of mutual aggression is truncated, and the reality sense of the body image is blurred and stunted. It is possible, Khan thinks, that it is because of their healthy infancies that these patients do not move into convinced perversion.

### THE CREATION OF COLLATED INTERNAL OBJECTS

Returning to perversions proper, Khan summarizes his thesis (1979). Freud (1905) saw that at the root of perversions was a piece of mental work. This work is done by a precocious ego-development, as described by Martin James (1960). What is created is, Khan thinks, a 'collated internal object', a complement to his ego collage, through which the pervert can experience and actualize only through specific sexual events. By this means perversions can be isolated psychoses which are compatible with normal living. The pervert's obsession is in some way akin to an artist's pursuit of his vision and actualization of it. Both devote much of their lives to the mental care and fruition of their obsessive passions. But here the similarity ends. With the pervert, he internalizes his mother's *idolized* image of him. The relation of this idolized self and object usurps much of the creative reparation devoted to others or their symbols which occurs in ordinary creativity. The key difference is that the one is a sexual acting, the other is not.

In this light the personality of the perverse person shows, at root, dissociations or splits. The original affective ego nuclei (Glover, 1943) have become fragmented, split or dissociated. There is a similar dissociation of the patient's felt environment. His early environmental objects are split and introjected in part aspects. This naturally occurs primarily with the representations of both father and mother. These disparate introjects slowly amalgamate into a *collated* internal object. The collage of self-and-object bits, Khan thinks, then comes to be used by the pervert as the equivalent of a transitional object. Within this collage, idolization of the part aspects of self and object takes place.

The normal transitional object is of course experienced as neither and both inside and outside the self. The collated object on the other hand is definitely internal but is then projected or externalized into a real external sexualized relationship.

### PERVERSION AND SADISM

Khan has said little about the part sadism and hate play in the perversions. At first sight, this seems surprising as most authors in the field give these a major role. Whereas Khan agrees with them, he makes the point that the mutually manipulative acting by both partners negates the effect of the sadism on each other. Paraphrasing Khan's point of view, one could say that sadism and hate, while present, are largely held in suspension by manipulative acting. Space does not allow us to discuss Khan's many contributions to specific perversions, which are original elaborations of his general thoughts about the subject.

## CONCLUSION

We have attempted to portray the Independents' extensive contributions to the question of character and its vicissitudes. Fairbairn and Winnicott in particular made profound general contributions to the subject. The former did this with his model of a psychic structure of a multiplicity of interacting sub-selves with objects. The latter introduced the concept of true self developing through transitional activity, which was contrasted with pathological false-self defence formations. Both men came to psychoanalysis when Klein's early ideas were prominently discussed in the British Psycho-Analytical Society.

Fairbairn even antedated Klein's paranoid-schizoid position. He postulated that its structuring was essential in development, and agrees with her that it precedes the depressive position. Winnicott, on the other hand, maintained that schizoid phenomena formed not a basic stage but a pathological byway. He conceived of early development in a different way, regarding the gradual cohesion of true-self experiences as being essentially formative for psychic structure. One could say, perhaps, that he comes nearer to Glover's concept of ego development from clusters of ego nuclei. Like most Independents, both Fairbairn and Winnicott accept Klein's concept of the depressive position.

It was Khan who fundamentally drew Fairbairn and Winnicott together and used them fruitfully in developing his theory of the schizoid nature of the perversions and the consequent development of collated character parts. Bollas has shown the importance of transitional activity in the healthy growth of true-self experiences and also how symbolization of affect and mood is dependent upon it. He sees character defects as consequences of inhibitions, distortions and *damage to the capacity to symbolize affects*. It is of note that this line of thinking has been pioneered by French and also American analysts and psychosomatists (Nemiah and Sifneos, 1970; McDougall, 1986, 1989) and influences their investigation of psychosomatic illness.

Balint, coming to the Independents from Ferenczi and the Hungarian school, has contributed to the study of the pathology of character with his concept of the basic fault. Whereas he did not introduce a model of psychic structure as such, he is clear that traumata from the maternal environment lead to faultiness of psychic structure which affects the infant as a whole. His contribution to the understanding of the genesis of borderline problems ranges alongside Fairbairn's schizoid character and Winnicott's false-self structure: all are based on the concept of early environmental traumata.

Most of the authors here give importance to the manic defences in pathogenesis. Klein introduced this concept (1935) and Winnicott elaborated it from his own conceptual viewpoint in his paper of 1935 (1958a). We have already pointed out that most Independents accept that the mastery of the depressive position is a necessary constellation of events prior to the classical oedipal conflict and is a pre-condition of healthy development. It is therefore a logical consequence that the manic defence, a failure to master the depressive position, is prominent in character pathology. The Independents' specific contribution here has been the link with environmental traumata in early childhood.

# 8  The Psychoanalytic Process – for the Patient

THIS AND THE two chapters following will be about the psychoanalytic process itself. They are divided up somewhat arbitrarily. This one will concern itself primarily with happenings on the patient's part and their understanding. The next will concentrate more upon events and knowledge within the analyst, and the third will dwell upon the interactions and understanding between both partners in the psychoanalytic venture. There is no pretence that this is an exhaustive study of psychoanalysis and its technique. It cannot even portray an Independent consensus, for there is hardly any, but it surveys certain lines of thought and method that have been voiced in recent years.

## EARLY DEVELOPMENT OF TECHNIQUE

When Breuer put the famous Anna O. under deep hypnosis, and so applied catharsis to treat her many hysterical symptoms, he thought that she was releasing intense strangulated affects which had not been abreacted appropriately at the time of the original traumata. Anna O. herself called her treatment chimney sweeping. Freud, holding a different theoretical position from the beginning about the aetiology of hysteria, also used catharsis in hypnosis, but soon discovered that the results were not as good as had been hoped for. The total success, Freud said, 'turned out to be entirely dependent upon the patient's relation to the physician and thus resembled the effect of "suggestion". If the relation was disturbed, all the symptoms reappeared, just as though they had never been cleared up' (Freud 1923a, p. 237). Moreover, there were patients who could not be properly hypnotized. In his *An Autobiographical Study* (1925) Freud related the incident which seems to have been, at least in part, instrumental in his decision to give up hypnosis: one day, when waking from a hypnotic trance, one of his patients threw her arms round Freud's neck. However, Freud always emphasized that the early treatment by hypnosis was of the greatest theoretical value, for it convinced him beyond any doubt that there was psychic material and content in the patient of which he had no conscious awareness.

## FREE ASSOCIATION AND THE FUNDAMENTAL RULE

When Freud visited Bernheim's clinic in Nancy he learned that the things which the patients experienced in the state of somnambulism were only apparently forgotten. If the physician insisted forcibly, the patients could remember them. It was from this that Freud took his guide, and he now resorted to forcing his unhypnotized patients to remember: he put his hand on their forehead and told them they would be able to remember when he put pressure there. It was the so-called pressure technique. He had to make an effort to urge and compel the patient to remember. The amount of effort required varied from one case to another and this was seen by Freud as a measure of the patient's resistance. Paula Heimann later (1950) pointed out that this could be seen as an example of counter-transference. Freud concluded that the patients had repressed ideas which were unacceptable to them so that remembering caused them unpleasant affects.

While he was applying the pressure technique, Freud discovered that patients had an abundance of ideas, but these were often held back from being communicated or from ever becoming conscious. They were simply felt to be too objectionable by the patients. Freud then gave up his pressure technique and encouraged the patients to pay attention to and 'listen' to whatever came to their minds – at the surface of their consciousness. They were asked to relate this with complete honesty and not hold anything back even though it might be judged disagreeable, nonsensical, unimportant or irrelevant.

This was a momentous step, for it changed the doctor–patient relationship from one of authority to one of partnership. In a short communica-

tion (Freud, 1920b), a reply to Havelock Ellis's criticism that free association makes psychoanalysis into a form of art, Freud acknowledges that
he did not discover free association since it has been used for centuries.
But he also draws attention to his theory of strict determinism behind the
patients' free associations. In this context he referred to a book by Börne,
a hero of his youth, which he had in part forgotten until Ferenczi showed
him one of the essays from it. Börne said 'And here follows the practical
application that was promised. Take a few sheets of paper and for three
days on end write down, without fabrication or hypocrisy, everything
that comes into your head. Write down what you think of yourself, of
your wife, of the Turkish War, of Goethe, of Fonk's trial, of the Last
Judgement, of your superiors – and when three days have passed you will
be quite out of your senses with astonishment at the new and unheard-of
thoughts you have had. This is the art of becoming an original writer in
three days' (Freud, 1920b, p. 265). Freud also mentioned that some
phrases, which for a long time he had thought were his own, were in fact
Börne's. For example, 'A disgraceful cowardliness in regard to thinking
holds us all back. The censorship of governments is less oppressive than
the censorship exercised by public opinion over our intellectual productions' or 'It is not lack of intellect but lack of character that prevents most
writers from being better than they are. . .Sincerity is the source of all
genius, and men would be cleverer if they were more moral' (1920b,
p. 265). Freud ends by saying that this hint might have brought to light
the fragment of cryptomnesia which may be suspected of lying behind
originality. Maybe it was the radical-liberal views of this hero of his
youth which influenced Freud, unknown to himself, when he developed
the partnership technique of free association in psychoanalysis.

The *fundamental rule* of free association for the patient also changed
the attitude of the analyst to the treatment situation. He no longer put
pressure upon the patient, but instead listened to him with *evenly suspended attention*, 'to surrender himself to his own unconscious mental
activity' (Freud, 1923a, p. 239). It was thought that this attitude would
best avoid reflection and construction of conscious expectation. Freud
thought that this was the best possible way for the analyst to 'catch the
drift of the patient's unconscious with his own unconscious' (1923a,
p. 239). It was thus possible to understand the patient's associations as
allusions and guess the material that was concealed in the patient.

## INTERPRETATION

Freud always maintained that there can be no strict rules about how to interpret, and it has been seen from the beginning as 'the art of psycho-analysis'. Over the years some technical guidelines have been agreed upon, which have been arrived at by experience, but it is here that the analyst's own style and the meeting of the patient's and analyst's uncon-sciouses is given full weight. However, from the beginning it was the patient's *resistance* to forgotten (defended against) material which in-itiated interpretation. The aim of this was to make the forgotten, uncon-scious material conscious and hence available to the patient's judgement. As long as the flow of free association was undisturbed, there was no need for the analyst to intervene. Classical analysis has always stressed that a vital part of the art of interpretation is its timing. If an interpreta-tion is given too early, before the patient is nearly there himself to receive it, he will either dismiss it – not hear it, one could say – or he will develop a hostile resistance to it. Most important thoughts and memories are recovered by the patient himself. The analyst is needed primarily to draw attention to that which is being resisted and therefore not available to be discovered by the patient's further free association on his own.

## TRANSFERENCE

Even before introducing the fundamental rule, Freud had observed that from time to time the patient suddenly stopped talking and claimed that nothing came to mind, it was a blank. On investigation, Freud found that, on such occasions, the patient had always been preoccupied with Freud himself: he either had a grievance against him, a forbidden wish towards him, or was experiencing him like a father or mother from the past. At first, Freud was irritated by this time-consuming, unnecessary complication, but then he saw that it invariably advanced the analysis. He understood it as a special form of resistance which the patient showed when further associa-tions, including remembering, had to be resisted because they came too close to repressed material. Instead of remembering, the patient then acted the memory in the emotional relationship with the analyst.

Freud had already seen that in a dream the unconscious wish has to be first transferred on to a day residue before it can find expression and satisfaction. In a similar light he now saw that transference of repressed, forbidden wishes, mainly about parental figures, on to the figure of the analyst took place, and that these were then re-enacted in the here and now of the analytic situation. Freud (1912a) said that it was not necessarily the most important bit of repressed material that manifested itself as a piece of transference; instead, it is that which is best suited for transference that is selected.

Freud (1912a) differentiated the positive, affectionate transference from the negative, hostile one. He divided the positive into a mild one of friendly, affectionate feelings which are admissible to consciousness and the transference of those feelings which betray repressed unconscious erotic sources. It is the latter and also the hostile transference which produce resistance, and interpretation is required to remove the resistances, particularly to remove them from the person of the analyst. The mild affectionate positive transference, however, is allowed to persist, for it is the vehicle of success. In this connection, Freud stated that it cannot be denied that the results of psychoanalysis rest upon suggestion, and this should be understood as influencing a person by means of the transference phenomena. But, unlike suggestion as used in hypnosis, it is here employed to achieve the patient's final independence and a permanent improvement in his psychical situation (1912a).

After the introduction of the structural model of the mind (1923b) and the revision of anxiety theory to that of signal anxiety (1926), positive and negative transferences were conceived of as repetitions of the patient's unresolved childhood relationships. Here the patient transfers on to the analyst the most important figures of his past and then relates to him with feelings and reactions towards these, which, however, are experienced as real in the here and now. The patient therefore reproduces an important part of his past life history and acts it instead of remembering and reporting it (1940).

It is the original ambivalent relationship to his parents which accounts for the patient's positive and negative transference repetitions. Freud maintained that transference should be interpreted early but not too early, so that neither love nor hate reach extreme heights. The analyst needs to gather material from various sources like dreams and parapraxes before making reconstructive interpretations. When we succeed in 'enlightening the patient on the true nature of the phenomenon of transference, we shall have struck a powerful weapon out of the hand of his resistance and shall have converted danger to gain. For a patient never forgets what he has experienced in the form of transference' (1940, p. 177).

The tripartite structure assumed in the later model of the mind (1923b) shifted the emphasis of classical analysis somewhat away from interpreting unconscious material which is resisted against. After this the stress became laid upon strengthening the ego in its various intra- and intersystemic relationships. Other resistances as well as that of transference now began to take on importance. There was ego-resistance in the form of gains from remaining ill and id-resistance in order to maintain habitual modes of obtaining drive satisfaction. Furthermore, resistances in the form of unconscious guilt feelings, and then as the expression of the need for punishment, have for many years been given predominant attention. This is known as defence analysis. Nevertheless, transference resistance has remained a nodal point of all analytic work.


## THE EFFECT OF TRANSFERENCE INTERPRETATION

Freud was mindful of the patient doing much of the analysis himself and believed in allowing mild positive transference feelings for the analyst to go on unhindered since they aided a co-operative analytic venture. It became a hallmark of the 'classical' school as a whole to abstain from making interpretations about the analytic transference unless it was manifesting itself as a *resistance*.

Sylvia Payne (1943, in King and Steiner, 1990) noted that certain departures from the classical method were being practised in Britain from the early 1920s onwards. Looking back on her early experiences she remembered the classical technique of Hanns Sachs in Berlin just as described above. What is more, his interpretations were mainly confined to summarizing only at the end of each session. Freud himself was recognized for being more active than this (Ruitenbeek, 1973). When Payne returned to London she was struck by the amount of interpretation throughout a session being reported by her colleagues. Not only this, she learned there was much interpretation of the transference relation from very early on and throughout the analysis. There was little worry about waiting for resistance to emerge. This was perhaps because the British had, maybe under Jones's influence, taken very early to the investigation of the patient's aggressiveness as a fundamental aspect of technique. They might then have taken to understanding early the patient's unconscious hostility, as distinct from his positive transference to the analyst, and interpreted it with the aim of easing anxiety and so allowing the analysis to progress.

It is of interest here that sensitivity to negative feelings towards the analyst seems to have been becoming marked even before the arrival of Klein. It was she, of course, who made the early interpretation of unconscious hostility to the analyst an important factor in her work, and this was one of the main features over which Anna Freud soon took issue (A. Freud, 1927, in King and Steiner, 1990).

It is probably true that many British Independents have continued this tradition of interpreting negative feelings in the patient about the analysis from quite early on. However, it is not on the whole regarded as good practice to make any such comments until the patient seems ready to receive and use them. Thus, although similar to Klein in their early sensitivity to negative feelings, many Independents would see themselves as closer to the more recent development of the classical model (Greenson, 1967) in recognizing the need to facilitate the therapeutic alliance and use the patient's positive feelings about the analysis.


## THE TEACHING OF SHARPE

Very early on, Ella Sharpe was giving a portrayal of many of the aspects of what were to become typical British Independent methods. Some regard her lectures to students on 'The technique of psycho-analysis' (1930) as a classic and they are still prized by students who read them, but they are perhaps not now well known. As well as clearly expounding and illustrating the fundamental aspects of psychoanalytic method, she mentions almost in passing several lines of thought that have become typically Independent since. She sees the analytic relationship as a form of unfolding a serious *dramatic play*. Sharpe also sees herself, the analyst, entering into a profound *dialogue with her own feelings* and hence having them as available for her use as possible. This was at a time before the espousal of the use of the countertransference when analytic neutrality was seen as a self-denial of feelings.

Within the realm of emotional attention to the patient and to his or her analytic transference from the first session onward. Sharpe saw *spon-*

*taneity* as essential. She understood neutrality as being the outcome of an open-minded flexibility of point of view, not of a laborious adherence to self-denial of emotionality. Perhaps most strikingly, she explicitly saw the central task of analysis as the freeing of a person's *ordinary creativity* – related by her to the Kleinian theme of repairing damaged objects. She perceived neurosis as fundamentally concerned with a person's *failure to know what properly to do with his life*. Here is a forerunner of sensitivity to the self-disorders. 'The people who enjoy the greatest ease. . .are those who have justified their existence to themselves. . .They have won through to a right to live. . .The psycho-neuroses I see as psychical miscarriages in the attempt to justify the right of the ego to exist' (1950, pp. 81–2). Nowadays it is common for a patient to give this as sufficient reason for wanting analysis; in those days other reasons, like suffering from psychoneurotic symptoms, were usually found first.

## THE THERAPEUTIC ACTION
## OF TRANSFERENCE INTERPRETATION

An important contribution, fundamental to the understanding of the development of ideas about technique in Britain, is James Strachey's paper 'The nature of the therapeutic action of psycho-analysis' (1934, 1969). He read it to the British Society in 1933, not long after Sharpe gave her lectures and seven years after Klein had come to settle in London. (His wife and he had helped to arrange for Klein to come in the first place.) The paper shows how deeply he, like many other British analysts, was affected by her thinking.

Strachey's paper has a dense clarity of thought which reveals that in the mid-1930s those later to divide into Kleinians and Independents shared a comprehension of transference interpretation. It was only later that they went their separate ways, when the Independents turned to more environmental, interactive and developmental interests, which also had an influence on their technique.

Strachey begins with a survey of ideas about technique, starting with a description of classical method. He then uses what he learnt from Klein to develop a view of transference generally and the analytic transference neurosis in particular. He starts from the classical description of the libidinal transference, but then points out that, in his opinion, for the child, hostile impulses, rather than libidinous ones, towards primary objects give rise to equally hostile super-ego feelings in return. 'His ego is left exposed to the pressure of a savage id on the one hand and a correspondingly savage superego on the other' (1969, p. 80). A neurotic vicious circle comes into being. It is perpetuated by oral mechanisms of introjection and projection. In unconscious phantasy, the savage super-ego is 'swallowed' into the ego by introjection. This is intolerable so its savageness is projected again, only to create an even purer and thus more severe super-ego. This raises renewed anxiety and is projected again, and so a vicious circle arises. By this means phantasy objects in the outer world become predominantly dangerous and hostile. The tyranny of an implacable super-ego constitutes the neurotic predicament. This model of unconscious phantasy would still be adhered to by many Independents, as one of the major components in neurotic anxiety – but not necessarily the only one.

Strachey now discusses the therapy of this state of affairs. To begin with, the analyst, by his instructions to free associate and his tolerant attitude, acts as an 'auxiliary super-ego', kinder than the patient's own. The patient gets a glimpse of a less hostile critical agency. But soon the fear of the implacable super-ego gains ascendancy again. However, there is now ground to facilitate change: the analyst has become a composite image, he is an object of the patient's libidinous and hostile id impulses, a representative of his implacable super-ego, but he is also perceived as a tolerant person. If the analyst catches the moment when the patient's id impulses are in an ascendant state, and hence when the implacable super-ego is at its clearest, and he then makes an interpretation linking himself with the primitive objects, there is a chance that the patient will be able to see the difference between his phantasy of the analyst as an implacable super-ego and what he is really like.

This immediate, here-and-now transference interpretation facilitates a form of reality testing by the patient. Strachey calls it a *mutative interpretation*. This is effective only in small doses, repeatedly applied in slightly different contexts each time. It cannot be effective if 'id energy is too intense' – that is, when desire for gratification is too imperious, for the patient's ego is then too weak and unstable to assimilate the complexity of the situation. Interpretations are mutative only when 'quantities of energy are minimal'. Psychic change comes about by a series of very small steps.

Strachey does not contend that other, non-transference, forms of interpretation are useless. He makes it plain that they must form the matrix within which mutative interpretations can grow. But the mutative transference interpretation, he says, is the essential ingredient of psychic change.

## CLASSICAL AND OBJECT-RELATIONS POINTS OF VIEW COMPARED

We have noted that Strachey was quite clear about using a combination of classical analytical thinking with Melanie Klein's formulations. Before going further it will be useful briefly to compare the British object-relations view of transference and its interpretation, which was particularly associated with Melanie Klein but which was also expressed by Strachey, with the classical view. The distinctions between the two have been of concern for many years and our summary here predominantly utilizes the symposium on the subject at the 1955 International Psycho-Analytic Congress, especially the overview by Zetzel (1956).

Originally, transference was conceived of as a displacement on to the analyst of repressed wishes and these soon came to be recognized as phantasies from early childhood. The transference neurosis was seen as a compromise formation like any neurotic symptom. Freud himself saw the sexual transference as predominantly resistant in nature and asserted that the patient's transference to the analyst should be interpreted only when it was halting ongoing, reflective analytic work by the patient. Resistance, a result of defence activity, could be diminished by interpretation of the content of the repressed. With the coming of the structural point of view, the super-ego, regarded as the heir to oedipal conflicts, was now seen as playing a part in the transference situation. The analyst was thus not only the object, by displacement, of infantile sexual wishes, but also the representative of parental prohibitions.

In the 1920s and 1930s, Sterba and Bibring, essential developers of classical technique, postulated a therapeutic split whereby an identification with the analyst was an essential feature of the transference. This was clarified further by Bibring himself who introduced the concept of therapeutic alliance between patient and analyst. A differentiation could then be made between the transference neurosis and the transference as therapeutic alliance. It was the transference neurosis that provided the seat of resistance.

In agreement with Freud, the classical analysts of the time were clear that analysis can proceed only from the surface to the depths. Deep transference interpretation early on was considered, and is still considered by many, at best to be meaningless to a patient and at worst to increase resistance. Though interpretation of the transference is here considered to be vital, it is not the only agent of change. Reconstruction and the working through of the neurosis in terms of the experience of every level of childhood fixation and development are also considered essential.

In summary, the classic point of view, centrally practised by perhaps the majority of analysts throughout the world, could be said to encompass the following. Premature interpretation is to be avoided. Patients must be free to commence and continue analysis for themselves. Interpretation at depth commences only when resistance is encountered. The therapeutic alliance is to be distinguished from the transference neurosis and the former needs to be encouraged. Interpretation of the transference is only one avenue of therapeutic progress, others are extra-transference investigation, reconstruction and working through at every stage of development.

Melanie Klein's approach to transference interpretation rests upon her conception of primitive phantasy: this is that the infant and child has ideas about, or misinterprets, events under the influence of his drives. Any relationship, in childhood and later, is timelessly open to being endowed with and misinterpreted by such phantasies – the relationship with the analyst included. The Kleinian view, agreeing with Strachey, would thus probably be that, since a phantasy is a misinterpretation, albeit an unconscious one, the best way to rectify this is also by interpretation. What is more, again like Strachey, the best occasion to rectify the phantasy is when it is directed straight towards the analyst and can be experienced as such, in all immediacy, by both the analyst and the patient. Hence the unique value put upon the here-and-now transference interpretation.

Heimann, then speaking as a Kleinian at the 1955 conference (Heimann, 1956), affirmed that psychic change essentially comes about *only* by precise, explicit transference interpretation made by the analyst, in the way described by Strachey. Later Kleinians (for example, Segal, 1981,

p. 70; Joseph, 1989) including many of those practising today, would agree with this.

British Independents must be recognized as, in part, growing out of this background, and nowadays they also still agree that transference interpretation is a *fundamental* for psychic change. But they do not, on the whole, subscribe to the view that only transference interpretation should be given automatically from the start. As will be seen, they recognize that, particularly in regressed states, the patient may attach quite different meanings to the words of an interpretation from those intended by the analyst. Transference interpretation, baldly given, is not seen as the universal panacea for resistance. So, Independents also value other therapeutic avenues, like reconstruction, extra-transference interpretation and other modes to evoke change in pathological structures.

It is of interest to note a certain dilemma that the British Independents find themselves in, due to their historical circumstances. They have been well rooted in the classical tradition, since many of their forebears went to study in Vienna or Berlin. But they also have roots in the Kleinian tradition, and it is with this that they, as object-relations exponents, are often equated by analysts from other countries. However, we will see that nowadays many of the methods of the Independents bear strong resemblances to classical technique, perhaps often more than to the Kleinian. These resemblances would be: emphasis upon the therapeutic alliance, care about premature interpretation of the transference, reconstruction and the careful working through of neurotic problems at each level of emotional development. However, the language used is often rather different from that of the classical tradition, for instance 'mutuality' is often used when others would speak of alliance. What is more, it must be admitted that many Independents are likely to be unaware of their classical roots and thus cannot attest to the affinities between the two. It must also be added that there are many differences from both classical and Kleinian methods. These will unfold in the coming pages.

## LATER STUDIES OF THE FUNCTION
## OF TRANSFERENCE INTERPRETATION

Independents have written steadily upon this subject. They have emphasized and spelt out its importance rather than introducing an original new theme, so we will not dwell long here. Balint (1939, 1968) had a good deal to say in his review of technique; Heimann (1956) and King (1973) summarized much work; Little (1951) and Khan (1960b) have written at length. Klauber (1981, 1987) did likewise, emphasizing many times that much change takes place without explicit and precise interpretation. Interpretations are however essential for the *consolidation* of emotional work that has already been done. There is a useful overview by Kohon (1986).

Stewart (1987) described and summarized six types of transference interpretation from a broad spectrum of object-relations points of view. They were:

i. Interpretations aimed at understanding a drive-anxiety-defence conflict between patient and analyst in an anaclitic type of object relationship.

ii. An extension of (i) in having two simultaneous conflicts of a similar and complementary nature.

iii. Interpretations aimed at understanding the sensibility and vulnerability of patient and analyst in a narcissistic type of object relationship.

iv. An extension of (iii) to include the interpretation of failure to achieve such understanding.

v. Interpretations aimed at understanding the atmosphere or mood between patient and analyst which might be in either type of object relationship.

vi. Interpretations aimed at understanding the patient's unconscious response to the analyst's interpretations.

(Stewart, 1987, p. 204)

Just as important as these, Stewart emphasizes the problem for the patient when the analyst overloads him with interpretations. He also says that this makes it plain that some types of transference interpretation are better not made. He places stress upon the transference value of silence on the part of the analyst at certain crucial moments.

Recently, Bollas (1987) has portrayed in some detail the importance of transference interpretations in the facilitation of the patient's self-analytic capacity. This is an ability to 'receive news from the self' (p. 236). Bollas says that this is the capacity for introspection. 'The arrival of news, from dreams, daydreams, passing incomplete thoughts, inspirations, observations of the other, and idiomatic acts in our lived life, belongs to the arena of experiencing oneself which follows recognition of our being' (p. 237). That which aims to keep out 'news' which the self cannot bear is termed defensive activity. One mode that Bollas emphasizes is projective identification. However, 'If I dare to be there where I am to hear news from myself, and if I can maintain that wish without aggressively seeking its accomplishment, then dream recollections, memories and the like will be evoked by this receptivity' (p. 238).

The analyst who involves the patient in long and complex interpretations will hinder this self-analytic capacity in the patient. What is more, Bollas thinks that a patient is very sensitive to the *idiom* of the activity of his particular analyst. The analyst cannot, and should not try to, expunge this particularity of his own but accept it as something that the patient will be using in his own analytic working. Transferences from the past will be taking place in modifying this idiom, and they will be enriching it. But the idiom is also present and *used* by the patient to express his past history and parts of his present self in the present living of the analytic relationship.

## THE PATIENT'S REGRESSION IN ANALYSIS

This is one of the most controversial aspects of explorations by British Independents. As is well known, regression is essentially a developmental concept, and in its broadest sense it is simply the reverse of progression or, psychologically speaking, a return to a state that was paramount earlier in development. It can encompass the whole of a person's psychological being or be restricted to a narrow range of functioning. What we are concerned with first here, however, is a benign form of regression, as first brought to attention by Anna O. in her talking cure, when she needed to repeat and act over again events and moods from her earlier life which she could not consciously recall. Regression in the therapy led to repetition and, with the analyst's help, thence to remembering. Breuer in his treatment of her was interested only in catharsis, but Freud, himself interested in *defences*, saw that re-enactment in the treatment involved regression by which the patient avoids painful memories. Ever since, regression has been seen as largely defensive and is dealt with by appropriate interpretation.

Ferenczi in Budapest determined to investigate the analytic treatment of patients who had been referred to him because they were in such a state of regression that they seemed unable to use the ordinary contained therapeutic regimen. He tried out at first a 'parameter' of active frustration. Then he resorted to other departures from normal technique, to forms of care and gratification to see what might work. In his diary (Dupont, 1988), Ferenczi made meticulous notes of each trial, of its apparent results, with arguments for and against that tactic. He was using an enthusiasm which could be seen as rash, but was painstakingly honest and empirical. As Michael Balint points out in his introduction to the diary, each experiment must be judged to have ended, by and large, in failure, but the methods had been tested and our knowledge took a step further forward. Ferenczi was being essentially scientific in his method.

Balint and Winnicott, particularly, followed up Ferenczi's search for the method of handling people who could not, or would not, progress within the usual limits of analytic technique. Though very different in character, and stating their ideas in very different languages, their findings bear striking similarities.

## WINNICOTT'S USE OF REGRESSION
## AS A TREATMENT DEVICE

Winnicott summarizes his thesis upon this subject in his paper, 'Metapsychological and clinical aspects of regression within the psychoanalytical set-up' (1954). He begins his argument by discriminating three categories of patient. First, there are those who 'operate as whole persons' and whose difficulties are in *inter*personal relations. For these, classical analysis is undoubtedly the treatment of choice. Winnicott thinks traumata have occurred, and difficulties have developed, predominantly in prelatency or oedipal times. Second, there are patients whose personal wholeness as people cannot totally be taken for granted. For instance, there is often only a dawning of recognition of real dependency on others. Here analysis of *mood* is crucial, and with it will emerge failures in the stage of concern, or the depressive position, to use Klein's term. No special new analytic technique is necessary, but it makes special demands upon the analyst. The moods can be so vehement that great care must be taken by the analyst to remain emotionally engaged with the patient while at the same time surviving as an analysing person in the face of the patient's profound attacks. Here patient and analyst are dealing with the emotional 'weaning' problems of the mother–child relationship.

The third category of patient includes those whose analyses must be concerned with developmental stages before the stable achievement of space-time unit status. This period needs what Winnicott calls 'management'. The analyst has to take up a holding function for the patient, and, as he stressed, ordinary analytic work has to be held in abeyance over long periods. Here the patient will have regressed to a stage of primitive emotional development when the mother's actual holding of the infant is needed. This regression has to be met and therapeutically used.

It was reiterated by Winnicott many times that for most patients the normal, consistent interpretative analytic mode was both necessary and sufficient. But some people suffered from an endless sense of futility and meaninglessness in life. They had often had years of classical analysis and felt all right while it lasted but relapsed when it was finished. Winnicott, like Ferenczi, saw these as a special category of patient, no doubt borderline psychotic in nature. Winnicott in fact called them psychotic, though not in a clinical psychiatric sense. Analysis was still possible but, he thought, only in modified form. He, again like Ferenczi, saw that such a patient often regressed in analysis to such a degree that his mature ego could not be relied on to recover itself either during the sessions or after. There was thus a severe regression, not necessarily to overt psychosis but to dependency on others, the analyst in particular. Winnicott decided to meet this with *ego care* for the patient. He felt he was rewarded in the long run by remarkable therapeutic progress in patients where there had largely been failure before.

Recalling the concept of the true self, originating in the innate potentialities of the baby, Winnicott postulates that a patient in his third category has suffered very early trauma to this potentiality. A false self has then taken over in compliantly relating to the external world in order to protect the original potentiality. If this false self fails, psychosis may take over as a 'last resort' defence of the true original self. The false self is thus, in a way, the normality of psychosis. A defence of the true self has taken place by a *freezing of the failure situation*. The way Winnicott sees this is perhaps similar to the earliest dissociations of the ego as described by Glover (1943). The freezing can be undone only by a regression to and beyond the frozen situation as part of the analytic healing process.

With these borderline self-disorders the false self has become such a 'caretaker' of the true self that it may be only after years of ordinary analysis, and when trust has sufficiently developed, that this caretaking can be handed over to the analyst and healing regression can take placc.

Winnicott goes on to consider two sorts of primary situation that need to be returned to by regression. The first sort is infantile *success* situations, the second is early *failures* – traumata. In the long run, they both need to be experienced and evaluated. In most neurotic conditions these returns are probably best conceived of as going back to fixations of good and bad *instinctual* conflict experiences. But, Winnicott insists, we must also put accent on *ego development*; this is essential when considering false-self phenomena. When we do this, the ego's development in an environment must be allowed to emerge. In this case the environment concerned is the one originally provided by the nursing mother. Winnicott maintained that, at the beginning, the environment must adapt nearly totally to the infant. However, he also stated that infants can increasingly accommodate to some environmental failure without lasting impairment. It is interesting to compare this model with observations by recent infant researchers (Stern, 1985).

Without an adequately adaptive environment, however, there will be impingement and trauma. In the stage of primary narcissism, Winnicott stresses, 'The environment is holding the individual, and *at the same time* the individual knows of no environment and is at one with it' (1958a, p. 283). He is pointing to the need during therapy to find primitive non-differentiated fusion states, in order to dissolve the old false modes of defensive character-structure. Using Matte-Blanco's terminology, these fusion states can be called symmetrized ones. Without discovering the possibility of their dissolution, Winnicott thinks the old modes will be returned to.

It is the reaching of this fusion in analysis that is essential yet fraught with so much danger, for, like the infant, the patient's dependency must be well-nigh total, and this is most painful and disturbing.

At about this point Winnicott introduces one of his most often-quoted notions when he says 'it is from psychosis that a patient can make a spontaneous recovery, whereas neurosis makes no spontaneous recovery and the psychoanalyst is truly needed. In other words, psychosis is closely related to health, in which innumerable environmental failure situations are frozen but are reached and unfrozen by the various healing phenomena of ordinary life, namely friendships, nursing during physical illness, poetry etc. etc.' (1958a, p. 283).

He goes on to specify the main criteria differentiating ordinary or classical technique of analysis from that required when there is the need for regression to find the true self. He points out that the usual analytic method involves the following: reliability of setting, time and attention; sessions of known, limited duration; the analyst 'expresses' love by his thoughtful interest and his hate by strictness in time-keeping and fees. The aim of analysis is to get in touch with a process in the patient, to understand and communicate by interpretation in words; resistance implies suffering, and this can be allayed by interpretation; there is a very clear distinction between fact and phantasy, for instance, the analyst is not hurt by a dream; the absence of talion can be counted upon. Put in other words, Winnicott summarized as the analyst being 'relied upon to behave himself'.

In contrast, Winnicott's position about the regressed patient is: psychotic illness is related to environmental failure at an early stage; here *futility* and *unreality* belong to a false self which protects the original potentiality of the true self; a setting is required to reproduce early mothering; it invites regression by its reliability. The regression is an organized return to dependence; here the patient and analytic setting merge into the early success of primary narcissism. Progress occurs when the re-emerged true self can meet environmental failures without false-self defences. Because of this, psychotic illnesses can be relieved only by special environmental provision interlocked with regression; the mark of success in the emergence of renewed true-self experiences is the receding of the sense of futility and the coming of the feeling of life being worthwhile.

What Winnicott was willing to offer these patients can be understood from his many case reports, as in *Playing and Reality* (1971a) and 'Fragment of an analysis' (1972). One sees from these how overtly undramatic the analyses were. His observations are so subtle that the reader may see them as just the same as any other analysis; only with careful re-reading does the difference appear.

It cannot be in doubt that psychotic and many borderline patients must fail to keep to the rules of classical analysis. Regressive tendencies being interpreted by that technique as defences leads to the analyses becoming stalemates. Winnicott saw a different course: it involved recognizing that the patients' mature egos did not recover from the regressive pull of the setting, so that these patients were often unable to look after themselves. What then is disputed by many analysts is whether this regression involves more than useless defence. Both Winnicott and Balint believed it did – that regression was necessary for change. What is more, Winnicott and Balint saw that regression meant that the patient's ego was impaired, albeit temporarily, and someone had to take over care.

Winnicott often tried to take over a large part of the caretaking himself. He worked out such things as very extended sessions, telephone conversations, sessions at odd times, etc., to accommodate to what he saw as the patient's ego needs. He also tried many forms of freedom for the patient and modes of feeding and physical holding. Here he was trying to bring the analytic setting into an equation with the facilitating aspects of the earliest environment. It was not quite the same as Sechehaye's *Symbolic Realisation* (1947) but close to it. Alexander's 'corrective emotional experience' bore some apparent similarity, but was distinctly different, for this involved active pre-planning by the analyst of corrective experiences, whereas ego-satisfactions were never initiated by Winnicott; they only evolved.

Other analysts who, like Winnicott, have systematically treated psychosis have also had to ensure that the twenty-four-hour ego care of the patient was provided. By definition, the ego in psychosis cannot organize living independently; someone else has to take over responsibility. Federn was the first to treat psychosis by analytic methods in the 1920s, and he relied on helpers, like Mrs Schwingh, who were specially gifted with psychotics, to take over twenty-four-hour care. Other British analysts, like Little, Bion and Rosenfeld, systematically relied on skilled outside help, often from psychiatric institutions. Winnicott often tried to keep his patients out of hospital. He has been condemned for this by some colleagues, for the sometimes comic but, to their eyes, reprehensible events that then occurred. In evaluating these condemnations it must be remembered that he was never accused of behaving unethically with a patient. It should also be remembered that this was forty years ago, and also that Winnicott, like Ferenczi, was attempting to help these people for whom classical analysis had so far proved ineffective.

Some criticism of Winnicott in this regard is perhaps justified. This is not about his seeing the need for ego care, but that he as the analyst was probably attempting to do more of it himself than was optimal or even possible. It seems that, like Ferenczi, he later gave up many of his more active techniques.


## MICHAEL BALINT AND THE USE
## OF THE PATIENT'S REGRESSION

Winnicott's style of writing was brilliant, often poetic, and his subtle observations often lead to intuitive insights. But he was not scholastic and, on the whole, did not bother to discuss other authorities' points of view on the subject in hand.

Balint's last book, *The Basic Fault* (1968), finally comes in many ways to rather similar conclusions to Winnicott. But its form is very different and shows the strength and value of his reasoning. He read widely in psychoanalysis, and moves to and fro describing different theoretical positions, then tries to portray both their strengths and weaknesses.

Balint starts by discussion of analytic therapy, maintaining that a precondition for a patient's successful internalization of interpretations is a fairly good ego structure in the first place. The analytic method of Freud, as seen in the case histories, almost always uses only words to convey meanings. And further, there is the assumption that they have their conventional meanings. There is no searching for gesture, intonation, etc. This verbalization, Balint thinks, requires a certain level of self–object development – the three-person 'oedipal' level. Freud, he says, had no hesitation in describing the child's mental experiences and emotions in this 'language of adults', and seems to have tacitly assumed that the feeling structures of the very young are closely similar to those of adults. Balint thinks that analysts are quite aware of pre-verbal levels in analytic sessions, but these levels, where intonation of words predominate, have to be converted into adult words to be worked with.

However, there are some patients who cannot take in words like this, so that they remain largely uninfluenced by them. They are, Balint says, usually then described as 'deeply disturbed', 'profoundly split', 'seriously schizoid', 'highly narcissistic' or the like. Such patients cannot follow the usual presupposition that interpretations are going to be experienced simply as interpretations by words with agreed meanings. To them the analyst's words often mean something quite else. For instance, they may be expressions of love, hate or indifference by the analyst. Ferenczi called this 'The confusion of tongues between the child and the adults' (1926).

Seen in this light, analytic treatment gives the patient two directions in which to use its facilities: to mobilize towards thought at the verbal level or, in the transference, to regress to find a better solution.

Balint thereupon postulates his thesis of the basic fault: the 'disturbed' patients, who do not react to words with their usually agreed meaning, seem to suffer from a primitive pre-verbal fault. It is not a conflict or a split, but rather a misalignment of the whole pattern of a structure. It is not at the level of internal conflict, but experienced simply as a faultiness within the self in relation to things.

When a patient is experiencing at this level, 'The only thing that can be observed is a feeling of emptiness, being lost, deadness, futility and so on, coupled with an apparently lifeless acceptance of everything that has been offered' (1968, p. 19).

Balint then turns to look at the analyst's reactions. At the oedipal level he is rarely tempted out of his sympathetic passivity, but, when in touch with the basic fault area, it is very much more difficult to keep neutrality. He may get immediately involved, or become over-sympathetic, defensively irritable or authoritarian.

Having considered these two levels, the three-person oedipal and the two-person basic fault level, Balint turns to the area of creation. Here there is no awareness of outside things of importance, the person is on his own, and his main concern is to produce something out of himself. At this level of experience, just as the externality of objects is of no concern, so also transference is of no interest as we ordinarily know it. Balint points out that he is in good company here, as divergent analysts like Fairbairn, Hartmann and Winnicott know the region, so also, later, did Heimann (1989).

Balint then discusses the question of the treatment of the narcissistic states generally and stresses how vitally important it is for the analyst to prove that he is capable of working in *harmony* – in *tune* – with the patient. With a neurotic person working at the oedipal level this can more or less be taken for granted but not with those that are injured narcissistically – in other words at the basic fault level.

Behind the basic fault lies the experience of primary love. It is very close to primary narcissism, but for Balint there is a great difference. Primary love occurs in its purest form *in utero*. Then, with the beginning of emergence from it, comes the state of the need *to be loved* in conflict-less innocence and harmony. As it is a need to be loved it is an object relation but not one that is concerned with the distinction of self and other. Here two individuals, originally mother and child, interpenetrate in a harmonious mix-up. Conflict is not yet felt but traumata in this state create basic (narcissistic) faults.

Turning back to the therapeutic situation, Balint begins to work out the argument that, if illness at the basic fault level is to be taken care of, then the patient must be allowed to regress to states, albeit optimally only transiently, that are of the harmonious, innocent nature of primary love with the analyst. This on the whole is facilitated by the analyst's tolerance and understanding concern. Balint shows how any analysis involves regression, but at the basic fault words begin to be meaningless, intonation and gesture are more sensitively monitored, the analyst's mood is uncannily recognized by the patient.

The patient has become more interested in the state of the analyst than in himself. When this is happening, Balint says, we know we have reached the region of a basic fault. A new kind of therapeutic task then faces the analyst.

It is something more akin to stimulating, or perhaps even to creating, a new willingness in the patient to accept reality and to live in it, a kind of reduction of resentment, lifelessness, etc., which appear in his transference neurosis as obstinacy, awkwardness, stupidity, hypercriticism, touchiness, greed, extreme dependence, and so on.

(Balint, 1968, p. 88)

Balint now moves over to consider this in the light of analytic technique. Classical technique, he thinks, can sometimes largely fail the patient, for he is related only at the oedipal-verbal level. Such technique is no doubt safe, but of what use is it when it fails? Likewise there are hazards inherent in concentration upon consistent interpretation and nothing else. Here he is taking issue with the Kleinians. We have come to accept, he thinks, that analysis deals only with experiences of a sufficiently low intensity that they can be expressed in words. With this assumption, analysts can become masters of word-play – confident, knowledgeable and perhaps overwhelming of the patient, who then slips into the position of the weak partner in the analytic enterprise. As with many weak partners in ordinary life, the patients become prone to idealize the analytic relation and the stronger partner – the analyst. If the patient begins to express complaint, his defensiveness is interpreted, a fault is found in *him* rather than an investigation of the relationship or the analytic environment being carried out.

Balint thinks that technique like this may accept the facts of the basic fault 'But attributes it, as it were, to the *patient's own fault*, in terms of what he has done in his fantasy to his internalized objects' (1968, p. 107). Balint then turns to the only way forward that he can see, that of allowing the regression to progress. He then examines the dangers inherent in this, and goes back to Ferenczi, whose experiments, he states, were mostly doomed to fail. Balint is particularly wary, probably more so than Winnicott was, of the 'grand experiment' with the 'worthwhile' case (Main, 1957). He says that he has never seen any such grand attempt succeed. Something seems to go wrong with the two-person relation between analyst and patient: sincerity in particular becomes idealized and in this climate illusion is more likely to bloom than truth. Worse still, the tolerance of the analyst can become his indulgence, both of himself and of the patient. The patient's greed may then be so provoked that it becomes akin to a ravenous addiction, imperiously demanding satisfaction until some other form of control is resorted to.

Balint emphasizes that regression could be tolerated in analysis so long as it is a temporary measure only, but it must not be accepted as a solution. He then proposes that if the analyst accepts this regression as an acceptable state of affairs, some remarkable therapeutic developments can happen. Balint gives one or two illustrations. For instance, he shows how even a bit of *acting* within the analytic situation, encouraged even by the analyst, can bring about a 'new beginning' for the patient. Thus acting, which can be regressive in nature, may not simply be a pathological resistance – it may be a preliminary stage in change.

He postulates more generally that with a regression, if allowed by the analyst, the patient may move into a state of innocent, trusting primary love, or '*arglos*' state, as he terms it using the German word. The patient seems then to be almost entirely *absorbed into his area of creation*. Here differentiation from the analyst is minimal, and it is important that the analyst recognizes and responds positively to the state. The analyst does not also have to become totally absorbed, but he must be quiet, accepting and even encouraging. The analyst *must not resist* the progress of this state. He must present no abruptness or 'hard edges'.

Balint also seems to think that small token real gratifications from the analyst are sometimes necessary, like holding a hand, to assure the patient of his well-meaningness. It is not clear how necessary Balint thought this was. Quite clearly the benign regression could often take place without it.

With the establishment of steady absorption in the area of creation, in the 'arglos' mood, *new beginning* experiences are possible. This involves changes in cathexis of self and objects but also amounts to a new *discovery*. It opens up new ways of loving and hating the analyst and new ways of being and doing elsewhere. He considers the new beginning to have the following features: noisy symptoms occur to start with but these subside into a mood of tranquillity; gratifications never reach orgastic end-pleasure; all such new beginnings occur *in the transference*. They lead to a changed relation with the analyst; they also lead to character changes; they involve going back to a point *before* the faulty development started. At the same time a new way is found more suited to present reality and for progression to occur. There is regression for the sake of progression.

Whereas this is a clear statement of the clinical situation when a regression to the level of the basic fault occurs, Balint remains aware of the hazards inherent in regression, and he begins to tease out the possibility of two forms of regression: benign and malign.

One form of regression seems to be aimed only at *gratification*, and this is the *malign* form. But there is another form which seems to be aimed at *recognition*, of the patient's plight by the analyst, and recognition of reality by the patient himself. With this a new beginning seems to be possible. This *benign regression* has the following features: there is not much difficulty in establishing a mutual, innocent, arglos trustingness; it leads to new beginning and real discovery; it is regression for the sake of recognition – mainly of the patient's internal problems; there is only a moderate intensity of demand or 'need'; there is an absence of severe hysteria and of genital orgastic elements in the regressed transference.

In contrast, malignant regression has such features as: the arglos mood breaks down; desperate clinging often ensues; there are attempts at new beginnings but with the threat of spirals of demand; the regression aims at gratification by external action, and this is of particularly high intensity; there are usually signs of severe hysteria in the picture clinically, and genital-orgastic elements in the transference can appear at any level. In this way Balint has shown how to look for the signs of readiness for benign regression, and how to be wary of malignancy. At its best he has shown how to pave the way for the patient who is getting ready for a new beginning.

## BALINT AND WINNICOTT ON REGRESSION COMPARED

Both men have sometimes been severely criticized, by Kleinian and also by more classical analysts. It is worth recalling the following points: from the point of view of clinical psychiatry the patients described by Winnicott with wide regressions in analysis were not psychotic, they were borderline, very disturbed none the less, with a profound sense of futility and emptiness. It was their massive *regression to dependency* that had to be managed, not their psychosis.

The technique that raised the greatest indignation has, as happened with Ferenczi, been that of the acceptance by both Balint and Winnicott, at times, of the patient's desire for physical contact, such as hand or head holding, which critics say must have had eroticism in it.

These physical-holding techniques were a fashion of some forty years ago and have not stood the test of time within the British Independents. Both Balint and Winnicott themselves seem to have relinquished the method later in their careers. It was perhaps Balint himself who, with his exploration and differentiation of the dangers of malignant regression, did most to end this particular experimentation.

Have the experiments of Ferenczi, Balint, Winnicott, Little and others served any purpose other than simply to disprove their own technical hypotheses? Some comparative considerations may throw light on this question. Though using very different idioms, it is remarkable how similar the findings of Balint and Winnicott are. They both postulate a certain form of ego pathology based on pre-verbal traumatic experience – the basic fault and the false self. The central symptom for both is the same: a sense of futility and emptiness of a far-reaching kind. Both prescribe the need for regression to a pre-ambivalent, pre-object differentiated state within the analytic setting. For this to be enabled they both agree that the analyst must provide a facilitating environment with no abruptness, no 'hard edges', better to veer towards acceptance than comprehensiveness and precision of interpretation.

Both also agree that such regressive circumstances allow for the re-establishment of a 'primary' state, of 'true self' or 'primary love'. With this, states of fusion or non-differentiation with the present object world are established, albeit transiently. This 'state of innocence' provides the ground for the relating of innate and primitive somato-psychic patterns to the present external world in a new way. It had previously been impeded by profound mistrust, backed by gross defences. With this both workers assert that the schizoid sense of futility can give way to new purposes of living.

## RECENT CONTRIBUTIONS ON REGRESSION

As mentioned in earlier chapters, the possibility of benign regression to a state of undifferentiation between self and object is held by many British Independents. Not only is it central for both Balint and Winnicott, it is so also in Little's (1957, 1960, 1966) work on basic unity. It was worked out, perhaps even before all the others, by Milner (1952, 1987) and also Khan (1960b, 1974b) and James (in Giovacchini, 1972). Milner also shows how important such de-differentiation is in creativity. It is also central to Matte-Blanco's (1975, 1988) thinking in his concept of symmetrization. Later analysts, like Klauber (1981) and Stewart (1989), again observe the importance of such states in the analytic process (see Chapter 10).

Balint and Winnicott both wrote about individuals with very severe pathology. But it seems that more generally there are many patients who *partially* operate in certain areas with false defensive parts of themselves which will be akin to basic faults. Thus perhaps everyone has certain aspects of functioning that are basically faulted. If this is so, then work on regression spreads to virtually every patient we see. Winnicott in fact said that every analysis will provide *moments of regression* to earliest dependency when frozen traumata come to the fore.

This does not mean that the extensive facilitation of regression, advocated in certain cases by Balint and Winnicott, ought to be followed in most cases. Most patients regress within the limits of the session and move out of it both to understand it in the session and to leave at the end. Maybe the term 'regression in the service of the ego' (Kris, 1952) can be applied here. It will depend upon the analyst's approach to regression, whether it is interpreted as a defence or whether he provides the facilitating setting and attuned analytic environment at those times when the patient can optimally use them in benignly regressive ways. The judgement of such times is a prime clinical concern.

Harold Stewart (1989) gives a detailed reconsideration of Balint's work at the basic fault level. He points to various directions of thought arising from it which have been taken up by many Independents in recent years. The first has been 'to avoid interpreting everything first as a manifestation of transference which is one present fashion in interpretive technique' (1989, p. 224).

The second is not to behave as a sharply contoured object. The third is not to behave omnipotently but to accept the experience of the regression.

These recommendations of accepting the experience of the regression and acting out without speedy interpretive work, meant that the emphasis was placed on mutual sharing of the experience in the analysis and that this is an important therapeutic agent in its own right and not simply as the vehicle for therapeutic insightful interpretations.

(Stewart, 1989, p. 224)

Stewart also thinks that there is a contribution by the analyst to the form a regression takes.

The more the analyst's technique was suggestive of omniscience and omnipotence, the greater is the danger of malignant regression. In addition to this, I would say that interpretations in sexual terms concerning sexual phantasies and conflicts, if given early in the analysis or else when the patient is regressed to the basic fault level, can easily lead to mental states of over-stimulation and over-excitement which may easily lead to severe acting out in a malignant fashion.

(Stewart, 1989, p. 227)

Stewart then recalls a patient he had reported in a previous paper (1977) as an example of the handling of an apparently malignant regression.

The patient, who felt divided into a good and an evil part, had developed a compulsive desire to know if I had an erection during the session, which changed into the active state to feel if I had one. This was at first controlled by interpretations. . .but these soon proved to be of little avail. . .she attempted physically to force me to let her feel if I had an erection or not. I naturally physically restrained her and she soon stopped and I was then faced with the problem of future tactics. . .I had reason to be fairly certain that she would not have heard my warning threat [to end treatment] as anything but a challenge. . .I decided that the only course for me to take was to continue to physically restrain her. . .in fact, after a few weeks of this and much analytic interpreting in the sessions when she felt she was good and not evil, this behaviour stopped, never to be repeated and it proved to be an important step forward in her progress towards health.

(Stewart, 1989, p. 227)

Christoper Bollas (1987) considers regression in another benign light and gives a detailed consideration of the events that occur when there is a 'moment' of benign regression to dependency during a session. It can be described as follows: the patient becomes unaware of the analyst's presence; he is in a kind of twilight state when he enjoys the sensation of lying on the couch and is listening, perhaps, to the cars passing or the ticking of a watch; thoughts then arise in response to these sensations; there is a losing oneself inside the sensations; there is thus a subtle transition from sensing the properties in the outside world to sensing them inside; it is a transitional or *intermediate* area of experiencing as Winnicott would term it; the patient reports being amid something new which Bollas believes is a shift from reception to evocation. It is from this internal state that a dream may suddenly be recalled or a memory emerge; the patient may find himself profoundly moved by the imaging, he may 'see what it is all about', he may discover something about mother or father or self that he has never *thought* before but must have 'known'; finally there is the need to tell the analyst.

Such a regression is a far cry from the malign ones discussed by Balint and Stewart. This is regression working healthily in the course of an ordinary analysis. It is what an analyst encounters any day, and many Independents tend to conceptualize usefully in terms of a regressive context.

## CONCLUSION

We have already been coming to some conclusions. Our first was not new: that a certain amount of regression by the patient is a natural part of analysis. It has defensive aspects but is also benignly harnessed in analytic work. This would be universally agreed; what is more controversial is what the analyst should do when faced by regression. Are there occasions when it is appropriate for him to act in ways other than simply to speak? We have been recounting experiments along these lines and seen that, by and large, Independents have decided not to continue with these active modifications of technique.

Some analysts have condemned the experiments by Balint, Winnicott, Little *et al.*, but the Independents take a quite different view. Probably because of their roots in English empiricism, they see these experiments as akin to Freud's 'pressure technique' – in hindsight perhaps misguided, especially if continued for long, but honest, courageous and essential as scientific tests.

The Independents' argument would continue: psychoanalytic technique is certainly not in a state of sufficient perfection to call a halt to further exploration. With the continued necessity for exploration, experiment by trial and error must be an essential part of the analytic armoury. Without it no true advance can be made. In any exploratory experiment, it is usual to hope that the theory to be tested will be correct enough to minimize error, but error is nevertheless essential to locate the limits of a hypothesis. With this in mind, the registration of error is as important as the correctness of a response, and sometimes more so. In this sort of exploratory activity, error is best not regarded with horror but as a painful yet valuable event. This attitude, essential to any scientific venture, is supported by an empirical ethic which is in turn supported by an emotional strength; it is this which lies deep in the roots of the Independents.

Being emotionally rooted means that controversy about such matters can be ill-tempered, and this has certainly been the case over the question of the handling of regression. The Independent's empirical point of view has the apparent weakness that it can seem to give assent to carelessness about errors. Thus, Independent technique has been accused of being generally vague and sloppy. This fundamentally misunderstands its aim. Commitment to open-mindedness in any endeavour requires self-discipline of a high order when complex issues are being evaluated. This is certainly the case with analysis. It should also be added here that the Independents' empirical ethic gives no encouragement to that quality of cruelty which can emerge in the minds of strict adherents to a doctrine after it has started to become sterile.

# 9 The Psychoanalytic Process – The Analyst's Contribution

THE BRITISH INDEPENDENTS' views on the analytic process can hardly be understood without knowing their underlying theory and preconceptions of infant and child development, and these have been spelt out throughout this book. We have seen how the Independents have extended Freud's view by their particular interest in the first two years of life, and in this context they have been impressed by the effects of early traumata upon later development, adult personality and pathology. It is this emphasis on early traumata that marks the Independents' contribution. They have consequently laid stress upon the fateful influence of the facilitating environment on later development. This mode of thinking can also be applied to the analytic situation as a facilitating one and where Independents could be said to have developed the idea, modifying Winnicott, that 'there is no such thing as a patient – only a patient with a therapist'.

This sense of patient with analyst in a joint venture and at the same time needing to be in dialectic dialogue also comes, however, directly from the experience of analysis itself. As discussed in the last chapter, the treatment of very ill, regressed patients could not but impress upon analysts the strength of their own emotional reactivity as they sat behind the couch. It stimulated interest in the countertransference, which led to its actual usefulness to the analyst in his work. This was widened to a recognition of the importance of the analyst's affective response generally. It is this that will be the subject of this chapter. This affectivity in turn led Independents recently to dwell upon the ongoing affective interaction between patient and analyst within the psychoanalytic venture.

This vision of interactivity involves conceiving of two minds as being one unit as well as two. It is an identical view to that derived, via a different route, by Rickman (Chapter 2) – that the theory of psychoanalytic technique must be based on a two-body psychology. The two-person or *conversational* nature of the dialogue between patient and analyst is returned to time and again in Independent thinking. While it is no doubt true that analysts in general will subscribe at some point to a two-body psychology when thinking of the therapeutic relationship, much theory about technique seems to have developed upon a one-body psychology, namely the analyst focusing mainly upon the patient's *intra-psychic* world. In consequence, this has largely led to the ignoring of the effect of the analyst upon the patient. The Independents have not fallen into this trap — if anything, they have erred in the opposite direction.

We have seen that Independents stay committed to Freud's developmental schemata and, as a consequence of their emphasis upon an environment-trauma theory of causation, they maintain Freud's original interest and belief in the value of *reconstruction*. We will be noting here the Independents' concern with recognizing the *reality* of what the patient has had to manage, at a cost, both in the past and in the present. This burden upon the patient can at times even come from the analyst himself. This is not to say that every memory from the past is believed as it stands, but rather that memories of things past, as opposed to pure fantasy, are *elaborations* by fantasy of events that actually happened. They are close here to the views of Ernst Kris (1952) in his important longitudinal studies in America.

The use of reconstruction presupposes a theoretical structure of child, adolescent and adult development. Here Independents have often used work from other researchers, particularly from Anna Freud and her colleagues, but also from other countries and from non-analysts like Piaget. It is quite against an Independent's philosophy to confine himself to the use of the writings only of close colleagues.

The developmental point of view has led the Independents' theory of technique into *pre-verbal* activity, which means emphasis on the intra-psychic experience of both patient and analyst. We discussed the patient in the last chapter and will now turn in more detail to the analyst's affective experiences.

## THE ANALYST'S COUNTERTRANSFERENCE

Freud (1910a) first introduced the concept of countertransference, and analysts at the time understood this as referring to the analyst's pathological emotional reaction to the patient. This reaction would be based on the analyst's own infantile transferences which hindered the appropriateness of his work with the patient. There was only one way to deal with this – more analysis. If self-analysis failed then one must seek it with someone else. Other analysts, like Heimann (1950), have agreed with this but also conceived of some manifestations of countertransference in a rather different light. The matter is controversial to the present day.

The British, particularly the Independents, can claim, with Racker in Brazil, to be the source of much of the new thinking about the *use* of the countertransference. However, the interest did not start in Britain but in Hungary. In the 1920s Ferenczi was carrying out his explorations into therapeutic work with patients who seemed unable to use the classical technique. He attempted to be as openly honest with his patients as they were expected to be with him, and this naturally led to the question of the analyst's emotional reactions to the patient. So the study of countertransference was in the air. Freud disapproved of Ferenczi's ventures, but after Ferenczi's death his student Michael Balint determined to experiment in ways that followed his teacher. He was perhaps less impetuous than Ferenczi and came to reaffirm classical technique for most problems.

**BALINT**

In his investigations of technique Balint naturally came upon the question of countertransference and there is a paper 'On transference and countertransference' (1939) by him and Alice Balint, his first wife. They conceive of the countertransference as the analyst's *normal*, non-pathological transference to the patient. They start by pointing out that anyone is liable to react emotionally to expressions of emotion – and this equally includes analysts. How can this be reconciled, wonder the Balints, with Freud's invocation that the analyst should be like the surface of a well-polished mirror, or like the sterility of the surgeon – both lifeless conditions?

Recognizing that there are great differences in atmosphere created by the characteristic sytles of different analysts, they spell out some of these.

Analysts, for instance, differ about such matters as when to start interpreting (as Strachey told us), what to interpret, the way to say it and so on. They conclude that there are as many ways to conduct an analysis as there are analysts and patients.

> Looked at from this point of view the analytic situation is the result of an interplay between the patient's transference and the analyst's counter-transference. . .[there] is no such thing as the 'sterile method of analysing'. . .Our patients, with very few exceptions, are able to adapt themselves to most of these individual atmospheres and to proceed with their own transference, almost undisturbed by the analyst's counter-transference. This implies that all of these techniques are good enough to enable patients with average disturbances in the development of their emotional life to build up a transference which is favourable to analytic work. . .
>
> One must reluctantly admit that for the average neurotic patient these individual variants of technique do not greatly matter. . .
>
> The objective task demands that a patient analysed in any of the many individual ways shall learn to know his own unconscious mind and not that of his analyst. The subjective task demands that analysing shall not be too heavy an emotional burden, that the individual variety of technique shall procure sufficient emotional outlet for the analyst. A sound and adequate technique must therefore be doubly individual. . .
>
> Returning to Freud's metaphor, we see that the analyst must really become like a well polished mirror – not, however, by behaving passively like an inanimate thing, but by reflecting without distortion the whole of his patient. The more clearly the patient can see himself in the reflection, the better our technique; and if this has been achieved, it does not matter greatly how much of the analyst's personality has been revealed by his activity or passivity, his severity or lenience, his methods of interpretation, etc.
>
> (Balint, 1939 [1965, pp. 206–7])

This is a rather little-known paper in the Anglo-Saxon world, but it can be said to reflect the beginning of a new era of psychoanalytic technique. Looking back now after fifty years, this passage in itself is a portrayal of much of Independent philosophy towards emotional responsiveness and its place in technique today, even though it was written before Balint had started his journey to come to Britain.

It is important to be clear that the Balints were extending the usage of the term countertransference from the narrower one applying it to the pathological emotional response of the analyst, to a wider one covering any emotional reaction by the analyst. This broader definition has tended to become recognized usage even though its looseness is conducive to lack of subtlety and to misunderstandings. Pearl King (1978) has suggested the term 'the analyst's affective response' to distinguish it from the countertransference proper.

### WINNICOTT

Apart from his ongoing work with children, Donald Winnicott had also been preoccupied during the early 1940s with exploring the possibilities of analysis with adult psychotic and borderline patients. He called these 'research analyses'.

One of the first papers to come from these experiences was 'Hate in the counter-transference' (1947b). Here he tries to convey that it is very important indeed for an analyst to be quite at home with his hatred if he is going to tackle the treatment of psychotic patients. He will not only experience it but also need to use it constructively.

He goes on to make an important differentiation between the following: first, abnormal countertransference feelings; then, the identification tendencies of the analyst which are different for each practitioner and make his work of a different quality from that of any other analyst (this is the same point as that made by the Balints); last, 'truly objective' countertransference – this is the affective response of the analyst arising from a particular patient's behaviour. Such a response might be hate if a patient is behaving in a truly nasty and hateful way.

Winnicott is stressing that it is very important for the analyst to continue to be aware of his own affects so as to be able to distinguish these all the time in his work. It is of note that he, like the Balints, has widened his definition of countertransference beyond Freud's usage, so in more recent terminology he might have called it 'Hate in the analyst's affective response'.

He sees that psychosis involves the experience of 'coincident love–hate' – their indistinguishability, in other words. It is this intrusive emotional confusion that makes hate and hatefulness omnipresent in the treatment of such illnesses. A consequence is that there will be times when the analyst's hate will be *justified* – for self-preservation, for example. Here the patient with fragile self-esteem may not be able to be told about it by the analyst, but the analyst must never deny the hatred to himself. Winnicott thinks that it is the mark of the ending of a good analysis that such feelings of hatred, among others, can belatedly perhaps be avowed quite openly to the patient.

He points out that hatred, being a *self-protective* device, needs to be able to be freely experienced when appropriate. What is more, there are many forms in the *structure* of the psychoanalytic *setting* that stand in, as it were, for hatred. Winnicott says this about the setting:

> For the neurotic the couch and warmth and comfort can be *symbolical* of the mother's love; for the psychotic it would be more true to say that these things *are* the analyst's physical expression of love. The couch *is* the analyst's lap or womb and the warmth *is* the live warmth of the analyst's body. And so on.
>
> (Winnicott, 1958a, p. 199)

The strict timing of the analytic hour gives a structure to the ending of the session. It is an occasion for the expression of, or symbolic of, the analyst's hatred. Incidentally, Winnicott is here pointing out the symbolic equations of psychosis a decade before they came into common usage (Segal, 1957). He is also giving an example of the psychotic symmetrization which Matte-Blanco was soon to be formulating. Similar ideas were beginning to grow in America from such as Searles and Fromm-Reichmann, and from Sechehaye in France.

Winnicott is pointing out again that it is this capacity to confuse utterly that makes hatred so commonplace in the work with psychotic patients. He reiterates that it can be quite justifiable, healthy and 'all right' to feel that you cannot stand a patient. Self-protection is as necessary for an analyst as it is for a mother with a young baby. In his inimitable way, he then contemplates mothers' hatred for their babies – which is just as applicable to analysts.

> A mother has to be able to tolerate hating her baby without doing anything about it. She cannot express it to him. If, for fear of what she may do, she cannot hate appropriately when hurt by her child she may fall back on masochism, and I think it is this that gives rise to the false

theory of a natural masochism in women. The most remarkable thing about a mother is her ability to be hurt so much by her baby and to hate so much without paying the child out, and her ability to wait for rewards that may or may not come at a later date.

(Winnicott, 1958a, p. 202)

He goes on to affirm 'It seems to me doubtful whether a human child as he develops is capable of tolerating the full extent of his own hate in a sentimental environment. He needs hate to hate' (p. 202). Such simple, seemingly thrown-away comments about everyday life were the strengths of Winnicott. We can begin to see how the tolerance, even enjoyment of and certainly the use of the analyst's affective response was beginning to come alive in Britain in the 1940s.

## HEIMANN

It was Paula Heimann's paper 'On counter-transference' (1950), read at the Amsterdam Congress of 1949, that is generally regarded as the starting point of specific interest in the use the analyst makes of the affective response. Heimann said that her paper was stimulated by seminars with students who often felt afraid and guilty when they became aware of having feelings towards their patients. They had misunderstood Freud's emphasis on the analyst's neutral attitude when he said that his task is comparable with that of a surgeon and that the analyst functions as the patient's mirror.

Heimann postulates that the countertransference, the analyst's feelings towards the patient, should be kept conceptually separate from the analyst's transference to him. Countertransference is an integral part of the analyst's comprehensive understanding of the patient's allusions to hidden aspects of his communications. On the whole, analysts are hardly aware of their countertransference feelings, but they can become important indicators clinically when they are at odds with the cognitive understanding of the patient's material. It is at this time that countertransference becomes a most helpful tool for understanding the patient. Heimann illustrates this with a short clinical vignette.

In the third week of his analysis a promiscuous divorced patient told Heimann that he was going to marry a woman he had met only a short time before. She was not particularly taken aback by this sort of news. It was, she knew from long experience, to be expected as an acting out of resistance in the transference. But somehow she also felt a strange deep apprehension and worry. This puzzled her for her worry was much stronger than she would have expected from such acting out.

Later during the session the patient recounted a dream which helped her begin to unravel things. This was: 'He had acquired from abroad a very good secondhand car which was damaged. He wished to repair it, but another person in the dream objected from reasons of caution. He had, as he put it, "to make him confused" in order that he might go ahead with the repair of the car' (1950, p. 82). Heimann saw that the car from abroad was herself, and that 'the other person' stood for the part of the ego who aimed for security and happiness and also for the analysis as a protective object. This led to another part of the ego of the patient, that which wished Heimann to be damaged, which was understood as the patient's infantile anal attacks on the mother. The patient's masochistic as well as sadistic potentialities had already been the subject of a previous session.

The dream helped Heimann to understand that her unconscious had grasped the seriousness of the patient's capacity to damage the analysis – hence her sense of worry at the beginning of the session. The crucial point she then makes is that she had *missed understanding in good time* the patient's communication. This was that the wanting to marry a woman who had had a rough ride, as the patient had said (like Heimann the refugee), was a self-destructive, masochistic attempt at repair of the analyst (mother) whom he had damaged in sadistic attacks. Instead of being the patient's supplementary ego and perceiving the nature of his acting out, Heimann had done something else: instead of understanding, she had *introjected* the patient. This had then given her the countertransference feelings of worry and concern that she could account for only later in the session when the dream was recounted. Heimann says:

the analyst's immediate emotional response to his patient is a significant pointer to the patient's unconscious processes and. . .helps the analyst to focus his attention on the most *urgent* [our italics] elements in the patient's associations and serves as a useful criterion for the selection of interpretations.

(Heimann, 1950 [1989, p. 77])

She concludes:

> In my view Freud's demand that the analyst must 'recognize and master' his counter-transference does not lead to the conclusion that the counter-transference is a disturbing factor and that the analyst should become unfeeling and detached, but that he must use his emotional response as a key to the patient's unconscious. This will protect him from entering as a co-actor on the scene which the patient re-enacts in the analytic relationship and from exploiting it for his own needs. . . .I do not consider it right for the analyst to communicate his feelings to his patient. In my view such honesty is more in the nature of a confession and a burden to the patient.
>
> (Heimann, 1950 [1989, p. 78])

Heimann is using the term countertransference here in a much more specific way than did either the Balints or Winnicott. For her the use is restricted to incidents when there is a time-lag between the analyst's unconscious and conscious understanding of the patient's communication. Instead of comprehending the patient's projections in good time, on such occasions the analyst unconsciously introjects the patient and experiences a consequent puzzling sense of unease.

It could be said that Heimann's 1950 paper had almost created the specific clinical use of the countertransference and thence the analyst's affective response.

In a later contribution to a symposium on countertransference (1960) Heimann expressed her concern that her earlier paper may have been misunderstood. She said she was now sometimes meeting students who made interpretations based on their feeling responses without giving due weight to what the patient had actually said to them. She also addressed the ongoing debate about what Freud might have meant in his scarce remarks on countertransference and whether or not he simply meant that it was the analyst's transference to the patient. She was of the opinion that transference and countertransference were fused. She said:

> In my experience, when I have afterwards (with proverbially easy hindsight) scrutinized incidents of counter-transference, successfully used as indication of processes in the patient, I concluded that the time-lag between my unconscious and my conscious understanding

was due in part to transference factors which I had not recognized at the time.

(Heimann, 1960 [1989, p. 156])

Heimann developed a further formulation in a later paper (1969). Here she states that many instances of so-called projective identification should be defined as re-activation in the patient of his infantile experiences with his rejecting and intrusive mother. In her opinion, the infantile ego does not actively introject a bad object but 'is helpless against its intrusion because the barrier function was not yet effective' (1969, p. 224). Such passively endured bad experiences form a substructure in the budding psychic apparatus. This substructure is then seen as the bad internal object.

When, in analysis, the patient identifies with such an intrusive and rejecting bad internal object, and the analyst does not perceive this in good time, he will then unconsciously introject the 'bad-object-identified' patient. It causes countertransference problems since the re-enactment may be missed and then the patient will be perceived as rejecting and intrusive. Heimann said:

'Projective identification' occurs as a counter-transference phenomenon, when the analyst fails in his perceptive functions, so that, instead of recognizing in good time the character of the transference, he on his part unconsciously introjects his patient who at this point acts from an identification with his rejecting and intruding mother, re-enacting his own experiences in a reversal of roles.

(Heimann, 1969, p. 230)

We can see that Ferenczi's original ideas have been carried forward and refined, first by the Balints and Winnicott, then picked up again and further clarified and reassessed by Heimann. At the time of her first paper on the subject Heimann was one of Mrs Klein's collaborators, but this paper, unlike those for the Controversial Discussions under her name, was worked out by herself alone. It was in fact rather disapproved of by Melanie Klein, who never came to believe in the use of the countertransference as portrayed by Heimann. As is well known, Kleinian analysts later took up the use of the countertransference vigorously and fruitfully (e.g. Rosenfeld, 1987). They have tended to use the analyst's feelings to detect hidden projective identifications by the patient into the analyst.

Countertransference for them thus seems to be the manifestation of projective identification as an interpersonal phenomenon. It has been a major step of the past half-century.

Independents vary, of course. Many systematically use this Kleinian way of looking out for hidden projective identifications. However, most would also agree with and use Heimann's way of investigating counter-transference feelings as indicators that the analyst has missed something the patient is communicating. It is the countertransference which alerts the analyst to search for hidden allusions in the patient's communications. We would conclude that emotional responses to the patient need to be viewed in several different ways.

## LITTLE

A year after Heimann read her paper, Margaret Little (1951) was also extending ideas on countertransference. In several papers she gives a wealth of lively clinical material illustrating its use. Like Ferenczi, she went so far as to argue for the usefulness for the analyst on occasion to analyse his own emotional reactions *with* the patient. As with many innovations, limits have to be discovered empirically by some daring practitioner exploring further than others to see where uselessness begins. This has probably happened over the question of 'public' self-analysis by the analyst, for it has not caught on. Most would agree with Heimann that such revelations are a burden to the patient. This is considered in detail by Bollas (1987, 1989) and will be discussed in the next chapter.

## KING

Perhaps the best summary of work in this area has been given more recently by Pearl King (1978). Like Winnicott she moves easily backwards and forwards between infancy and analysis, using the former as an illustrative metaphor for the latter. An infant cannot be studied in isolation, only in relation to mother, or substitute. The affects of mother and infant attune with each other – and so do patient and analyst. More recently, of course, infant researchers, in both Europe and America, with modern recording techniques have gone into the fine detail of the vital mother–infant relation.

King points out how the all-important analysis of affects is most difficult to accomplish when *traumata* have occurred at *pre-verbal* periods of a patient's development. But these can begin to be uncovered from the analyst's careful monitoring of his own affects. She notes that she is following the lead of Winnicott and Heimann.

She stresses that countertransference as a pathological phenomenon must be clearly distinguished from the analyst's other affective responses.

I *define this affective response of the analyst* as the perception by the analyst of feelings and moods, unrelated to his personal life, and which may even feel alien to his normal way of reacting, but which, when placed in the context of the patient's material and the psychoanalytic setting, illumine and render meaning to those transference phenomena that are in the process of being experienced, consciously or unconsciously, by the patient.

(King, 1978, p. 330)

Like Heimann and most others, King does not believe in the analyst sharing his own affective reactions with the patient. But she stresses that the analyst's self-awareness is essential all the time. When the analyst finds himself feeling in ways that are not ego-syntonic then he must examine whether this is an instance of 'classic' pathological countertransference to be self-analysed – whether he is being in effect the 'victim' of the patient's intrusive projective identifications or whether there is some other pre-verbal instigating circumstance.

King illustrates her contentions with a case example of a patient who was less than a year old when her mother went into hospital for several months. This trauma was thus definitely of pre-verbal origin. It was naturally difficult to analyse, and King shows how she systematically went about it by using the examination of her own affective responses. She concludes:

But if the analyst is to remain free to use his own affects to understand aspects of his patient's unconscious conflicts, he must maintain an attitude of neutrality or 'non-attachment' (to borrow a term from Eastern philosophy). I believe, however, that such an attitude 'is a crucial factor in the curative process and one of our main therapeutic tools'.

(King, 1978, p. 334)

King here makes it clear that she wishes to see an ego-syntonic equivalent for the analyst of a therapeutic *split* of the ego in the patient. In doing this she gives Freud's demand for neutrality a new meaning.

Picking up this idea about neutrality from King and putting it in a slightly different way, we can see that neutrality is a function of a freedom to reflect on and move, both outwardly and inwardly, from different positions of affective appraisal and then to bring them together in new constellations.

We see that, from the starting point of the idea of the countertransference in its narrowest sense, a number of Independents have developed concepts of clinical practice that centre on the affective interaction of the analyst with the patient and that amount to a philosophy of the nature of the therapeutic interaction, which Rycroft investigated in an important paper in the 1950s.

## AFFECTS AND WORDS

### RYCROFT

In 'The nature and function of the analyst's communication to the patient' (1956b, 1968a) Charles Rycroft starts out from Susanne Langer's work (1942) and points out that human behaviour is not just food-getting but a language: every move can be a gesture. However, since classical metapsychology is a 'single mind' system, psychoanalysis often does not do full justice to human communicativeness. Rycroft expressly goes on to see man as a social animal. Psychodynamics is then clearly the study of the development of interpersonal relations and psychopathology that of the ways in which this might break down.

He emphasizes that affects play an essential part in communication. An affect is, optimally, perceptible by others because of the perceivers' capacity to empathize, that is, to attune or evoke a complementary affect in themselves. Because of this complementarity, upon which the analytic method is based, Rycroft proposes that there must be developed a metapsychology of interpersonal relations to clarify our theories of symbolism and technique. It is of interest that, except in the work of systems theorists, this has not developed further.

Rycroft then goes on to make a very important differentiation between signs and symbols (see also Chapter 3). He proposes that gestures and *intonations* are *signs* or signals of the presence of affects, whereas *metaphor* and *dream* images are *symbols* for they indicate *conceptions of affects*. He points out that the dividing line between a sign and a symbol is often not clear. It is a region which clearly deserves more scrutiny than it has received. Rycroft, disagreeing with Jones, then asks that fully discursive words should be allowed to join non-discursive symbols on equal terms as symbols. Discursive words are certainly agreed by the conventions of language, but they can also convey conceptions about affects and are used thus in psychoanalysis.

Analysis is seen as a mode whereby interpretations help the patient to discriminate progressively between his phantastical and his real relationship with the analyst. Hence it becomes easier for him to be aware of his feelings and thoughts and then to communicate them. This is very close to Strachey (1934) on interpretation. However, for Rycroft, the increased capacity to be aware and communicate is not solely due to the intellectual content of verbal interpretations. The analyst will at the same time have been making many *implicit* communications. These might be such as 'I am still here and listening' or 'I remember what you said last week and last year' or 'You have interested me enough for me to remember'. They might go further to 'You are not the first person to have felt like this' or 'I am not admonishing you' and so on. The first group of communications tells about the analyst being interested by the patient, the second gives the patient permission to be himself.

These, Rycroft stresses, are affective communications from the analyst, even though they may not be overt expressions. They are made by signs rather than by discursive verbal symbols: they are inferred from the phrasing of words but not from their specific meaning. They are likely to be muted because they are uttered by the analyst, but they are none the less affects. They could intellectually be stated in words, but this would be worse then useless. The natural way to judge the presence of an affect is to look for the signs of it, the verbal nuance, cadence, intonation and so on. These are not easily capable of deceit. A communication, Rycroft thinks, given only in dead words makes the listener doubt the sincerity of the speaker.

In a subsequent paper, 'An enquiry into the function of words in the psycho-analytic situation' (1958), Rycroft starts with words as essentially

secondary process symbols associated largely with conscious and preconscious levels and thus with detailed communicability. Because of the level
at which words operate, their use ordinarily implies the mind functioning
at a level of self–object differentiation. However, words can still obviously
be used in psychoanalysis for the resolution of conflicts dating from
before speech. Here, one use of words in analysis is for their permissive
function – as mentioned a few paragraphs back. Rycroft then reiterates
in greater detail than before his main contention, that much of what
happens in analysis is by sign–gesture, intonation and the physical setting
of the consulting-room. He makes plain that he is restating what Balint
(1939) and Winnicott (1949a) had been saying.

Rycroft then tackles a difficult subject which, on the whole, can only
be talked around even though it is of central importance. This is the
attempt to define the analyst's therapeutic attitude. 'Benevolent neutrality' won't quite do, because it is actually a combination of two contradic-
tions. He sees the therapeutic attitude as an enduring disposition of
emotional tendencies or affective potentialities. The mood, vigour, feeling, concentration, etc., of the analysis may change from day to day, but
the disposition or potentiality to analyse must remain. A vital aspect of
this he sees as having been brought out by Sterba (1934), who points to
the analyst's readiness to participate *imaginatively* in the patient's inner
and outer life rather than doing so by direct involvement.

Words are used day in day out with different penumbras of meaning
and different functions by both the patient and the analyst. For instance,
words may be used by intonation to discharge oral, anal, urethral, phallic
or genital impulses. Here they are often projectiles, and when a patient is
in such a projectile state he will be prone to interpret the analyst's words
as projectiles also, and so on.

Every interpretation has a web of affective meanings, only a few of
which enter the focus of consciousness. The same is true of every association by the patient. Each interpretation 'can be thought of as a detail of a
total interpretative pattern which emerges during the course of the analysis' (Rycroft, 1968a, p. 80). The meaning of any one interpretation can
only be understood in the whole setting of the unfolding sequence. It is
part of a gestalt. Every word has its particular range of often concrete
meaning for any individual, and this is made even more specific by the
context at any particular time. Rycroft gives an instance here of the
analyst's consistent use of the word 'castrated' to indicate the experience

of feeling emasculated or unmanned. For a particular patient, for a very long time, it meant only anatomical castration and nothing else. This is the same point as made by Balint (1968) when he says how at the basic fault words can cease to have their common meaning for a patient.

Rycroft moves on to pointing out how intuitively sensitive most people are to the intonational, syntactical and linguistic habits of others. It is by these meanings between and behind words that we judge others' moods and character. Sensitivity to these are the finest tools of the analyst's trade. We use them in becoming aware of mood, anxiety, affect, defence and character.

Rycroft concludes by spelling out a consequence of the recognition that analysis is about communication between two people. As it is between two people, we must, he insists, consider the psychology of the analyst as well as that of the patient, and this will be the subject of the next chapter.

# 10 The Psychoanalytic Process – The Dialogue of Patient and Analyst

WE HAVE BEEN trying to see how both patient and analyst contribute to the psychoanalytic process, which can be seen as two-person, yet a unity. It is this clinical approach to the emotionality of the analytic encounter that marks the strongest thrust of Independent work in the past two decades.

It is now about twenty years since both Balint and Winnicott died, and more recent work clearly has many roots in their thought. The best-known writers in this recent line of thinking about technique are Khan, Klauber, Enid Balint, Limentani, Little, Stewart, Coltart, Symington, Casement, Bollas, Pedder and Parsons.

## KLAUBER

John Klauber was knowledgeable about psychoanalytic theory, but more interested in writing on other matters. He was a courageous innovator in thinking and writing about the emotionality of technique. He exemplified the spirit, both in strengths and weaknesses, of the British Independent analyst. Klauber published two selections of papers: *Difficulties in the Analytic Encounter* (1981) and a much shorter posthumous one, primarily made up of lectures to undergraduates about what constitutes the essence of psychoanalysis, *Illusion and Spontaneity in Psycho-Analysis* (1987). In the latter, an introductory paper by Symington gives a valuable summary of his work.

Klauber was interested in the admixture of phantasy and reality – namely illusion. He pointed out that the received view, from the time of

Strachey onwards, was that cure came about by the patient being brought to the stage where he was able to make judgements about reality un-clouded by illusory or delusory ideas. Klauber saw things differently and stated that this was achievable only through the *agency of illusion*. The transference is, he says, a *dramatization* of the patient's illusions and the analytic setting is a stage that enables this to occur.

> We cannot live by reality alone. We need the illusions which touch reality 'with a celestial light'. That is why religion is so important in all societies, not excluding – however much we may object to religion – the esoteric forms that often pervade scientific societies.
>
> (Klauber, 1987, p. 8)

It is through illusion that we comprehend reality. Illusion has value for the patient as well as for all of us. This is a philosophy close to that of Winnicott, but Klauber's discourse is more that of the learned historian which he was before taking up medical studies.

Although he knew that psychoanalysis was a very difficult and impor-tant activity, Klauber reasoned that it should be capable of being part of the life of any thinking man; in this sense it is ordinary and should not be idolized. It has been said that he demythologized psychoanalysis. For instance, he recognized that patients actually knew a lot about their analysts. 'When the patient visits the psychoanalyst for a consultation, it is not only the psychoanalyst who makes an assessment – the patient also attempts to make an assessment of the analyst' (1987, p. 10). This has been discussed by other analysts, like Greenson (1967), in different con-texts, but Klauber has his own lucid way of putting things. He took great care to describe, in just the right words, what an experience felt like.

From early in his career Klauber stressed the necessity of authenticity. It was only later, after he had rigorously mastered the technique, that he said that, for his own sake, an analyst needs also to be spontaneous, but, more than this, the patient needs him that way in order to be able to use him.

> It is spontaneity which allows the unconscious to work or, rather, which allows its more direct expression. . .I know of no metapsycho-logical proposition which demands that our spontaneous reactions should always be filtered through the secondary processes. In fact the spontaneous processes are responsible for the artistic and most creative

aspects of the analysis, and can be almost as clever and perceptive in their operations as they are in dreams.

(Klauber, 1987, p. 33)

He often reiterates that transference is such a powerful emotional activity that it is not necessary to set up a totally neutral setting, even if this were possible. It weaves itself round whatever setting is there. This is just about the same view as the Balints (1939) put forward many years before.

Klauber was led to the opinion also that therapeutic change did not occur through transference interpretation alone. This view was held by Balint too and, as we have seen, is a strong tradition among Independents generally. Klauber, like Freud, believed that *truth* was the agent of psychoanalytic cure, and this could never be the possession of any isolated group or faction. 'The human mind is satisfied, and in some sense healed, by what it feels as truth' (1981, p. 6). Symington summarizes this view when he says, 'Truth is a flighty lady and will never allow any one idea, person, group of persons, ideology, religion or school to possess her' (in Klauber, 1987, p. 51). This is the same as Winnicott's insistence upon the value of authenticity.

It was not possible, Klauber thought, for any analyst to hold a continuous, totally neutral stance in relation to his patients, and over all aspects of each patient's character, even if this were desirable. This was not to say that the analyst was to be thoughtlessly self-indulgent about the expression of his prejudices, but rather that the analyst's feelings are detectable by the patient anyway and it is best to recognize this possibility openly. He did not agree with Little's (1986) opinion that the analyst's self-analysis with a patient may sometimes be valuable. It is, however, the analyst's open-mindedness about the revision of his opinions that is the vital form of his neutrality.

Some analysts might feel contempt for the colleague who says he needs his patients. Klauber faced this but drew attention to something which is obvious but rarely spoken about. He says:

Patient and analyst need one another. The patient comes to the analyst because of internal conflicts that prevent him from enjoying life, and he begins to use the analyst not only to resolve them, but increasingly as a receptacle for his pent-up feelings. But the analyst also needs the patient in order to crystallize and communicate his own thoughts, including some of his inmost thoughts on intimate human problems which only grow organically in the context of this relationship. They cannot be shared and experienced in the same immediate way with a colleague, or even with a husband or wife. It is also in his relationship with his patients that the analyst refreshes his own analysis. It is from this mutual participation in analytic understanding that the patient derives the substantial part of his cure and the analyst his deepest confidence and satisfaction.

(Klauber, 1981, p. 46)

Klauber placed great importance on interpretation, particularly transference interpretation. But, as we have said, he did not believe it was the only prime agent in cure. Independents think it is a prime precept that, before any particular theory, the analyst must be open to deep *emotional contact with his patient*. Klauber believed that pathological jealousy, perversion and paranoia had roots in that level called schizoid by Fairbairn, basic fault by Balint, false self by Winnicott, and at-the-level-of-psychotic-anxieties by the Kleinian school. He had the hunch that if emotional contact was made here, then the patient was healed by it. If the analyst himself was already healed at this deep level, then he might be better able to pass this on to his patients. Winnicott referred to something similar when he spoke of moments of healing. Perhaps this happens in any emotional encounter that is deeply moving.

He was close to classical technique on the subject of the mild positive transference, which is the agent of continuity and should not be analysed, but Klauber has his own elaboration. During analysis, what the patient seeks is a gratifying object relationship, but through interpretation this desire is frustrated. Instead the patient receives understanding, and a relationship develops based upon use of identification with this understanding mode rather than object relating. Interpretation therefore puts boundaries to the analytic relationship and defines its role. This is the same point as Rycroft (1956b) was at pains to make. Symington (in Klauber, 1987) illustrates this with a metaphor. It is like a man who buys a plot of land to build a house on. The plot must have boundaries for it to be acquired, but the house is built on the land not the boundary.

The making of emotional contact comes from one place only: from the spontaneous creative core of each individual, both patient and analyst. It is worth repeating that above all Klauber draws our attention to careful spontaneity. This must be distinguished from impulsiveness and can be used only after mastery of a rigorous technique. Spontaneity comes from the ego searching for a truth, whereas impulsiveness comes from the id rebelling against a super-ego injunction.

Klauber believed in talking more freely than would be customary in some models, but he was clear that detachment traumatized the patient. A silent analyst repeats what was an original trauma for many patients, a too-distant parent who is silent on emotional matters. The silence could reveal the original trauma but Klauber was convinced that it was rarely an agent for change.

He went on to point out something which is hardly remembered by most analysts. The *beginning* of an analysis is a trauma for the patient, who is at that time stirred to be aware of a whirling welter of feelings that his consciousness has never had to process before. De-traumatization starts with interpretation and also by the patient beginning to make partial identifications with the analyst. This requires sounds, intonation and words from the analyst – not a silent repetition of the trauma. Klauber believed that the spontaneity of the analyst facilitates the maximum freedom of expression by the patient at that time. The patient might, with this new freedom, feel angry and hostile to those who have in the past enslaved him. He may even become omnipotently extravagant with this new freedom. But better, Klauber felt, for this to be given its head than be stamped on. By this means, omnipotence – which is needed in small doses – could be better integrated by the patient himself.

Integration of a phantasy with the ego was what gives imagination its significance. It was this that the analyst must foster and not so much the minutiae of detailed phantasies.

Klauber believed in the classical view of the slow release into consciousness of warded-off ideas as defences are undone. But he also became aware that this benign process could be interfered with by the analyst's attitudes. Sometimes that which was classed as resistance in the patient had been provoked by the analyst.

For benign unfolding to proceed, it is necessary for the analyst to be in emotional attunement or contact with the patient. For this, a lack of defensiveness is necessary in the analyst as well as in the patient; only in this way can the analyst 'be with' him.

Klauber was clear that in the analytic dialogue the patient cathected the analyst with illusions. He then goes on to investigate the analyst's specific way of cathecting the patient.

The analyst has to identify with his patient's mental and emotional processes in order to achieve empathy, but the identification involved in empathy is not enough. It is too transient and too uncontrolled. In order to achieve continued and deeper understanding, he must not only empathize with his patients but scrutinize their mental processes critically, continually testing the empathic identifications which he holds inside him with his intellect and with the affects which finally determine his judgement. That is, he must hold the patient inside himself cathected with just the right degree of ambivalence, absorbing some parts of the image into himself and holding others at a distance.

(Klauber, 1981, p. 50)

From the patient's side Klauber gives this summary of how the transference unfolds within the structured situation behind the analytic process.

The fact that the patient begins a flight from reality in which he substitutes ingrained images from childhood for the analyst is evidence that his mind cannot stand the strain of the relationship. Basically he attempts to supply himself with the image of the early mother who satisfied in compensation for that of the analyst, who frustrates (though it may sometimes seem the other way round). These two images, one from the present, one from the past, cannot be held separate for an indefinite time. The longings that recognition stirs are too primitive: the mother's first response to her baby is rather surprisingly but significantly called 'recognition behaviour', and to be recognized is a fundamental human need. The images therefore become confused – in psychoanalytic language they are condensed. The System Unconscious, which can appreciate likenesses but cannot discriminate, has taken over. The task of analysis is then to use the discriminating power of the ego to study a greater range of likenesses that would otherwise have been available and to differentiate one from another.

(Klauber, 1981, p. xxix)

This description of the functions of appreciating likenesses and discriminating differences is close to Matte-Blanco's (1975) mode of formulation. It seems that Klauber is suggesting that the appreciation of likenesses is fostered particularly by the attunement and mutuality between analyst and patient, while their discrimination is fostered particularly by explicit confrontation and interpretation. It is perhaps here that a difference of emphasis lies between British Kleinians and Independents. Perhaps Kleinians, in their writing and teaching, emphasize the analyst's 'confrontation' (Greenson, 1967), whereas the Independents speak more about facilitation. Many analysts would agree that both aspects are needed in the analytic process, so that each group is emphasizing a different side of the same coin.

In the psychoanalytic process towards cure Klauber saw both interpretation and other things as vital.

> The experience of timelessness is a mystical experience of profound value, and an essential prerequisite of cure, but it is not the cure itself. Nor does the cure consist only in the secondary evaluation of the primary emotional experience. The cure consists in the fact that the patient's comparison and differentiation of the experience makes possible a new development, in which he can again lose the power of discrimination in terms of a new unconscious synthesis of reality and illusion.
>
> (Klauber, 1987, p. 11)

Interpretations are crucial as a consolidation.

> Interpretations are never final formulations, and the process of analytical working through could in part be defined as the gradual modification of the interpretations by cooperative work until they satisfy both partners.
>
> (Klauber, 1981, p. 133)

Klauber's originality lay in saying, in a verbal language of feeling, that which was not verbal. He succeeded by a careful searching for the words which simply describe experiences in detail. The direct voicing of what for him was obvious was frequently controversially received by his colleagues. He felt that analysis was about telling the truth as you know it. This often took a good deal of courage.


## STEWART

Most recently Harold Stewart (1987, 1989, also in private communication) has been addressing himself to the question of agents for psychic change. In his forthright way he summarizes Independent and other views with clarity, and comes to a conclusion similar to that of Klauber, that, though transference interpretation, particularly that with a 'here and now' immediacy, is a central factor, it cannot be the only agent of change. He lists as also essential: extra-transference interpretations; re-constructions; therapeutic regression; and techniques to overcome an analytic impasse (see also Chapter 8). Here Stewart is voicing a view that is close to a classical one, but with an added emphasis on investigation and use of therapeutic 'de-differentiation' by means of benign regressions. He thus considers that mutuality, or partial de-differentiation between patient and analyst, is an essential in the analytic process, and many Independents would probably agree with him. In the field of the use of benign regression, Stewart values, particularly, the analyst's silence – not for provocative purposes, but when the patient needs time to unfold himself without intrusion.

## ENID BALINT

Enid Balint, in a series of clinical papers stretching over several decades (1959, 1963, 1973, 1987, and in private communication), is also concerned with benign regression in the analytic situation. Like other Independents, she sees that many self-disorders appear to have roots in very early maternal failures. Mothers who fail to know what their infants are really experiencing is one traumatic condition that specially interests her. The pain and terror arising from such traumata readily repeat themselves in the regressive circumstances of the analytic situation.

## KHAN

Masud Khan was particularly concerned with the treatment of patients suffering from ego-disorders resulting from cumulative traumata. He emphasized the essential role of *reconstruction* during the earlier phases of analysis. We have already seen (Chapter 7) such disorders as being the outcome of an often silent accumulation of minute traumata due to the failure of the mother's functioning as a shield protecting her infant and child from anxiety.

Khan thinks that such patients often repeat the elements of their primary infantile relations in minute detail in relation to specific aspects of the analytic situation and to characteristic attributes of the analyst. The attributes are then felt as important *things* rather than as being expressions of a person. Whenever the patient comes across areas of stress, to which the defects in his ego react so that he cannot cope, he manages or avoids them by acting out. However, this must be distinguished from the acting out of neurotic patients with an intact ego. They are in flight from conflict and guilt, not from the panic of being unable to cope. Patients with ego defects due to cumulative traumata often react automatically by taking *flight into reality* whenever they meet a repetition of one of their nodal developmental crises in analysis. It is not conflict, Khan thinks, but their encounter with unmanageable affectivity in the clinical situation which activates the re-enactment.

Khan stresses that steady observation of the patient over long stretches of time is necessary and this may include a temporary tolerance of the patient's attempts to bring the analyst under his omnipotent control. This will enable the analyst to reconstruct the original traumata and their developmental vicissitudes and then to interpret them in regard to their repetition in the analytic situation. This aims at helping the patient perceive what he himself has made the analyst see and register. It may then be possible for him to begin to tolerate that inner panic which compelled him towards this particular re-enactment in the first place. It will also strengthen the patient's confidence in the analytic process. With an increased capacity to feel dependence, the patient is more likely to be able to make regressive use of the analytic situation.

In such ways the analyst provides a function that is akin to that of a mother as a protective shield: he becomes the patient's auxiliary ego. Khan took pains to point out that this methodology should not be mistaken either for a corrective emotional experience type of therapy or for one where the analyst considers himself to have actually become the primary object for the patient in the transference.

Khan believed that a consistent use of the countertransference helps the analyst evaluate the patient's needs in terms of the ego processes involved. By this means he can provide a certain protective shield with regard to specific functions where there was an original lack of it. If, as is usual, the analyst has tuned himself to feel the strain of the clinical process, he is the more capable of assuming that distance which enables him to register, perceive and reconstruct what is happening in the clinical situation.

## LIMENTANI

Adam Limentani is an experienced clinician and highly esteemed teacher of psychoanalysts. His writing predominantly concerns itself with clinical elucidation rather than theory. Like other Independents he has also written considerably upon emotionality. His paper 'Affects in the psycho-analytic situation' (1977) contains a valuable review of the literature and discusses many clinical topics which represent the mainstream of Independent thinking. He warns about the over-emotional analyst:

> we could hardly overlook the affects as they are often the immediate reason why patients seek treatment. . .The vicissitudes of the affects in the analytic situation can, and in my contention are, controlled by the analyst. . .his [the analyst's] thinking and feeling will have far-reaching effects on the course of an analysis. . .A patient will often respond with increasing persecutory anxiety to an excessively *feeling* approach because it can be experienced as seduction, teasing and, finally, frustrating.
>
> (Limentani, 1977, pp. 172–3)

His knowledge of theory enables him to be pointedly critical at times:

> Green (1973, p. 104) has commented on the absence of such a[n] [affect] theory in the writings of Melanie Klein, who has influenced many authors who have dealt with this subject. . .A theory of affects, as such, may be irrelevant to the Kleinian psychology, which could hardly be said to neglect them. However, some amongst our Kleinian colleagues create the impression that all one has to do in order to clarify the most obscure clinical situation is to locate the paranoid or depressive anxiety. It is not always easy to relate this attitude to clinical experience.
>
> (Limentani, 1977, p. 174)

Limentani substantiates many of his points with clinical material. He describes, for instance, how a very disturbed patient, who has gone through a successful first analysis largely at the level of 'symbolic equations' with his analyst, may need a second analysis to work this through with the aim of symbolizing affect at a more discursive level.

Limentani also makes the valuable point that, with patients who have never really 'lived' their lives in the past, a second analysis may be necessary. This would be used to work through again old and discarded affect states by reconstruction of the first analysis, which would often have been swamped by recollections and reconstructions, but in the course of which the patient had found a past in the first place. In such cases, it is only during the second analysis that Greenacre's (1975) point, that reconstructions bring the child and adult together, can become relevant.

In his well-known paper 'A re-evaluation of acting-out in relation to working through' (1966), and also in 'On some positive aspects of the negative therapeutic reaction' (1981), Limentani reassesses acting out and the negative therapeutic reaction. He evaluates the positive, communicative, value of acting out, as opposed to seeing it simply as a destructive, instinctual action due to lack of ego control and without other meaning. Likewise, he maintains that the negative therapeutic reaction can be seen as an acting out in the transference; it can be understood as a stubborn defence against the re-experiencing of pain and psychic suffering associated with early trauma. Thence, it may be conceived as a valuable indicator that more working through is needed. The emphasis on early trauma, affect, reconstruction and the handling of the transference and countertransference is a good example of an Independent analyst at his clinical work.

## PEDDER, PARSONS AND OTHERS

Recent thinking by the newer generation of British Independents bears a striking resemblance to Klauber's approach of looking at analysis as the work of a collaborating and antagonistic dialogue within a relationship that is seen as more symmetrical in form than was envisaged in Freud's Victorian era.

Jonathan Pedder, in Independent fashion, moves between and shows the coherence of many different authors' theories: there is 'Attachment and new beginning: some links between the work of Michael Balint and John Bowlby' (1976); 'Psychotherapy play and theatre' (1977) and 'Transitional space in psychotherapy and theatre' (1979), both of which are centrally using Winnicott; there are also works on grief, loss and mourning (1982, 1985) which use Bowlby and his colleagues among others; and there are many papers on analytic psychotherapy.

Michael Parsons searches, also open-mindedly, for an essence at the heart of things, like realizing with a patient the simple truth that 'distinguishing fantasy from reality really matters' (1986, p. 475). Though using the language of Bion and Matte-Blanco, he speaks like Klauber when he says:

'What really matters about this analysis?' is a question for which patient and analyst must each seek an answer, and both must allow it to take them by surprise. There is a parallel between the patient's need to give up his established ways of coping and the analyst's need not to cling on to his familiar ways of understanding.

(Parsons, 1986, p. 487)


## CASEMENT

Patrick Casement's book *On Learning from the Patient* (1985) has become much valued and widely used as a textbook for psychotherapists. In British Independent style he puts forward just what the title says: how a therapist can provide himself with a discipline of self-examination so that he is more sensitive to listening to the patient's most urgent communications than to his own theories or emotive preconceptions. The book is a series of case studies used to present a mode of 'internal supervision' by the analyst of himself. A similar method had been suggested some years before by Langs (1976) in America. Casement shows how, when puzzled in or between sessions, he sets about consciously identifying in imagination with how the patient might be hearing him, the analyst. In this way Casement seriously and clearly works through a great many impasse situations with his patients.

He explores many aspects of therapeutic discourse and moves adroitly and convincingly from one case example to another. These underline Casement's overriding message, which is that understanding the patient's dynamic movements in the therapeutic interaction is of paramount importance. Because they are outside Casement's express purpose on this occasion, many questions of technique, of how to tackle defence and resistance for instance, are naturally put on one side for the purposes of this particular book.

## COLTART

Another important but controversial contribution to the dialogue of patient and analyst is a paper by Nina Coltart (1986, and in Kohon, 1986a), 'Slouching towards Bethlehem. . .or thinking the unthinkable in psychoanalysis'. The title is taken from a short poem by W. B. Yeats called 'The Second Coming'. A few lines will indicate Coltart's reason for its use.

> The darkness drops again; but now I know
> That twenty centuries of stony sleep
> Were vexed to nightmare by a rocking cradle,
> And what rough beast, its hour come round at last,
> Slouches towards Bethlehem to be born?

Coltart, even more than Klauber, does not bother with systemization of theory but is much concerned clinically. In this paper she muses aloud about some of the underlying qualities of the analytic life and soon comes to the point that every analysis starts out as a mystery – something vital in the patient 'slouches towards Bethlehem waiting to be born'. She is stressing that we are concerned with potentialities in the patient – and also in ourselves. Taking her cue explicitly from Bion, she moves from one epigrammatic thought about the analytic process to another, as, 'it seems to me undesirable that one should communicate certainty about a patient to a patient, or at least, only very occasionally' (in Kohon, 1986, p. 191). This appreciation of the analyst's uncertainty in the idiom of his activity with the patient is typical of many Independents. It probably stems in part from their intellectual background in empiricism.

How strangely diametrically opposed this seems to be to the often proffered advice to students that on the whole it is not a good idea to express oneself with doubt to a patient because it is likely to be muddling to him. Here are a few more thoughts by Coltart:

The act of faith may feel like a spontaneous regression to complete unknowing, and may well be accompanied by dread; it can be disturbing to the analyst and seem like a serious self-induced attack on his ego, which in a way it is. . .

During phases like this in analysis it is true to say that one does not *think* at all during some sessions. . .

Certainly I believe that one not only can but should enjoy psychoanalytical sessions.

(Coltart, in Kohon, 1986, pp. 191, 192, 196)

One point she made in this paper has aroused much controversy. She is picking up the need for spontaneity as used by Winnicott and Klauber. She calls it 'the analyst's act of freedom', borrowing explicitly from Symington, whose contribution will be discussed later.

She describes an impasse with a patient who had reached a state 'which breathed psychosis' for months.

He slouched and humped himself grimly and disjointedly up and down my stairs and in and out of my room. His gaze, when he glanced at me, was shifty, evil, and terrified. He was as if possessed. When I spoke about what I saw and felt, he glowered, grunted and sank further into an ungainly heap. He had never wanted to lie on the couch, so all this was face-to-face. I carried dark and heavy projective identifications, to put it one way, which I tried in vain to decode to him, until I was almost as saturated in despair as he was.

One day, without really thinking it out clearly. . .I simply and suddenly became furious and bawled him out for his prolonged lethal attack on me and on the analysis. I wasn't going to stand for it a second longer, without the remotest idea *at that moment* of what alternative I was proposing! This outburst of mine changed the course of the analysis. . .

. . . we came to see how much, to his own surprise and horror, this man had needed to live out, and have *experienced and endured by another person without retaliation*, his primary hatred of a genuinely powerful mother. . .

I had given up trying to 'understand' this patient, given up theorizing and just sat day after day without memory or desire in a state of suspension, attending only with an empty mind to him and the unknowable truth of himself, which had shaped his life, until such a moment as I was so *at one* with it that I knew it for the murderous hatred it was, and had to make a jump for freedom – his as well as mine, though I did not think that out at the time – by shouting. These acts of faith can feel dangerous.

(Coltart, in Kohon, 1986, p. 195)

Coltart has been severely criticized for this intervention by some who see it simply as impulsive bad analysis, while she has been just as much appreciated by others for being courageous enough to put something before us which is not usually spoken about but thought to be valuable – as some patients will testify. Still other analysts have regretted that this one episode has been taken out of context and clouded the essence of a long and arduous analysis. Those who have heard longer and more detailed descriptions of this analysis know that it was a model of great care and sensitive restraint. Stewart (1977, 1987, 1989) has reported similar occasions of affective expression in analysis with equal clarity and has received the same mixed reactions.

## SYMINGTON

Neville Symington has also considered expressions like these, but in a more theoretical way. His paper 'The analyst's act of freedom as agent of therapeutic change' (1983, and in Kohon, 1986) starts with describing certain assumptions about a patient that any analyst can easily slip into. For instance he had a patient who was paying very much less than his other patients.

I used to sigh to myself and say inwardly, 'poor Miss M, £x is the most I can charge her'. . .It was part of the furniture of my mind and I had resigned myself to it in the same way that I reluctantly resigned myself to the English weather. So the analysis went on. . .until one day a startling thought occurred to me: 'Why can't Miss M pay the same as all my other patients?'.

(Symington, 1983, p. 283)

Symington then proposed putting the fee up. Miss M wept rather piti-fully for a couple of sessions but then resolved to meet the challenge. She extricated herself from a job where the boss called her 'little Mary', took another for more money and gave the push to a parasitic boyfriend 'because she had been able to give the push to a parasitic analyst'. These events were followed by other favourable ones.

Symington follows this with an even more dramatic example, and then looks at the events and sees that he 'was a prisoner of an illusion about the patient's capacities. I had been lassoed into the patient's self perception and I was just beginning to extricate myself from it' (1983, p. 283). He goes on to consider the psychotic and neurotic manifestations of this *lassoing* or illusory stranglehold and comes to the following conclusions.

> My contention is that the inner act of freedom in the analyst causes a therapeutic shift in the patient and new insight, learning and development in the analyst. The interpretation is essential in that it gives *expression* to the shift that has already occurred and makes it available to consciousness. The point though is that the essential agent of change is the *inner* act of the analyst and that this inner act is perceived by the patient and causes change.
>
> (Symington, 1983, p. 286)

Symington seems to be thinking that, at one level, the analyst and patient make a single system. Where this involves an illusory world of the patient, as all transferences must in part be, then the analyst is prone to be lassoed into the patient's illusions. It is a *corporate* activity. As the analyst proceeds, he slowly disengages himself from it and the corporate activity transforms itself. There are shared illusions which the analysis slowly undoes.

Symington uses an analogy with reading a difficult passage from Kant and says:

> I may understand it straight away but, on the other hand, I may not. If I do not it is because I have a false idea and this blinds the intellect. I will be able to understand when I can banish the false idea and allow the idea that Kant is proposing to be grasped by my intellect. I may be quite resistant to doing so. . .To understand Kant I need to adopt a passive attitude so that I can become receptive to his ideas but I must actively be prepared to banish mine. At the moment of understanding I become Kant, as it were, through an action of the ego, whereby I dispel my superego contents and because of this I remain separated and

become slightly more of an individual. At the moment of understanding activity and passivity come together and form a single psychological event.

Now in the psychoanalytical situation, something very similar occurs. The patient's communications and the analyst's feelings and thoughts become the raw material out of which understanding arises. The analyst does not only have his own false ideas to clear away but needs to be passive to the analytical process and combating the resistance that he and the patient are locked into. The attempt to understand is being continuously sabotaged by a parallel process that stimulates and fosters false ideas.

(Symington, 1983, p. 289)

Symington then draws his argument together by saying that 'people are individuals yet part of a corporate entity' (1983, p. 291). One such corporate enterprise, towards falsity sometimes, but also towards truthfulness, is psychoanalysis.


## BOLLAS

In two recent books (1987, 1989), Christopher Bollas articulates a movement that is felt by many Independent psychoanalysts, and particularly by those of the more recent generation. We will describe his ideas at greater length than those of other writers, because, in a lucid style, he draws together and makes intelligible many of the streams of thinking about technique that are running within the Independents at this time. The background ideas are about the analyst's reflections on his own affective responses to the patient's mood and emotional communications within the session. Bollas says:

I believe what I describe is a form of play in the analytic situation. . .I disagree both with those analysts who systematically and rigorously translate the patient's discourse into transference interpretations (all in the name of pure analysis) and with those who believe that each patient needs constant affective and interpretive adjustment from the analyst in order to feel understood. The first practice erodes the analysand's self-analytic capability. . .the second practice expels the analytic element from the scenes of the analytic situation, as the clinician seeks positions of identification with the analysand to provide an empathetically attuned response.

(Bollas, 1989, p. 74)

It will be recalled that Bollas borrows from Winnicott and conceptualized in the first place from the notion of the patient's true-self potentials that have probably been stunted into the creation of false-self or defensive structures. The aim is to help the patient find his own authentic ways of being spontaneous, and this cannot be achieved by the analyst himself being false and inauthentic. The analyst must use his own true self. He must, however, distinguish this from impulsiveness and self-indulgence. Each analyst needs to find his own *idiom* of true analytic working. 'Personal idiom always mediates the unconscious and its laws. Psychoanalysts make interpretations, they invent meanings; they do not discover the meaning conveyed by the patient. No two analysts would say the same thing to the same patient' (1989, p. 73).

The analyst must however be aware of his idiom with the patient. To this end he must treat himself as one of the objects of scrutiny in the analytic process, and by doing so he must be his own subject. At the same time he is an object being used by the patient for his own purposes. The awareness of the *patient's use of him* is central. Thus the analyst needs to move between awareness of his own self and the patient's use of him. Bollas applies this philosophy, and he starts with regard to the recognition of the patient's positive and creative aspects:

> I am puzzled by the fact that in the psychoanalytic literature, the rigorous analysis of destructive processes and the negative transference are presented as if this were a particularly onerous task. My experience is that most analysands are consciously troubled by their destructive thoughts, feelings and actions. . .I try to grapple with what I consider to be a worrying exclusion. . .the psychoanalysis of the patient's life instincts: his love of the analyst, his creative integrations in analytic work, his admirable accomplishments in life.

(Bollas, 1989, p. 77)

Bollas goes on to mention a manic-depressive patient he had treated and says:

One feature of my work with him, my intense confrontations of his delusions, was contingent upon my celebration of his capabilities. I do not think that. . .[he] would ever have been able to bear my confrontative analysis of him had I not also enjoyed his creativity.

(Bollas, 1989, p. 83)

Looking at the other side of this celebration, he cautions:

The problem we face in celebrating the analysand is in not allowing this to be a form of stimulation, gratification or false self adaptation. . . many analysands mistrust the analyst when he comments on a constructive side of their personality. This is often the result of sheer strangeness. . .This may be because, sadly, they have rarely received such recognition from a parent. . .When this is true, the analyst needs to follow up a celebration with an analysis of the patient's response, including their real confusion over how to receive such a communication. . .the patient may experience the analyst's comment as unbelievable because it seems to fulfil an intense though secret wish on the analysand's part. . .[or he] understands such interventions as only valuable because the analyst seems to approve. . .this may necessitate analysis of the false self.

(Bollas, 1989, pp. 87–8)

With activities such as this in mind, Bollas surveys the wide scope of endeavor that the analyst must encompass. He deduces that:

The analyst's interpretive work. . .can only generate insight in the other. . .I am concerned that some psychoanalysts, who place a particularly high value on the unwavering interpretation of the here and now transference, seem to believe that by a constant translation of a patient's discourse *into* transference interpretations, the patient will move from a primitive level of functiong to a less fractured state of mind. . .The question arises: is this analytic work insightful? Has the patient enhanced his understanding of himself and developed a capacity for insight? The answer is yes and no.

(Bollas, 1989, p. 94)

He then develops some conclusions:

Psychoanalytic work must vary according to the immediate emotional reality of the session. . .[but] each of the schools in some respects polemicizes a single feature and analytic life. Each Freudian should also be a Kohutian, Kleinian, Winnicottian, Lacanian and Bionian, as each of these schools only reflects a certain limited analytic perspective.

(Bollas, 1989, p. 99)

He discusses the uses of the analyst's personality:

Analysands sometimes evolve the true self through use of different parts of the analyst's personality. They use the analyst's thoughtfulness, humour, sensuality, doubt, aggression, language capacity, memory, critical-interpretive ability, phantasy life, uninterpretiveness, maternal holding function, paternal presence – a list of personality elements that is virtually endless. . .No analyst is ever neutral once he has met the patient. . .no two patients ever use the analyst's personality elements to achieve specific functions in the same way. . .The psychoanalyst's multiple function, then, refers to the analyst's *usefulness* as an object. . .Although the psychoanalyst enhances the movement of the true self through object usage if he can make elements of his personality available to the patient, this should be accomplished authentically. . .it is absolutely incorrect, in my view, to provide the patient with empathy, celebration, aggression, or even analysis, if such provision is not authentic. The patient's unconscious use of the analyst's true conviction is vital to his eventual well-being.

(Bollas, 1989, pp. 101–7)

One particular facet of Bollas's ideas about technique is one that has been much addressed in previous pages – the use by the analyst of his own emotional responsiveness. Bollas's narrative starts with a consideration of the hysterical character:

It is an essential feature of clinical work for the analyst to reflect on his experience as the patient's object. . .Masud Khan (1975) has written that one aspect of hysterical enactment is the need to compel the other into becoming a witness-accomplice. . .[she] compels the analyst to observe her introjects by means of a kind of performance art. . .

[One patient, Jane] was capable of suddenly violent scenes designed to coerce someone into capitulating to her needs. . .I became aware that she was affecting me but not in any lasting way, since my laughter, or my near-tearfulness, was so immediately evoked by her that I never felt I was actually taking in what she was talking about. . .Jane communicated through the senses. She was attractive and knew it. Her body-gesture syntax led me to view her as a spectacle, luring me away from a thoughtful consideration of her internal life. On occasion, I was less inclined to listen to the content of what she was saying than to be snared by the musicality of her vocal delivery. . .But seeing is not knowing and hearing is not understanding. It is as if the sensational discourse undermines true communication. . .

One aspect of my countertransference was my representation of the transferred maternal introject, as I had become unwilling to be moved beyond the sensational to the cognitive and reflective. . .I was forced into being the mother's outline. . .Hysterics, therefore, do not believe in using language for the reciprocal exchange of feeling and meaning because the mother did not give the hysteric a continuous experience of finding through language adequate transformation of unintegrated and instinctual states.

It is the analyst who becomes the patient's object, not the other way round. Each patient handles us differently, as the object of their transference. . .Hysterical conversion still exists. The primary difference is that in the past the hysteric converted psychic content into a numbed object that was a part of *her* body, whereas now it is the analyst who suffers the effect of hysterical conversion. It is as if my mind (my capacity to be empathically analytic) were numbed by my analysand and as if I. . .were oddly indifferent to the presence of pain in the patient. . .If the repressed is to return it must come from me, for in the hysteric's conversion states the return of the repressed emerges from the psychoanalyst's countertransference.

(Bollas, 1987, pp. 189–99)

Having been introduced to the subject through the analyst's experience of hysteria, we can now consider more generally the *expressive uses of the countertransference*. Bollas thinks that the analyst is compelled to relive elements of the patient's infantile history through his countertransference, through his affective, internal response to the patient. Bollas says:

Disturbed patients, or analysands in very distressed states of mind, know they are disturbing the analyst. Indeed it is as if they need to place their stress in the analyst. . .'Alongside the analyst's freely and evenly hovering attention which enables the analyst to listen simultaneously on many levels', writes Paula Heimann, 'he needs a freely roused emotional sensibility so as to perceive and follow closely his patient's emotional movements and unconscious phantasies' (1960, p. 10). . .the analyst 'must turn his own unconscious like a receptive organ towards the transmitting unconscious of the patient' (Freud, 1912b, p. 115).

The psychoanalyst's establishment of mental neutrality is akin, in my view, to the creation of an internal potential space (Winnicott, 1974), that functions as a frame (Milner, 1952) through which the patient can live an infantile life anew without the troublesome impingements of the clinician's judgements. . .

By establishing a countertransference readiness I am creating an internal space which allows for a more complete and articulate expression of the patient's transference speech. . .Patients create environments. Each environment is idiomatic and therefore unique. . .The capacity [of the analyst] to bear uncertainty. . .[enables] the patient to manipulate us through transference usage. . .To answer the question 'how does the patient at a preoedipal level employ us?', we must turn to the countertransference and ask of ourself, 'how do we feel used?'. . .

Because the analyst is the other patient, sustaining in himself some inter-subjective discourse with the analysand, it is essential to find some way to put forward for analytic investigation that which is occurring in the analyst as a purely subjective and private experience. It is essential to do this because in many patients the free associative process takes place within the analyst, and the clinician must find some way for his internal processes to link the patient with something he has lost in himself. . .the analyst needs to play with the patient, to put forth an idea as an object that exists in that potential space between the patient and the analyst, an object that is meant to be passed back and forth between the two. . .The gradual non-traumatic use of my own subjectivity is an essential element in my work.

(Bollas, 1987, pp. 200–8)

Bollas goes on to define in detail what he calls the *direct use* of the countertransference or affective response of the analyst.

By direct use of the countertransference I mean that quite rare occasion, one which may be of exceptional value to the effectiveness of the analysis, when the analyst describes his experience as the object.

(Bollas, 1987, p. 210)

A summary of a clinical experience illustrates what Bollas means by this.

> [Helen] would pause for a long time, often as much as several minutes, and then she would resume her account as if there had been no interruption. . .she had had a spell of psychotherapy with an analyst who was exceedingly interpretive. She told me that she was accustomed to saying just a bit about something, and the analyst would translate her fragment into a full interpretation about some aspect of her relation to him. . .so I said I thought she was waiting for me to intervene like her previous analyst. She agreed with this, and for some time I thought that this was perhaps the crux of the matter. . .No such luck. Instead I found the situation quite unchanged. . .I knew that I felt irritated. . .during these pauses. . .I began to feel bored and sleepy. . .I decided that the material expressiveness of the patient's mental life was now in me. . .I proceeded to tell her that her long pauses left me in a curious state, one in which I sometimes lost track of her, and it seemed to me that she was creating some sort of absence that I was meant to experience. . .she seemed to disappear and reappear without announcement of either action.
>
> The patient was immediately relieved when I spoke up for my own subjective state. . .In making my experience available to the patient, I put in the clinical potential space a subjective scrap of material that was created by the patient, and by expressing myself I gave a bit of something of Helen's self back to her. . .After some time. . .she told me how distracted and otherworldly her mother was, and how the mother had only been able to relate to a small portion of her as a child, leaving Helen to live through her childhood in secrecy and in dread of her true self.
>
> (Bollas, 1987, pp. 211–13)

Finally, Bollas sees the transference–countertransference interaction as something which is half-known but not properly thought about; Bollas calls this an *unthought known*. With this in mind he makes it clear that:

> it can be valuable for the clinician to report selected subjective states to his patient for mutual observation and analysis. . .I do not think that most interpretations should be either statements of feelings or senses within the analyst or direct disclosures of the position in which the analyst finds himself. Such is the near-phobic dread of this area of

technique within psychoanalysis that I shall state that the analyst must use such interventions sparingly. . .each analyst must be thoroughly tuned in to the patient's unconscious response to his intervention. . .

The analyst's disclosure of a selective subjective state of mind is not equivalent to the expression of affect (for example, 'you make me angry') or the revelation of an unanalysed feeling or phantasy. . .More mental work goes into the evolution of the statement 'I feel' or 'I sense' than I bring to interpretation proper. . .the psychoanalyst's relation to the unthought known is *thoughtful*, even though the core of significance has yet to be discovered.

(Bollas, 1987, pp. 230–2)


## CONCLUSION

Emphasis has been placed in this chapter on the need for the analyst to make emotional contact with, and conceptualize about, the specific personal details of the patient's actual feeling state of the moment. This openness may be assisted by a particular theory, but, in the last analysis, the openness of the analyst's mind must take precedence over a particular theoretical orientation.

We have been describing a tendency among Independents to view the analytic process, not only from its confrontative aspects, but also from those of unity and mutuality between patient and analyst. Confrontation and mutuality with the patient in analysis seem to be two, apparently contradictory, aspects of an issue of great sensitivity. There can be little doubt that the confrontation of unconscious phantasy, particularly in its defensive aspects, is the fundamental key to the psychoanalytic process. The Kleinian tradition has performed a service to psychoanalysis by emphasizing important, hitherto unrecognized, aspects of phantasy and defensive process that require confrontation. In doing this they have, rightly, tended to polemicize confrontation. The Independents respect this point of view. They too consider that it is a primary necessity for the analyst to centre himself upon a distance from the patient that is optimal for objectivity. However, recognizing the need to facilitate the patient's own spontaneous propensity to analyse, they have put forward the importance of mutuality and, hence, have perhaps tended to polemicize this. It seems that a *movement*, in thought and feeling, between the two aspects is essential on the part of the analyst. However, since confrontation and mutuality can be felt to be such antipathetic emotions, feelings run high when the two sides are polemicized. This would seem to be a dialectic process that is fraught with aggravation, yet is central to the evolution of analysis.

With this in mind it seems that we might now be in a position to reassess and make a new statement about analytic *neutrality*. Neutrality is basically essential to facilitate a patient's reverie, untroubled by demands from the analyst. It has often been thought that emotional expression by the analyst must violate this neutrality. Yet in these pages we have seen some expressions of the value of the analyst carefully communicating, at certain times, something from his emotional core. Is there some general theoretical way that the dividing line between a useful expression and a deleterious one can be construed? It seems that a viewpoint utilizing, not only Bollas and Winnicott, but also the logical precision of Matte-Blanco might be helpful.

Bollas has introduced us to the concept of the shared potential space between analyst and patient (he also calls it *the intermediate space*, a term introduced originally by Winnicott [1971a]) and related this to neutrality. Briefly, going back to the beginning with regard to transitionality: a transitional object is one that is experienced as part of the self and also not part of the self. A transitional or potential space is, likewise, an area of experience that is felt as both self and not-self. An intermediate space is an interpersonal phenomenon: one where two or more people experience that there is a *commonality between them but that they are separate* – the other is experienced as of the self and yet other.

It is in this intermediate space that Bollas, following Winnicott, makes plain that the serious 'play' of analysis must occur; it is here that creative transformations seem to occur. Can we say any more about the characteristics of this space? First, the term 'space' can only be a metaphor drawn from experience of the physical world, yet it is not essentially a physical matter. What, however, is essential is that the activity must involve the experience of its belonging to the self and not-self at the same time. Furthermore, this must occur in *both* participants. This is what the present writer has called a 'symmetrization between selves' (Matte-Blanco, 1975; Rayner and Tuckett, 1988). In this particular symmetrization, the self and another are felt to be the same, fused, identified, in harmony, attuned (Stern, 1985) or as one. It is an essential experience in mutual empathy. However, transitional and intermediate experiences are not just simple interpersonal symmetrizations. These would become crude loss of boundary. In a transitional activity there is also the awareness that the other is not of the self. In Matte-Blanco's terms, a symmetrization and an asymmetrization 'lean upon' each other. It is an activity using an essential paradox. The other *is* self (symmetrical) and *not*-self (asymmetrical) concurrently.

If this paradox is the defining characteristic for therapeutic play to occur, then this psychic condition of self = other = not-self must be maintained for therapeutic activity to occur. It seems that this is the essence of the analyst's neutrality. To maintain neutrality, the analyst must always have available a capacity to be identified with the patient and yet separate, to feel the same as, and different from, to be together and apart, in sympathy and antipathy, and so on.

When defences come into play this combination overbalances and neutrality is lost. It will be clear that the patient cannot be expected to maintain neutrality; its exemplar and guardian must be the analyst himself. When the analyst loses this combination then he has stopped analysing, and he will be likely to impinge upon the patient in untherapeutic ways.

However, it will be becoming evident that expression of affect by the analyst is not precluded by this neutral mode. What must be maintained by the analyst is the paradoxical activity between identification and dis-identification. This in itself is a subtle activity which requires much skill, commitment and self-discipline.

Under these conditions, if an affect is communicated by the analyst, there must simply be a *readiness* to move in thought to its negation and its converse. Thus, if the analyst communicates, say, that he is being made cross by the patient, then neutrality demands that he move in thought away from this position to envisage converse and other affects about the patient. This is ordinary analytic reflectiveness. When, on the other hand, an analyst simply 'emotes' and says something like 'I'm fed up with you' and leaves it at that, then the analyst is expressing himself from one set position only. The paradoxical identification and dis-identification, or self = other = not-self state, is fractured. Put in another way, analysis has stopped when there is no movement by the analyst in his identifications of and with the patient. It is the paradoxical movement of affect-thought by the analyst that seems to be essential to neutrality, not grey inexpressiveness.

There seem to be links between this neutral mode of movement in thought and the empirical mode, which we described in Chapter 8 as being at the heart of the Independents' philosophy. Their avowedly tolerant attitude, which values trial and error, probably affects their idiom of interpretative activity in the clinical situation. Like the registration of an erroneous hypothesis in scientific activity, an interpretation that has error in it is likely to be painful and even seem foolish after the event. However, just as in a scientific experiment, it can none the less be valuable – even essential.

Friendly tolerance, which is really present and not just an ideal among the Independents when they meet together, has the disadvantage that it may excuse lax thoughtlessness. However, it also facilitates exploration in unknown territories of thought, which is just as important for a patient as it is for the analyst.

# 11 Beyond the Couch: The Applications of Psychoanalysis

ERNEST JONES WAS a pioneer in illuminating the cultural sciences with psychoanalytic understanding. Even by 1911–12 his output of papers was prodigious. He had great breadth of scholarship, but so impatient was he that quantity often won over grace of style. However, his introductions to analysis for the educated public are among the earliest in English and are still a pleasure to read.

Jones was one of the first in the field of psycho-history. He strove to show that aspects of a creative work can be well understood, not simply as a thing in isolation, but as the product of its creator's character traits in interplay with life events. Not long after Freud's monograph on Leonardo (1910b), Jones followed with a short study of Andrea del Sarto (1913a). Why, asked Jones, did such a supreme master of technique and of the portrayal of beauty fail to move the viewer's heart and thus lack true greatness? The answer, Jones found, lay in del Sarto's marriage: his wife was very beautiful and his favourite model, but she was greedy and tyrannical. Under her influence he was alienated from his family and friends, and his art steadily declined. However, he seems to have delighted in giving in to her every whim. Jones suggests that del Sarto gladly gave up his authenticity, to use a present-day term, for his wife's sake, and with this his true art forsook him. Allied to this, Jones also noted, was del Sarto's latent passive femininity married to his wife's active masculinity. Nowadays, perhaps, del Sarto could also be viewed from the point of view of false-self compliance.

He wrote other short psycho-biographies on the poet von Kleist (1911d), on Louis Napoleon (1913b) and on the chess master Paul Morphy (1931b). Not a psycho-biography, but most famous in this genre, is Jones's essay on Hamlet and Oedipus (1910b), later expanded into a book (1949). What is it, Jones asks, that inhibited Hamlet's will in his resolve to kill Claudius, and led to the vacillations which make the core of the play? Jones gives an oedipal explanation: it is because Hamlet sees in Claudius that sexual usurper who is also his own infantile self. Hamlet slips away from this realization into female passivity. This, alternating with his active desire to revenge his loved father, makes for the vacillation.

In contradistinction to those scholars who maintain that knowing an author's life casts no useful light on the nature of a work of literature, Jones naturally sees Hamlet's indecision as a reflection of Shakespeare's own unconscious emotionality. Jones puts great weight, for instance, upon the passive femininity in Shakespeare's character and upon the thesis that the play was written within a year of the death of his own father. Critics, however, have pointed out the shaky evidence for both these ideas (Brome, 1982).

Jones's understanding, not only of Shakespeare, but also in his study of Paul Morphy the chess master (1931b) has been ridiculed by many scholars. Yet he is, with justification, respected by the psychoanalytically inclined. For those who maintain that a work of literature or art is best studied in its pure form, in isolation, psycho-history is an irrelevance, but, for those who wish to enquire into the personal and emotional roots of the artefacts of culture, Jones is an inspiring pioneer.

Jones was not content to rest with these applications of analysis. A list of some of his titles will indicate his scope. For sociology and politics there are: 'A linguistic factor in English characterology', 'The island of Ireland', 'The inferiority complex of the Welsh', 'The psychology of constitutional monarchy', 'The psychology of quislingism', 'The Jewish question'. For anthropology and folklore there are, for instance: 'The symbolic significance of salt', 'Psychoanalysis and anthropology', 'Mother right and the sexual ignorance of savages'. For the study of religion there are: 'The God complex', 'The madonna's conception through the ear' and 'A study of the Holy Ghost'. Some of these, like 'The God complex', are brilliant and historic; others display Jones's vast reading but are less relevant. (They are all published in Jones 1974a or 1974b.)

Jones was also indefatigable in reading papers and giving talks to groups of other professionals and to the public. The other members of the British Psycho-Analytical Society were also tireless in giving papers and talks through the 1920s and 1930s. There were hundreds by the Glovers, Flugel, Rickman, Isaacs, Riviere, Searl, Sharpe, Chadwick and others. Their efforts did justice to the vital importance of psychoanalysis in humankind's cultural history. No journal seemed to be too grand or too humble to publish their contributions.

J. C. Flugel, an academic psychologist of distinction at the same time as being a practising analyst, wrote widely on matters of social and humanistic concern. His *Psycho-Analytic Study of the Family* (1921b) was the first book in English on this subject. The *Psychology of Clothes* (1930) is also a classic in the study of social movements. His *Man, Morals and Society* (1945), aiming to use psychoanalytic insights to address ethical questions for the postwar world, became a best seller with the educated public.

John Rickman, as much as Flugel, had a profound sense of social concern allied to a grasp of individual and group processes. His psychologically informed commentaries on the politics of the time appeared frequently in the British medical press in the years leading up to the Second World War, and these were appreciated enough to be often reprinted in daily newspapers.

Returning to the study of art and literature, Ella Sharpe must take pride of place. Much less prolific than Jones, her writings betray her wide knowledge and subtle feeling for literature and have a grace of style that Jones often lacked. 'Francis Thompson, a psycho-analytical study' (1925) is psycho-history. In Thompson, a leading English religious poet of the nineteenth century, Sharpe traces out lines of emotionality in his work to do with his profound identification with his mother and abysmal dread of and loneliness at the thought of leaving her. In 'The impatience of Hamlet' (1929) she takes issue with Jones, suggesting that it is not a tragedy of procrastination but of impatience. No doubt realizing that Shakespeare was England's greatest 'psychoanalytic' contributor to the world, she wrote other works on the playwright, but she died before completing the book she had hoped to write. Though psycho-history has often been criticized, its advent has changed the face of ordinary biography. None is now complete without a consideration of childhood roots and their part in the subject's later life, even though many biographers disavow any psychoanalytic heritage.

Since the war, work of literary interpretation has hardly kept up the pace of earlier years. From the Independents there has been Mitchell's work on feminism (1972, 1974, 1978, 1982, 1984) and passing papers about art and literature, particularly by Rycroft (1955), Pedder (1977, 1979a), Maxwell (1981), Hildebrand (1986) and Parsons (1990). There is a notable contribution in the work of John Padel. His book *New Poems by Shakespeare* (1981) is primarily a work of literary scholarship, and psychoanalysis is hardly mentioned. But without Padel's long clinical experience and psychoanalytic sensitivity it is doubtful whether he would have found the inspiration to work out the thesis of his study.

Padel addresses himself to the puzzling lack of meaningful order in the published sequence of Shakespeare's sonnets. Basing himself upon the style and content of the sonnets, Padel re-orders them into separate poems, usually of three or four sonnets each. These poems can then be seen to be commentaries upon life events. What is more, they are seemingly written to a single person. Following many scholars before him, he sets out to ask whether the sonnets may indeed have been written for one person, and settles for an affirmative answer. Not for the first time, he considers that they were written for William Herbert, Earl of Pembroke. Turning to historical documents of the Herbert family, he suggests that the sonnets were commissioned by Herbert's father and mother (the sister of Sir Philip Sidney, the poet) on various occasions, sometimes to celebrate a birthday but more often to provide a philosophical homily to persuade the young man to forsake his selfish ways and to settle down into marriage and responsible adulthood.

The care and detail of Padel's literary scholarship place him in a different category from writers in the same region, like Jones. It is the use of an analytic background together with this scholarship that gives his studies a special dimension. Though Padel leads the way into a new area of measured scholarship using psychoanalysis, at present probably few among the Independents have sufficient scholarship in the arts or classics to follow him. One exception is Parsons's (1990) new approach to the works of ancient Greece. Of course in the region of visual art there are Milner's many works (1950a, 1958, 1969, 1987; see also Chapter 4).

## PSYCHOANALYSIS AND OTHER PROFESSIONS
## BETWEEN THE WARS

Jones, and Glover also, were thoroughgoing in telling the educated public about psychoanalysis, but primarily they were committed to creating a band of independent-minded analytic thinkers, who could also work together as a team. They succeeded, and psychoanalysts respected themselves and were respected as members of a serious therapeutic discipline. Jones and Glover were not, however, interested in co-operating as equals with other professionals. Thus, with clinical psychiatrists and non-Freudian psychotherapists, as well as with other helping professions, contact remained sporadic until after the Second World War when Jones's and Glover's influence in the British Society had waned.

## WINNICOTT

An exception to Jones's embargo was Donald Winnicott's work. A paediatrician first of all, he saw several tens of thousands of mothers and babies over his professional lifetime. This quantity of empirical data outstretches most of that upon which more formal scientific research is based.

Starting outside analysis, Winnicott was one of the first great exponents of creating an interface in data and theory in both directions with other professions. The applications of analysis he made were more than just telling others about psychoanalytic understanding of a subject, though he was a master of popularization. He also drew in understanding from other fields, particularly his speciality of medicine and also social work, to contribute to analytic theory.

It was the mothers and babies who came for routine checks to his hospital out-patient clinics who provided the evidence which inspired him in his understanding of infant development. It was from here that his conviction of the crucial centrality of the environmental factor in child development and its pathology grew. Thus, paediatrics and psychosomatics were at the core of his consideration of analytic theory, just as child psychiatry and biology were at the heart of Bowlby's.

Already in his first book, *Clinical Notes on Disorders of Childhood* (1931a), his psychoanalytic understanding was helping to transform him into a paediatrician who believed in the importance of children's feelings. He described children's symptoms, like shyness, enuresis, fidgetiness, eczema, and showed they were no longer simply physiological malfunctions, but intelligent and therefore intelligible solutions, of a sort, to human emotional conflict.

The function of the professional was, for Winnicott, to enhance the facilitating environment provided by mothers. With this in mind, it was a duty of an analyst to move for some of the time from behind the couch into the applied field. Phillips (1988) summarizes this:

In Winnicott's view experience was traumatic for the child if it was incomprehensible, beyond the child's grasp. The onus was on the mother, at first, to present the world to the infant in manageable doses. And the onus on those helping mothers and infants, Winnicott believed, was to protect this process. 'If it be true, or even possible,' he writes, 'that the mental health of every individual is founded by the mother in her living experience with her infant, doctors and nurses can make it their first duty not to interfere. Instead of trying to teach mothers how to do what in fact cannot be taught, paediatricians must come sooner or later to recognise a good mother when they see one and then make sure that she gets full opportunity to grow to her job' (Winnicott, 1965 p. 161).

(Phillips, 1988, p. 2)

With the coming of the war in 1939 Winnicott became a psychiatric consultant to the government's scheme of evacuating children from their homes in areas liable to bombing. It turned out to be a unique opportunity to assess the relative importance of environmental provisions. He came to the conclusion that children with good early parental experiences were better able to make constructive use of their new environment. We can see here his paediatric and psychiatric work informing his later psychoanalytic theory as much as his analysis of patients was informing his preventive psychiatry.

He felt he must tell the world at large what he had the unique opportunity to find in his clinic and consulting-room, so he gave hundreds of talks, in person and on the radio, and wrote innumerable articles for parents and various professional groups with the aim of altering them to the new ways of understanding interpersonal emotionality and human development. The ordinary technical language of psychoanalysis was alien to him so he found his own. He was often idiosyncratic, and also at times contradictory, in his attempts to communicate in words his impressions of the earliest experiences of a baby with mother. Though these were pre-verbal experiences, he described them with an evocative fluency that was nearer to poetry than scientific diction.

Second to paediatrics, his greatest professional influence was probably through teaching social workers. His second wife, Clare, was an active social worker, senior administrator and lecturer, as well as psychoanalyst. In Britain after the war, psychiatric social workers, engaged with the mentally ill and in child guidance, had a central core of their training that was analytically informed, much of it from Winnicott's lead. This was well established for many years, but, about two decades ago, after a great increase in the legal powers and the size of the profession in Britain, there was a move away from specialization to an almost exclusive adherence to generic social-work training. With this came a turn away from long-term individual casework responsibility in the teams run by the local government authorities. The psychoanalytic element in much training and practice waned. It has not yet caught on again within social work itself. But the last decade has seen an enormous growth in psychotherapy and counselling by many members of all the caring professions in Britain. Much of this is analytically informed, often to a high standard – but sometimes imperfectly so.

Winnicott was still drawing on his paediatric experience when, later in his career, he worked exclusively as an analyst and child psychiatrist in a well-known teaching hospital. Seeing that long-term analysis was out of the reach of the majority, for both financial and geographical reasons, he worked out a mode of psychotherapeutic consultation (1971b) with children and also their parents. He worked with a swift interpretativeness that used his great intuitive gifts.

Winnicott assumed that everyone, child or adult, has a primary wish to be understood. He did not start with the conventional idea that a patient is essentially more evasive than communicative. Rather, he saw children and adults as potentially just as collaborative as antagonistic. Because of this, his psychoanalytic presence, as with many other Independents, might not seem so imposing as that of some classical or Kleinian analysts.

Here is a short fragment from an early example of a therapeutic consultation by Winnicott.

an intelligent girl of twelve who had become nervous at school and enuretic at night. No one seemed to have realized that she was struggling with her grief at her favourite brother's death. . .events had taken place in such a way that she never experienced acute grief, and yet grief was there waiting for acknowledgement. I caught her with an unexpected 'you were very fond of him weren't you?' which produced loss of control, and floods of tears. The result of this was a return to normal at school and a cessation of the enuresis at night.

(Phillips, 1988, p. 52, quoting Winnicott, 1964, p. 212)

Though never formally setting out on set-piece family therapy, he would quickly engage with parents as and when they were co-operatively available. Sometimes he would work, like Freud with little Hans's father, with parents, helping them to manage at home while hardly seeing the child himself. He worked with great daring and flair. He never believed that his methods could be taught through general principles. Some have thought since that this was not completely right. But his thought was in line with the belief that mothers cannot be taught to be good-enough mothers. They can only be enabled to use their potentials. For him, teaching was facilitating the learner's potentials. Thus, he did not believe in the founding of a 'school' where certain general principles could be taught.

## BOWLBY

John Bowlby might seem the antithesis of Winnicott, but they had much in common. Both were inspired in their teens by Darwin. Both had a feeling for personal individuality, the community and humankind at large, in equal proportions, though it was Winnicott who emphasized the aloneness of the self. Both engaged with problems of illness and human development on a wide social scale in ways that neither Freud nor Klein ever personally attempted. Both devoted much of their lives, and inspired many others, to facilitating environmental provisions for the healthy growth of children. Both achieved rare success beyond the realm of psychoanalysis in what they attempted.

There is no need to dwell further upon the world-wide importance of the work of Bowlby – this has been attempted at some length in Chapter 5. It will be recalled that, like Winnicott with paediatrics, Bowlby tried to feed the conclusions, drawn from his studies of biological and statistical research, back into the psychoanalytic culture for therapeutic use in Britain. But, as we have noted, he has perhaps had less success, in this one particular area only, than Winnicott.

## PSYCHOANALYSIS – IN ISOLATION
## OR WITHIN THE COMMUNITY?

The years leading up to the Second World War still saw Ernest Jones, as its long-standing president, assisted by Edward Glover, keeping the British Psycho-Analytic Society in rather lofty isolation from those other institutions, like the Tavistock Clinic, which practised psychotherapy less rigorously but which were probably more in touch with the British people generally. For instance, for many years all students of psychoanalysis were forbidden by Jones to work at the Tavistock Clinic. This was finally broken when Bion, who was a mature and respected psychiatrist while still a student of psychoanalysis, simply refused to obey Jones, and no action was taken against him.

At the same time, there was much dissatisfaction with Jones and Glover among the established members of the Society. Not only did the membership think that they were high-handed in their offices, but also that they were not concerned enough about the social issues of the well-being of ordinary people at large. The country was now on the verge of being engulfed by war and this brought into the open a sense of duty and concern for the community and for humankind in general. These emotions were never far beneath the surface among many – probably most – British liberal intellectuals of the time, and now they surfaced with vigour. One important underlying upheaval leading to the Controversial Discussions of 1942-3 was revolt against the policies of Jones and Glover, particularly their isolationist attitude to the community at large. This was quite separate from the controversies between Anna Freud and Melanie Klein which have since gained fame.

Concern about the part psychoanalysis can play in the life of the community was thus deeply entrenched among the members of the British Society from long before the war. This tradition has been strongly carried on, without a break, ever since, especially by the Independent stream. It could be said that there have always been two contrasting directions of duty among British psychoanalysts: one is towards clarifying and strengthening psychoanalysis itself, while the other is towards using it for the benefit of others. They must naturally go hand in hand, but sometimes they have acted in opposition.

Those who feel a duty to use analysis in the service of others can, sometimes rightly, be accused of watering down, or obscuring, analytical essentials. On the other hand, the 'pure' analyst can, also rightly, be accused of sterile self-absorption. Over recent decades, many Independents have sometimes felt that the other two groups, the Kleinians and the Anna Freudians, were often too exclusively concerned with analytic purity and were shrinking psychoanalysis into self-absorption. On the other hand, the Independents themselves were criticized, often even condemned, for being too concerned with the functions of analysis in society and thus becoming analytically inefficient. Independents, who recognized that analytic rigour must go hand in hand with a service to the community, felt that this condemnation was unjustified. At all the events, many Independents claim that it has been they particularly who, often against resistance from others, have engaged psychoanalysis in useful interchange with the community in which it lives.

John Rickman, though at the centre of the Psycho-Analytical Society, had an attitude very different from Jones's isolationist trend. His sense of the equal importance of the individual inner world, the group, the community and humankind at large has already been noted. Though younger than Jones, and his assistant as a pioneer, he had a depth of sympathy and breadth of social vision that Jones perhaps lacked. His qualities came to the fore, most usefully for the future of psychoanalysis, in an unusual way during the Second World War years.

## WARTIME, THE NORTHFIELD EXPERIMENT, RICKMAN

At the start of the war, many younger analysts joined the Medical Corps of the army. Though not so young, Rickman also joined and became an inspiration to the many psychiatrists and social scientists who crossed his path and became interested in analysis.

Many of these army psychiatrists and scientists became concerned with therapeutic activity, not just individually but in groups and in the culture of a community. Their ideas certainly stemmed from Freud, and particularly from his way of just listening to patients for hours on end, and to everything they said. But ideas came from other areas as well.

The army in wartime, both in psychiatry and in combat units, quickly seized upon new thinking, much of it coming from Kurt Lewin and other 'gestalt' psychologists, about the workings of groups. People like Tom

Main, researching such things as high and low morale in combat units, picked up the importance of group influences, and particularly *mutuality*, in supporting against personal depression, disaffection and panic in battle. Wise soldiers, of course, have always intuitively understood the importance of this mutuality.

The vital necessity of mutuality between people alerted researchers to the object-relations point of view in psychoanalysis. They began to see that classical instinct theory is necessary but not sufficient. Real human relations, and their internal representatives, matter for well-being as much as instincts and the internal phantasies that express them.

Another component in understanding came from an unexpected source. For years, during the early part of the war, a large army was waiting in Britain. It trained hard but the boredom of thousands of men had to be combated. One way devised was to have each unit spend several hours a week discussing general current affairs with their officers. It came to be the one place where an unheard-of thing was allowed – soldiers were free, and expected, to argue with their officers. Here was an equality of exploration in thought. Many officers objected to this, for it seemed a subversive innovation. However, it won the day for the time being, as it staved off boredom and enhanced morale.

In time many of the analytically interested psychiatrists and social scientists found their way to Northfield in Birmingham. This was one of several army hospitals treating soldiers with 'war neuroses'. It is famous in the history of psychodynamic endeavour, for it was here that many of the innovations of the postwar years originated. The later founders of the Tavistock Institute of Human Relations, like Wilfred Bion, Elliot Jaques, Henry Dicks, Tommy Wilson, Harold Bridger, Isabel Menzies Lyth, Eric Trist and Jock Sutherland met each other through the Northfield workers. So also did Tom Main, Clifford Scott, Millicent Dewar and Michael Foulkes, the classical Viennese analyst, who was one of the originators of group therapy.

A moving force behind the analytic thinking central to the work at Northfield was Rickman. Main has given him first place of honour in his gratitude to those there, calling him the 'hidden hero of psychoanalysis' (Main, 1989). During the Russian Revolution he had set up and run makeshift hospitals on behalf of the British Quakers, and he had plenty of experience of institutions and groups of all sorts. Later, as Jones's main administrative colleague, he had been a prime mover in developing the Institute of Psycho-Analysis in London with its sophisticated structure which has run well for very many years. His understanding of medicine and analysis, as well as of the behaviour of groups and institutions, together with his great generosity and acumen, gave a central inspiration to these workers in wartime. It was Rickman, of course, who first differentiated psychological theories on the basis of whether they were one-body, two-body, three-body or multi-bodied in nature. He was using a mode of thought that has become second nature to many Independent psychoanalysts. It leads to the importance of 'moving in thought' – between systems of ideas and between levels of systems, as opposed to focusing within one mode in a 'pure' but tunnel-visioned way.

Perhaps it was from his family background, with its Quaker meetings, that Rickman also came to recognize the value of, and to develop, the way of facilitating a group to wait, often in silence, for emotional spontaneity to arise.

## THE TAVISTOCK INSTITUTE OF HUMAN RELATIONS, THE WORK OF BRIDGER, TRIST AND THEIR COLLEAGUES

One of the fruits of Northfield has emerged in work with industry and large organizations.

Eric Trist recently recalled the beginning of this development: that during the war years and particularly at Northfield, 'There was a great coming together of psychoanalysis with the social sciences – as a result of the emergence of the object relations approach, which, in the eyes of us at the Tavistock Institute, unified the psychological and social fields' (Trist in L. Klein, 1989, p. 50). It is useful to note Trist's stress here upon object relations as adding a new dimension to the instinct theory, which by itself could not become a unifying ground.

With the coming of peace, many of the old friends kept together and became founders of the Tavistock Institute of Human Relations. For forty years this has been a privately funded research and consultancy organization used by industry and other large organizations. It is allied to and shares a building with, but is not part of, the Tavistock Clinic, which is a National Health Service institution. Founder members included Bion, who was analysed by Rickman and then by Klein, Jaques, who was an analyst with Klein but later became a distinguished academic in social science, and Tommy Wilson, who became an analyst but spent his life working with industry. Trist, analysed by Heimann, did not train as an analyst but remained a social scientist, becoming chairman of the Tavistock Institute and perhaps its most distinguished theoretical thinker and writer.

Harold Bridger, a teacher of mathematics before the war, found his way via officer selection to the Northfield group. He trained as an analyst with Heimann but has devoted the major part of his life to the Tavistock Institute's consultancy work in industry and other large organizations. He has written little, and colleagues like Trist may be more scholarly, but as a facilitator of others he is outstanding.

After the 'great coming together' of the 1940s, the interplay of ideas between analysis and the social sciences became static until recent years when 'the conditions of society on the one hand and theoretical advances on the other are bringing psychoanalysis and the social sciences together again' (Trist, in L. Klein, 1989, p. 50). This rapprochement has centred upon Bridger's concern with the theory and management of *transitions*.

Social scientists have noted that, with developments, particularly in production and in communications technology, a state of rapid, continuous, almost exponential change is taking place in social systems throughout the world. Change on this scale has been unknown before in human history.

With the external environment in rapid flux, organizations large and small are called upon to be ready to transform many of their functions if they are to survive, let alone flourish. It is speculated – and doubted by other social scientists, it must be admitted – that this is a state of affairs in which a *social natural selection* and survival of the fittest takes place in commerce, industry and, at a lesser pace, also in government. The Darwinian frame of reference, also beloved of many British Independents, is evident here.

Macro-social conditions under these circumstances are in a state of 'white-water' turbulence. Incidentally, the mention of white water brings us into the region of mathematical chaos theory.

Bridger understood that institutions must learn to *manage transitions* efficiently or perish. Better, he thought, to prepare for change with conscious intent than passively hope for the best. He then set about informing his colleagues of Winnicott's conceptualization of *transitional phenomena* (Winnicott, 1971a). He stressed particularly the role of play, illusion and make-believe in the transitional 'third area'. Kurt Lewin (1935) had, many years earlier, introduced the notions of psychological space, boundaries and permeability at a border, when investigating group dynamics, while Winnicott developed similar notions from the study of the individual psyche. But it was from Winnicott that Bridger received the inspiration to think particularly about the active management of transitions.

Bridger (Ambrose, in L. Klein, 1989) drew attention to the value of considering separate phases of transition. Anthony Ambrose, a psycho-analyst also associated with the Tavistock Institute for many years, has theorized upon this in detail. He says that the basic feature of transitional learning is active, exploratory learning, not a passive kind as when a person is shown what to do. 'Transitional learning. . .refers to the process whereby an individual who, having gained new insight into why he behaves in a peculiar way in a particular situation, gradually realises the implications for his whole character structure. In other words, he extends an insight into one part of his behavioural or psychic system to the system as a whole in which the part is embedded' (Ambrose, in L. Klein, 1989, p. 153).

A first aspect of transitional learning is an essential scanning of the external and internal conditions of an institution and its individuals. Old ideas and practices must be scrutinized in order to relinquish those that are no longer appropriate. This is, perhaps, akin to the analyst's free-floating attention. Second, comes discovery, choice and implementation of new ideas found to be effective in the changed situation. Here there may be necessity for profound paradigm shifts or changes in basic as-sumptions. This needs to occur both on the part of individuals working together and also at the level of groups within the institution. Group shifts cannot take place without transitions within individuals and, vice versa, there cannot be stable transformations in individuals without group change. The third aspect of transition is that of getting at the real meaning, the deeper implications of the dissonance that is being expe-rienced within the system.

Winnicott, following Melanie Klein, stressed that in the child, transi-tion was mediated by play and a similar function operated in adults. Bridger suggests that a similar process, which he calls 'design' and which involves transitional space activity between the planners, must be acti-vated in institutions. It is like the play of a child, but with more conscious thought and personal responsibility involved (Trist, in L. Klein, 1989). Jaques in his seminal book *The Changing Culture of a Factory* (1951) was looking in a similar direction but without today's sense of urgency.

The similarity will also be noticed between Bridger's organization in transition and Tom Main's (1989) therapeutic community, discussed below. There is in fact at least one actual treatment community, Peper Harow for very disturbed adolescents, run on lines close to those of Main but which owes its original inspiration to Bridger. Main and Bridger were colleagues at Northfield. There is also the Cotswold Community which derives much inspiration from Donald Winnicott.

With the problem of institutional transitions taking on a new urgency, work on this is being used by organizations and government agencies in much of western Europe and the US. Bridger, Trist, Ambrose and their colleagues have thus founded the Institute for Transitional Dynamics in Switzerland. This is an international organization expressly studying institutional change.

## THERAPEUTIC COMMUNITY, THE WORK OF TOM MAIN

A courageous Northfield experiment was conducted by another leading force in psychoanalytic thinking, Wilfred Bion, and it became a milestone. He had shown that the natural self-discipline of soldiers can be damaged if their officer takes upon himself all disciplinary responsibility. However, this can be reversed if the officer uses his rank only to help the soldiers fashion their own self-disciplinary functions in frank, spontaneous, Quaker-like, free, purposive discussion. But there was then trouble from a different direction: before the soldiers achieved this self-disciplined excellence there were weeks of uncontrolled ill-discipline. Bion had the nerve to stand this, but the higher military authority in the hospital did not, and Bion was posted elsewhere. This caused some indignation among Bion's scientific colleagues, but Tom Main, a younger psychiatrist at the time, regarded it as an important fact that, in attending to the plight of his soldier patients, Bion had not noticed the plight of higher authority (personal communication by Main; see also Main, 1989).

Main set about an exercise in systems-theory thinking (1946) before the term had even been invented. He saw Northfield Hospital as a *community* of interdependent systems. He also recognized that each system in it, from the human individual to the hospital as a whole in its relation to the army as a whole, needed for its own health to monitor, explore and modify its own functions. This discursive activity was by its nature therapeutic. Discussion is necessary for health; therapy for Main is part of ordinary life.

Warned by Bion's experience, Main saw to it that he took note of, and engaged with, all the systems involved when he initiated something new. It proved a complex task, but at least, as Tom Main said, he was not sacked. It was this idea of the necessity of the self-monitoring of all systems in an organization that gave birth to Main's original concept of a therapeutic community.

After the war Main was appointed as medical director of the Cassel Hospital, which is a small hospital for the treatment of neuroses. Main determined to fulfil his dream of creating a therapeutic community. He was convinced that in order to achieve this, he and the therapeutic staff had to become analytically trained, which in due course they were. With about a hundred beds and all patients receiving individual analytic therapy, the hospital went into the new National Health Service in 1948.

From his time at Northfield, Main had realized that various socially accepted defensive structures operated in any ordinary hospital. Thus, a dichotomy was often created whereby there were, on the one hand, patients who were ill and helpless and, on the other, staff who, by definition, were healthy and competent. This basic assumption might seem valid enough for many purposes in a general hospital. However, researches by Menzies Lyth (1988), a Kleinian analyst, exposed this myth years ago, and Main himself was clear that it was certainly not appropriate in a hospital for neurotic disorders. Main wanted to create a model hospital community that was self-examining in all its systems.

No one was excluded from this community activity. Not only patients and clinical staff, but administrative and clerical staff, cooks, cleaners, porters and gardeners had access to consultation groups. A great deal of time was, and is, taken up in investigating and defining roles and functions; no one is exempt. Every relationship is subject to scrutiny and definition. Tensions in working together are searched for and hunted down all the time. It is a very verbose process, but no one is likely to feel half-hearted in such an ambience. Main regards therapeutic thinking as a sort of 'informed common sense'. This is the nature of the language used.

There is continuous need to define and redefine roles and functions, but it is all direct, full of feeling, rarely precious or esoteric.

Main's idea, that *any* health-seeking system must be self-monitoring, exploratory of its relations and capable of self-modification, is obvious. But no one had really thought of it so comprehensively before and, with the perennial human propensity to split, deny and project unpleasant experiences, it is very easy to lose this understanding. In an individual enterprise culture like Britain or America, often with evaluation being made by financial ideals only, there is often an endemic ignorance of, even attack upon, this sense of self-examining communality. But without such examination, it is likely that the health of any community and its individual members may be threatened. Main presided over the therapeutic community at the Cassel Hospital for about thirty years until his retirement in the mid-1970s.

One of the few cost-effectiveness studies of psychotherapy in Britain was carried out at the Cassel. It was found that many of the patients had been out of work for very long periods prior to treatment, but after treatment they had nearly all found work and stayed employed for several years. On a financial measure alone, the benefit is obvious (Denford, 1983).

Community methods have made it possible for very disturbed families to be worked with psychotherapeutically. Many of these families are on the local authority's 'at risk' register and may be the subject of a treatment order from the court. One of the directions that has been initiated is the treatment of families sent by the court because a member has been found guilty of child sexual abuse. This work is reflected in the book *The Family as In-patient* (Kennedy, Heymans and Tischler, 1987).

The Cassel has achieved a world-wide reputation, though its methods have not been copied exactly by many whole institutions in Britain. However, many multi-disciplinary teams in institutions have taken up the Cassel model of self-examination and its precepts have spread to many countries.


## THE TAVISTOCK CLINIC, THE WORK
## OF JOHN D. SUTHERLAND

The Tavistock Clinic, an out-patient clinic founded in 1920, for a long time was regarded as the 'poor relation' of the British Psycho-Analytic

Society and for many years was shunned by Jones and Glover. With the war years came their withdrawal, and the Society became much more of a participant with the outside community. With the end of the war in 1945, there was a new spirit of forward-looking optimism in the country, together with a recognition of the necessity for communal awareness and action. In 1948 the National Health Service came into being, and with this there was a unique opportunity for co-operation between the two organizations. The Tavistock staff often worked full time at the clinic, and were paid for this, while training in psychoanalysis during the evenings. This has continued very satisfactorily for over forty years. Recently the Tavistock has re-established its own qualifying training in psychoanalytically orientated psychotherapy without discouraging training by the Institute of Psycho-Analysis.

Under Jock Sutherland's chairmanship from the late 1940s till the late 1960s the Tavistock Clinic grew in size and competence to the world-renowned institution that it is today. Its activities are too wide for justice to be done to them within the scope of this book. Sutherland, once a lecturer in psychology who then trained in medicine and psychiatry, was himself originally a student of Fairbairn in Edinburgh. He is, in character and knowledge, the quintessence of the unassuming, open-minded Independent psychoanalyst (Sutherland, 1952, 1958, 1969, 1980, 1989). Basing his cogent thinking on group methods and social science as much as on the inner world of his psychoanalytic work, he bears much comparison with Rickman. The influence of both has been great. Under Sutherland's aegis many different departments with differing theoretical backgrounds flourished. For instance, though largely founded by John Bowlby, the child therapy training at the Tavistock has been predominantly Kleinian in background. However, many of the child psychiatrists, like Bowlby himself, were definitely not, yet both flourished. Adult department consultants like Balint, Ezriel, Kellnar and Thompson were Independents or, like Turquet and Gosling, Kleinian, and they also flourished together. Sutherland was not a charismatic leader like Main, but he was a great leader none the less of a different stature. His mode was more suitable for the fostering of a mature institution that was polyglot and of great size.

On retirement from the Health Service, Sutherland moved back to his native Scotland and founded the Scottish Institute of Human Relations, based on the Tavistock model. Here, with a handful of analytic colleagues, all incidentally of Independent persuasion, he has spent his retirement in building up analytic and therapeutic training resources in Scotland.

The chairmen of the Tavistock Clinic have all had a Kleinian background since Sutherland left. However, its atmosphere must have a liberating essence, for no chairman since then has been thought to be tainted with sectarianism; all have been greatly respected for their judicious breadth of vision and open-mindedness.

## PSYCHOANALYSTS WORKING IN THE HEALTH SERVICE

Work by British psychoanalysts in Health Service and other national institutions has naturally not been confined to the Cassel and Tavistock. It has become a tradition that many work, at least part time, as consultants or in other posts in many of London's teaching hospitals, in psychiatric, psychotherapy and child guidance clinics, as well as in education and student counselling services. For many years, around 75 per cent of British analysts have worked, at least part time, in the public service. Some regard a psychoanalyst who works in this applied field as showing him or herself to be only partly interested in psychoanalysis, but this is definitely not the philosophy or the practice of the Independents.

## ANALYTIC THINKING IN BRIEF PSYCHOTHERAPY,
## IN SEXUAL AND MARITAL THERAPY AND
## IN GENERAL MEDICAL PRACTICE:
## THE WORK OF MICHAEL AND ENID BALINT

The writing of Michael Balint was, like Donald Winnicott's, very extensively about the applications of psychoanalysis. Inspired by Ferenczi, Balint was always searching for new uses for the analytic method and experience. He saw that, even though full analysis might be the treatment of choice, it was often not available at times of crucial need. Like Winnicott, he came later to the conclusion that full analysis was often not even the treatment of choice. A sufferer's life position might well be such that long-term self-exploration was of no interest to him but shorter-term self-exploration could none the less be deep and changes could be established which were lasting. With this in mind he was in the forefront of the powerful British Independent tradition of turning outward and applying analysis for the use of others and also finding others' ideas that might be of use to analysis.

From the early 1950s until his death Balint did much of his writing, especially on applied subjects, with Enid Balint, his wife. Though not usually named as co-author, her discussions informed much of his later writing. She brought her own particular, less mercurial mode of clinical analytic thinking to their work.

There were three directions towards which the Balints turned: brief focal analytic therapy, sexual and marital therapy and the use of selected analytic concepts by general practitioners. All of these contained variations of the first mentioned, focal therapy.

In the early 1950s, Balint, working part of his time as a consultant at the Tavistock Clinic, called together a group of his colleagues, including Main and others from the Cassel Hospital, to make up a 'workshop' to study the possibilities of brief therapy. Within the setting of the National Health Service this sort of work with individual adult patients, up to about thirty sessions with an average of fifteen, was often all that was economically possible under the prevailing conditions. Over the next decade this study group worked out the basic principles for this type of therapy.

In contrast to analysis, where the slow unfolding of emotional structures was allowed to proceed at the patient's speed, the aim of brief therapy was 'to go in fast, work at depth and come out quick', as it used to be put by members of the group. This needed the formulation of a clear, conscious plan of action from the outset. The therapist needed to be very well informed analytically to be able to detect unconscious structures. Optimally, he also needed to be monitored throughout by colleagues in order to maintain the confidence, clarity and consistency that the work demanded. The first essential requirement was psycho-diagnostic skill. Patients were always seen by a psychotherapist and a psychologist, both analytically trained, using their differing diagnostic methods. An assessment was made of the patient's predominant character structures and then, within this setting, of the nature of the unconscious conflicts which were centrally manifest and predominant in the current crisis.

If a patient seemed to be of such a character that he was preoccupied by diffuse, amorphous, hence more-or-less objectless, long-term anxieties and was consequently prone to withdraw into his own self-deluding inner world, then brief therapy would not be indicated. The level of such problems could readily be diagnosed as 'at a one- or two-person level of functioning'. On the other hand, if a patient was worrying about conflicts that directly involved himself with other people and moreover was aware that he might be playing a part in creating the problems, then brief therapy would be more likely to be considered. Put in that mixture of classical Freudian and Kleinian terminology that Independents often have adopted, it was often said that 'for focal therapy a patient's conflicts needed to be experienced with depressive concern at the three-person-oedipal level'.

The assessment then proceeded by the reports of the two initial assessors being discussed by the workshop and a treatment plan being defined. This laid out the focus of conflict that seemed to be pressing and was thus readily available for brief work. The therapist was left free to carry out the treatment according to his own judgement but he had to record carefully every session and be able to be answerable to the group for his interpretations and actions. Close criticism was the norm in the discussions. This included the therapeutic work by Balint himself, who could on occasion be subject to merciless criticism. Workshop decisions were evolved democratically.

It was found that, so long as patients were carefully selected and the duration of treatment was explicitly stated and understood at the start, some profound work and change at unconscious levels could be effected. What is more, so long as pain and anger about termination were carefully tackled, the problem of chronic regression to dependency upon the therapist was minimal.

Balint and Winnicott were alike in expounding the possibility of doing useful brief psychotherapeutic work. For his part, Winnicott never formulated general principles that could be taught, maintaining that such 'schooling' was impossible. Balint, on the other hand, set out with his colleagues with the explicit intention of finding principles which, within limits, could be taught to those who were psychoanalytically grounded. This grounding was essential in order to be able to detect and work systematically with unconscious emotional structures in conflict.

The methods of brief therapy along the lines first worked out by Balint and his workshop are now widely and internationally known and practised. Teams at the Cassel under Denford and at the Tavistock under John Wilson were still active at the time of writing.

With one exception (1972), the Balints themselves wrote little about focal therapy. This was left to Michael Balint's pupil, David Malan, whose world-renowned books (Malan, 1963, 1976a, 1976b, 1979) on the subject have become classics in this field. In them, brief therapy technique is laid out with clarity of theory and detailed case description. Malan's early work, for which he is most famous, is concerned, first, with describing the technique, but then going on to a searching statistical validation of the brief therapeutic method. As the therapies were brief, and very careful case records were taken in each case studied, and as follow-up studies over years were systematic, statistical analysis was possible and was stringently carried out. Certain clinically meaningful factors were seen to emerge and were shown to be statistically significant.

For instance, Malan highlighted in this way that intense emotional involvement, on both sides of the therapeutic relationship, was present in successful outcomes. High motivation for change on the part of the patient, allied with enthusiasm by the therapist, seemed to be optimal. A high correlation between successful outcome and the repeated use of parent–therapist transference interpretation was consistently found. Malan also found that the early diagnosis of a dynamic focus, first by the therapist and then by the patient, was conducive to optimal outcome. Therapists are not usually very interested in statistical analysis. Malan was an exception, and his findings, such as that upon the parent–therapist transference link, gave therapists a greater confidence in the use of those aspects of the method that had been affirmed statistically.

Those who have worked in this focal way will affirm that, so long as selection is careful, brief therapy can be long-lasting and useful. Those who have known only the methods of long-term analysis often find this hard to believe, even though the evidence is clearly laid out in the published works. Malan is trenchantly critical of this attitude taken by many analysts when he says:

> Here we find an extraordinary state of affairs – one of the unfortunate consequences of the psychoanalytic tradition, according to which. . .
> Only one method of treatment is available, regardless of the social class or intelligence of the patient, and the nature of the problem. The method is not applicable to large numbers, nor to the less intelligent, less educated, underprivileged, less introspective, or less motivated types of patient.

Therefore, patients are chosen to suit the therapy, not the therapy to suit the patient.

All methods of treatment that are not the pure gold of analysis are depreciated. Therefore, the briefer and more 'superficial' methods are not explored, because they are assumed *a priori* to be ineffective in the long run. Since these methods are not explored, the fact that they can sometimes be remarkably effective is never discovered.

Since all treatment is long-term, all vacancies are rapidly blocked, and waiting lists grow to the point at which the length of wait for therapy is quite unrealistic. . .There is thus an inability to treat the patient in his acute state. . .Thus, probably, chronic maladaptive patterns are left to form and become established.

(Malan, 1976b, p. 4)

Malan's later work has turned away somewhat from statistical validation to introducing psychotherapy to student practitioners. He has also attempted to find more powerful focal methods than the ones we have described, which seem to have gained little support from his colleagues. They will not be discussed here.

At about the same time as the start of the brief therapy workshops, Enid Balint had been one of the founder-members of the Tavistock Institute's Family Discussion Bureau, which has since been called the Institute of Marital Studies. Here a method of parallel therapy of the two marital partners by two separate therapists was worked out. The two therapists would regularly meet together, with a third acting as a supervisor. The work was not so defined nor necessarily so brief as that of focal therapy, but it bore strong affinities with it. This technique was further developed over the years and continues to this day.

Rather later in the 1950s, Michael Balint became a consultant to the Family Planning Association. This was an organization of doctors and nurses concerned with contraceptive advice and prescription. Later the work was taken into the National Health Service, but its teaching and training have expanded and continue within the Institute of Psychosexual Medicine. Family planning practitioners naturally found that many emotional conflicts came to the fore during their consultations, especially at physical examination. It was with a view to responding to these emotional problems that the practitioners called in Michael Balint. With them he developed a method of investigation and training through workshops which he had begun with general practitioners. It is a mode that has come to be used world-wide.

After some years Balint gave up his work with family planning practitioners and handed it over to his old student and, later, colleague, Tom Main. For nearly thirty years Main continued and expanded this work. A form of brief therapy has been developed and is carried out by the planning practitioners themselves. Among many other findings, it has been noticed, for instance, that the time of the physical examination in such consultations is often a 'moment of truth' (Main, 1989) when emotional problems reach a critical point and can be worked upon by doctor and patient over a very short time.

Michael and Enid Balint are perhaps most famous in Britain and internationally for another area of applied analysis. This is their introduction of selected analytic concepts into general medical practice.

Balint, himself the son of a general practitioner, developed a unique directness of rapport with GPs. During the early 1950s he began to meet weekly with small groups of practitioners to discuss the patients in their practices and the handling of them. The pioneer work, described in *The Doctor, His Patient and the Illness* (Balint, 1957b), concerned itself with an investigation of the nature of their practice.

> My first task, therefore, is to state the problem that we are to investigate. Briefly, the problem is this: why does it happen so often that, in spite of earnest efforts on both sides, the relationship between patient and doctor is unsatisfactory or even unhappy? Or in other words, why does it happen that the drug 'doctor', despite apparently conscientious prescription, does not work as intended? What are the causes of this undesirable development and how can it be avoided?
>
> (Balint, 1957b, p. 5)

In the course of the next two decades many studies upon the psychodynamics of aspects of general practice were completed by Balint or his colleagues. There were, for instance, *Treatment or Diagnosis: A Study of Repeat Prescriptions* (Balint et al., 1970), *Night Calls* (Clyne, 1961), *Asthma, Attitude and Milieu* (Lask, 1966), and *Six Minutes for the Patient* (E. Balint and Morell, 1973b), to quote just a few.

At the same time the Balints were developing a mode whereby a general practitioner might make systematic psychotherapeutic interventions in the course of his ordinary work. This is spelt out in their *Psychotherapeutic Techniques in Medicine* (M. Balint and E. Balint, 1961). Through the medium of their weekly workshops, some GPs developed considerable skill in engaging with some of their patients, often within the few minutes ordinarily available, at a deep and meaningful emotional level. Probably from knowing him or her for a long time, the doctor would often have a clear idea of the patient's characteristic idiosyncrasies and thence be able to detect and quickly engage with immediate, yet by no means superficial, conflicts that were assailing the patient at the time. The similarity between the brief therapy workshops and those of the family planning doctors soon becomes apparent.

The Balints carefully distinguish the technique they have developed from reassurance or common-sense psychology. Nor do they think of it as akin to hypnosis or suggestion. It is essentially an interpretative method aimed at unveiling anxiety and undoing defences. It requires a secure combination of sensitivity to character structures together with a tough spontaneity when confronting patients with their fruitless but well-encrusted habits. There is no doubt that GPs, with their long personal acquaintance with their patients, seeing them at their most vulnerable times, are in a specially good position to be therapeutically effective. It is none the less impressive what can be achieved in weekly workshops with a leader experienced in this type of work.

There have been few proponents of the workshop method with focal therapies who have had the flair that Michael Balint possessed. But the mode has more than survived, not only at the Tavistock and the Cassel but in many other places in Britain, Europe and America. A recent book by a child therapist shows the development of a combination of Winnicott's method with that of the Balints when dealing with problems of sleeplessness in infants and young children (Daws, 1989).


CONCLUSION

This record of the application of psychoanalytic ideas in many fields of work by British Independents since the Second World War speaks for itself. The contributions by such as the Balints, Bowlby, Bridger, Main, Sutherland and Winnicott are valued world-wide in their fields, but behind them has been the contribution of many of their Independent colleagues. However, it has to be said that it is not only Independents who have been innovators by going out to introduce analytic concepts into other fields and so enhance the work of their practitioners. Analysts of Kleinian and contemporary Freudian orientation have done the same. What has distinguished the Independents, however, is that, as a group of colleagues, they have felt committed to, and supported one another in, taking psychoanalytic findings into the community. They have helped develop new methods so that a wider range of people can benefit from psychoanalytic knowledge. The majority of them have also stayed committed to psychoanalytic practice in their own consulting-rooms, as the earlier chapters of this book testify. They have, in fact, engaged in a two-way traffic of ideas – from the consulting-room to the outside world and from work and theory in other fields into the consulting-room.

Behind those Independents whose contributions we have mentioned are scores of others, many of whom have published hundreds of papers (a selection of these is included in the bibliography at the end of this volume), but there are very many more, unpublished, who have lectured and taught over many years.

Perhaps of as great importance, there has been a very strong surge of interest in analytic therapy throughout Britain in the past two decades. Thirty years ago there were two organizations concerned with work with adults, both in London, which carried out formal training in this area. These were the Institute of Psycho-Analysis and the Jungian Institute of Analytical Psychology. Now there are several dozen psychotherapy institutions throughout the country concerned with training. Some are systematically analytic and of high quality, others less so, but the trend is unmistakable and probably irreversible. It seems that analytical psychotherapy and counselling have come to stay as an essential part of our culture in the future. Here too, many psychoanalysts, of all orientations, not just Independents, have helped create and raise standards by their work as therapists, supervisors, lecturers, seminar leaders and organizers.

Of what use will psychoanalysis be in the future? In one field at least the signs are clear: it seems that psychotherapy will need psychoanalysis to provide a consistent core of scholarly and deep, theoretical and technical discourse. Conversely, psychoanalysis will need psychotherapy in order to become widely useful in the community and to have a source of new and provocative data. How the two modes – the one based upon long-term, very frequent, interpersonal engagement, the other upon shorter or less frequent contact – will converse together, use each other and be fruitful remains for the future to say.

# 12  Conclusions

## THE CLASSICAL BACKGROUND, KLEIN AND INDEPENDENT THEORY

**W**E MUST REITERATE that this book and, even more, these conclusions cannot but be the writer's own biased and idiosyncratic vision of Independent analysts' work. Justice has not been done to some writers, while more than justice has been given to others. Nevertheless, we have faithfully tried to portray some strong strands of ideas that seem to have grown from Britain. But a loose association of minds is most unlikely to produce only these particular strands; even less likely would be a unanimous consensus about the essence of Independent philosophy and work. With this warning in mind, let us begin to draw the arguments of this book together.

Presided over by Ernest Jones in the 1920s and 1930s, British psychoanalysts rooted themselves directly and deeply in Freud's classical theory and technique. Training and tradition have continued in Britain from this beginning so that the Independents are still firmly based on classical thinking. At the same time, the British had their own kind of liberal, empirical, humanistic ideology and culture which they brought to the shaping of analysis. It was probably their islanders' stubborn independence from mainland Europe that contributed to the welcome for Melanie Klein in London. The later 1920s and 1930s saw the British welding Klein's ideas together with classical method in a unique way. The fruit of this 'marriage' began to emerge in the vivacious clinical style of such as Sharpe and Brierley. The philosophy of open-mindedness about psychoanalytic matters was well established by the time that the Freuds came to London in 1939. Controversy between them and Klein soon became acute. However, the majority of the British Society wished to ally themselves exclusively with neither side, but to be free to draw from both

– and from others as well. When the division into groups became formalized in the later 1940s, the majority of the Society reluctantly gathered into a group which was first entitled 'Middle' and later called Independent.

The sequence of the book emphasized the fact that theoretical orientation and philosophy have shaped Independent technique.

We defined the philosophy of open-mindedness which holds Independents together, and showed how this means that they cannot be a school which polemicizes any single theoretical or technical point of view. There is good reason for such schools to thrive within a wider association. This is the way ideas are developed. However, such an association cannot, by its philosophy, uphold or fight exclusively for any one school. Nevertheless, certain themes of thought have flourished.

## AFFECTS, THEIR SYMBOLIZATION AND CREATIVITY

Flugel, Glover and Brierley in the 1930s emphasized the conceptual importance of affects. Brierley in particular showed that affects contain self-and-object relations – together with drives towards new affect or self–object states. They, and later King and Limentani, seem to point to affects as basic conceptual elements. Feelings are perhaps the stuff, or conceptual units, of a psychoanalytic 'calculus'.

Following the philosopher Susanne Langer, Independents, like Milner, Rycroft and Bowlby indicated that affects are structured states or activities of intuitive evaluation which comprehend in several directions at once. They take in the conditions of the environment and the body as well as psychic objects as integrated configurations. Affects are ego activities *par excellence*, not just representations of drives. Only in pathology are feelings set against thought, for in health they are essential preliminary stages of deep thinking processes.

On symbolization, we saw how Milner and Rycroft both used Langer to distinguish discursive, secondary process, verbal-logical symbolization, whose main function is to communicate about conditions in physical space. This can be distinguished from non-discursive, presentational, psychoanalytic or isomorphic symbolization, which is epitomized by the symbols of dreams. This form of symbol is a vehicle for communicating affect appraisal states. Analysis uses both sorts or symbols.

We saw that metaphor participates both in this primary process, iso-morphic symbolism and also in more discursive modes. Several writers showed the importance of the capacity to symbolize affects for ordinary psychic health. Psychosomatists in several countries have done likewise.

Milner saw artistic creativity as the expression of communicating truthfully, by manifold symbolizations, about complex feeling states. Art is about the truthful symbolization of inner feelings, whereas science is about the truthful symbolization of the external physical world. Probably taking a cue from Milner, Winnicott saw creativity as ordinary by sug-gesting that it is an expression of an individual's innate, physiologically based true self and is the essence of human health. He deduced from this that psychological ill-health stems in part from falsification of true-self feelings. This would happen in thoughtless compliance with others and in alienation from true, innately based potentials. The ego is then distorted or damaged. At the same time, Winnicott tried to portray the essentially paradoxical nature of the conditions under which creativity takes place. The medium which a creative activity uses must have a transitional, 'me yet not-me', paradoxical quality in it. The concept of transitionality is perhaps Winnicott's greatest contribution to our understanding of cul-tural activity. It has the widest applicability.

One theme running through many Independents' ideas is the impor-tance and value of moving into and out of states of self–object de-differentiation. There is the 'delusion of unity' of Sharpe, the 'illusion of unity' of Milner, the 'basic unity' of Little, the 'primary love' and 'arglos state' of Balint, the 'symmetrization' or 'homogenization' of Matte-Blanco and Winnicott on 'merging' and transitional phenomena in the third area, that of 'illusion'. Milner in particular showed how a rhythm occurred in the movement in and out of these states in truly aesthetic creativity.

## THE SELF AND FACILITATING, OR TRAUMATIC, ENVIRONMENT

The development of self within its environment is perhaps the particular mark of Independents' theory and has specially affected their technique. Fairbairn, Balint, Bowlby and Winnicott considered the infant's begin-nings and enlarged Freud's model of oral-libidinal satisfaction. They all assumed fateful experiential states from the word go, and maintained that the human organism grows especially through affection with intimate persons. This is a biological need. The viewpoint stems from Freud's basic model of libidinal development, but, perhaps because of the British bent towards the Darwinian-biological way of thinking, the human infant is always conceived in relation to his human environment. It is a prime constituent of the object-relations point of view. Each author culled his own particular view, but for all of them the innate potentials of an infant meet a facilitating, or at times traumatic, environment.

For these four thinkers, and for many Independents, it is environmental traumata impinging upon the immature psyche that are the basic pathogens fateful for later development. Such a view is not inimical to classical theory. It elaborates certain aspects of later Freud. Nor is it inimical to concepts of the internal world which have been Klein's gift. It gave rise to Fairbairn's particularly sophisticated structural model of the mind.

However, there are distinct differences from Kleinian theory, at least in its earlier form before Bion tried to rectify matters with his concept of the container. These differences seem to have brought out slight but important differences in clinical approach. Klein, as we have understood her, saw the basic pathogenic situation as stemming from aggression and destructiveness, manifestations of the death instincts, being in conflict with the libido of the life instincts from the beginning. Such conflicts may have been exacerbated by environmental factors but they are conflicts between drives and fundamentally intra-psychic in origin. The involvement of external objects is originally brought about by the infant projecting aspects of his or her internal world into them. Herein lie the pathogens of an individual's later interpersonal relationships. Such a model makes possible a one-person or solipsistic model of psychopathology. It probably patterns the situation for the Kleinian analyst in clinical work. His task is to confront the patient's solitary world of internal objects, in particular his phantasy-dominated defensive structures against intolerable internal pain. For this, it is seen as optimal for the analyst to maintain a consistent position at a distance from the patient which is sufficient for explicit verbal interpretation.

Such a basic clinical position is essential. But the Independents' point of view about pathogenesis is that the original psychic pathogen is not intra-psychic, but at the interface between the individual and his environment. Innately based somato-psychic potentials meet the environment and may be stunted, distorted or falsified by its impingements. The child's ego has much to put up with. The psychic structure of an adult will inevitably carry memory traces, however distorted, of early traumata. Here the internal world with its defence structures remains just as important as for the Kleinian school in the therapeutic endeavour. However, for the Independent, psychopathology contains memory elements of actual happenings that were not simply created by the patient's impulses and phantasies.

When re-experiencing of these traumata is in the ascendant, the analyst is seen as needing to move his responsiveness somewhat closer to the patient – to active communality of communication about the 'here and now'. The Kleinian approach, seeing aggressive impulses as the basic pathogen, seems to consider that consistent interpretation of these provides the necessary help for intra-psychic change. The Independent, seeing the patient's ego struggling with environmentally derived impingements, on these occasions tends towards finding an attunement with the patient's predicaments. There is a therapeutic mutuality between analyst and patient about past pre-verbal experiences that are being revived. Verbalization may then be of a rather mirroring kind which describes the here and now, often by using metaphors. However, this does not preclude the finding of objective distance when resistance against unconscious conflicts is in the ascendant again. Such resistance may be manifested by the patient's trickery, malice, stupidity or other distortions. It is here that countertransference plays a central role in judging the patient's immediate affect state. From this, differentiation can be made between regressions to early pre-verbal traumata in the service of the ego and regressions as resistances. Little has been said in this book about the technique of dealing with resistance for it is well covered by both classical and Kleinian writers. Here, as often, the Independents lean on others.

It is often thought that the Independent's stress on the environment is inimical to the analyst addressing himself fully to his patient's inner world. For instance, Bowlby's theory has been condemned as anti-analytic because he addresses himself directly to the early situation of the infant. However, an analyst's ignorance of Bowlby's research means that vital data are not available for analytic understanding. The fact that findings about attachment are derived from places other than the therapeutic situation makes them no less relevant to the clinician.

Another consequence of the Independents' interest in the individual in his environment concerns the place given to hate, aggressiveness, sadism and masochism. They have no doubt of aggression's great power and its part in evil of any kind, be it personal or social. Perhaps because of their Darwinian roots, Independents tend to differ rather from Klein's theory and to see aggressiveness itself as also essential to survival. They are particularly interested in its value for the survival of the separate self. It is viewed as one of Freud's 'ego-preservative instincts'. The task of analysis is then to uncover how in pathology this natural aggressiveness has become perverted into unchecked sadism and masochism which is destructive of living, individually or in groups.

Heimann (1989) addressed the relevance of death instincts. She suggested a differentiation between a biologically rooted life instinct, which enhanced an aggressive instinctual potential, and cruelty in its various manifestations. The latter she conceived of as a typical human property, always signifying early traumata. This line of thought probably approximates to the approach of many Independents.

## INTROJECTIONS THROUGHOUT CHILDHOOD AND THEIR RECONSTRUCTION IN ANALYSIS

Though Fairbairn, Balint, Winnicott and Bowlby began by conceiving of very early traumata, they, and later Independents like Khan and James, have stressed that traumata do not lie solely in infancy. Because of the omnipresence of memory in human development, introjection and internalization of relations with objects in the environment are continually taking place. Later internalizations are shaped or distorted by their precursors. Every developmental phase has its own crucial characteristic qualities which can be sundered by traumata during that time as well as being made vulnerable by earlier ones. This view is naturally consonant with, and fundamentally uses, the findings of Anna Freud and her school as well as other, particularly American, psychoanalysts with special interests in development.

For the majority of Independents, fundamental psychic structure is not completed in infancy but continues throughout childhood, adolescence and beyond. Therapeutic psychoanalysis must entail detailed reconstruction of essential aspects of each phase of development and its working through. Early phases of such work will be through transference repetition, but later conscious, verbal recollections and reconstructions will be central. By such means the patient finds his own particular language to address the past that is within him. It is through knowledge of his past, as not the same as his present yet also alive, that a person knows and achieves an ability to live with himself.


## CHARACTER STRUCTURE AND PATHOLOGY

We noted that, though mankind has been fascinated by character since the dawn of history, it has only been with the coming of psychoanalysis that an individual character can actually be engaged with, be understood and even be modified through the means of a systematic method. The key British thinker on structure was Fairbairn. The 'schizoid personality' of Fairbairn, with its emphasis on splitting, points towards the alienation of aspects of the self from essential core experiences. So too does the 'basic fault' of Balint and 'false self' of Winnicott. All emphasize different aspects and in certain ways contradict each other. Fairbairn, like Klein, sees the schizoid position as developmentally prior to depressive experiences. However, Balint and Winnicott did not see a developmental line from a schizoid to a depressive position. These positions were seen as of great importance in pathology, but they were variations, even digressions, from the healthy course of maturation. Nevertheless, all three authors point towards underlying self-disorders where neurotic symptoms or character traits may be various, but there is always an underlying experience of futility.

Masud Khan linked these different views within his picture of schizoid characteristics. He then drew upon Glover, Gillespie and Limentani who had shown that perversions were ways of protecting, yet also a flaw in, the reality sense. From this premiss, he then developed his highly articulated theory of the perversions, and showed how they were orgasmically acted-out dreams. By 'sexualization across the splits' in the personality, discrepant parts of the self were transiently 'as if' united in orgasmic experience with another person. They were then denied or defused and lost from experience till the next time around.

Other borderline character deformations have been described, like Winnicott's anti-social tendency and Balint's philobat and ocnophil defence structures. More recently we have Bollas's normotic, ghostline and anti-narcissist personalities, and Limentani's vagina-man. These are contributions to the work of character analysis.

The specific contributions of Independents to the understanding of neuroses have been to emphasize possible underlying self-disordered features which lie in borderline psychotic regions. On the whole, they work with classical analytic theories which they regard as sufficient to comprehend neurotic disorders, particularly when recent developments, mainly from America, are also taken into account. Independents have aimed at enlarging the scope of analytic therapy in the direction of self-disorders rather than at transforming theory and therapy.

## THE ANALYTIC PROCESS

The Independents tend to consider that the need for the analyst to keep emotional contact with the patient's actual feeling state must be paramount. This openness may be assisted by a particular theory, but, in the last resort, disciplined, self-scrutinizing openness to the patient must take precedence over obedience to a prescribed theoretical orientation.

Fundamentally the Independent approach to therapy is a non-controversial one of perceiving and interpreting the patient's communications in terms of their resistant or defensive content. As for any psychoanalyst, the aim is always hermeneutic in nature, to enhance meanings by verbal interpretation.

Glover, Sharpe, Heimann, King, Klauber and Stewart all wrote about the centrality of the analytic transference and the need for its consistent interpretation along the lines first enunciated by Freud. Both Winnicott and Balint also stressed that most analysts' work concerns neurotic problems which involve three-person, oedipal-level intra-psychic conflicts. These create defensive structures and resistances which are best met by the analyst's consistent decoding of their manifestations in order to reveal the painful conflicts behind them.

Recent analysts, British, American and European, have been concerned with the borderline regions of the self-disorders. Here projections and introjections hold sway more emphatically than repressions. It is here that developments from classical technique such as the use of countertransference and the analyst's affective response play a vital part.

## TRANSFERENCE INTERPRETATION

In 1934 Strachey made a bridge between classical and Kleinian theory. He argued in proper classical fashion that neurosis concerns the development of powerful phantasies about present relations that have been transferred from the past. In the transference neurosis these repeat themselves with insistence towards the person of the analyst. If the analyst can show the patient the discrepancy between his phantasy and the reality of the analyst then work towards change has begun. He argues that transference interpretation has a clarity and immediacy that make it an essential mutative step. Most Kleinians would agree with this.

Independents also tend to see precise verbal interpretation of the 'here and now' transference as essential. But it is only one function in the analytic cure. It is most applicable, and subject to the least misunderstanding, when transference feelings in the patient are acutely active and near to conscious awareness. This is likely to be when the patient's oedipal-level conflicts are uppermost. The time for the analyst to interpret in such a transferential way must be judged by listening to the affects of the patient's associations. This will use the sensitivity of the analyst's affective responsiveness and countertransference.

## REGRESSION

Many Independents are of the opinion that, at times, other activities of the analyst provide a setting for formal interpretation and are needed to achieve therapeutic change. Like all analysts, they accept that regression can be used as an ordinary defensive device to avoid the re-emergence of intra-psychic conflicts. After Freud, it was Ferenczi who began to explore the possible value of regression. It was then Balint and Winnicott, followed by Little, who investigated this issue in detail. Winnicott thought that even major regressions to helplessness and dependency (rather than to overt psychosis, as is often thought) were necessary in some cases manifesting the self-disorders of profound false-self or as-if characters. Regression was necessary in order to repeat in the transference relationship the origin of the patient's overall false structures and thence find again the true self with its innate somato-psychic potentials. In a rather similar manner, Balint discriminated benign regressions from those that were impulse ridden and malign. He considered that benign regression in the transference to the area of the basic fault was essential for a therapeutic change or new beginning from the basic fault level.

The physical holding techniques associated with these experiments by Ferenczi, Balint, Winnicott and Little have, to many, made all the findings about regression suspect. It is sometimes a subject of unpleasant invective. We noted that Balint stressed that Ferenczi's experiments largely failed, but the reading of his diaries shows his basically scientific frame of mind about these matters. Perhaps because of their roots in English empiricism, Independents appreciate the necessity of experiments like these. They often value trial and error in the course of analysis itself, where some errors can be as useful as correctness.

Extended parameters, like holding, applied during the treatment of severely disturbed people, have never been given wide acceptance. It seems to have been a bit of a fashion in the 1940s and 1950s, but, as far as we know, few analysts have attempted them since. When a colleague has tried to use an extended parameter, maybe with a dare-devil in him, he has usually found that this has had to be worked through 'in abstinence' later – as Freud had warned. It is at this stage that the analyst needs considerable sensitivity and skill. Eissler (1953) pointed out that the success or failure of an extended parameter depends upon this stage. It has been the necessary and courageous publication of papers by authors like Winnicott, Balint and Little which has helped this understanding. We are not talking here of instances when ethical limits have been breached, a subject of a quite different order and one which never arose with these authors.

It is remarkable how similar are Winnicott and Balint on the value of regression. They both posit a character structure based on pre-verbal traumata – basic fault and the false self. The symptom in both cases is a sense of futility and emptiness. Both prescribe the need for the patient to regress, albeit often briefly and transiently, to states of pre-object differentiation with the analyst. It is not the detail of exact verbal interpretations that matters in the finding of this regressed state but a facilitating idiom of quality to the analytic environment provided by the analyst. At such times, the analytic milieu optimally has no hard edges, it is better to err towards empathy than towards confrontation and to kindness rather than to severity. Such gentleness of mood is a requisite at the time when the patient is progressing out of character defence to a regression which is benign and in the service of the ego. This analytic milieu is provided by the quiet of the room and in its furnishing, but also by the consistency of the analyst's presence, his attunement with the patient, and the affective tone and modulation of his words.

When problems are at pre-oedipal and pre-verbal levels, defensive structures will be maintained predominantly by projective and introjective activities by the patient, not least in the analysis. This will entail countertransference feelings by the analyst as he becomes the recipient of the projections. This has been carefully worked out in recent decades by Kleinian analysts, and most Independents avail themselves of this understanding.

Many Independents also make a point of working with the patient's identifications with unintegrated introjects which result in a reversal of roles. Here, as Heimann showed, the analyst is simply left at the same receiving end as the patient was when an infant. In summary, regression is not always only defensive.

The emphasis on the value of benign regression to de-differentiation, and movement out of it, is a mark of many Independents. Here they often write about patients with severe borderline character pathology. However, it seems that many, perhaps all, neurotic patients operate with partially faulted or false aspects or parts to themselves; perhaps everyone does. Thus, every analysis will at times entail movements by the patient between regression and progression which require corresponding movements of affective responsiveness by the analyst. Descriptions of faults and falsity may illuminate subtle aspects of many defensive structures in any patient.

## THE ANALYST'S AFFECTIVE RESPONSIVENESS

Drawing attention to the importance of the establishment and use of times of mutuality, when the analyst's empathy is manifest, has been one of the major contributions of the Independents. It is close to Greenson's concept of the therapeutic alliance. Alice and Michael Balint (1939), in their pioneering paper, introduced the idea of countertransference feelings as often not pathological but useful. All analysts have different styles of emotionality, these are often well known by patients and it is best to recognize this. There is no such thing as sterile analysing. The quiet emotionality of the analyst is the milieu or ground upon which the patient develops his own expressiveness. This is the philosophy of many Independents.

Winnicott (1949a) differentiated pathological from necessary, and even valuable, hate by the analyst and pointed out the occasions, albeit rare, when this can be usefully expressed. Heimann's (1950) classic paper showed how the analyst might use her countertransference to detect when she had missed something in the patient's prior communications and had instead unconsciously introjected the patient, giving rise to the analyst feeling strangely disturbed. King (1978) introduced the terminology of the 'analyst's affective response', restricting the term 'countertransference' to what it says it is, a phantasy from the past in the analyst. Many of the analyst's affective responses may contain much to be taken note of besides repetitions from the past.

With acknowledgement of the analyst's feeling responses, the process of analysis can be seen as an often muted, affective dialogue between both participants. Such a description of analysis is open to much misunderstanding. It is often thought of as suggesting an undue emotional involvement by the analyst rather than being a straightforward description of the state of affairs in the analytic conversation. In fact it requires severe discipline, since there is no comfort for the analyst in the certainty of a simple prescribed technique.

Kleinian theory of technique seems to tend to confine the use of countertransference feelings to being a means of locating the patient's projective identifications into the analyst. Many Independents make use of their own feelings in this way and have been helped by the Kleinian formulations, which have a valuable clarity. However, many Independents, like Heimann, also often ask themselves what they themselves may be contributing to the patient's particular mode of projectiveness.

## SPONTANEITY IN THE ANALYTIC DIALOGUE

We have noted how Strachey in 1934 had proposed that cure came about when the analyst's words have shown to the patient that his phantasy of the analyst had untrue elements in it. By this precise verbal activity the patient came to make affective judgements about the analyst that were less clouded by illusory phantasy. John Klauber did not disagree with this as a formulation of one aspect of what was happening. But he showed that cure from the patient's phantastical illusions was only to be achieved by the agency of illusion itself. Here is another example of the use of paradox, which is central to the Independent mode of thought. It may be by dramatization, illusion *par excellence*, which stirs affect in the analytic setting, so that change is set in motion. Freud himself saw analytic activity as having play in it; Winnicott explored this fully, and it has recently been stated most trenchantly by Joyce McDougall (1986, 1989).

To facilitate the spontaneous emergence of dramatization in the patient, the analyst needs to lead the way, Klauber and others have thought, by an underlying freedom to be intuitive and spontaneous himself. Winnicott similarly emphasized that analysis towards the patient's experience of true-self feeling comes through the agency of the analyst's own true self. The spontaneous processes in both the patient and the analyst are responsible for that which is creative in the analytic situation. Affective truth, as manifest in spontaneity of utterance and often through the dramatic medium of metaphor and illusion, is an agent of psychoanalytic cure.

## THE PATIENT'S OWN ANALYSING PROCESS AS PARAMOUNT

Taking the lead from Freud (1912a) and the Balints in 1939, Klauber and others think that the patient's transference develops so powerfully that no analyst need or should attempt a consistent front of emotionally grey or sterile neutrality. The analyst's first task is to make emotional contact, or to attune, with the patient – and to keep it as best he can. Klauber was even of the opinion that a patient might be healed by this alone on occasion. There is among Independents a scepticism about the exclusive attendance upon the minutiae of transference reactions, and the making of only meticulous formal verbal interpretations about them.

In the final analysis, it is interpretation by the patient himself which leads to change. Mutation can come about through a multiplicity of means and not only from the analyst's verbalized insights. Freud (1939) saw this when he noted that emotional change can occur through friendships and not just upon the couch.

Integration of split-off and isolated phantastical structures into the functioning of the central realistic self is what gives a person's imagination its significance. It is this the patient needs and which the analyst should foster, rather than restricting both patient and himself to the minutiae of detailed phantasies. The patient's need to be known is not to be confused with being intruded upon or interfered with.

Klauber expressed the view of many Independents when he saw that the analyst himself could interfere with the benign process of undoing defences. For instance, like Balint and Stewart, he saw that the lofty omniscience of an analyst was anti-therapeutic. On the other hand, the finding of mutuality and a sense of corporateness or alliance could be a non-specific benign agency. This must not, however, be confused with controlling seductiveness on the part of patient or analyst.

As with most useful intellectual activity, a dialectical process has occurred among the Independents on this subject. For instance, Limentani (1977) provided a valuable counterweight here by pointing out the burden upon a patient created by an analyst being over-emotive, a viewpoint a good number of Independents agree with. More recently, Casement has continued this tradition of enquiry into the analyst's contributions for good and ill in the analytic process, by developing a systematic mode of self-examination and consciously examining himself from the patient's point of view.

## EXPLICIT COMMUNICATION OF AFFECT BY THE ANALYST

The stage was set for another controversy by Coltart's 1985 paper in which she reported the heavy psychotic silence of a patient for many months and knew it for a murderous hatred. She uttered an expression of freedom by shouting that she was not going to stand for it a minute longer. This seemed to change the course of the analysis.

Here Coltart had been in empathy with the patient, identifying with him. She was suffering under her sympathetic attunement with him, which was none the less necessary for her to understand the patient. She refers to it as a bid for freedom, but a limit was also set for the patient by her expostulation.

Symington theorized upon this issue of freedom. We have just raised its counterpart, the function of a limit. He noted that empathy often leads to being 'lassoed' by the patient. The present writer has followed Stern (1985) and has referred to this as 'attunement' by the analyst with the patient. We suggest that such a stage is always necessary. A therapeutic process perhaps needs acts of freedom of true-self spontaneity by both the patient and analyst. However, this must remain controversial at the present time.

When the emotionality of the patient is well within the analyst's intellectual-verbal level of comprehension, then his spontaneous utterances will take the shape of verbally formulated interpretations. But these are impossible in psychotic and borderline phases, as in Coltart's example. The only alternative to formulated interpretation may be seen by some to remain simply silent. However, others, like Stewart, adjudge this to be an unresponsive milieu that can have 'hard edges'. Other ways may be necessary to express freedom of differentiation, and to set limits of tolerance. Such responsiveness may have errors in it but be necessary in the trial-and-error learning that is the analytic process.

Put in other words, sequences of resonance and dissonance are parts of the progress of therapeutic change. Explicit, full, verbal interpretations, in the last analysis by the patient himself, are the essence and aim of this chain, but often occur only late in analytic mutation. Full interpretations are essential for consolidation of emotional shifts which will have already started in the course of earlier trial-and-error work. One aspect of trial and error will be the analyst's apparent mistakes and ineptitude, which, however, are inevitable.

There is mutuality in this sequence, the analyst engages with the patient, attunes and then disengages to relate to the patient from another position. For therapeutic usefulness he must link his new point of view about the patient to previous ones; this can only be done by verbal means. The analyst is introducing a change of key in the dialogue. A new mutual activity between the two protagonists may then beneficially evolve.

The critical moments in these sequences seem to be the times of transition from attunement or fusion between patient and analyst to a dis-identification. This process bears comparison with the discords between mother and infant that occur prior to new developments in life.

## THE MULTIPLE FUNCTIONS OF THE ANALYST

Bollas's exposition of his technique is one that many Independents would probably agree with. Here use is made of the concept of the patient's innate true-self potentials that will have been distorted by false-self defensive structures. The analyst must find the optimal use of his own true-self potentials. This amounts to his own natural idiom of intuition with the patient. The analyst must also be aware of the effect of his own idiom upon the patient. There must be a continuous shift of awareness of self to patient and back. Such intuitive awareness is often threatened by the malice and trickiness of a patient. Under such circumstances the traditional analytic distance, and countertransference awareness, is invaluable.

A number of Independents think that the notion of aggressiveness as the exclusive centre of therapeutic endeavour can become misplaced. Many patients actually find it easier to be aware of and deal with their aggressiveness than their life instincts. The same holds true for creativity. Patients are often unused to valuing and showing their accomplishments. For such states of affairs a two-pronged activity is necessary. It is essential to confront defensive phantasy with its falsity and at the same time to affirm the healthily creative in the patient. This can be done only when it is overtly manifest in the patient's communications. The analyst must here become a judge of authentic creativity of ideas, and this is, in effect, essentially an aesthetic judgement, though it most often relates to everyday activities. Such affirmation can be valid only when the analyst is not encouraging a false, compliant, charming or seductive aspect of the patient.

This task of affirmation spells out the multiplicity of functions that are part of the analytic process. Precise, formal verbal interpretation is only one of them. In the last analysis it is the patient who must have the insight, and the analyst is then an auxiliary and facilitator, albeit an essential one. He must work with what, for the patient, is the emotional immediacy of the session. There is a danger in any psychoanalytic school when it polemicizes one facet only of the multiple aspects of the analytic situation, hence Bollas's saying that every Freudian needs to be also a Kohutian, a Kleinian, a Lacanian and a Winnicottian at times.

The patient may evolve different true-self aspects through the use of different authentic aspects of the analyst. However, he may also be stuck upon a false use of him. The study of the use of the analyst is important. For instance, in hysterical characters, the patient's repressed body functioning may first be manifest in the analyst's countertransference, where he becomes aware of strange unwanted feelings in his own body. By locating these the analyst can be making a first step in handing them back for the patient to find a rightful place for them.

The analyst, some Independents think, can sometimes usefully express his own countertransference feelings to the patient, and this is a source of considerable controversy. Those who do it maintain that it clarifies and enhances the immediacy of the analytic process; those who refrain stress that the patient may be burdened by what he experiences as the analyst's personal revelations.

## ANALYTIC NEUTRALITY

Though deep commitment by the analyst is a basic necessity, a funda-mental neutrality about what the patient does is nevertheless absolutely essential. The patient must be free of intrusive demands from his analyst's emoting and disturbances in the consulting-room. These are likely to be experienced as impingements, conducive to false-self perpetuation and defensive structures.

Nevertheless, certain expressions of affect by the analyst may not necessarily destroy neutrality. When analysis is proceeding creatively, a shared or intermediate 'space' is transitional between the two protago-nists. Under these circumstances something shared is felt to be part of each person's self and yet not part of it too. It has, therefore, the character of a transitional paradox. If this 'mid-way' shared space is truly transitional, then it is neutral. Transitionality gives it all the properties of neutrality; it paradoxically belongs to each, and yet not, for it belongs to both. This is what any neutral zone is.

Therapeutic interaction is a form of playing. It seems here that patient and analyst are *potentially free to be evaluative* of an idea, activity or feeling when engaged in this transitional activity. To do this, they must be free to be able to move in thought from affirming an idea to negating it, from owning to disowning, and from it being part of the self to its being not-self. This does not mean that each must actually go through all these motions, but there must be a freedom of choice to do so. In this context, the transitionality of a dialogue lies in the potential *reversibility* of ideas by both protagonists.

When this movement of feeling and thought is interrupted and one of the protagonists defensively disowns an idea, that is, denies and projects it from the self, or intrudes violently upon the other with an idea, then of course transitionality and neutrality are lost. Exploratory play ceases and this is most likely to happen when anxiety about instinctual love or hate emerges.

This occurs repeatedly in the course of analysis. When it does, then the analyst must be more than ever careful to retain his neutrality and transitionality. But the patient is now in resistance and needs confrontation; mutual playfulness and transitionality are now not called for. Rather, a neutrality, as first defined by Freud and practised by all analysts over many years, is still needed in its traditional, objective, cool, 'like a surgeon' form.

## BEYOND THE COUCH AND APPLICATIONS OF ANALYSIS

Before the Second World War, British analysts were very active in informing the public about Freud's ideas. They also applied psychoanalytic concepts to the understanding of cultural phenomena, art and literature. They were critics, as it were, viewing an activity from the outside. With one or two notable exceptions, they did not participate in the activity themselves. It was not till during and after the Second World War, when Britain was in a ferment of social ideas, that analysts began to participate as equals with others in their activities.

Maybe because most of their pioneers were born in Britain and naturally had a mutuality with other natives, it is indubitably true that it was largely the Independents who led the way to analysts participating equally with other professions in mutual work.

The movement towards applying analysis was resisted by many analysts at every stage in history and has caused bitterness. Jones and Glover condemned the analytic therapy of the pre-war Tavistock Clinic and virtually forbade participation with other professionals too. After the Second World War it took many years of lobbying, pressure and pleading for the British Psycho-Analytic Society to come round to the founding of an official section or forum for the presentation and discussion of applied work. Prejudice against such applications has come from members in all three groups. The rationale against the application of analysis has naturally been that it weakens and then falsifies true analytic work. Such an argument undoubtedly has some validity, but some of those who have been most distinguished in applied fields have also creatively contributed much to the theory and technique of analysis.

More positively, the insistence upon maintaining a very frequent, five times per week, basis to analytic training has ensured the continuing growth of work upon character analysis which must be at the core of our profession. However, there has been a price to pay for this: it has meant that, with very few exceptions, pure psychoanalysis in Britain is confined to one tiny area in north-west London. At the same time many centres of analytic therapy have recently been established. Some of these, in London and other cities, are calling on analysts for help in training activities. Independents led the field into this area of training and were often condemned for doing so, but now analysts from all three groups are actively participating. What is more, psychoanalysts hold many consultant psychotherapist, psychologist or social work appointments, where they introduce psychoanalytic concepts to students and to multidisciplinary teams. Here again the Independents were predominant as pioneers, but others have followed strongly.

These developments have led to a curious division between what could be called 'pure psychoanalysis', based on five times a week therapy, and less frequent contact, which is usually called 'psychoanalytically orientated psychotherapy' and can be of various natures. More often than not, it is not an assessment of the patient's needs which decides what therapy is offered but extraneous factors of various kinds.

Apart from the needs of patients, it is an open question at the present time whether it is best to maintain psychoanalysis in its pure form in one institution only for the whole of Great Britain. This might facilitate a tight-knit group of experts, but leaves it to individual analysts to go out more or less alone into the applied field and to other parts of the country. On the other hand, a concerted effort is being envisaged to spread psychoanalysis, with its proper training facilities, more evenly throughout the country. Naturally there are arguments both ways, and it is outside our scope to discuss them here.

## THE INDEPENDENTS' CONTRIBUTION

What the Independents have given has been very specific but essential for psychoanalysis throughout the world.

Long before Winnicott was fully conceptualizing about transitionality, British Independent analysts like Sharpe, Rickman and Brierley, Milner and Rycroft were pointing in that direction by their work on symbolization and creativity. Undoubtedly they were originally stimulated by the work of Melanie Klein among others, but it was also an interest in regression to de-differentiation and out again, and in transient fusion states in exploratory playing, that pointed to transitionality and to healthy creativity. The study of creativity has been a prime contribution to understanding the analytic process.

Freud, by his enunciation of the pleasure and reality principles, emphasized a dichotomy of the mind into internal and external. After years of pathfinding by earlier British Independents, it remained for Winnicott to demonstrate the essence of something else beside – the transitional or third area of the mind.

Fairbairn was perhaps in a similar mood when he said in effect that his therapeutic aim in analysis was to help the patient change from a 'closed system' of one intra-psychic life, to an 'open system' where he or she was free to be interpersonal with several others.

Perhaps it has been this ease with the third area, hand in hand with an empiricist and Darwinian past, that directed attention to the individual in an environment, but also made it easy for Independents to go out into the field of applied psychoanalysis. For it is with a facility in thinking about matters of the third area that analysts have much to say that can readily be assimilated by others. They can teach about many matters of feeling, such as loss and mourning. Here defences and resistance to the sexual unconscious, which need a grasp of classical analysis to comprehend, play only a part. There is much beyond this, comprehensible to any reflective person, which is also vital for human life, and still the province of psychoanalytic thinking.

To their tradition of open-minded empiricism and humanism the Independents have added their theory in terms of transitions and creativity. They have brought, perhaps, a mood of paradox, of mutuality yet examination, of spontaneity yet discipline, into the dialogue of emotions which is clinical psychoanalysis. They have fun exploring yet keep to the rules imposed by reality. The Independent contribution is only a part of the whole fabric that is psychoanalytic knowledge, but it is a valuable one.

# Bibliography

Authors who are Independent psychoanalysts are marked with an asterisk (\*). The place of publication is London unless otherwise stated.

Abelin, E. L. (1981) 'Triangulation', in R. Lax, ed. *Rapprochement*. New York: Jason Aronson.

Ambrose, A. (1989) 'Key concepts to the transitional approach to managing change', in L. Klein, ed. *Working with Organisations*. Tavistock.

\*Arden, M. (1984) 'Infinite sets and double binds', *Int. J. Psycho-Anal.* 65: 443–52.

—— (1985) 'Psycho-analysis and survival', *Int. J. Psycho-Anal.* 66: 471–80.

—— (1987) 'A concept of femininity', *Int. Rev. Psycho-Anal.* 14: 237–424.

\*Balfour, F., Clulow, C. and Dearnley, D. (1986) 'Shared phantasy and therapeutic structure in brief marital psychotherapy', *Br. J. Psychother.* 3: 12–20.

——, Malan, D., Heath, E. and Bacal, H. (1968a) 'A study of psycho-dynamic changes in untreated neurotic patients', *British Journal of Psychiatry* 114: 525–51.

——, Malan, D., Rayner, E., Bacal, H. and Heath, E. (1968b) 'Psycho-dynamic assessment of the outcome of psychotherapy', in R. Porter, ed. *The Role of Learning in Psychotherapy*. Edinburgh: Churchill.

——, Malan, D., Hood, V. and Shooter, A. (1976) 'Group psychotherapy: a long-term follow-up study', *Archive of General Psychiatry* 33: 1303–15.

\*Balint, E. (1959) 'Distance in space and time', in M. Balint, *Thrills and Regressions*. Hogarth.

—— (1963) 'On being empty of oneself', *Int. J. Psycho-Anal.* 44: 470–80.

—— (1972) 'Fair shares and mutual concern', *Int. J. Psycho-Anal.* 53: 61–5.

—— (1973) 'Technical problems found in the analysis of women by a woman analyst', *Int. J. Psycho-Anal.* 54: 195–201.

—— (1987) 'Memory and consciousness', *Int. J. Psycho-Anal.* 68: 475–84.

—— and Balint, M. (1966) *A Study of Doctors*. Tavistock.

—— and Morell, J. (1973) *Six Minutes for the Patient*. Tavistock.

\*Balint, M. (1932) 'Character analysis and new beginnings', in Balint (1965).

—— (1933) 'On transference of emotions', in Balint (1965).

—— (1935) 'Critical notes on the theory of the pre-genital organization of the libido', in Balint (1965).

—— (1936) 'The final goal of psychoanalytic treatment', *Int. J. Psycho-Anal.* 17: 206–16, and in Balint (1965).

—— (1937) 'Early developmental states of the ego, primary object of love', in Balint (1965).

—— (1939) 'On transference and counter-transference' [with Alice Balint], *Int. J. Psycho-Anal.* 20: 223–30, and in Balint (1965).

—— (1942) 'Contributions to reality testing', *Br. J. Med. Psychol.* 19: 2–12, and in Balint (1957a).

—— (1947) 'On genital love', *Int. J. Psycho-Anal.* 29: 34–40, and in Balint (1965).

—— (1950) 'Changing therapeutic aims and techniques in psychoanalysis', *Int. J. Psycho-Anal.* 31: 117–24, and in Balint (1965).

—— (1951) 'On love and hate', in Balint (1965).

—— (1952) *Primary Love and Psycho-analytic Technique.* First edition. Tavistock.

—— (1955) 'Friendly expanses – horrid, empty spaces', *Int. J. Psycho-Anal.* 36: 127–41.

—— (1957a) *Problems of Human Pleasure and Behaviour.* Hogarth.

—— (1957b) *The Doctor, His Patient and the Illness.* New York: International Universities Press.

—— (1958a) 'Three areas of the mind', *Int. J. Psycho-Anal.* 39: 328–40.

—— (1958b) 'The concepts of subject and object in psychoanalysis', *Br. J. Med. Psychol.* 31: 161–72.

—— (1959) *Thrills and Regressions.* Hogarth.

—— (1965) *Primary Love and Psycho-analytic Technique.* Enlarged edition. Tavistock.

—— (1966) 'Psycho-analysis and medical practice', *Int. J. Psycho-Anal.* 47: 54–62.

—— (1968) *The Basic Fault.* Tavistock.

—— et al. (1970) *Treatment or Diagnosis: a Study of Repeat Prescriptions.* Tavistock.

—— and Balint, E. (1961) *Psychotherapeutic Techniques in Medicine.* Tavistock.

—— and Balint, E., Gosling, G. and Hilderbrand, P. (1966) *A Study of Doctors.* Tavistock.

—— and Lorand, S., eds. (1956) *Perversions, Psychodynamics and Psychotherapy.* New York: Random House.

—— , Ormstein, P. and Balint, E. (1972) *Focal Psychotherapy.* Tavistock.

*Barnett, B. (1978a) 'The Balint group and unconscious mental life', in A. S. Prangshvill and A. Sherzia, eds. *The Unconscious*, vol. 3. Tbilisi, USSR: Metshiereta Publishing House.

—— (1978b) 'Learning, training and freedom to feel', in H. Blackham, ed. *Education for Personal Autonomy*. Bedford Square Press.

—— (1979) 'Balint, the doctor and fear of being unscientific', in P. Hopkins, ed. *The Human Face of Medicine*. Pitman.

—— (1987) 'Intervention, professionalism and the child', *School Psychology International* 8: 1–10.

*Bentovim, A. *et al.* (1988) *Child Sexual Abuse within the Family*. Wright.

Bion, W. (1963) *Elements of Psycho-Analysis*. Heinemann.

—— (1967) *Second Thoughts*. Maresfield.

*Birksted-Breen, D. (1975) *The Birth of a First Child*. Tavistock.

—— (1986) 'The experience of having a baby', *Free Associations* 4: 22–36.

—— (1989a) *Talking with Mothers*. Free Association Books.

—— (1989b) 'Working with an anorexic patient', *Int. J. Psycho-Anal.* 70: 29–40.

Blum, H. P. (1983) 'The position and value of extra-transference interpretations', *J. Amer. Psychoanal. Assn* 31: 587–617.

*Bollas, C. (1974) 'Character, the language of self', *Int. J. Psycho-Anal. Psychother.* 3: 397–418.

—— (1979) 'The transformational object', *Int. J. Psycho-Anal.* 60: 97–107.

—— (1982) 'On relation to the self as an object', *Int. J. Psycho-Anal.* 63: 347–59.

—— (1983) 'Expressive uses of the counter-transference', *Contemporary Psychoanalysis* 19: 1–34.

—— (1987) *The Shadow of the Object*. Free Association Books.

—— (1989) *Forces of Destiny*. Free Association Books.

*Bowlby, J. (1940a) *Personality and Mental Illness*. Kegan Paul.

—— (1940b) The influence of early environment in the development of neurosis and neurotic character', *Int. J. Psycho-Anal.* 21: 154–78.

—— (1944) 'Forty-four juvenile thieves', *Int. J. Psycho-Anal.* 25: 19–52, 107–27.

—— (1949) 'The study and reduction of group tensions in the family', *Human Relations* 2: 101–20.

—— (1950) *Personal Aggressiveness and War*. Kegan Paul.

—— (1951) *Maternal Care and Mental Health*. Geneva: WHO.

—— (1953a) *Child Care and the Growth of Love*. Harmondsworth: Penguin.

—— (1953b) 'Some pathological processes set in train by early mother-child separation', *Journal of Mental Science* 99: 265–72.

—— (1956) 'The effects of mother-child separation', *Br. J. Med. Psychol.* 29: 48–73.

—— (1957) 'An ethological approach to research in child development', *Br. J. Med. Psychol.* 30: 230–40.

—— (1958) 'The nature of a child's tie to his mother', *Int. J. Psycho-Anal.* 39: 350-73.

—— (1960a) 'Separation anxiety', *Int. J. Psycho-Anal.* 41: 80-113.

—— (1960b) 'Grief and mourning in infancy and early childhood', *Psychoanal. Study Child* 15: 9-52.

—— (1960c) 'Ethology and the development of object relations', *Int. J. Psycho-Anal.* 41: 313-17.

—— (1961) 'Process of mourning', *Int. J. Psycho-Anal.* 42: 317-40.

—— (1963) 'Pathological mourning and childhood mourning', *J. Amer. Psychoanal. Assn* 11: 500-41.

—— (1969) *Attachment and Loss*, vol. 1, *Attachment*. Hogarth.

—— (1973) *Attachment and Loss*, vol. 2, *Separation*. Hogarth.

—— (1976) 'Psychoanalysis as art and science', *Int. Rev. Psycho-Anal.* 6: 3-14.

—— (1979) *The Make and Breaking of Affectional Bonds*. Tavistock.

—— (1980) *Attachment and Loss*, vol. 3, *Loss*. Hogarth.

—— (1981) 'Psychoanalysis as a natural science', *Int. Rev. Psycho-Anal.* 8: 243-56.

—— , Robertson, J. and Rosenbluth D. (1952) 'A two year old goes to hospital' *Psychoanal. Study Child* 7: 82-94.

*Brafman, A. (1978) 'The family, the child and the psychiatrist', in J. Connolly, ed. *Therapy Options in Psychiatry*. Pitman.

—— (1988) 'Infant observation', *Int. Rev. Psycho-Anal.* 15: 45-52.

*Brearley, M. (1985) *The Art of Captaincy*. Hodder.

*Bridger, H. (1985) 'Northfield revisited', in M. Pines, ed. *Bion and Group Psychotherapy*. Routledge.

—— and Coles, R. (1969) 'The consultant and his roles', *Br. J. Med. Psychol.* 42: 231-43.

—— and Higgin, G. (1965) *The Psychodynamics of an Intergroup Experience*. Tavistock.

*Brierley, M. (1932) 'Some problems of integration in women', *Int. J. Psycho-Anal.* 13: 433-45.

—— (1936) 'Specific defeminants in feminine development', *Int. J. Psycho-Anal.* 17: 163-71.

—— (1937) 'Affects in theory and practice', *Int. J. Psycho-Anal.* 18: 256-63.

—— (1939) 'A prefatory note on internalized objects', *Int. J. Psycho-Anal.* 20: 241-50.

—— (1942) 'Internal objects and theory', *Int. J. Psycho-Anal.* 23: 107-14.

—— (1943) 'Theory, practice and public relations', *Int. J. Psycho-Anal.* 24: 119-27.

—— (1944) 'Metapsychology as process theory', *Int. J. Psycho-Anal.* 25: 97-109.

—— (1951) *Trends in Psycho-Analysis*. Hogarth.

—— (1969) 'Hardy perennials in psycho-analysis', *Int. J. Psycho-Anal.* 56: 447–52.

Britton, R. (1989) 'The missing link', in R. Britton *et al. The Oedipus Complex Today*. Karnac.

Brome, V. (1982) *Ernest Jones, Freud's Alter Ego*. Caliban.

*Brown, D. (1959) 'The relevance of body image to neurosis', *Br. J. Med. Psychol.* 32: 249–21.

—— (1965) 'Body image and susceptibility to contact dermatitis', *Br. J. Med. Psychol.* 38: 261–67.

—— (1977) 'Drowsiness in the counter-transference', *Int. Rev. Psycho-Anal.* 4: 481–92.

—— (1985) 'The psychosoma and the group', *Group Analysis* 18: 93–100.

—— (1989) 'A contribution to the understanding of psychosomatic processes in groups', *Br. J. Psychother.* 6: 5–9.

—— and Pedder, J. (1979) *Introduction to Psychotherapy*. Tavistock.

——, Tantom, D. and Kalucy, R. (1982) 'Sleep scratching and dreams in eczema', *Psychotherapy and Psychosomatics* 37: 26–35.

*Browne, N. (1980) 'Mirroring in the analysis of an artist', *Int. J. Psych-Anal.* 61: 493–503.

—— (1986) 'Some enuretic derivatives in adult analysis', *Int. J. Psycho-Anal.* 67: 449–57.

*Carpy, D. (1989) 'Tolerating the counter-transference: a mutative process', *Int. J. Psycho-Anal.* 70: 287–94.

*Casement, P. (1982a) 'Some pressures on the analyst for physical contact during reliving of an early trauma', *Int. Rev. Psycho-Anal.* 9: 279–86.

—— (1982b) 'Samuel Beckett's relationship to his mother tongue', *Int. Rev. Psycho-Anal.* 9: 35–44.

—— (1984) 'The reflective potential of the patient as mirror to the therapist', in J. Raney, ed. *Listening and Interpreting*. New York: Jason Aronson.

—— (1985) *On Learning from the Patient*. Tavistock.

—— (1986a) 'Interpretation: fresh insight or cliché?' *Free Associations* 5: 90–104.

—— (1986b) 'Counter-transference and interpretation', *Contemporary Psychoanalysis* 22.

—— (1987a) 'The experience of trauma in the transference' in J. Klauber, *et al. Illusion and Spontaneity in Psycho-Analysis*. Free Association Books.

—— (1987b) 'Between the lines', *Br. J. Psychother.* 4: 86–93.

—— (1990) *Further Learning from the Patient*. Routledge.

Cassirer, E. (1953) *Philosophy of Symbolic Forms*. Cambridge, MA: Harvard University Press.

Cavell, M. (1988) 'Interpretation, psychoanalysis and the philosophy of mind', *J. Amer. Psychoanal. Assn* 36: 859–80.

Chasseguet-Smirgel, J. (1984) *Creativity and Perversion*. Free Association Books.

Clancier, A. and Kalmanovitch, J. (1987) *Winnicott and Parodox*. Tavistock.

Clyne, M. (1961) *Night Calls*. Tavistock.

*Cohen, N. (1982) 'On loneliness and the ageing process', *Int. J. Psycho-Anal.* 63: 149–55.

*Coltart, N. (1985) 'The treatment of a transvestite', *Psychoanal. Psychotherap.* 1: 65–79.

—— (1986) 'Slouching towards Bethlehem . . . or thinking the unthinkable in psychoanalysis', in G. Kohon, ed. *The British School of Psychoanalysis*. Free Association Books, pp. 185–99.

—— (1987) 'Diagnosis and assessment of suitability for analysis', *Br. J. Psychother.* 4: 127–34.

*Conran, M. (1976a) 'Schizophrenia as incestuous failure', *Schizophrenia* 75: 203–10.

—— (1976b) 'Incestuous failure', *Int. J. Psycho-Anal.* 57: 477–82.

—— (1985) 'The patient in hospital', *Psychoanal. Psychotherap.* 1: 31–43.

Davis, M. and *Wallbridge, D. (1981) *Boundary and Space*. Karnac.

Daws, D. (1989) *Through the Night*. Free Association Books.

*Denford, J. (1981) 'Going away', *Int. J. Psycho-Anal.* 313–32.

—— (1983) 'Selection and outcome in in-patient psychotherapy', *Br. J. Med. Psychol.* 56: 225–43.

Deutsch, H. (1942) 'Some forms of emotional disturbance and their relation to schizophrenia', in H. Deutsch (1965) *Neurosis and Character Types*. New York: International Universities Press.

*Douglas, G. (1956) 'Psychotic mothers', *Lancet* 21 January: 124–95.

—— (1963) 'Puerperal depression and excessive compliance with the mother', *Br. J. Med. Psychol.* 36: 271–86.

Dupont, J. (1988) *The Clinical Diary of Sandor Ferenczi*. Cambridge, MA: Harvard University Press.

Eissler, K. (1953) 'The effect of the structure of the ego on psycho-analytic technique', *J. Amer. Psychoanal. Assn.* 1: 104–43.

Erikson, E. H. (1950) *Childhood and Society*. Penguin.

*Evans, J. (1966) 'Analytic group therapy with delinquent adolescents', *Adolescence* 1: 180–96.

—— (1975) 'Depression in adolescents', *Proceedings of the Royal Society of Medicine* 68: 565–66.

—— (1980) 'Ambivalence', *Journal of Adolescence* 34: 273–84.

—— (1982a) 'Adolescent group therapy and its contribution to the understanding of adult groups', in M. Pines, ed. *Evolution of Group Therapy*. Routledge.

—— (1982b) *Adolescent and Pre-Adolescent Psychiatry*. New York: Grune & Stratton.

—— and Acton W. (1972) 'A psychiatric service for the disturbed adolescent', *Br. J. Psychiatry* 120: 429–32.

*Eyre, D. (1975) 'A contribution towards the understanding of the confusion of tongues', *Int. J. Psycho-Anal.* 56: 449–54.

—— (1978) 'Identification and empathy', *Int. Rev. Psycho-Anal.* 5: 351–9.

*Fairbairn, R. (1936) 'The effect of a king's death upon patients undergoing analysis', *Int. J. Psycho-Anal.* 17: 228–84.

—— (1940) 'Schizoid factors in the personality', in Fairbairn (1952).

—— (1941) 'A revised psychopathology of the psychoses and psychoneuroses', *Int. J. Psycho-Anal.* 22: 250–79, and in Fairbairn (1952).

—— (1943) 'The repression and the return of bad objects', *Br. J. Med. Psychol.* 19: 327–41, and in Fairbairn (1952).

—— (1944) 'Endopsychic structure considered in terms of object relations', *Int. J. Psycho-Anal.* 25: 60–93, and in Fairbairn (1952).

—— (1952) *Psycho-Analytic Studies of the Personality*. Routledge.

—— (1954) 'Observations in defence of the object relations theory of personality', *Br. J. Med. Psychol.* 28: 144–56.

—— (1964) 'A note on the origin of male homosexuality', *Br. J. Med. Psychol.* 37: 31–2.

Fenichel, O. (1946) *The Psychoanalytic Theory of Neurosis*. Kegan Paul.

Ferenczi, S. (1916) *First Contributions to Psychoanalysis*. Boston, MA: Badger Press.

—— (1925) *Thalassa: A Theory of Sexuality*. Karnac Reprints.

—— (1926) *Further Contributions*. Hogarth.

—— (1951) *Final Contributions*. New York: Basic.

Fisher, C. (1965) 'Psychoanalytic implications of recent records of sleep and dreaming', *J. Amer. Psychoanal. Assn.* 13: 197–303.

*Flugel, J. C. (1917) 'Freudian mechanisms as factors in moral development', *Br. J. Psychol.* 8: 477–89.

—— (1920) 'On the character and married life of Henry VIII', *Int. J. Psycho-Anal.* 1: 24–37.

—— (1921a) 'On the biological basis of sexual repression and its sociological significance', *Br. J. Med. Psychol.* 1: 225–80.

—— (1921b) *The Psycho-Analytic Study of the Family*. Hogarth.

—— (1924) 'Polyphallic symbolism and the castration complex', *Int. J. Psycho-Anal.* 5: 155–96.

—— (1929) 'On the moral attitude to present day clothes', *Br. J. Med. Psychol.* 9: 60–91.

—— (1930) *The Psychology of Clothes*. Hogarth.

—— (1933) *A Hundred Years of Psychology*. Duckworth.

—— (1934) *Men and their Motives*. Kegan Paul.

—— (1942) 'Sublimation: its nature and conditions', *British Journal of Educational Psychology* 13: 1–80.

—— (1945) *Man, Morals and Society*. Duckworth.

—— (1955) *Studies in Feeling and Desire*. Duckworth.

Freud, A. (1926) *The Psychoanalytical Treatment of Children*. Imago, 1946.

—— (1936) *The Ego and the Mechanisms of Defence*. Hogarth.

—— (1956–65) *Research at the Hampstead Child-Therapy Clinic and Other Papers*. Hogarth.

—— (1965) *Normality and Pathology in Childhood*. Hogarth.

—— (1971) *Problems of Psychoanalytic Technique and Therapy*. Hogarth.

Freud, S. (1900) *The Interpretation of Dreams*. in James Strachey, ed. *The Standard Edition of the Complete Psychological Works of Sigmund Freud*, 24 vols. Hogarth, 1953–73, vol. 4–5.

—— (1901) *The Psychopathology of Everyday Life. S.E.* 6.

—— (1905) *Three Essays on the Theory of Sexuality. S.E.* 7, pp. 125–243.

—— (1908a) 'Character and anal erotism'. *S.E.* 9, pp. 167–76.

—— (1908b) 'Creative writers and daydreaming'. *S.E.* 9, pp. 143-9.

—— (1910a) 'The future prospects of psychoanalysis'. *S.E.* 9, pp. 139–52.

—— (1910b) *Leonardo da Vinci and a Memory of his Childhood. S.E.* 11, pp. 63–138.

—— (1911) 'Formulations on the two principles of mental functioning'. *S.E.* 12, pp. 215–27.

—— (1912a) 'Dynamics of transference'. *S.E.* 12, pp. 99–110.

—— (1912b) 'Recommendations to physicians practising psycho-analysis'. *S.E.* 12, pp. 111-21.

—— (1912c) 'A note on the unconscious in psycho-analysis'. *S.E.* 12, pp. 260–6.

—— (1913a) 'On beginning the treatment'. *S.E.* 12, pp. 121–44.

—— (1913b) 'The disposition to obsessional neurosis'. *S.E.* 12, pp. 317–26.

—— (1914a) 'On narcissism'. *S.E.* 14, pp. 73–104.

—— (1914b) 'Remembering, repeating and working through'. *S.E.* 12, pp. 147–56.

—— (1915a) 'Observations on transference love'. *S.E.* 12, pp. 159–71.

—— (1915b) 'Instincts and their vicissitudes'. *S.E.* 14, pp. 117–40.

—— (1915c) 'Repression'. *S.E.* 14, pp. 146–58.

—— (1915d) 'The unconscious'. *S.E.* 14, pp. 166–217.

—— (1916) 'Some character types met most in psycho-analysis'. *S.E.* 14, pp. 311–36.

—— (1917) *Mourning and melancholia, S.E.* 14, pp. 3–39.

—— (1920a) *Beyond the Pleasure Principle. S.E.* 18, pp. 7–66.

—— (1920b) 'A note on the prehistory of the technique of analysis'. *S.E.* 18, 263–5.

—— (1923a) 'Two encyclopaedia articles'. *S.E.* 18, pp. 242–62.

—— (1923b) *The Ego and the Id. S.E.* 19, 3–68.

—— (1925a) 'Some psychic consequences of anatomical differences between the sexes'. *S.E.* 19, pp. 213–60.

—— (1925b) *An Autobiographical Study. S.E.* 20, pp. 3–74.

—— (1926) *Inhibitions, Symptoms and Anxiety. S.E.* 20, pp. 37–178.

—— (1931) 'Female sexuality'. *S.E.* 21, pp. 225–46.

—— (1933) *New Introductory Lectures. S.E.* 22, pp. 112–36.

—— (1937) 'Analysis Terminable and Interminable'. *S.E.* 23, pp. 209–54.

—— (1939) *Moses and Monotheism. S.E.* 23, pp. 7–140.

—— (1940) *An Outline of Psychoanalysis. S.E.* 23, pp. 144–208.

\*Ghaffari, K. (1987) 'Psychoanalytic theories on drug addiction', *Psychoanal. Psychotherap.* 3: 39–51.

\*Gill, H. (1970) 'The influence of parental attitudes on the child reactions to sexual stimuli Family Process', *Family Process* 9: 20–9.

—— (1982) 'The life context of the dreamer and the setting of dreaming', *Int. J. Psycho-Anal.* 63: 475–82.

—— (1987) 'Effects of oedipal triumph', *Int. J. Psycho-Anal.* 68: 251–60.

—— (1988) 'Working through resistances of intrapsychic and environmental origin', *Int. J. Psycho-Anal.* 69: 535–50.

—— and Sutherland, J. (1964) 'The significance of the one way vision screen', *Brit. J. Med. Psychol.* 37: 16–31.

—— and Sutherland, J. (1967) 'Psycho-diagnostic appraisal', *Brit. J. Med. Psychol.* 40: 62–71.

\*Gillespie, W. H. (1940) 'A contribution to the study of fetishism', *Int. J. Psycho-Anal.* 21: 401–5.

—— (1952) 'Notes on the analysis of sexual perversions', *Int. J. Psycho-Anal.* 33: 397–402.

—— (1953) 'Extra-sensory elements in dream interpretation', in G. Devereux, ed. *Psychoanalysis and the Occult.* New York: International Universities Press, pp. 373–82.

—— (1956a) 'The general theory of sexual perversion', *Int. J. Psycho-Anal.* 37: 396–403.

—— (1956b) 'The structure and aetiology of sexual perversion', in S. Lorand, ed. *Perversions, Psychodynamics and Therapy.* New York: Random House, pp. 28–41.

—— (1956) 'Experiences suggestive of paranormal cognition in the psychoanalytic situation', in P. Wolstenholme and E. Miller, eds. *Extrasensory Perception*, J. & A. Churchill, pp. 204–20.

—— (1963) 'Some regressive phenomena in old age', *Br. J. Med. Psychol.* 36: 203–9.

—— (1964a) 'Contribution to symposium on homosexuality', *Int. J. Psycho-Anal.* 45: 203–9.

—— (1964b) 'Psychoanalytic theory of sexual deviation with special reference to fetishism', in I. Rosen, ed. *The Pathology and Treatment of Sexual Deviation*, Oxford: Oxford University Press, pp. 123–45.

—— (1968) 'The psychoanalytic theory of child development', in E. Miller, ed. *Foundations of Child Psychiatry*. Pergamon: pp. 51–69.

—— (1969) 'Concepts of vaginal orgasm', *Int. J. Psycho-Anal.* 50: 495–97.

—— (1971) 'Aggression and instinct theory'. *Int. J. Psycho-Anal.* 52: 155–60.

—— (1975) 'Woman and her discontents: a reassessment of Freud's views on female sexuality', *Int. Rev. Psycho-Anal.* 2: 1–9.

—— (1989) 'The legacy of Sigmund Freud', in J. Sandler, ed. *Dimensions of Psycho-analysis*. Karnac.

Giovacchini, P., ed. (1972) *Tactics and Techniques in Psychoanalytic Therapy.* Hogarth.

Glover, E. (1925) 'Notes on oral character formation', *Int. J. Psycho-Anal.* 6: 131–54.

—— (1928) 'The aetiology of alcoholism', *Proceedings of the Royal Society of Medicine* 21: 45–50.

—— (1928) *The Technique of Psycho-Analysis.* Baillière, Tindall & Cox.

—— (1929) 'The psychology of the psychotherapist', *Br. J. Med. Psychol.* 9: 1–16.

—— (1931) 'The therapeutic effect of interpretation', *Int. J. Psycho-Anal.* 12: 397–417.

—— (1932a) 'Common problems in psychoanalysis and anthropology: drug, ritual and addiction', *Br. J. Med. Psychol.*, 12: 109–31.

—— (1932b) 'On the aetiology of drug addiction', *Int. J. Psycho-Anal.* 13: 63–73.

—— (1935) *War, Sadism and Pacifism.* Allen & Unwin.

—— (1936) 'War and pacifism', *Character and Personality* 4: 100–21.

—— (1936) *The Dangers of Being Human.* Allen & Unwin.

—— (1939) *Psychoanalysis: A Handbook.* Staples, revised 1949.

—— (1940a) *The Psychology of Fear and Courage.* Harmondsworth: Penguin.

—— (1940b) 'The mental strain of war', *The Highway* 13: 1–40.

—— (1943) 'The concept of dissociations', in Glover (1968).

—— (1945) *An Examination of the Klein System of Child Psychology.* New York: International Universities Press.

—— (1947a) *Basic Mental Concepts.* Imago.

—— (1947b) *The Social and Legal Aspects of Sexual Abnormality.* Institute for the Scientific Treatment of Delinquency.

—— (1948) 'Pathological character formation', in S. Lorand, ed. *Psycho-Analysis Today*. Allen & Unwin.

—— (1949) 'An outline of investigation and treatment of delinquency', in T. R. Eissler, ed. *Searchlights on Delinquency*. New York: International Universities Press.

—— (1950) *Freud or Jung*. Allen & Unwin.

—— (1953) *Psycho-Analysis and Child Psychology*. Imago.

—— (1956) *The Early Development of Mind*, vol. 1, *Selected Papers*. Imago.

—— (1957) *The Psychology of Prostitution*. Institute for the Treatment of Delinquency.

—— (1960) *The Roots of Crime*, vol. 2, *Selected Papers*. Imago.

—— (1961) 'Some recent trends in psycho-analytic theory', *Psychoanal. Q.* 30: 86–107.

—— (1964a) 'Aggression and sado-masochism', in I. Rosen, ed. *The Pathology and Treatment of Sexual Deviation*. Oxford: Oxford University Press.

—— (1964b) 'Freudian or Neo-Freudian', *Psychoanal. Q.* 33: 17–52.

—— (1966) 'Metapsychology of metaphysics', *Psychoanal. Q.* 35.

—— (1967) 'In praise of ourselves', *Int. J. Psycho-Anal.* 48: 499–503.

—— (1968) *The Birth of the Ego*. Allen & Unwin.

—— (1969) 'Bibliography of the works of Edward Glover', *Psychoanal. Q.* 38: 532–49.

—— and Brierley, M. (1940) *An Investigation of the Technique of Psycho-Analysis*. Ballière, Tindall & Cox.

Green, A. (1973) *Le discours vivant. La conception psychoanalytique de l'affect*. Paris: Presses Universitaires de France.

—— (1977) 'Conceptions of affect', *Int. J. Psycho-Anal.* 58: 129–56.

—— (1986) *On Private Madness*. Hogarth.

Greenacre, P. (1953) *Affective Disorders*. New York: International Universities Press.

—— (1968) 'Perversions, some genetic considerations', *Psychoanal. Study Child* 23: 47–62.

—— (1975) 'On reconstruction', *J. Amer. Psychoanal. Assn.* 14: 9–27.

Greenberg, J. R. and Mitchell, S. A. (1983) *Object Relations in Psychoanalytic Theory*. Cambridge, MA: Harvard University Press.

Greenson, R. (1967) *The Technique and Practice of Psychoanalysis*. New York: International Universities Press.

Grolnik, S. and Barkin, L. (1978) *Between Reality and Phantasy*. New York: Jason Aronson.

Grotstein, J. (1981) *Splitting and Projective Identification*. New York: Jason Aronson.

Guntrip, H. (1973) *Personality Structure and Human Interaction*. Hogarth.

Hall, C. (1966) *The Meaning of Dreams*. New York: Basic.

Hartmann, E. (1984) *The Nightmare*. New York: Basic.

*Hayley, T. (1990) 'Charisma, suggestion, psycho-analysts, medicine-men and metaphor', *Int. Rev. Psycho-Anal.* 17: 1–10.

*Hayman, A. (1962) 'Some aspects of regression in non-psychotic puerperal breakdown', *Br. J. Med. Psychol.* 35: 135–42.

—— (1965) 'Verbalization and identity', *Int. J. Psycho-Anal.* 46: 455–60.

—— (1969) 'What do we mean by "ID"?', *J. Amer. Psychoanal. Assn.* 17: 353–80.

—— (1972) 'Some interferences with the analysis of an atypical child', *Psychoanal. Study Child* 27: 476–504.

—— (1974) 'Some unusual anal fantasies of a young child', *Psycho-Anal. Study Child* 29: 265–76.

—— (1986) 'On Marjorie Brierley', *Int. Rev. Psycho-Anal.* 13: 383–92.

—— (1989) 'What do we mean by "phantasy"?', *Int. J. Psycho-Anal.* 70: 105–14.

*Heimann, P. (1942) 'A contribution to the problem of sublimation and its relation to process of internalization', *Int. J. Psycho-Anal.* 23: 8–17, and in Heimann (1989).

—— (1949) 'Some notes on the psycho-analytic concept of introjected objects', *Br. J. Med. Psychol.* 22: 8–15, and in Heimann (1989).

—— (1950) 'On counter-transference', *Int. J. Psycho-Anal.* 31: 81–4, and in Heimann (1989).

—— (1952a) 'A contribution to the re-evaluation of the Oedipus complex - the early stages', *Int. J. Psycho-Anal.* 33: 84–92, and in Heimann (1989).

—— (1952b) 'Preliminary notes on some defence mechanisms in paranoid states', *Int. J. Psycho-Anal.* 33: 208–13, and in Heimann (1989).

—— (1952c) 'Notes on the theory of the life and death instincts', in M. Klein, P. Heimann, S. Isaacs and J. Riviere *Developments in Psycho-Analysis*. Hogarth, pp. 321–37, and in Heimann (1989).

—— (1952d) 'Certain functions of introjection and projection in early infancy', in M. Klein, P. Heimann, S. Isaacs and J. Riviere *Developments in Psycho-Analysis*. Hogarth, pp. 122–68.

—— (1954) 'Problems of the training analysis', *Int. J. Psycho-Anal.* 35: 163–8.

—— (1955a) 'A contribution to the re-evaluation of the Oedipus complex – the early stages', in M. Klein, P. Heimann, and R. E. Money-Kyrle, eds. *New Directions in Psycho-Analysis*. Tavistock, pp. 23–38, and in Heimann (1989).

—— (1955b) 'A combination of defence mechanisms in paranoid states', in M. Klein, P. Heimann, and R. E. Money-Kyrle, eds *New Directions in Psycho-Analysis*. Tavistock, pp. 240–65, and in Heimann (1989).

—— (1956) 'Dynamics of transference interpretations', *Int. J. Psycho-Anal.* 37: 303–10, and in Heimann (1989).

—— (1957) 'Some notes on sublimation', in Heimann (1989).

—— (1958) 'Notes on early development', in Heimann (1989).

—— (1960) 'Counter-transference', *Br. J. Med. Psychol.* 33: 9–15, and in Heimann (1989).

—— (1962a) 'Contribution to discussion of "The curative factors in psychoanalysis"', *Int. J. Psycho-Anal.* 43: 228–31.

—— (1962b) 'Notes on the anal stage', *Int. J. Psycho-Anal.* 43: 406–14, and in Heimann (1989).

—— (1964) 'Comments on the psycho-analytic concept of work', in Heimann (1989).

—— (1968) 'The evaluation of applicants for psycho-analytic training', *Int. J. Psycho-Anal.* 49: 527–39, and in Heimann (1989).

—— (1969) Postscript to 'Dynamics of transference interpretation (1956)', in Heimann (1989).

—— (1970) 'The nature and function of interpretation', in Heimann (1989).

—— (1975a) 'Sacrificial parapraxis – failure or achievement?' *Annual of Psychoanalysis* 3: 145–63. New York: International Universities Press.

—— (1975b) 'From "cumulative trauma" to the privacy of the self', *Int. J. Psycho-Anal.* 56: 465–76.

—— (1977) 'Further observations on the analyst's cognitive process', *J. Amer. Psychoanal. Assn.* 25: 313–33.

—— (1978) 'On the necessity for the analyst to be natural with his patient', in Heimann (1989).

—— (1980) 'About children and children no-longer', in *Psychoanalytici aan het woord*, Deventer: Van Loghum Slaterus BV, pp. 289–307.

—— (1989) *About Children and Children No-longer*, M. Tonnesmann, ed. Routledge.

—— and Isaacs, S. (1952e) 'Regression', in M. Klein, P. Heimann, S. Isaacs and J. Riviere *Developments in Psycho-Analysis*. Hogarth, pp. 169–97.

—— and Valenstein, F. (1972) 'The psychoanalytical concept of aggression: an integrated summary', *Int. J. Psycho-Anal.* 53: 31–5.

Hermann, I. (1936) 'Clinging-going-in-search', reprinted in *Psychoanal. Q.* (1976) 45: 5–36.

*Hildebrand, P. (1966) 'Structural aspects of the Tavistock training', in M. Balint *et al. A Study of Doctors*. Tavistock.

—— (1976) 'Reflections on the future of psychoanalysis', *Int. Rev. Psycho-Anal.* 3: 1–14.

—— (1983) 'The contemporary relevance of the psycho-dynamic tradition', in D. Pilgrim, ed. *Psychology and Psychotherapy*. Routledge.

—— (1986) 'The Caledonian tragedy', *Int. Rev. Psycho-Anal.* 13: 39–49.

—— (1988) 'The other side of the wall – a psycho-analytic study of creativity in later life', *Int. Rev. Psycho-Anal.* 15: 353–64.

Hinshelwood, R. (1989) *A Dictionary of Kleinian Thought.* Free Association Books.

*Hobson, R. P. (1980) 'The question of egocentrism: the young child's competence in the coordination of perspectives', *Journal of Child Psychology and Psychiatry*, 21: 325–31.

—— (1982) 'The question of childhood egocentrism: the coordination of perspectives in relation to operational thinking', *Journal of Child Psychology and Psychiatry* 23: 43–60.

—— (1983) 'The autistic child's recognition of age-related features of people, animals and things', *British Journal of Developmental Psychology* 1: 343–52.

—— (1984) 'Early childhood autism and the question of egocentrism', *Journal of Autism and Developmental Disorders* 14(1): 85–104.

—— (1985) 'Self-representing dreams', *Psycholanal. Psychother* 1(3): 43–53.

—— (1986a) 'The autistic child's appraisal of expressions of emotion', *Journal of Child Psychology and Psychiatry* 27: 321–42.

—— (1986b) 'The autistic child's appraisal of expressions of emotion: a further study', *Journal of Child Psychology and Psychiatry* 27: 671–80.

—— (1987) 'The autistic child's recognition of age and sex-related characteristics of people', *Journal of Autism and Developmental Disorders* 17(1): 63–79.

—— (1989a) 'On sharing experiences', *Development and Psychopathology* 1: 197–203.

—— (1989b) 'Beyond cognition: a theory of autism', in G. Dawson, ed. *Autism.* New York: Guilford.

—— and Lee, A. (1989) 'Emotion-related and abstract concepts in autistic people: evidence from the British Picture Vocabulary Scale', *Journal of Autism and Developmental Disorders* 19: 601–23.

——, Ouston, J. and Lee, A. (1988a) 'What's in a face? The case of autism', *Brit. J. Med. Psychol.* 79: 441–53.

——, Ouston, J. and Lee, A. (1988b) 'Emotion recognition in autism: coordinating faces and voices', *Psychological Medicine* 18: 911–23.

*Hood, C. (1975) 'Child care and development', Mills & Boon.

*Hood, J. (1964) 'On therapeutic intervention in the child guidance setting', *Journal of Child Psychotherapy* 2: 7–13.

Hopkins, J. (1987) 'Failure of the holding relationship', *Journal of Child Psychotherapy* 13: 5–18.

*Hopper, E. (1981) *Social Mobility.* Blackwell.

—— (1985) 'The problem of context in group-analytic psychotherapy', in M. Pines, ed. *Bion and Group Psychotherapy.* Routledge.

Hughes, J. (1989) *Reshaping the Psychoanalytic Domain.* Berkeley, CA: University of California Press.

*James, M. (1960) 'Premature ego development', *Int. J. Psycho-Anal.* 41: 288–94.

—— (1962) 'Infantile narcissistic trauma', *Int. J. Psycho-Anal.* 43: 69–79.

—— (1964) 'Interpretation and management in the treatment of pre-adolescents', *Int. J. Psycho-Anal.* 45: 494–502.

—— (1966) 'Anxiety, socialization and ego development in early infancy', *Int. J. Psycho-Anal.* 47: 230–5.

—— (1968) 'Psycho-analysis and childhood', in J. Sutherland, ed. *The Psycho-Analytic Approach.* Tavistock.

—— (1972) 'Preverbal communications', in P. Giovacchini, ed. *Tactics and Techniques in Psychoanalytic Therapy.* Hogarth.

—— (1979) 'The non-symbolic role of psycho-somatic disorder', *Int. Rev. Psycho-Anal.* 6: 413–22.

Jaques, E. (1951) *The Changing Culture of a Factory.* Tavistock.

*Jones, E. (1910a) 'Freud's theory of dreams', *American Journal of Psychology* 21: 283–308.

—— (1910b) 'The Oedipus complex as an explanation of Hamlet's mystery: a study in motive', *American Journal of Psychology* 21: 72–113.

—— (1910c) 'On the nightmare', *American Journal of Insanity* 66: 383–417.

—— (1911a) 'The psychopathology of everyday life', *American Journal of Psychology* 22: 477–527, and in Jones (1948).

—— (1911b) 'The relationship between dreams and psychoneurotic symptoms', in Jones (1948), pp. 251–72.

—— (1911c) 'Some instances of the influence of dreams on waking life', *Journal of Abnormal Psychology* 6: 11–18.

—— (1911d) 'On dying together', in Jones (1974a).

—— (1912) 'The symbolic significance of salt in folklore and superstition', in Jones (1974b).

—— (1913a) 'The influence of Andrea del Sarto's wife on his art', in Jones (1974a).

—— (1913b) 'The God complex', in Jones (1974b).

—— (1913c) 'Hate and anal erotism in the obsessional neurosis', in *Papers on Psycho-Analysis,* 2nd edition, pp. 540–8.

—— (1913d) *Papers on Psycho-Analysis,* 1st edition. Ballière, Tindall & Cox.

—— (1915) 'The repression theory in its relation to memory', *British Journal of Psychology* 8: 33–47.

—— (1916) 'The theory of symbolism', *British Journal of Psychology* 9: 181–229, and in Jones (1948).

—— (1918) 'Anal-erotic character traits', *Journal of Abnormal Psychology* 13: 261–84, and in Jones (1948).

—— (1920) 'A linguistic factor in English characterology', *Int. J. Psycho-Anal.* 1: 256–61, and in Jones (1974a).

—— (1921) 'Persons in dreams disguised as themselves', *Int. J. Psycho-Anal.* 2: 420–3.

—— (1922a) 'Introjection and projection', *Int. J. Psycho-Anal.* 3: 119.

—— (1922b) 'The island of Ireland', in Jones (1974b).

—— (1923a) *Essays in Applied Psychoanalysis.* International Psycho-Analytic Press.

—— (1923b) 'A psycho-analytical study of the Holy Ghost', in Jones (1974b).

—— (1926a) 'Deprivation of the senses as a castration symbol', *Int. J. Psycho-Anal.* 7: 236–7.

—— (1926b) 'The origin and structure of the super-ego', *Int. J. Psycho-Anal.* 7: 303–11, and in Jones (1948).

—— (1927a) 'Child analysis', *Int. J. Psycho-Anal.* 8: 387–91.

—— (1927b) 'Discussion on lay analysis', *Int. J. Psycho-Anal.* 8: 174–98.

—— (1927c) 'The early development of female sexuality', *Int. J. Psycho-Anal.* 8: 459, and in Jones (1948).

—— (1928a) 'The development of the concept of the super-ego', *Journal of Abnormal and Social Psychology* 23: 276–85.

—— (1928b) *Psycho-Analysis.* Ernest Benn.

—— (1928c) 'Psychoanalysis and the artist', *Psyche* 8: 73–88.

—— (1928d) 'Psychoanalysis and folklore', in *Essays in Applied Psycho-Analysis* (1951) 2: 1–21, and in Jones (1974a).

—— (1929a) 'Fear, guilt and hate', *Int. J. Psycho-Anal.* 10: 383–97, and in Jones (1948).

—— (1929b) 'The inferiority complex of the Welsh', *Essays in Applied Psycho-Analysis* (1951) 1: 128–32, and in Jones (1974a).

—— (1930a) 'Jealousy', in Jones (1948).

—— (1930b) 'Psychoanalysis and psychiatry', in Jones (1948).

—— (1930c) 'Psychoanalysis and biology', *Essays in Applied Psycho-Analysis* (1951) 1: 135–64.

—— (1930d) 'Psychoanalysis and the Christian religion', *Essays in Applied Psycho-Analysis* (1951) 2: 198–211, and in Jones (1974b).

—— (1931a) *On the Nightmare.* Hogarth.

—— (1931b) 'The problem of Paul Morphy: a contribution to the psychoanalysis of chess', *Int. J. Psycho-Anal.* 12: 1–23, and in Jones (1974b).

—— (1933) 'The phallic phase', *Int. J. Psycho-Anal.* 14: 1–33, and in Jones (1948).

—— (1935) 'Early female sexuality', *Int. J. Psycho-Anal.* 16: 263–73, and in Jones (1948).

—— (1937) 'Love and morality', *Int. J. Psycho-Anal.* 18: 1–5.

—— (1941) 'Evolution and revolution', *Int. J. Psycho-Anal.* 22: 193–208.

—— (1947) 'The genesis of the super-ego', in Jones (1948).

—— (1948) *Papers on Psycho-Analysis*, 5th edition. Ballière, Tindall & Cox; Baltimore, MD: Williams, 1950.

—— (1949) *Hamlet and Oedipus*. New York: Norton.

—— (1953) *Life and Work of Sigmund Freud*, vol. 1. Hogarth.

—— (1955) *Life and Work of Sigmund Freud*, vol. 2. Hogarth.

—— (1957) *Life and Work of Sigmund Freud*, vol. 3. Hogarth.

—— (1959) *Free Associations: Memories of a Psychoanalyst*. Hogarth.

—— (1974a) *Psycho-Myth, Psycho-History,* vol. 1 (*Essays in Applied Psychoanalysis*, American Edition). New York: Hillstone.

—— (1974b) *Psycho-Myth, Psycho-History*, vol. 2. New York: Hillstone.

Joseph, B. (1989) *Psychic Equilibrium and Psychic Change*. Routledge.

*Kennedy, R. (1984) 'A dual aspect of the transference', *Int. J. Psycho-Anal.* 65: 471–83.

—— (1987) 'Struggling with words: aspects of the psycho-analysis of a male homosexual', *Int. J. Psycho-Anal.* 68: 119–28.

—— (1990b) 'A severe case of communication disorder', *Internation Journal of Psychiatry* 71: in press.

—— and Benvenuto, B. (1986) *The Works of Jacques Lacan: An Introduction*. Free Association Books.

——, Heymans, A. and Tischler, L., eds (1987) *The Family as In-Patient*. Free Association Books.

—— (1991) *Freedom to Relate*. Free Association Books.

*Khan, M. (1960a) 'Clinical aspects of the schizoid personality', *Int. J. Psycho-Anal.* 40: 430–7, and in Khan (1974b).

—— (1960b) 'Regression and integration in the psychoanalytic setting', *Int. J. Psycho-Anal.* 41: 130–46, and in Khan (1974b).

—— (1962a) 'Dream psychology and the evolution of the psycho-analytic situation', *Int. J. Psycho-Anal.* 43: 21–31, and in Khan (1974b).

—— (1962b) 'The role of infantile sexuality in early object relations in female homosexuality', in I. Rosen, ed. *The Pathology and Treatment of Sexual Perversions*. Oxford: Oxford University Press.

—— (1963) 'The concept of cumulative trauma', *Psychoanal. Study Child* 18: 283–306, and in Khan (1974b).

—— (1964) 'Ego, distortion, cumulative trauma and the role of reconstruction in the analytic situation', *Int. J. Psycho-Anal.* 45: 272–9, and in Khan (1974b).

—— (1965a) 'The function of intimacy in acting out in the perversions', in

J. Slovenko, ed. *Sexual Behaviour and the Law*. Springfield, MA: Thomas, and in Khan (1979).

────── (1965b) 'Foreskin fetishism and its relation to ego pathology in male homosexuality', *Int. J. Psycho-Anal*. 46: 64–80, and in Khan (1979).

────── (1966) 'The role of phobic and counter-phobic mechanisms and a separation anxiety in the schizoid character formation', *Int. J. Psycho-Anal*. 47: 306–13, and in Khan (1974b).

────── (1969a) 'An essay on Balint's researches on the theory of psycho-analytic technique', *Int. J. Psycho-Anal*. 60: 237–48.

────── (1969b) 'The role of the collated internal object in perversion formation', *Int. J. Psycho-Anal*. 50: 555–65, and in Khan (1979).

────── (1970) 'Towards an epistomology of the process of care', *British Journal of Medical Psychology* 43: 64–77.

────── (1972a) 'Dread of surrender to resourceless dependence in the analytic situation', *Int. J. Psycho-Anal*. 53: 225–30, and in Khan (1974b).

────── (1972b) 'Exorcism of the intrusive ego, alien factors in the analytic situation', in P. Giovacchini, ed. *Tactics and Techniques in Psychoanalytic Therapy*. Hogarth.

────── (1973) 'The role of illusion in the analytic space and process', *Annual of Psycho-Analysis* 1: 231–46, and in Khan (1974b).

────── (1974a) 'Ego orgasm in bi-sexual love', *Int. Rev. Psycho-Anal*. 1: 143–50, and in Khan (1979).

────── (1974b) *The Privacy of the Self*. Hogarth.

────── (1975) 'Freud and the crises of responsibility in modern therapeutics', *Int. Rev. Psycho-Anal*. 2: 25–45, and in Khan (1983).

────── (1976) 'The changing use of dreams in psycho-analytic practice', *Int. J. Psycho-Anal*. 57: 325–30.

────── (1978) 'Secret and potential space', in Khan (1983).

────── (1979) *Alienation in Perversions*. Hogarth.

────── (1983) *Hidden Selves*. Hogarth.

────── (1988) *If Spring Comes*. Routledge.

*King, P. (1962) 'The curative factors in psycho-analysis', *Int. J. Psycho-Anal*. 43: 225–34.

────── (1968) 'Alienation and the individual', *British Journal of Social and Clinical Psychology* 7: 81–92.

────── (1973) 'The therapist–patient relationship', *J. Anal. Psychol*. 18: 1–8.

────── (1978) 'Affective responses of the analyst to the patient's communication', *Int. J. Psycho-Anal*. 59: 329–34.

────── (1983) 'The life and work of Melanie Klein in the British Psycho-Analytical Society', *Int. J. Psycho-Anal*. 64: 251–60.

────── (1986) 'The life cycle as indicated by the transference in the psycho-analyses of the middle aged and elderly', *Int. J. Psycho-Anal*. 61: 153–60.

—— (1989) 'Activities of British psycho-analysts during the Second World War', *Int. Rev. Psycho-Anal.* 16: 15–34.

—— and Steiner, R., eds. (1990) *The Freud/Klein Controversies.* Routledge.

*Klauber, J. (1966) 'An attempt to differentiate a typical form of transference in neurotic depression', *Int. J. Psycho-Anal.* 47: 539–45.

—— (1967) 'The significance of reporting dreams in psycho-analysis', *Int. J. Psycho-Anal.* 48: 424–32, and in Klauber (1981).

—— (1968a) 'The dual role of historical and scientific method in psycho-analysis', *Int. J. Psycho-Anal.* 49: 80–9, and in Klauber (1981).

—— (1968b) "The psycho-analyst as a person', *Brit. J. Med. Psychol.* 41: 315–23, and in Klauber (1981).

—— (1972a) 'The relation of transference and interpretation', *Int. J. Psycho-Anal.* 53: 385–91, and in Klauber (1981).

—— (1972b) 'Psycho-analytic consultation', in P. Giovacchini, ed. *Tactics and Techniques in Psychoanalytic Therapy.* Hogarth.

—— (1974) 'Notes on the psychical roots of religion', *Int. J. Psycho-Anal.* 55: 249–56, and in Klauber (1981).

—— (1976) 'Some little described elements of the psycho-analytical relationship', *Int. Rev. Psycho-Anal.* 3: 283–90.

—— (1977) 'Analyses that cannot be terminated', *Int. J. Psycho-Anal.* 58: 473–7, and in Klauber (1981).

—— (1980) 'Formulating interpretations in clinical psycho-analysis', *Int. J. Psycho-Anal.* 61: 195–202, and in Klauber (1981).

—— (1981) *Difficulties in the Analytic Encounter.* Free Association Books.

—— (1983) 'Psycho-analytic societies and their discontents', *Int. J. Psycho-Anal.* 64: 675–86.

—— et al. (1987) *Illusion and Spontaneity in Psycho-Analysis.* Free Association Books.

Klein, J. (1987) *Our Need for Others and its Roots in Infancy.* Tavistock.

Klein, L. ed. (1989) *Working with Organisations.* Tavistock Institute of Human Relations.

Klein, M. (1928) 'Early stages of the Oedipus complex', in Klein (1948).

—— (1930) 'The importance of symbol formulation in the development of the ego', in Klein (1948).

—— (1932) *The Psycho-Analysis of Children.* Hogarth.

—— (1935) 'A contribution to the psycho-genesis of manic-depressive states', *Int. J. Psycho-Anal.* 16: 145–74, and in Klein (1948).

—— (1940) 'Mourning and its relation to manic depressive states', *Int. J. Psycho-Anal.* 21: 125–154, and in Klein (1948).

—— (1946) 'Notes on some schizoid mechanisms', *Int. J. Psycho-Anal.* 27: 99–110, and in Klein (1952).

—— (1948) *Contributions to Psycho-Analysis*, Hogarth.

—— (1957) *Envy and Gratitude*. Tavistock.

——, P. Heimann, S. Isaacs and J. Riviere (1952) *Developments in Psycho-Analysis*. Hogarth.

——, P. Heimann and R. E. Money-Kyrle, eds. (1955) *New Directions in Psycho-Analysis*. Tavistock.

—— and J. Riviere (1937) *Love, Hate and Reparation*. Hogarth.

*Kohon, G. (1984) 'Reflections on Dora: the case of hysteria', *Int. J. Psycho-Anal.* 65: 75–84.

—— (1985) 'Objects are not people', *Free Associations* 2: 19–30.

——, ed. (1986a) *The British School of Psycho-Analysis: The Independent Tradition*. Free Association Books.

—— (1986b) 'Countertransference an Independent view', in Kohon (1986a).

—— (1987) 'Fetishism revisited', *Int. J. Psycho-Anal.* 68: 213–28.

Kohut, H. (1971) *The Analysis of the Self*. Hogarth.

*Kreeger, L. (1974) 'Psychotherapy in the past, present and future' and 'Psychotherapy with adults', in V. Varma, ed. *Psychotherapy Today*. Constable.

——, ed. (1975) *The Large Group: Dynamics and Therapy*. Constable and Maresfield.

—— and de Mare, P. (1974) *Introduction to Group Treatments in Psychiatry*. Butterworth.

Kris, E. (1952) *Psycho-Analytic Explorations in Art*. New York: International Universities Press.

Langer, S. (1942) *Philosophy in a New Key*. Cambridge, MA: Harvard University Press.

—— (1953) *Symbolic Logic*. New York: Dover.

—— (1967) *Mind: An Essay on Human Feeling*, vol. 1. Baltimore, MD: Johns Hopkins University Press.

—— (1972) *Mind: An Essay on Human Feeling*, vol. 2. Baltimore, MD: Johns Hopkins University Press.

—— (1982) *Mind: An Essay on Human Feeling*, vol. 3. Baltimore, MD: Johns Hopkins University Press.

Langs, R. (1976) *The Therapeutic Interaction*. Jason Aronson.

Laplanche, J. and Pontalis, J. B. (1973) *The Language of Psycho-Analysis*. Hogarth.

Lask, A. (1966) *Asthma: Attitude and Milieu*. Tavistock.

Laufer M. and M. E. (1984) *Adolescence and Developmental Breakdown*. New Haven, CN: Yale University Press.

*Layland, R. (1981) 'In search of a loving father', *Int. J. Psycho-Anal.* 62: 215–24.

—— (1984) 'The use of a mistress and the internal sexual mother', *Int. J. Psycho-Anal.* 65: 323–9.

Lewin, B. (1948) 'Inferences from the dream screen', *Int. J. Psycho-Anal.* 29: 224–31.

Lewin, K. (1935) *A Dynamic Theory of the Personality.* New York: Macmillan.

*Lewis, E. and Casement, P. (1986) 'Interruption of mourning by pregnancy', *Psychoanal. Psychother.* 2: 45–52.

Likierman, M. (1989) 'Clinical significance of aesthetic experiences', *Int. Rev. Psycho-Anal.* 16: 133–50.

*Limentani, A. (1966) 'A re-evaluation of acting out in relation to working through', *Int. J. Psycho-Anal.* 47: 274–82.

—— (1968) 'On drug dependence', *Int. J. Psycho-Anal.* 49: 578–90.

—— (1972) 'The assessment of analysability', *Int. J. Psycho-Anal.* 53: 352–61.

—— (1974) 'The training analyst and difficulties associated with psycho-analytic training', *Int. J. Psycho-Anal.* 55: 71–7.

—— (1976) 'Object choice and actual bi-sexuality', *International Journal of Psycho-Analytic Psychotherapy* 5: 205–17.

—— (1977) 'Affects and the psycho-analytic situation', *Int. J. Psycho-Anal.* 58: 171–97.

—— (1979a) 'Clinical types of homosexuality', *Br. J. Med. Psychol.* 50: 209–16.

—— (1979b) 'The significance of transsexualism', *Int. Rev. Psycho-Anal.* 6: 379–99.

—— (1981) 'Some positive aspects of the negative therapeutic reaction', *Int. J. Psycho-Anal.* 62: 379–90.

—— (1984) 'To the limits of male homosexuality', *Journal of Analytic Psychotherapy and Psychopathology* 2: 115–29.

—— (1989) *Between Freud and Klein.* Free Association Books.

Lindemann, E. (1944) 'Symptomatology and management of acute grief', *American Journal of Psychiatry* 101: 123–38.

—— (1979) *Beyond Grief.* New York: Aronson.

*Little, M. (1951) 'Counter-transference and the patient's response to it', *Int. J. Psycho-Anal.* 32: 32–4, and in Little (1986).

—— (1957) 'The analyst's total response to his patient's needs', *Int. J. Psycho-Anal.* 38: 240–54, and in Little (1986).

—— (1958) 'On delusional transference', *Int. J. Psycho-Anal.* 39: 134–8, and in Little (1986).

—— (1960) 'On basic unity', *Int. J. Psycho-Anal.* 41: 377–84, and in Little (1986).

—— (1964) 'The balancing of the function of the ego', *Int. J. Psycho-Anal.* 45: 261–72, and in Little (1986).

—— (1966) 'Transference in borderline states', *Int. J. Psycho-Anal.* 47: 476–85, and in Little (1986).

——— (1986) *Toward Basic Unity*. Free Association Books.

*MacCarthy, B. (1966) 'Work with parents in an in-patient adolescent unit', *Journal of Child Psychotherapy* 1.

——— (1979) 'Incest and psychiatry', *Irish Journal of Psychotherapy* 2: 17–36.

——— (1987) 'Incest victims', *Psychoanal. Psychother.* 2: 157–68.

McDougall, J. (1986) *Theatres of the Mind*. Free Association Books.

——— (1989) *Theatres of the Body*. Free Association Books.

McDougall, W. (1908) *Social Psychology*. Methuen.

Mahler, M., Pine, F. and Bergmann, A. (1975) *The Psychological Birth of the Human Infant*. New York: International Universities Press.

Main, M., Kaplan, N. and Cassidy, J. (1985) 'Security in infancy, childhood and adulthood'. In I. Bretherton and E. Waters *Growing Points of Attachment Theory and Research*. Monograph Society for Research in Child Development no. 209. 50: 66–104.

*Main, T. (1946) 'The hospital as a therapeutic institution', *Bulletin of the Menninger Clinic* 10: 66–70, and in Main (1989).

——— (1947) 'Clinical problems of repatriates', *J. Mental Science*, 391: 354 63, and in Main (1989).

——— (1957) 'The ailment', *Br. J. Med. Psychol.* 30: 129–45, and in Main (1989).

——— (1958a) 'Perception and ego function', *Br. J. Med. Psychol.* 31: 1–8, and in Main (1989).

——— (1958b) 'A fragment on mothering' in E. Barnes, ed. *Psycho-Social Nursing*. Tavistock, and in Main (1989).

——— (1961) 'Mothers with children in a psychiatric unit' in E. Barnes, ed. (1968) *Psycho-Social Nursing*. Tavistock, and in Main (1989).

——— (1962) 'Psychoanalysis and psychosomatic illness', in P. Hopkins and H. Wolff, ed. *Principles of Treatment of Psycho-somatic Disorders*. Pergamon, and in Main (1989).

——— (1967) 'Knowledge, learning and freedom from thought', *Australian and N. Zealand Journal of Psychiatry* 1: 64–71, and in Main (1989).

——— (1975) 'Some psychodynamics of large groups', in L. Kreeger, ed. *The Large Group*. Constable, and in Main (1989).

——— (1983a) 'The concept of the therapeutic community', in M. Pines, ed. *The Evolution of Group Analysis*. Routledge, and in Main (1989).

——— (1983b) 'Pre-hysterectomy states', in K. Draper, ed. *Practice of Psycho-Sexual Medicine*. Libbey, and in Main (1989).

——— (1989) *The Ailment and Other Psycho-analytic Essays*. Free Association Books.

*Malan, D. H. (1959) 'On assessing the results of psychotherapy', *Br. J. Med. Psychol.* 32: 86–98.

——— (1963) *A Study of Brief Psychotherapy*. Tavistock.

—— (1976a) *Towards the Validation of Dynamic Psychotherapy*. New York: Plenum.

—— (1976b) *The Frontier of Brief Psychotherapy*. New York: Plenum.

—— (1979) *Individual Psychotherapy and the Science of Psychodynamics*. Butterworth.

—— , Bacal, H., Heath, E. and Balfour F. (1968) 'A study of psychodynamic changes in untreated neurotic patients', *British Journal of Psychiatry* 114: 525–38.

—— , Bacal, H., Heath, E. and Balfour F. (1975) 'Psychodynamic changes in untreated neurotic patients II', *Archive of General Psychiatry* 32: 110–28.

—— , and H. Phillipson (1957) 'The psychodynamics of diagnostic procedures', *Br. J. Med. Psychol.* 30: 92–102.

Mannoni, O. (1971) *Freud: The Theory of the Unconscious*. Verso.

Masters, W. H. and Johnson, V. E. (1965) *Human Sexual Response*. Boston, MA: Little, Brown.

*Matte-Blanco, I. (1940) 'Some reflections on psycho-dynamics', *Int. J. Psycho-Anal.* 21: 253–79.

—— (1943) 'An approach to the problems of spatial extension in the mind', *Int. J. Psycho-Anal.* 24: 180–90.

—— (1959) 'Expression in symbolic logic of the characteristics of the system unconscious', *Int. J. Psycho-Anal.* 40: 1–5.

—— (1975) *The Unconscious as Infinite Sets: An Essay in Bi-Logic*. Duckworth.

—— (1976) 'Basic logico-mathematical structure in schizophrenia', in D. Richter, ed. *Schizophrenia Today*. Pergamon.

—— (1981) 'Reflecting with Bion', in J. Grotstein, ed. *Do I Dare Disturb the Universe?* Beverley Hills, CA: Caesura Press.

—— (1988) *Thinking, Feeling and Being*. Routledge.

*Maxwell, H. (1981) 'Oedipus: another angle', *Int. Rev. Psycho-Anal.* 9: 163–6.

—— (1986) *An Introduction to Psychotherapy for Medical Students and Practitioners*. Bristol: Wright.

Meltzer, D. (1983) *Dream-Life*. Perthshire: Clunie Press.

Menzies Lyth, I. (1988) *Containing Anxiety in Institutions*. Free Association Books.

*Michael, R. (1968) 'Gonadal hormones and the control of primate behaviour', in R. Michael, ed. *Endocronology and Behaviour*. Oxford: Oxford University Press.

*Milner, M. (1934) *A Life of One's Own*. Chatto; Virago.

—— (1937) *An Experiment in Leisure*. Chatto; Virago, 1986.

—— (1943) 'The toleration of conflict', *Occupational Psychology* 17: 1–20.

—— (1944) 'Suicidal symptoms in a child of three', *Int. J. Psycho-Anal.* 25: 53–61, and in Milner (1987).

—— (1945) 'Some aspects of phantasy in relation to general psychology', *Int. J. Psycho-Anal.* 26: 144–52.

—— (1950a) *On Not Being Able to Paint.* Heinemann.

—— (1950b) 'A note on the ending of analysis', *Int. J. Psycho-Anal.* 31: 191–3, and in Milner (1987).

—— (1952) 'The role of illusion in symbol formulation', in M. Klein, P. Heimann and R. E. Money-Kyrle, eds. *New Directions in Psycho-Analysis.* Tavistock, and in Milner (1987).

—— (1956) 'The communication of primary sensual experience', *Int. J. Psycho-Anal.* 37: 278–81.

—— (1958) 'Psycho-analysis and art', in J. Sutherland, *Psycho-Analysis and Contemporary Thought.* Hogarth.

—— (1969) *The Hands of the Living God.* Hogarth.

—— (1987) *The Suppressed Madness of Sane Men.* Routledge.

*Mitchell, J. (1972) *Women's Estate.* Harmondsworth: Penguin.

—— (1974) *Psychoanalysis and Feminism.* Harmondsworth: Penguin.

—— (1984) *Women: The Longest Revolution.* Virago.

—— , ed. (1984) *Selected Writings of Melanie Klein.* Harmondsworth: Peregrine.

—— and Oakley, A., eds. (1978) *The Rights and Wrongs of Women.* Harmondsworth: Penguin.

—— and Rose, J. (1982) *Feminine Sexuality, Jacques Lacan and the Ecole Freudienne.* Macmillan.

*Muir, B. (1987) 'Is In-patient Psychotherapy a Valid Concept', in Kennedy, R. *et al.* (eds.) *The Family as In-Patient.* Free Association.

—— and Varchevker, A. (1975) 'Acting out, rebellion and violence', in S. Meyeson, ed. *Adolescence and Breakdown.* Allen & Unwin.

Nemiah, J. and Sifneos, D. (1970) 'Affect and fantasy in patients with psychosomatic disorders'. In O. Hill, ed. *Modern Trends in Psychosomatic Medicine.* Butterworth.

*Padel, J. H. (1972) 'The contribution of W. R. D. Fairbairn', *Bulletin of the European Psycho-Analytical Federation* 2: 13–26.

—— (1975) 'That the thought of hearts can mend', *Times Literary Supplement* December 19.

—— (1978) 'Dream interpretation - an object relational approach', in J. Fosshage and C. Loew, eds. *Dream Interpretation.* New York: Spectrum.

—— (1981) *New Poems By Shakespeare.* Herbert.

—— (1985a) 'Ego in current thinking', *Int. Rev. Psycho-Anal.* 12: 273–84.

—— (1985b) 'Was Shakespeare happy with his patron?', *Psycho-Analytic Psychotherapy* 1: 25–42.

—— (1986) 'Narcissism - a Fairbairnian view', *British Journal of Psychotherapy* 3: 256–64.

—— (1987) 'Freudianism: later developments', in R. Gregory, ed. *Oxford Companion to the Mind.* Oxford: Oxford University Press.

—— (1989) 'Shakespeare's Sonnet 20', *Int. Rev. Psycho-Anal.* 16: 171–8.

—— (1990) 'Fairbairn's thought on the relationship between inner and outer worlds', *Free Associations*, in press.

Palombo, S. (1978) *Dreaming and Memory.* New York: Basic.

Parkes, C. M. (1972) *Bereavement. Studies of Grief in Adult Life.* Tavistock.

*Parsons, M. (1984) 'Psycho-analysis as vocation and marital art', *Int. Rev. Psycho-Anal.* 11: 453–62.

—— (1986) 'Suddenly finding it really matters: the paradox of the analyst's non-attachment', *Int. J. Psycho-Anal.* 67: 475–88.

—— (1990) 'Oedipus at Colonus', *J. Analyt. Psychol.* 35: 19–40.

*Payne, S. (1935) 'A conception of femininity', *Br. J. Med. Psychol.* 15: 18–33.

—— (1936) 'Post war activities and the advance of psychotherapy', *Br. J. Med. Psychol.* 16: 51–65.

—— (1950) 'The fetishist and his ego', in R. Fliess, ed. *The Psycho-Analytic Reader.* Hogarth.

*Pedder, J. (1976) 'Attachment and new beginning: some links between the work of Michael Balint and John Bowlby', *Int. Rev. Psycho-Anal.* 3: 491–97.

—— (1977) 'Psychotherapy, play and theatre', *Int. Rev. Psycho-Anal.* 4: 215–23.

—— (1979a) 'Transitional space in psychotherapy and theatre', *Br. J. Med. Psychol.* 52: 377–84.

—— (1982) 'Failure to mourn, and melancholia', *British Journal of Psychiatry*, 141: 329–37.

—— (1985) 'Loss and internalisation', *Br. J. Psychother.* 1: 164–70.

—— (1986) 'Reflections on the theory and practice of supervision'. *Psychoanalytic Psychotherapy* 2: 1–12.

—— (1987) 'Biographical contributions to psychoanalytic theory', *Free Associations* 10: 102–16.

—— (1988) 'Termination reconsidered', *Int. J. Psycho-Anal.* 69: 495–505.

—— (1989a) 'How can psychotherapists influence psychiatry?', *Psychoanalytic Psychotherapy* 4: 43–54.

—— (1989b) 'The proper image of mankind: some comments on the evolution of psycho-analytic theory', *Br. J. Psychother.* 6: 70–80.

—— and Brown, D. G. (1979b) *Introduction to Psychotherapy: An Outline of Psychodynamic Principles and Practice.* Tavistock.

Peterfreund, E. (1971) *Information Systems and Psychoanalysis.* New York: International Universities Press.

Phillips, A. (1988) *Winnicott*. Fontana.

Piaget, J. (1950) *The Psychology of Intelligence*. Routledge.

—— (1951) *Play, Dreams and Imitation in Childhood*. Routledge.

—— (1953) *The Origins of Intelligence in the Child*. Routledge.

*Pitt-Aikens, T. (1989) *Loss of the Good Authority*. Harmondsworth: Penguin.

—— and Ellis, A. T. (1986) *Secrets of Strangers*. Duckworth.

*Pratt, J. (1958) 'Epilegomena to the study of Freudian instinct', *Int. J. Psycho-Anal.* 39: 1–8.

Racker, H. (1968) *Transference and Countertransference*. Hogarth.

*Raphael-Leff, J. (1984) 'Myths and modes of motherhood', *Br. J. Psychother.* 1: 6–30.

—— (1985a) 'Fears and fantasies of childbirth', *North American Journal of Pre and Peri Natal Psychology* 1: 14–18.

—— (1985b) 'Facilitators and regulators, participators and renouncers: mothers' and fathers' orientations towards pregnancy and parenthood', *Journal of Psychosomatic Obstetrics and Gynaecology* 4: 169–84.

—— (1986a) 'Psychological processes of infertility', *British Journal of Sexual Medicine* 13: 28–9.

—— (1986b) 'Facilitators and regulators: conscious and unconscious processes in pregnancy and early motherhood', *Br. J. Med. Psychol.* 59: 43–55.

—— (1989) 'Where the wild things are', *International Journal of Perinatal Studies* 1: 79–89.

—— (1990a) 'The baby-makers – psychological sequelae of technological intervention for infertility', in P. Fedor-Freybergh, ed. *Prenatal and Perinatal Psychology and Medicine: Encounter with the Unborn*, vol. 2. Carnforth: Parthenon Press.

—— (1990b) 'If Oedipus was an Egyptian. . . - an Osirian alternative to the Oedipal myth', *Int. Rev. Psycho-Anal.* 17: 309–35.

—— (1990c) *Psychological Processes in Childrearing*. Chapman & Hall.

*Rayner, E. (1971) *Human Development*, Allen & Unwin, 3rd edition, 1986.

—— (1981) 'Infinite experiences, affects and the characteristics of the unconscious', *Int. J. Psycho-Anal.* 62: 403–12.

—— (1986) 'Psychoanalysis in Britain', R. Fine, ed. *Psychoanalysis Round the World*. New York: Haworth.

—— and Hahn, H. (1964) 'Assessment for psychotherapy', *Br. J. Med. Psychol.* 37: 331–43.

—— and Tuckett, D. (1988) 'An introduction to Matte-Blanco's reformulation of the unconscious', in Matte-Blanco (1988).

*Rickman, J. (1921) 'An unanlysed case, anal erotism occupation and illusions', *Int. J. Psycho-Anal.* 2: 424–31.

——— (1928a) 'On some standpoints of Freud and Jung', *Br. J. Med. Psychol.* 8: 44–8.

——— (1928b) *Index Psycho-Analyticus 1893–1926.* Hogarth.

——— (1928c) *The Development of the Psycho-Analytical Theory of the Psychoses.* Baillière Tindall & Cox.

——— (1929) 'On quotations', *Int. J. Psycho-Anal.* 10: 242–48.

——— (1932) 'The psychology of crime', *Br. J. Med. Psychol.* 12: 264–8.

———, ed. (1936) *On the Bringing up of Children.* Kegan Paul.

——— (1937a) 'On "Unbearable" ideas and impulses', *American Journal of Psychology* 20: 248–53.

———, ed. (1937b) *Psycho-Analytic Epitomes.* Hogarth.

——— (1939a) 'Sexual behaviour and abnormalities', *British Encyclopaedia of Medical Practice* 2: 110–25.

——— (1939b) 'The general practitioner and psycho-analysis', *The Practitioner* 143: 192–8.

——— (1940) 'On the nature of ugliness and the creative impulse', *Int. J. Psycho-Anal.* 21: 294–313, and in Rickman (1957).

——— (1950a) 'On the criteria for termination of analysis', *Int. J. Psycho-Anal.* 31: 200–5, and in Rickman (1957).

——— (1950b) 'The role and future of psychotherapy with psychiatry', *Journal of Mental Science* 96: 181–9, and in Rickman (1957).

——— (1950c) 'The factor of number in individual and group dynamics', *Journal of Mental Science* 96: 170–3, and in Rickman (1957).

——— (1951a) 'Reflections on the functions and organisation of a psycho-analytical society', *Int. J. Psycho-Anal.* 32: 218–32, and in Rickman (1957).

——— (1951b) 'Number and the human sciences', in W. Muensterberger, ed. *Psycho-Analysis and Culture.* New York: International Universities Press, and in Rickman (1957).

———, ed. (1953) *Psycho-Analytic Epitomes.* Hogarth.

——— (1957) *Selected Contributions to Psycho-Analysis.* Hogarth.

——— and Bion, W. (1943) 'Intra-group tensions in therapy', *The Lancet* 678: 27 November 1943.

Robertson, J. (1958) *Young Children in Hospital.* Tavistock.

——— (1982) *A Baby in The Family.* Harmondsworth: Penguin.

Rosen, I. (1964) *The Pathology and Treatment of Sexual Deviation.* Oxford University Press.

Rosenfeld, H. (1987) *Impasse and Interpretation.* Tavistock.

Rutter, M. (1972) *Maternal Deprivation Reassessed.* Harmondsworth: Penguin.

Ruitenbeek, H. (1973) *Freud as we Knew Him.* Detroit: Wayne State University Press.

*Rycroft, C. (1951) 'A contribution to the study of the dream screen', *Int. J. Psycho-Anal.* 32: 178–84, and in Rycroft (1968a).

—— (1953) 'Some observations on a case of vertigo', *Int. J. Psycho-Anal.* 34: 241–47, and in Rycroft (1968a).

—— (1955) 'On idealization, illusion and catastrophic disillusion', *Int. J. Psycho-Anal.* 36: 24–9, and in Rycroft (1968a).

—— (1956a) 'Symbolism and its relation to the primary and secondary process', *Int. J. Psycho-Anal.* 37: 469–72, and in Rycroft (1968a).

—— (1956b) 'The nature and function of the analyst's communication to the patient', *Int. J. Psycho-Anal.* 37:114–16.

—— (1958) 'An enquiry into the function of words in the psycho-analytic situation', *Int. J. Psycho-Anal.* 39: 408–15, and in Rycroft (1968a).

—— (1960) 'The analysis of a paranoid personality', *Int. J. Psycho-Anal.* 41: 59–69, and in Rycroft (1968a).

—— (1962a) 'On the defensive function of schizophrenic thinking', *Int. J. Psycho-Anal.* 43: 32–9, and in Rycroft (1968a).

—— (1962b) 'Beyond the reality principle', *Int. J. Psycho-Anal.* 43: 388–93, and in Rycroft (1968a).

——, ed. (1966) *Psycho-Analysis Observed.* Constable.

—— (1967) 'The God I Want', in H. Mitchell, ed. *The God I Want.* Constable.

—— (1968a) *Imagination and Reality: Psycho-analytic Essays 1951–61.* Hogarth.

      (1968b) *A Critical Dictionary of Psycho-Analysis.* Nelson.

—— (1968c) *Anxiety and Neurosis.* Allen Lane.

—— (1971) *Reich.* Fontana.

—— (1979) *The Innocence of Dreams.* Hogarth.

—— (1985) *Psycho-Analysis and Beyond.* Hogarth.

Sachs, H. (1923) 'Zur Genese der Perversionen', *Int. Zeitschr. S. Psychoanal.* 7: 172–84.

Sandler, J., Dare, C. and Holder, A. (1973) *The Patient and the Analyst.* Allen & Unwin.

Sechehaye, M. A. (1947) *Symbolic Realisation.* New York: International Universities Press.

Segal, H. (1957) 'Notes on symbol formulation', in Segal (1981).

—— (1981) *The Work of Hanna Segal.* New York: Jason Aronson.

*Sharpe, E. F. (1924) 'Vocations', in *Social Aspects of Psycho-Analysis*, Williams & Norgate.

—— (1925) 'Francis Thompson, a psycho-analytical study', *Br. J. Med. Psychol.* 5: 329–40.

—— (1927) 'On child analysis', *Int. J. Psycho-Anal.* 8: 380–2.

—— (1929) 'The impatience of Hamlet', *Int. J. Psycho-Anal.* 10: 270–76, and in Sharpe (1950).

—— (1930) 'Certain aspects of sublimation and delusion', *Int. J. Psycho-Anal.* 11: 12–18, and in Sharpe (1950).

—— (1930–1) 'The technique of psycho-analysis', *Int. J. Psycho-Anal.* 11: 251–77, 361–85 and 12: 24–60, and in Sharpe (1950).

—— (1935) 'Similar and divergent unconscious determinants underlying the sublimations', *Int. J. Psycho-Anal.* 16: 180 91, and in Sharpe (1950).

—— (1937) *Dream Analysis.* Hogarth.

—— (1940) 'An examination of metaphors', *Int. J. Psycho-Anal.* 21: 201–19, and in Sharpe (1950).

—— (1943) 'Cautionary tales', *Int. J. Psycho-Anal.* 24: 41–6, and in Sharpe (1950).

—— (1946) 'From King Lear to the Tempest', *Int. J. Psycho-Anal.* 27: 19–34, and in Sharpe (1950).

—— (1947) 'The psycho-analyst', *Int. J. Psycho-Anal.* 25: 140–5.

—— (1950) *Collected Papers.* Hogarth.

*Sinason, M. (1986) 'Setting up the Willesden Centre for Psychological Treatment', *Psychoanalytic Psychotherapy* 2: 217–26.

*Sklar, J. (1985) 'Some uses of psycho-analysis in the National Health Service', *Psychoanalytic Psychotherapy* 1: 45–53.

—— (1986) 'Splitting of the Ego', *Psychoanalytic Psychotherapy* 2: 29–38.

—— (1989) 'Gender identity: 50 years from Freud', *Br. J. Psychother.* 5: 46–52.

—— and Puri, I. (1989) *Notes for the M.R.C. Psych Examination, Part I.* Butterworth.

Spillius, E. B. (1988a) *Melanie Klein Today, I Mainly Theory.* Tavistock.

—— (1988b) *Melanie Klein Today, II Mainly Practice.* Tavistock.

Spitz, R. (1965) *The First Year of Life.* New York: International Universities Press.

*Stephen, K. (1922) *The Mis-use of Mind: A Study of Bergson's Attack on Intellectualism.* Kegan Paul.

—— (1935) *Psycho-Analysis and Medicine: A Study of the Wish to Fall Ill.* Cambridge: Cambridge University Press.

Sterba, R. (1934) 'The fate of the ego in analytic therapy', *Int. J. Psycho-Anal.* 15: 117–28.

Stern, D. (1985) *The Interpersonal World of the Infant.* New York: Basic.

*Stewart, H. (1961) 'Jocasta's crimes', *Int. J. Psycho-Anal.* 42: 424–30.

—— (1963) 'A comment on the psychodynamics of the hypnotic state', *Int. J. Psycho-Anal.* 44: 372–4.

—— (1966) 'On consciousness, negative hallucinations and the hyperoid state', *Int. J. Psycho-Anal.* 47: 50–3.

—— (1968) 'Levels of experience of thinking', *Int. J. Psycho-Anal.* 49: 709–11.

—— (1973) 'Experience of dreams and the transference', *Int. J. Psycho-Anal.* 54: 345–48.

—— (1977) 'Problems of management in the analysis of a hallucinating hysteric', *Int. J. Psycho-Anal.* 38: 167–76.

—— (1979) 'The scientific importance of Ernest Jones', *Int. J. Psycho-Anal.* 60: 397–403.

—— (1981) 'The technical use, and experiencing of dreams', *Int. J. Psycho-Anal.* 62: 301–7.

—— (1985) 'Changes of inner space', *Int. J. Psycho-Anal.* 66: 255–64.

—— (1987) 'Varieties of transference interpretation', *Int. J. Psycho-Anal.* 68: 197–206.

—— (1989) 'Technique at the basic fault regression', *Int. J. Psycho-Anal.* 70: 221–30.

—— (1991) *Psychic Experience and Problems of Technique.* In press. Routledge.

Stoller, R. J. (1974) *Sex and Gender.* Taresfield Reprints.

*Strachey, A. (1922) 'Analysis of a dream of doubt and conflict', *Int. J. Psycho-Anal.* 3: 154–62.

—— (1943) *A New German-English Psycho-Analytical Vocabulary.* Baillière, Tindall & Cox.

—— (1957) *The Unconscious Motives of War.* Allen & Unwin.

*Strachey, J. (1930) 'Some unconscious factors in reading', *Int. J. Psycho-Anal.* 11: 322–31.

—— (1931) 'The function of the precipitating factors in the aetiology of the neurosis', *Int. J. Psycho-Anal.* 12: 326–30.

—— (1934) 'The nature of the therapeutic action of psycho-analysis', *Int. J. Psycho-Anal.* 15: 127–59, also (1969) reprinted in *Int. J. Psycho-Anal.* 50: 275–92.

——, ed. (1954–74) *The Complete Psychological Works of Sigmund Freud, Standard Edition,* vols. 1–24. Hogarth.

*Sutherland, J. D. (1941) 'Three cases of anxiety and failure in examinations', *Br. J. Med. Psychol.* 19: 73–81.

—— (1952) 'Psychological medicine and the National Health Service', *Br. J. Med. Psychol.* 25: 71–85.

——, ed. (1958) *Psycho-Analysis and Contemporary Thought.* Hogarth.

—— (1963) 'Object relations theory and the conceptual model of psychoanalysis', *Br. J. Med. Psychol.* 36: 109–24.

—— (1969) 'Psycho-analysis in the post-industrial society', *Int. J. Psycho-Anal.* 50: 673–82.

—— (1971a) *Towards Community Mental Health.* Tavistock.

—— (1971b) *The Changing Role of the Psychotherapist*. Tavistock.

—— (1978) 'The self and personal object relations', in S. Smith, ed. *The Human Mind Revisited*. New York: International Universities Press.

—— (1980) 'The British object relations theorists: Balint, Winnicott, Fairbairn, Guntrip', *J. Amer. Psychoanal. Assn.* 28: 829–60.

—— (1989) *Fairbairn's Journey into the Interior*. Free Association Books.

—— and Gill, H. (1964) 'The significance of the one-way vision screen in analytic group psychotherapy', *Br. J. Med. Psychol.* 37: 185–202.

—— and Gill, H. (1967) 'Psycho-diagnostic appraisal in the light of recent theoretical developments', *Br. J. Med. Psychol.* 40: 299–316.

Suzuki, T. (1953) *Essays in Zen Buddhism*. Rider.

*Symington, N. (1980) 'The response aroused by the psychopath', *Int. Rev. Psycho-Anal.* 7: 291–8.

—— (1983) 'The analyst's act of freedom as agent of therapeutic change', *Int. Rev. Psycho-Anal.* 10: 783–92.

—— (1985) 'Phantasy effects that which it represents', *Int. J. Psycho-Anal.* 66: 349–58.

—— (1986) *The Analytic Experience*. Free Association Books.

*Tonnesmann, M. (1979) 'Containing stress in professional work', *Social Work Service* 21: 34–41.

—— (1980) 'Adolescent re-enactment, trauma and reconstruction', *Journal of Child Psychotherapy* 6: 23–44.

—— , ed. (1989) P. Heimann *About Children and Children No-longer*. Routledge.

Trist, E. (1989) 'Psychoanalytic issues in organisational research and consultation', in L. Klein ed. *Working with Organisations*. Tavistock Institute of Human Relations.

—— et al. (1962) *Organisational Choice*. Tavistock.

*Trowell, J. (1986) 'Physical abuse of children: some considerations when seen from the dynamic perspective', *Psychoanalytic Psychotherapy* 2: 63–73.

*Tuckett, D. (1983) 'Words and the psycho-analytic interaction', *Int. Rev. Psycho-Anal.* 10: 407–13.

—— (1985) *Meetings Between Experts*. Tavistock.

—— and Rayner, E. (1988) 'An introduction to Matte-Blanco's reformulation of the Freudian unconscious', in Matte-Blanco (1988).

Tustin, F. (1981) *Autistic States in Children*. Routledge.

*Wallbridge, D. and Davis, M. *Boundary and Space*. Karnac.

*Winnicott, D. W. (1931a) *Clinical Notes on Disorders of Childhood*. Heinemann.

—— (1931b) 'Fidgetiness', in Winnicott (1958a).

—— (1931c) 'A note of normality and anxiety', in Winnicott (1958a).

—— (1935) 'The manic defence', in Winnicott (1958a).

—— (1938) 'Shyness and nervous disorders in children', in Winnicott (1964).

—— (1940) 'The deprived mother', in Winnicott (1957).

—— (1941a) 'The observation of infants in a set situation', *Int. J. Psycho-Anal.* 22: 229–49, and in Winnicott (1958a).

—— (1941b) 'On influencing and being influenced', in Winnicott (1964).

—— (1942) 'Child department consultations', *Int. J. Psycho-Anal.* 23: 139–46, and in Winnicott (1958a).

—— (1945a) *Getting to Know Your Baby*. Heinemann.

—— (1945b) 'Primitive emotion and development', *Int. J. Psycho-Anal.* 26: 137–43, and in Winnicott (1958a).

—— (1945c) 'The only child', in Winnicott (1964).

—— (1945d) 'Twins', in Winnicott (1964).

—— (1946a) 'What do we mean by a normal child?', in Winnicott (1964).

—— (1946b) 'Aspects of juvenile delinquency', in Winnicott (1964).

—— (1947a) 'The child and sex', in Winnicott (1964).

—— (1947b) 'Hate in the counter-transference', in Winnicott (1958a).

—— (1948a) 'Childrens' hostels in war and peace', *Br. J. Med. Psychol.* 21: 175–81.

—— (1948b) 'Paediatrics and psychiatry', *Br. J. Med. Psychol.* 21: 229–40, and in Winnicott (1958a).

—— (1949a) *The Ordinary Devoted Mother and her Baby*, Nine Broadcast Talks Privately Published, and in Winnicott (1964).

—— (1949b) 'Mind and its relation to the psychosoma', in Winnicott (1958a).

—— (1950a) 'Some thoughts on the meaning of the word democracy', in Winnicott (1965).

—— (1950b) 'Aggression in relation to emotional development', in Winnicott (1958a).

—— (1951) 'Transitional objects and transitional phenomena', in Winnicott (1958a).

—— (1953) 'Psychosis and child care', *Br. J. Med. Psychol.* 26: 68–74, and in Winnicott (1958a).

—— (1954) 'Meta-psychological and clinical aspects of regression', in Winnicott (1958a).

—— (1955b) 'Childhood psychosis: a case managed at home', in Winnicott (1958a).

—— (1954) 'The depressive position in normal emotional development', in Winnicott (1958a).

—— (1956a) 'Clinical varieties of transference', *Int. J. Psycho-Anal.* 37: 386–88, and in Winnicott (1958a).

—— (1956b) 'Primary maternal preoccupation', in Winnicott (1958a).

—— (1956c) 'The Antisocial Tendency', in Winnicott (1958a).

—— (1957a) *The Child and the Family: First Relationships.* Tavistock.

—— (1957b) *The Child and the Outside World: Developing Relationships.* Tavistock.

—— (1958a) *Collected Papers: Through Paediatrics to Psycho-Analysis.* Tavistock.

—— (1958b) 'The capacity to be alone', *Int. J. Psycho-Anal.* 39: 416–20, and in Winnicott (1965b).

—— (1958c) 'Child analysis in the latency period', in Winnicott (1965b).

—— (1959) 'Is there a psychoanalytic contribution to psychiatric classification', in Winnicott (1965b).

—— (1960a) 'Counter-transference', *British J. Medical Psychol.* 33: 17–21, and in Winnicott (1965b).

—— (1960b) 'String', *Journal of Child Psychology and Psychiatry* 1: 49–52, and in Winnicott (1965b).

—— (1960c) The theory of the parent-infant relationship', *Int. J. Psycho-Anal.* 41: 585–95, and in Winnicott (1965b).

—— (1960d) 'Ego distortion in terms of true and false self', in Winnicott (1965b).

—— (1962a) 'The theory of the parent-infant relationship – further remarks', *Int. J. Psycho-Anal.* 43: 238–9, and in Winnicott (1965b).

—— (1962b) 'A personal view of the Kleinian contribution', in Winnicott (1965b).

—— (1962c) 'Ego integration in child development', in Winnicott (1965b).

—— (1963a) 'Dependence in infant care, child care and in the psycho-analytic Setting', *Int. J. Psycho-Anal.* 44: 339–44, and in Winnicott (1965b).

—— (1963b) 'Development of the capacity for concern', in Winnicott (1965b).

—— (1963c) 'Psychotherapy of character disorders', in Winnicott (1965b).

—— (1964) *The Child, the Family and the Outside World.* Harmondsworth: Penguin.

—— (1965a) *The Family and Individual Development.* Tavistock.

—— (1965b) *The Maturational Processes and the Facilitating Environment.* Hogarth.

—— (1966a) 'Becoming deprived as a fact', *Journal of Child Psychotherapy* 1: 5–12, and in Winnicott (1971b).

—— (1966b) 'Psycho-somatic illness in its positive and negative aspects', *Int. J. Psycho-Anal.* 47: 510–16.

—— (1967a) 'The location of cultural experience', *Int. J. Psycho-Anal.* 48: 368–72.

—— (1967b) 'Mirror role of mother and family in child development', in P. Lomas, ed. *The Predicament of the Family.* Hogarth.

—— (1968) 'Playing: its theoretical status in the clinical situation', *Int. J. Psycho-Anal.* 49: 591–9.

—— (1969) 'The use of an object', *Int. J. Psycho-Anal.* 50: 711–16.

—— (1971a) *Playing and Reality.* Tavistock.

—— (1971b) *Therapeutic Consultations in Child Psychiatry.* Hogarth.

—— (1972) 'Fragment of an analysis', 'Mother's appearance in the clinical material as an ego alien factor', both in P. Giovacchini, ed. *Tactics and Techniques in Psychoanalytic Therapy.* Hogarth, pp. 455–693 and 405–13.

—— (1973) 'Fear of breakdown', *Int. Rev. Psycho-Anal.* 1: 103–7.

—— (1974) *Playing and Reality.* Reprinted by Penguin.

—— (1977) *The Piggle: An Account of the Psychoanalytic Treatment of a Little Girl.* Hogarth.

—— (1984) *Deprivation and Delinquency*, edited by Winnicott, C., Shepherd, R., Davis, M. Tavistock.

—— (1986a) *Home is Where we Start From.* Harmondsworth: Penguin.

—— (1986b) *Holding and Interpretation: Fragments of an Analysis.* Hogarth.

—— (1987a) *Babies and their Mothers.* Free Association Books.

—— (1987b) *The Spontaneous Gesture*, ed. F. R. Redman. Cambridge, MA: Harvard University Press.

—— (1988) *Human Nature.* Free Association Books.

—— (1989) *Psycho-Analytic Explorations.* Cambridge, MA: Harvard University Press.

*Wright, K. (1976) 'Metaphor and symptom, a study of integration and its failure', *Int. Rev. Psycho-Anal.* 3: 97–109.

—— (1990) *Between Mother and Baby.* Free Association Books.

*Zachary, A. (1985) 'A new look at the vulnerability of puerperal mothers', *Psychoanlytic Psychotherapy* 1: 71–89.

Zetzel, E. (1956) 'Current concepts of transference', *Int. J. Psycho-Anal.* 37: 369–76.

# Index

This first edition of
*The Independent Mind in British Psychoanalysis*
was finished in February 1991

The book was commissioned by Robert M. Young,
copy-edited by Gillian Wilce,
indexed by Dennis Southers,
designed by Wendy Millichap
and produced by Bernard F. Horan
for Free Association Books and Jason Aronson Inc.